Edinburgh
Information Technology Series

VALENCY AND CASE IN
COMPUTATIONAL LINGUISTICS

S. Michaelson and Y. Wilks
Series Editors

H. L. SOMERS

VALENCY AND CASE IN COMPUTATIONAL LINGUISTICS

EDINBURGH UNIVERSITY PRESS

Edinburgh University Press
22 George Square, Edinburgh

Set in Linotron Times by
Wilmaset, Birkenhead and
printed in Great Britain by
Redwood Burn Ltd, Trowbridge

British Library Cataloguing
in Publication Data
Somers, H. L.
Valency and case in computational
linguistics.—(Edinburgh information
technology series; 3)
1. Linguistics—Data processing
I. Title
410'.28'5 P123
ISBN 0 85224 518 1

CONTENTS

PREFACE

This work concerns the application of two closely related linguistic theories to a range of computational language-processing tasks. As such it is divided into three distinct parts: the first presents a thorough review of the linguistic theories of Valency and Case of a number of authors; the second discusses and exemplifies a range of classic problems for Case; and the third consists of a discussion of the use of Valency and Case in Computational Linguistics and Artificial Intelligence in general, and in Machine Translation in particular.

It is rather interesting that in general linguistic circles, neither Case nor Valency receive much acclaim. Valency has never attracted much attention outside East and West Germany, and to a lesser extent the Soviet Union. This is all the more surprising when one considers that in Germany, Valency is effectively the standard linguistic theory, and is found in the most traditional of grammar books, as well as permeating most of the linguistic description emanating from those two countries. Case on the other hand attracted a large amount of attention during the 1970s, but now seems rather out of favour among theoretical linguistics. By contrast, in Computational Linguistics, Case is an extremely popular linguistic theory. How can this difference in attitude be explained? It will become clear in the pages that follow that there are indeed a number of theoretical problems with both Valency and Case, but the fact remains that for certain applications, both theories offer a degree of intuitive attraction. Probably the loss of interest in Case has more to do with the fact that the area of linguistics in which it has most to offer has receded from the forefront of interest. Theoretical linguistics has today returned to pure syntax, and strict grammatical and theoretical adequacy in grammars has replaced the interest in the relationship between syntax and semantics that Case more readily addresses. To put it bluntly, Case is too woolly for today's tastes. Computational Linguistics on the other hand is characterised by the ready dismissal of questions of theoretical nicety in favour of practicalities: individual problem cases do not tend to invalidate a Computational Linguistic theory – they are merely excluded from the theory and treated in some more or less *ad hoc* manner. Furthermore, semantics is regarded as an area of particular importance in this field, and so Case finds itself a place amongst the tools of the linguistic engineer rather than amongst the preoccupations of the theorist.

This book is therefore addressed to a variety of readers. For the Theoretical Linguist, here is, for the first time, an extensive survey of the field, describing first a number of key authors' individual approaches, and then taking a horizontal view of the problems that confront the theory. A number of new solutions are proposed, including a radical review of the traditional Valency distinction of 'complements' and 'adjuncts', and a new version of Case which, it is hoped, goes some way towards answering some of the problems discussed. For the Practical Linguist, the interest lies in seeing how a particular syntactico-semantic theory is put to work in the important and ever-growing field of Computational Linguistics. For the linguist who is unfamiliar with this field, the third part of this work will serve as an introduction to some of the issues in Natural Language Processing. For the established Computational Linguist and the Artificial Intelligence researcher, perhaps having only an informal training in Linguistics, here is a thorough appraisal of the theoretical background to a topic with which he or she will surely be familiar, but where detailed background information was until now dispersed and thus not readily available. Although all the relevant subfields of Computational Linguistics are addressed, there is a particular emphasis in the final chapter on Machine Translation, since it is here that, with the additional interest of multilingual questions, the practical usefulness of the theories is brought to the fore.

As an overview of Case and Valency, this work is a contribution to the theoretical field. But its main thrust is as a work of pragmatic application, and as such it is worth underlining here the innovations that are to be found in the pages that follow. In Valency theory, much attention is paid to the question of distinguishing 'complements' and 'adjuncts'. The large number of criteria for doing this are reviewed, and a test for this distinction in English is offered. But a more important suggestion is that the distinction is in fact not the clear-cut binary division so far assumed, and a revised scale of six degrees of valency-binding is offered. As regards Case, we investigate in particular the consequences of the 'one case per clause' and 'one case per argument' principles, recognising in these two constraints some of the main problems with Case in general. By allowing contraventions of the first of these two principles where one occurrence is valency-bound and the other is not, we offer a solution in terms of 'inner' and 'outer' cases to many of the traditional problems, while the 'dual roles' problem is addressed by our 'case grid' proposal, in which cases are defined on a two-dimensional grid: this also facilitates the expression of correspondences between related verbs with slightly different case frames. In the third part of the book, devoted to Computational Linguistics, we present a relatively coherent model for natural language analysis based on our view of Valency, and on the most attractive versions of Case as described in part I, and show how it can be applied in Machine Translation.

I am indebted to a great number of people for their help and support during the writing of this work. They are too numerous to mention, though they will recognise themselves in some of my example sentences. I wish nevertheless to acknowledge a particular debt to Rod Johnson, Paul Bennett, Pete Whitelock, Kieran Kilby and Yorick Wilks, in addition to all my friends and colleagues at CCL, and on the EUROTRA project.

Throughout this work, foreign language quotations are cited in my own translation. Examples in foreign languages are accompanied by a literal gloss and/or a translation as appropriate. Foreign technical terms are translated where this is felt to be necessary, and the translation is generally used thereafter.

H.L.S. Manchester, January 1985

PART ONE: THEORIES

In this the first of three parts we shall be looking closely at a number of approaches to Valency and Case to establish a detailed background to our general discussion of Case and its appropriateness to Natural Language Processing.

In Chapter 1 we consider the field of Valency grammar. Four approaches are considered in essentially chronological order, though in fact distinctions between these four are not always clear-cut. In his position as a forerunner or father-figure to the Valency movement, Tesnière deserves special mention, even though his elaboration of the basic idea remains largely problematic. Various early German linguists extended and consolidated Tesnière's ideas, but it is perhaps Helbig and Schenkel who, with their Valency Dictionary, firmly established the theory as a school of Linguistics. Developments along these lines by Heringer and Engel and Schumacher are briefly discussed.

By far the most researched question for Valency grammarians is the problem of how to distinguish complements and adjuncts, and we review the more important of the tests that do this. The section ends with my own proposal for distinguishing complements and adjuncts in English in the form of the 'do so' test. The remaining sections discuss the possible difference between syntactic and semantic valency (and here allusions to Case-like approaches are obvious), the treatment of syntactic classes other than verbs in a Valency framework, and finally, returning to the complement-adjunct distinction, a discussion of this very fundamental aspect of the model. The suggestion that there are not two but six distinct degrees of valency binding is presented, with some exploration of the consequences of this for Valency grammar in general.

In Chapter 2 we survey the work of Fillmore, the obvious father-figure in Case Grammar. Taking each of his relevant works in turn, and concentrating on discussing the issues rather than simply recapitulating Fillmore's proposals, we see a very clear development of Fillmorean Case both in terms of orientation and elaboration. From the earliest attempts at providing an alternative underlying structure within the TG framework, we see Fillmore diverted away from the phrase-structure approach, concentrating on Case as a useful device in the lexicon, relating near-synonymous verbs, and accounting for distributional polysemy. In his later works Fillmore takes on a more semantics/pragmatic approach with Case playing a part in defining the relationship between speakers' perceptions of given situations as reflected in the choice of syntactic structure and lexical verb selection.

The approach of Anderson discussed in Chapter 3 differs markedly from that of Fillmore. Couched firmly in Dependency framework, Anderson's 'localistic' Case grammar reflects syntactic more than semantic relations, with his reduction of the ever-growing Fillmorean set of cases to four essential relations defined on a two-by-two matrix. Although Anderson's version of Case has certain attractions, in particular his attempt at formal completeness, we find that its consequent lack in reflecting intuitively-felt relations between certain predicates and predications makes it of only marginal interest for our current needs.

In Chapter 4 we group together a number of Case-based approaches to syntax having in common the relation of case-frames for sentences to underlying verb-types. We consider in detail the work of Chafe, and developments of his basic model by Cook and Longacre. Here we find the useful notion that lexical entries for verbs specify not individual case-frames but rather verb 'features' from which case-frame configurations might be inferred by general rule. Although both Cook's and Longacre's elaborations of Chafe's original ideas are open to criticism in some of their details, the general approach is seen as having great merit. The chapter closes with a discussion of the apparently unrelated classification of event types developed by Dowty from original work by Vendler. It is shown that there are striking similarities in the results of the two theories, and the suggestion is made that some combination of the two approaches might be mutually profitable.

In Chapter 5 we consider the theory of 'Lexicase' by Starosta. Like Anderson's, Starosta's model seems to lay more stress on syntactic relations, although his range of cases is certainly more semantics-oriented, at least in nomenclature. However, we discover that Starosta strikes an uneasy balance between syntactic and semantic relations which leads to some inconsistencies and lack of clarity, and analyses of some phenomena seem particularly unsuited to multilingual language processing.

In the final chapter of Part I, we investigate Dik's Functional Grammar. At first sight, Functional Grammar seems to bring together many of the ideas discussed in previous chapters: there are clearly some elements of Valency grammar in the model, while Dik's description of predicate types and their associated predicate-frames is very reminiscent of the Chafe/Cook approach discussed in Chapter 4. The relating of semantic functions to syntactic functions also looks promising. However there are some problems with Dik's concept of syntactic functions, which seem to take on a character rather removed from the notion of elements in syntactic structure which would otherwise make Dik's model extremely attractive. A further detractor is Dik's attempts to insist on language universality for his concepts, which in some instances lead him to analyses which lack intuitive appeal.

Part I of this work as a whole then attempts to represent the broad spectrum of Valency and Case, and even if there seem to be some widely divergent approaches, it is hoped that the underlying unity of approach – in particular as a set of verb-centred models in which the syntactic and semantic relations of nominals to the central verb are of primary interest – becomes evident. For the most part, the relevance of each theory to automatic natural language processing is understated: we leave this until Part III. Nevertheless, the relative concentration on some aspects of a given approach at the expense of others is often a preparation for this later discussion, and we should always keep this end-goal in mind.

ONE

VALENCY

1. *Introduction*

In General Linguistics Valency grammar holds a rather strong position. In Germany – both East and West – Valency grammar is now regarded more or less as the 'classical' approach, both to the teaching of German as a foreign language, and to the linguistic description of German. Elsewhere however (at least until the 1980s, cf. Leech, 1981; Matthews, 1981; Roberts, 1981; Allerton, 1982) it has been more or less ignored, and this is all the more surprising when one considers how uncontentious the rudiments of Valency grammar are – the major problems are only encountered in the elaboration of the theory. Nevertheless, most of the work on Valency grammar is in German, and about German, though there is now a small but growing number of Valency treatments of other languages: for example Emons' (1974, 1978) works on English, Happ's (1978*a*) treatment of French and (1976, 1978*b*) Latin, and Rickmeyer's (1977) Japanese Valency dictionary.

In this chapter we shall attempt to characterise and comment upon the main threads of Valency theory in recent years, generally concentrating on those elements of most interest to us in terms of their relevance to the use of Case-like notions in natural language processing.

There exists a considerable wealth of material on Valency grammar, mostly in German. Several excellent overviews can be found: particularly worthy of recommendation are those of Emons (1974) and Biere (1976), while Schumacher and Trautz's (1976) bibliography is certainly a representative and probably exhaustive list of works up to that date. Following the style of most of those general works, we present first a brief historical view of the notion of Valency in German grammar, and then concentrate on the major points of discussion and disagreement in the theory.

2. *General review*

Most writers on the subject cite Tesnière (1959) as responsible for introducing the notion of Valency into modern linguistics, noting however that these early ideas were to undergo several modifications, particularly in the light of German linguistic data. A detailed description and discussion of Tesnière's model is given in Somers (1982*a*). We shall recapitulate here some of the main points.

Tesnière's grammatical model differed from the contemporary approaches in being strictly verb-centred. The key notion for Tesnière was that of dependency (*dépendance*) between the elements of the sentence, which entered into certain governor-subordinate (*régissant-subordonné*) relationships. The topmost governor in the sentence is generally the verbal element, and Tesnière's main interest was in the nature of the relationships between the verbal governor and its immediate subordinates. These are characterised by the distinction between 'actants' and 'circumstantials' (*circonstants*), actants being elements which are central participants in the process, while circumstantials (as their name implies) express the associated temporal, locational, etc. circumstances (p. 102).

Tesnière establishes (p. 102) a formal connection between nominals or their equivalent and actants on the one hand, and between adverbials or their equivalent and circumstantials on the other (p. 106).

The number of actants that a verb takes is important, and is stated as the verb's valency (*valence*) (p. 238). Possible verb valencies range from zero to three: avalent verbs take no actants, as exemplified by meteorological verbs like *rain* and *snow*, whose subject is purely formal and therefore does not have actant status; monovalent verbs are traditional intransitive verbs like *fall*; divalent verbs taking two actants are the traditional transitive verbs – Tesnière's example is *hit*; trivalent verbs are exemplified by *give*.

Tesnière distinguishes types of actants, naming them prime actant, second actant and third actant. Certain syntactic functions are associated with each type: the first actant is generally the subject, the second the object, and the third the indirect object. In inflected languages, says Tesnière, the association is with Nominative, Accusative and Dative. Furthermore, each of the three actants has its own typical semantic function: the first actant is the one which performs the action, the second undergoes the action, and the third is the one to whose benefit or detriment the action takes place.

As regards the possible distribution of actants, Tesnière is inconsistent. At one point (p. 108), he suggests that the order number of an actant can never be higher than the valency of the verb, i.e. the third actant only appears with trivalent verbs and so on, and conversely, a monovalent verb will always occur with a prime actant. Later however he states that 'It is not always necessary that all a verb's valencies be filled with their actants or that the verb be, so to speak, saturated. Certain valencies may remain unused or *free*' (pp. 239f) and, furthermore, he gives examples of monovalent verbs taking a second or third actant: *falloir* ('to be necessary') takes a formal subject and a direct object; German *warm sein* ('to be warm') has its only actant realised by a dative (1).

(1) Mir ist warm.
'I am warm'

Turning now to circumstantials, Tesnière first notes that, unlike actants, their number for any verb or sentence is indefinite (and may be zero). Considering the distinction between actants and circumstantials, Tesnière says: 'At first sight, the *distinction* between actants and circumstantials is precise. But on closer inspection it can be seen that it is difficult to fix with precision. . . . The third actant has certain of the characteristics of a circumstantial. Conversely, certain circumstantials are in some ways analogous with actants, so that one is led to consider carefully criteria which would enable actants and circumstantials to be differentiated' (p. 127). The criteria that Tesnière suggests are those of form 'Since the circumstantial can only be an adverb, it must, if it is a substantive, first receive an adverbial marker in the form of a preposition' (p. 128), and of sense: 'The actant is an integral part of the verb, so that it is often indispensible in order to complete the sense of the verb. . . . On the other hand, the circumstantial is essentially optional' (p. 128). Tesnière however recognises the frailty of these definitions. Third actants are often introduced by the so-called adverbial marker, while certain prepositional phrases look like actants from the closeness of their connection with the verb, as in (2).

(2) Alfred change de veste.
'Alfred is changing (his) jacket'

In the paper mentioned above (Somers, 1982*a*), the critical reaction to Tesnière's model is discussed in some detail. The two major criticisms however can be summed up as follows. First, it seems that in the elaboration of the model, Tesnière was too influenced by surface syntax and in particular French surface syntax. The association between prepositional phrases and circumstantials leads to some counter-intuitive labelling (cf. Gougenheim, 1960:145). Second, some dissatisfaction has been expressed at the apparent semantic motivation behind the distinction between actants and circumstantials (cf. Robins, 1961:86).

Indeed, many of Tesnière's problems stem from his attempt to reconcile the conflicting syntactic and semantic characterisations of his notions of actant and circumstantial. However, Tesnière was innovative in an important way, and even if there remains much to question in his presentation of the model, his work clearly laid the foundations for the approach to syntax discussed in this chapter.

At about the same time as Tesnière's work was being published, German grammarians began to adopt more and more Valency-like notions into their traditional grammars. Linguists also began to attempt to explore the theoretical possibilities of the approach, and to devise suitable notations. Notable in this respect are Helbig and Schenkel, whose *Wörterbuch zur Valenz und Distribution deutscher Verben* (1973), which first appeared in 1968, remains for many the seminal work in Valency grammar (cf. also Helbig, 1971). Conceived essentially for didactic purposes, it consists of a brief review of some Valency-like approaches to German syntax, an explanation of the author's own views of the theory, an introduction to the notation used, and then an extensive list of German verbs, grouped according to meaning and some syntactic properties.

As Helbig and Schenkel are regarded as central figures in the Valency world, it is of interest here to consider in some detail what they propose. Their presentation revolves around three central issues, the first of which is the consideration of the verb as the structural centre of the sentence. It is in this respect that both Valency and Case-like theories of grammar differ from contemporary views of grammar – compare the Chomskyan notion of the kernel sentence consisting of subject plus predicate (Chomsky, 1957:33) – and Helbig and Schenkel review some of the reasons for preferring a verb-centred approach. However, we shall not dwell on this matter, but refer the reader both to the appropriate sections of Helbig and Schenkel (pp. 24–31), and to the well-referenced discussion in Brinker (1977:103ff).

The second important issue is the distinction between Valency-bound elements – Helbig and Schenkel follow Tesnière in using the term 'actant' (*Aktant*) though 'complement' (*Ergänzung*) is otherwise more common – and 'adjunct' (*freie Angabe*), and the further subdivision of complements into obligatory and optional. An important consideration for Helbig and Schenkel, and for many other Valency grammarians, is the way in which this distinction can be made in practice. We shall discuss in detail in Section 3 the range of tests proposed to establish this distinction: Helbig and Schenkel favour the 'elimination test' (*Weglaßprobe* or *Eliminierungstest*) with which one is able to distinguish obligatory elements from optional ones, though the distinction of optional complements from adjuncts is not covered by this test. This highlights the fact that there seems to be an important difference between elements which are obligatory and those which are necessary – a neat distinction which calls into question the notion of acceptability of example sentences which may differ according to whether or not the context of an utterance is taken into account: we shall return later to this further question of communicative versus structural necessity of elements.

Helbig and Schenkel give a general definition of 'valency-boundness', based on the distinction between complements/actants and adjuncts: 'Both obligatory as well as optional actants (both are necessary elements) are bound by valency to the verb, are anchored in the syntactic frame of the verb and thus their number and type can be fixed. The adjuncts on the other hand (as unnecessary elements) are not bound to the verb, are unlimited in number and can for this reason be left out of or added to almost any sentence at will' (Helbig and Schenkel, 1973:33f).

This definition incorporates two important notions, one of which seems to be at the heart of Valency grammar, and the other of which appears to be a fundamental misinterpretation which, surprisingly, no other reviewer seems to have commented upon. The basic notion is that when an element in a sentence is described as 'valency-bound', this means that it is closely associated with the verb to the extent that its presence and appearance (i.e. surface form) are predictable from what we may call the 'valency pattern' of the verb. Indeed, it is precisely this information that Helbig and Schenkel attempt to capture in the formalism of their valency dictionary. However, their comment here on the nature of adjuncts seems to imply that adjunct status is somehow an inherent feature of some elements: thus adjuncts can be left out of or added to almost any sentence. What Helbig and Schenkel do not make clear is that elements can only be described with respect to a particular verb, and just as a certain element may be a complement with one verb but an adjunct with another (cf. *in*

London in (3) and (4)), so might an adjunct in one context turn out to be a complement in some other context, and thus it does not make any sense to describe the adjunct *in London* in (4) as insertable in or eliminable from any sentence almost at will, when it is clearly not 'freely eliminable' from (3):

(3) James lives *in London*.

(4) He looked for his friend *in London*.

A similar (and, I believe, misguided) approach can be seen in Matthews (1981:123ff), whose discussion centres around the question of which syntagmatic relations (e.g. subject, object, indirect object, locational adverbial etc.) are more or less usually valency-bound. The 'problems' he has, especially with indirect objects (pp. 128ff), stem from the fact that valency-boundness is not a feature of a syntactic function, but is determined by the individual verb itself.

Helbig and Schenkel (p. 35) contrast complements and adjuncts according to their place in deep structure, describing adjuncts as constituents of the sentence, while complements are constituents of the verb-phrase. Since the difference between complements and adjuncts lies in deep structure, as shown in (5), the criterion for their distinction must reflect this. The proposed 'backformation' test is discussed in Section 3.

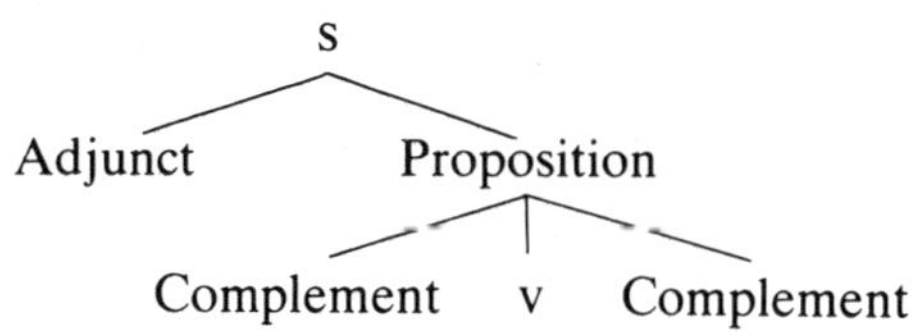

(5) (adapted from Helbig and Schenkel, 1973:35)

In the final section of their theoretical discussion, Helbig and Schenkel consider the relationships between traditional grammatical classes and roles and valency-boundness. They note that early Valency grammarians such as Tesnière and Brinkmann (1962) closely associated the notions of valency-boundness with certain syntactic functions: for both these writers the possibility of prepositional objects other than 'dative' as complements/actants was excluded, as were all adverbial phrases, even where they were admittedly obligatory in some sense.

The remainder of the theoretical section is concerned with explaining Helbig and Schenkel's own formalism for the dictionary entries. Each entry consists of three levels (*Stufen*): the first gives simply the numerical valence of the verb, distinguishing obligatory and optional elements. The second level gives the syntactic form of the valency-bound elements, i.e. category (substantive, prepositional complement, embedded sentence etc.) and surface case. In the third level the restrictions – principally semantic – on each case are sated. These are expressed within a small range of familiar markers (e.g. animate, abstract, human, action, local, modal), and generally accompanied by examples. The full entry for *wecken* ('wake'), for example, is as follows (p. 130): [S=substantive; n=nominative; a=accusative; p=preposition; d=dative]

I. wecken$_{2+(1)=3}$
II. wecken → Sn, Sa, (pS)
III. Sn → 1.±Anim (*Die Mutter, der Hund, der Wecker* weckt das Kind.)
[*The mother, the dog, the alarm clock* wakes the child]
2. Abstr (*Der Lärm* weckte ihn.) [*The noise* woke him]
3. Act (*Das Schreien* weckte ihn.)
[*The shouting* woke him]
Sa → +Anim (Ich wecke *das Kind, das Tier.*)
[I wake *the child, the dog*]
p=aus
pSd → Abstr (Die Mutter weckt das Kind *aus dem Schlaf.*)
[The mother wakes the child *from his sleep*]

It is interesting to note how polysemous verbs are represented: the different valency patterns of verbs are usually captured by having two (or more) entries one after the other. This is always the case when the numerical valency of the two variants differs, (see for example *öffnen* ('open'), p. 381), which, as in English, has both transitive and intransitive patterns. In this representation however, there is no way of relating the two variants and showing that the subject in the instransitive has the same semantic restrictions as the object in the transitive, or more importantly that one of the patterns can be derived from the other. This information is carried by an additional remark which lies outside the formalism of the dictionary entry. This method of differentiation of verbs is also occasionally used where the numerical valency pattern is identical, but where realisation at levels II and III may differ between variants. A good example is *bemerken* ('remark', 'notice'), whose 'second' arguments only partially overlap in syntactic form and semantic restrictions, and whose 'third' (optional) arguments require different prepositions (p. 380). Wherever possible however, differences in usage of verbs will be captured at the second and third levels only, where alternatives in syntactic form and/or semantic restrictions can be given. It is interesting to consider the apparent motivations behind the two possible representations of polysemous verbs, since no mention of this dichotomy is made in the introduction section of the book. It seems that in each case a decision has been made as to whether a different valency pattern – by which we might mean different possibilities in selection of syntactic form and/or different semantic restrictions – implies a different verb, or merely indicates internal variation possibilities. It is difficult to discern any consistent motivation.

At about the same time as Helbig and Schenkel, Heringer (1967, 1968) was developing an approach to Valency grammars. Heringer follows much the same lines as Helbig and Schenkel, although with two particularly interesting further developments. Heringer's consideration of the definition of 'complement' led him to consider more carefully what the term might mean: in his discussion of the distinction between complements and adjuncts, he notes that '. . . complements always complete the meaning of the verb. If a complement is missing, then the meaning of the verb is meant to be incomplete. Here too there are dangers, since temporal and locative adjuncts also complete the meaning of the verb, i.e. one must establish more exactly what one understands by "complete"' (Heringer 1968:429).

Heringer was led to introduce the important notion of 'ellipsis' as a possible cause of complement omission, so that 'Where homonymous verbs have different valencies they are either polysemous (or homographs), or there is an ellipsis. Ellipses are only possible with certain complements and in certain situations or contexts. They do not effect meaning. More likely is that the missing complements are understood' (Heringer, 1968:427). Yet since ellipsis is a feature of 'parole' (Heringer, 1967:15), its importance in the distinction of complements from adjuncts is bound up in the question of communicative versus structural necessity of elements, to which we shall return below.

The second development of Heringer's was his introduction of meaningful numerical annotation of valency 'formulae'. More or less equivalent to Helbig and Schenkel's level II, Heringer (1967:14) presents numerical subscripts which indicate syntactic forms of complements, with 1 for Nominative, 2 for Accusative, 3 for Dative, 4 for Genitive and 5 for prepositional complement.

This may not seem an important innovation, but it has certain implications for the formal representation of valency patterns, and in particular establishes a certain cohesion between the two essentially separate parameters of valency-boundness on the one hand, and syntactic function on the other. Heringer's formalism is in a sense a reversion to Tesnière's original conception, in that we can talk again of 'first actant' (i.e. e_1), meaning 'noun in nominative', 'second actant' (e_2), and so on down to 'fifth actant' (e_5) prepositional object, although it should be made clear that Heringer's numbering of complements does not in any sense imply a hierarchy of expected syntactic functions in the way that Tesnière's did (cf. above).

A similar, though more extensive formalism is used in Engel and Schumacher's (1976) valency dictionary: these authors distinguish ten types of complement, and in a useful table (pp. 22f) compare their nomenclature with that of other major Valency grammarians.

3. *Distinction of complements and adjuncts*

By far the most researched question in Valency grammar is the practical distinction of complements and adjuncts. The solution to this question is fraught with controversy however, and in this section we shall briefly review a number of the more important proposals. A rather more detailed treatment of this topic is to be found in Somers (1984). In the sections that follow, we use English examples, based wherever possible on the originals.

The 'elimination test' (*Eliminierungstest*) is described by Helbig and Schenkel as follows: 'We eliminate an element from the sentence and observe whether the remaining sentence is still grammatical or thereby ungrammatical. If it is still grammatical, then the eliminated element is not obligatory; if however it is ungrammatical, then the eliminated element is syntactically obligatory for the sentence to endure' (Helbig and Schenkel, 1973:33). In the examples below (1)-(3), the italicised element turns out to be not eliminable and therefore obligatory. Note that in this and most other tests, we deal with active declarative sentences as the basic forms. Thus, for example, the possibility of omitting deep subjects in imperatives, passives or infinitives does not come into consideration in this elimination test.

(1a) *I* visit *him* in Berlin.
(1b) I visit him.
(1c) *I visit in Berlin.
(1d) *I visit.
(2a) *He* put *the book under the table.*
(2b) *He put the book.
(2c) *He put under the table.

(2d) *He put.
(3a) *We* were expecting *him* the following Sunday at 12 o'clock at the station.
(3b) We were expecting him.
(3c) *We were expecting the following Sunday.
(3d) *We were expecting at the station.
(3e) *We were expecting at 12 o'clock.

The 'extraction method' (*Abstrichmethode*), introduced by Grebe (1966:468) looks very similar – cf. (4)-(5):

(4) The roses bloom ~~in our garden~~.
(5) The farmer ploughs his field ~~in the morning~~.

Brinker (1972:181), however, distinguishes between the elimination test and the extraction method. In the former, the test is to see whether the sentence with elements removed from it remains grammatical, and thus whether the element in question is obligatory or optional. In the latter however, the aim is to distinguish complements, whether obligatory or not, from adjuncts. The reason that we are not permitted to extract *his field* from (6a), even though this would leave (6b), which is still grammatical, is that in doing so we would change the basic meaning of the predicate.

(6a) The farmer ploughs his field.
(6b) The farmer ploughs.

Brinker calls elements like *his field* with *plough* 'semanteme constitutive' (*semantemkonstitutiv*), by which he means that as an element it constitutes part of the semanteme or meaning unit: 'An element will be called "semanteme constitutive" if its deletion leads to a change in the semantic value of the whole sentence, i.e. if the change of meaning associated with the deletion cannot be attributed to the deleted element alone' (Brinker, 1977:115). The test however is beset with difficulties, as Brinker (1972:180f) points out, since the all-important notion of 'meaning-unit' remains undefined, and therefore entirely intuitive. This, says Brinker, is no basis for an operational test.

Returning to the elimination test, we may quickly discover that it too runs into difficulties of interpretation. The main problem is that of course, as Vater (1977:25) points out, the elimination test is only able to separate obligatory complements on the one hand from all other optional elements on the other. But more seriously than this, the test relies on some notion of grammatical acceptablility which in turn is difficult to distinguish from 'communicative' completeness.

Rosengren (1970:48), Sommerfeldt (1973:96) and Ballweg-Schramm (1976:57) all suggest that the notions of obligatory versus optional and necessary versus eliminable are all quite independent. Notably, contexts can be found where an otherwise obligatory element can be omitted, and conversely where an essentially optional element becomes necessary.

Panevová stresses the need '. . . to distinguish between the obligatoriness of a participant at the semantic level and the necessity of the presence of an element that realized this participant at the level of surface syntax' (Panevová, 1974:7), and suggests that a semantically obligatory element might in different circumstances be at a syntactical level obligatory, 'potential' (i.e. optional), or even 'necessarily realised by zero' – compare Cook's (1973:92f) 'covert case roles', discussed in Chapter 4 Section 5.

If we accept the elimination test as a means of distinguishing obligatory complements on the one hand from optional complements and adjuncts on the other, we still require some means of distinguishing among optional elements between complements and adjuncts. Helbig and Schenkel's approach is the 'backformation test' (*Zurückführungstest*). Based on the notion that in deep structure complements are attached to the predicate, whereas adjuncts attach to the sentence, they propose (1973:37) a test which consists of reformulating the element in question as a relative clause: if this can be done without the resulting sentence being ungrammatical, and without changing the basic meaning (cf. Helbig, 1969:165), then the element that has been backformed can be said to be an adjunct. Buysschaert (1982:52ff) describes a similar test for English.

Steinitz (1969:31) (who also uses this test) gives several possible backformations for *in Berlin* in (7), while Helbig and Schenkel (1973:37ff) give a number of examples of positive and negative applications (8)-(10):

(7a) He visited her *in Berlin*.
(7b) He visited her, when he/she stayed in Berlin.
(8a) My friend lives *in Dresden*.
(8b) * My friend lives, when he is in Dresden.
(9a) He put the book *under the table*.
(9b) * He put the book, when he was under the table.
(10a) He died *in Dresden*.
(10b) He died, when he was in Dresden.

Examples are also given where the element in question may best be transformed into an accompanying sentence (11):

(11a) The children are playing *behind the house*.
(11b) The children are playing; the playing takes place behind the house.

Several commentators (Rosengren, 1970:49; Emons, 1974:73; Korhohnen, 1977:133; Vater, 1977:28) have described difficulties with this test. It is not always clear what criteria to use in choosing the appropriate form of the backformation, especially as regards choice of verb and subject for the embedded sentence. Example (9) is in any case badly chosen also because the main clause of the backformed sentence is in its own right ungrammatical (as the elimination test would show). Furthermore, it is especially difficult to transform nonlocative adverbials convincingly. Even assuming a 'correct' backformation, it remains difficult to judge whether the basic meaning has been changed. Finally, it is relatively easy to think up examples both of complements that are easily backformed (particularly optional ones), and of adjuncts that cannot be. The backformation test, then, does not seem to be very acceptable. Not only is the mechanism of its application unclear, but it does not regularly result in the desired analysis.

Anderson (1973:54) suggests a type of 'substitution test' based on the fact that in a sentence the morphosyntactic realisations of certain elements can be said to be strongly 'governed' by the choice of the verb, and this can be demonstrated by replacing that verb with another quasi-synonym, while other elements remain unaffected (12):

(12a) I have been waiting *for my friend for two hours.*
(12b) * I have been expecting *for my friend for two hours.*
(12c) I have been expecting *my friend for two hours.*

The concept that verbs govern specific cases or prepositions is well established, and lies at the heart of Valency grammar. But in fact as the basis for a test for distinguishing complements and adjuncts in this framework, the concept is not particularly useful, for several reasons.

First, the test may be inconclusive simply because the alternative verb chosen for the substitution test happens to have the same morphosyntactic valency pattern (13):

(13a) I was looking *for that book* yesterday.
(13b) I was searching *for that book* yesterday.

Second, some verbs have multiple valency patterns either through polysemy or through free variation in the surface realisation of complements, but such that the notion of the government by verbs of certain surface 'cases' (including prepositional phrases) seems not to apply. For those verbs taking a locative complement (especially verbs of motion like *go*, *walk*, etc.), a huge range of prepositions can introduce the complement. Third, the unacceptability of some elements with a given verb may be due not to the fact that the strong case government has been contravened, but simply that an adjunct may be semantically impossible with a given verb. Thus, for example, the unacceptability of (14a) is not explicable in terms of *meet* strongly governing *in* (14b), but to the fact that a directional adjunct is not appropriate with *meet*.

(14a) * I met him to Edinburgh.
(14b) I met him in Edinburgh.

Nevertheless, the concept of strong case government may be useful to a certain extent, and it does lead to some valid observations about the possible behaviour of elements. For example, a strongly governed preposition usually cannot be replaced by an alternative near-synonymous preposition, while in a prepositional adjunct it often can: compare example (15), suggested by Engel and Schumacher (1976:6), with (16):

(15a) Inge is arguing *with* her friend.
(15b) * Inge is arguing *in the company of* her friend.
(16a) Doris is travelling *with* her friend to Retzbach.
(16b) Doris is travelling *in the company of* her friend to Retzbach.

This strong government of prepositions is particularly effectively reflected in German syntax by the fact that such prepositions must usually be present in the surface structure when the complement they govern is an embedded sentence, as in (17).

(17a) Ich erinnere mich *daran*, als er in Wiesbaden wohnte.
'I remember when he lived in Wiesbaden'
(17b) Hinrich wartet *darauf,* daß die Tagung beginnt.
'Hinrich is waiting for the meeting to begin'
(17c) Wir halfen *dabei*, das Hi-Fi einzubauen.
'We helped to install the Hifi'

A similar construction is found in English pronominal and question forms (Herbst, 1984:4) – cf. (18):

(18a) She was certain that she had met Dennis.
(18b) She was certain *of* it.
(18c) What was she certain *of*?

Another feature that distinguishes complement and adjunct prepositional phrases is that they cannot be conjoined (except in the highly rhetorical device zeugma) (19)-(20):

(19) * He was waiting for his friend and (for) hours.
(20) * He looked over the document and my shoulder.

It is interesting to note that the preposition is often felt intuitively to be part of the verb: we distinguish *look at* and *look after*, we talk of the meaning of French *dépendre* as being 'depend on', and so on.

Some authors have regarded the intractability of strongly governed prepositions as the basis for a criterion of complement-adjunct distinction in prepositional phrases, noting further that such prepositions seem to be semantically empty: 'A result of the inexchangeability of the preposition is that generally it has no meaning of its own; in any case it would require a certain amount of contorted thinking to attribute to the *auf* ('for') in the verb *warten* (*auf*) ('wait (for)') a meaning of its own independent of the verb' (Engel and Schumacher, 1976:62).

The application of a test based on this concept gives certain positive results: if a preposition cannot be exchanged with another preposition having a similar meaning, and/or no meaning can easily be assigned to the preposition independent of the verb, then this is a strong indication that the prepositional element is a complement of the verb, and that the preposition is strongly governed by the verb. Unfortunately, a negative result of the test does not necessarily imply adjunct status. Notable examples of this can be provided by verbs of motion already mentioned.

It is appropriate at this stage to add our own test for the distinction of complements and adjuncts to those described above. We present briefly here what we shall call the 'do so' test, though for further discussion see Somers (1984:516ff).

Several authors (e.g. Quirk *et al.*, 1972:49, 582, 684–697; Palmer, 1974:23f, 161) have noted the use of *do* as a general proform for verbs, and in a famous article, Lakoff and Ross (1976) described the use of the phrase *do so* as a proform for the verb phrase. Thus (21a) may be reduced to (21b):

(21a) Harry went to Reading and Bev went to Reading.
(21b) Harry went to Reading and Bev did so too.

Lakoff and Ross (1976:105) suggest that this substitution is not possible with stative verbs, though the unacceptability of their example with *know* (22) is arguable, nor with predicative adjectives, whether stative or not (23).

(22) * Bill knew the answer, and Harry did so, too.
(23a) * John was heavy, and Bill did so, too.
(23b) * John was careful, and Bill did so, too.

The important observation however is that '. . . elements that may occur after *do so* are outside of the verb-phrase (are not constituents of VP), and elements that cannot occur are inside the verb phrase' (Lakoff and Ross, 1976:105). If we translate into Valency grammar terms, it would appear that the *do so* construction provides us with a reliable means of distinguishing complements and adjuncts. The fact that *tomorrow* occurs in the second part of (24) tells us that the corresponding element italicised in the first phrase is an adjunct.

(24) John took a trip *last Tuesday*, and I'm going to do so tomorrow.

Lakoff and Ross make the claim '. . . that *do so* replaces all of the constituents of the verb phrase and only these' (Lakoff and Ross, 1976:105) but (25) shows that this is erroneous.

(25) Bill bought Gladys a present in Manchester today on an impulse, and Roger did so too / and Roger did so in Bury / and Roger will do so tomorrow / but Roger did so after careful consideration.

However, this does not affect the applicability of our 'do so' test, which can be stated as follows: while a *do so* phrase can be the proform of anything up to the entire predication (less its subject), the minimum element that can be substituted is the predicate plus any complements (again, other than the subject). Thus from the unacceptability of the sentences in (26) we are able to confirm complement status for the italicised elements.

(26a) * I live *in Manchester* and Jock does so *in Salford*.

(26b) * Harold drives *a Volkswagen* and Rod does so *a Lancia*.

(26c) * The News lasts *for fifteen minutes* and the Weather Report does so *for five*.

(26d) * Pete bought a car *for £200* and Kieran did so *for £300*.

Notice incidentally that this test does not test for the complement status of the subject, but all other functions are covered. In the 'do so' test, it is not the fact that an element can be understood to be part of the proform that makes it a complement, but the fact that it cannot occur alongside the proform. The acceptability of (27) tells us nothing about the status of *yesterday*, whereas the unacceptability of the sentences in (26) tells us precisely that the italicised elements are complements.

(27) Mike started a new job yesterday and so did Fred.

Corresponding tests for languages that have similar constructions can be proposed: Happ (1978*a*:115) suggests one for French; Brinker's (1972:190f) test with the connective *und zwar* ('and what is more') seems to work in a comparable way for German; and the Japanese construction *mo . . . soo suru* is strikingly similar to the English *do so* (Somers, 1984:518).

4. *Syntactic versus semantic valency*

For the most part, Valency grammar is presented as a theory of syntax, where the valency pattern of a verb is a description of the syntactic patterns into which it enters, or which it governs. But there are versions of Valency grammar that strive to incorporate an appeal to the semantic characteristics of the arguments in a given predication. We have already seen that there is a certain conflict between the levels of expression and intention, as where the omission of an optional complement nevertheless implies its being 'understood': this is Heringer's (1968:427) notion of ellipsis, illustrated in (1), in which expression of the optional adjectival complement *bad* in (1b) is essentially vacuous for this use of *smell*.

(1a) The mushrooms smell.
(1b) The mushrooms smell bad.

Stötzel (1970) looks at other apparent contradictions in his treatment of reflexive verbs. He is concerned that although the syntactic valency of a reflexive verb might specify the reflexive pronoun as an obligatory complement, noting further that in this way certain pairs of transitive and intransitive-reflexive verbs could be said to have the same valency pattern (2), such verb pairs should be differentiated, in that intuitively there is some semantic distinction to be drawn.

(2a) Fritz ärgert mich.
FRITZ ANNOYS ME
(2b) Fritz ärgert sich.
FRITZ ANNOYS SELF
'Fritz is getting angry'

In a similar manner, meteorological verbs like *regnen* ('rain') can be said to be syntactically monovalent, but semantically avalent, the presence of the formal subject *es* on the 'expression level' (3a) being determined merely by the feature of German grammar that requires most verbs to have a subject in simple declarative sentences. English and French have a similar constraint (3b-c), though Italian and Spanish do not (3d-e).

(3a) Es regnet.
(3b) It is raining.
(3c) Il pleut.
(3d) Piove.
(3e) Llueve.

Stötzel does not suggest that semantic valency is more important, but merely that the two should be distinguished. Stötzel is criticised both by Emons (1974:60f) and by Biere (1976:162ff), not for his desire to distinguish two types of valency, but for not being able to show clearly the consequences of this distinction. The lack of operational criteria for distinguishing syntactic and semantic valency is highlighted by Emons, who suggests (1974:61) that it is only at the expression (syntactic) level that data are available, and that anything of interest at the intention (semantic) level must be regarded in relation to its expression. Biere (1976:163) on the other hand points out that, although Stötzel's distinction of the two types of information is well established, he uses only syntactic information to distinguish valency patterns.

The Arbeitsgruppe Marburg (1973) criticise Stötzel's ideas from a different angle: they suggest that it is only in the case of meteorological impersonal verbs, and of verbs taking a 'non-communicative' reflexive pronoun (e.g. *sich schämen* – 'be ashamed') that syntactic and semantic valency are at odds. In the latter case, they say that the verbal lexeme can be considered disjoint, while the former constitute a small and easily definable set of exceptions to a general rule: 'A theory . . . which is *redundant* for the description of the *overwhelming majority* of cases seems uneconomical, to say the least' (Arbeitsgruppe Marburg, 1973:20) [emphases mine]. We can regard Stötzel's failure to convince other Valency grammarians of the need to consider more closely the semantic level as perhaps partly due to the lack of any model of semantic valency with which he could more clearly express his insights. Such a model is of course provided by Case grammar, which at the time (1970) was only just gaining currency, and we can imagine Stötzel may have been unaware of Case grammar – at least until it was too late to incorporate it in his book.

Leech (1981) makes more explicit the correspondence between syntactic and semantic valency, using the example of *say* and *speak*, which on the surface are differentiated as being bivalent and monovalent respectively, while expressing 'the same basic meaning' (p. 198). The interest of this analysis is stressed: '. . . the point is that valency has both a syntactic and a corresponding semantic aspect. The definitions of *say* and *speak* differ in that *speak* incorporates a null argument; that is, the meaning of *speak* is roughly "to say *something*"' (Leech, 1981:198). Leech is careful to distinguish syntactic and semantic valency: 'Although the example of *say* and *speak* is oversimplified, it does show that syntactic valency is independent of what we might now fittingly call "semantic valency": the combinatorial possibilities of predicates and their terms. Both verbs *say* and *speak* express the same two-place predicate SAY, and yet their syntactic valencies are different' (Leech, 1981:198f). Leech goes on to exemplify different ways in which semantic valency patterns map onto syntactic ones, noting such phenomena as polyvalency of verbs (and resulting occasional ambiguities), and the optional 'realisation' of some valency-bound elements. Finally, Leech notes that it is not only verbs which have valency, but members of other word classes too. It is to this notion that we now turn our attention.

5. *Extensions to classes other than verbs*

While most of the work in Valency grammar has been concerned with verbs, many authors have been quite prepared to consider also that adjectives and nouns used predicatively should be analysed in a similar manner, and this issue has become more or less uncontentious. Several recent works on Valency have covered the predicative use of adjectives and (to a lesser extent) nouns, and some have indeed been wholly concerned with this topic (e.g. Sommerfeldt and Schreiber, 1974, 1975; Teubert, 1979). It is true that there has been some question whether a predicative adjective or noun is to be regarded as a complement of the copula, as in Engel and Schumacher (1976:72ff) or as the predicate *per se*, as Heringer (1970*a*:169ff) strongly proposes, or even some combination of these, as with Helbig and Schenkel's (1973:23) analysis of *böse sein* ('be angry') (1), in which *böse* ('angry') is a complement of *sein* ('be'), but *ihrer Tochter* ('with her daughter') is dependent on *böse*.

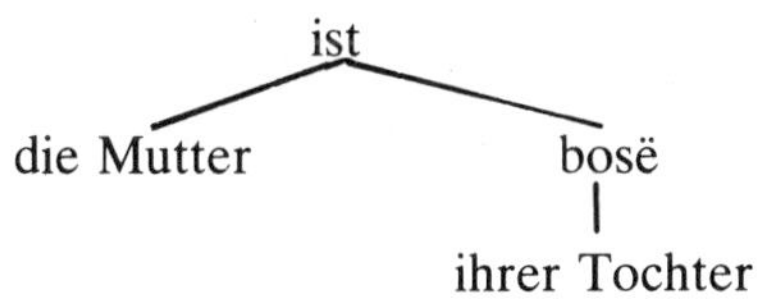

(1) Die Mutter ist ihrer Tochter böse.
'The mother is angry with her daughter'

However, there is a school of thought closely related to Valency grammar in which all or most word classes have some 'valency' attributed to them. This line of thought seems to be a feature of the Soviet approach to Valency – cf. references given by Helbig and Schenkel (1973:21, 81), amongst them Mel'čuk (1964) is notable – but is largely ignored by German Valency grammarians.

The notion that adjectives and nouns may enter into dependency relationships as governors is well recognised by early Valency grammarians, but the extension of this notion for non-predicative adjectives and nouns in the way that it is extended for verbs, with syntactic form and semantic restrictions of complements described, is largely not taken up.

As mentioned in the previous section, Leech (1981) briefly suggests that members of word-classes other than verb can have valency. He does not pursue the discussion in detail, but suggests *happy* as (in our terminology) monovalent, while '. . . an adjective like *glad*, although similar in meaning to *happy*, requires two elements to complete its meaning: *a is glad at/about b.* (This might be explained in everyday language by saying that *happy* signifies a simple 'unfocused' emotion, whereas *glad* represents an emotion which is 'focused' on some source or object of feeling.)' (Leech, 1981:199).

Among German Valency grammarians, the notion of non-verbal valency has only recently been given much attention. Korhohnen (1977:170ff) is able to show that there are certain respects in which it makes sense to regard non-predicative adjectives and nouns especially as having a 'valency pattern'. There is a clear sense in which nouns derived from verbs can be said to have a valency pattern which will correspond at the semantic level very closely to that of the verb, in that similar if not identical selection restrictions on arguments will apply, and at the syntactic level may be derivable from it by general rule (though admittedly these rules may be quite complex) – cf. (2)-(4).

(2a) The people are fighting for freedom.
(2b) The people's fight for freedom . . .
(3a) The boy gave his brother a book.
(3b) The boy's gift of a book to his brother . . .
(4a) The government raised $10m by indirect taxation.
(4b) The raising by the government of $10m by indirect taxation . . .

In their treatment of nominal valency, Sommerfeldt and Schreiber (1975, 1977) consider only nouns derivable from adjectives and verbs as we have so far, and conclude that nouns can have a maximum of three complements, all of which are naturally optional (since a noun can always stand alone). This seems an unexpected restriction, given that one can easily imagine nominalisations of verbs whose valency is greater than three, and indeed the restriction does not seem to hold, at least for English (5).

(5) Bill's purchase of a car from John for £150 . . .

It is conceivable that Sommerfeldt and Schreiber's upper limit results from their suggestion that noun complements can only be realised as genitives or prepositional phrases (1975:117), and that this method of noun group construction is less natural in German, where there is a preference to coin complex compound nouns.

Korhohnen (1977:172) suggests that for the most part the distinction of complement or adjunct status for arguments in noun groups (including nouns not derived from verbs or adjectives) is relatively straightforward, though this notion seems to be based on the dubious principle of free insertability of adjuncts (see Section 2). There are difficulties however with genitives, which by the criterion of free insertability generally look like adjuncts, but by the criterion of communicative necessity (see Section 3) appear to be complements.

Leech is very brief on noun valency, but his one statement does seem to suggest support for this treatment of nouns not derived from verbs: 'Nouns are a mixed category as regards valency: some nouns, e.g. those signifying natural kinds or artefacts, are univalent [i.e. monovalent in our terminology], in contrast to relational nouns such as *father*, *end*, *employee*, etc. which are bivalent' (Leech, 1981:199).

It is not clear what there is to be gained from considering nouns not immediately derivable from predicates as possible governors of valency patterns, especially when we concentrate on syntactic valency. Equally, it is clear that normalisations of predicates are amenable to the sort of analysis Valency theory affords. We should not leave the question of noun valency without drawing attention to the approach of Dependency theory (see Section 7), upon which Valency theory can be said to be based. In Dependency theory, as seen for example in the work of Tesnière (cf. Section 2), the relationship within a noun group between the noun and its modifiers (determiner, adjectives, etc.) is seen as one of governor and governed; but it seems that to attempt to describe these relationships in terms of 'valency' would flounder: patterning between heads and modifiers does not seem to be 'predictable' in the way that patterning within predicate groups is, and it is this patterning that is the basis of Valency grammar.

6. *On the binary nature of the complement-adjunct distinction*

Most Valency grammarians have taken for granted the basic distinction between complements and adjuncts and, as we have seen above, are more concerned with discovering operational means of establishing this distinction. In this section it is proposed to look more closely at this distinction, and to put forward the view that valency-boundness is not a simple binary feature in the argument-predicate relationship, but that there are additional values for valency-boundness, in particular for arguments which are to be regarded as neither valency-bound complements nor completely free adjuncts, but as lying in some intermediate area.

Let us take as our starting point the consideration of a verbal predication as a combination of predicate and arguments. This is relatively easy to exemplify with a verb-phrase, though the notions should also be extendable to nominalisation of predicates. In a verbal phrase like (1), it is relatively clear that by any account only *yesterday* is circumstantial and therefore an adjunct, the other elements *the man*, *a car* and *from the salesman* being complements of the verb *buy*.

(1) The man bought a car from the salesman yesterday.

The intuitive notion that Valency grammar is attempting to capture is that some elements are central to the predication, and some are peripheral, and furthermore that these correspond to complements and adjuncts respectively. Another way of saying the same thing is that central participants (complements) pertain to the predicate itself, while peripheral participants (adjuncts) pertain to the predication as a whole. A more striking example is provided in (2):

(2) On behalf of the Commission the committee yesterday granted Portugal 100 000 EAUs for her disaster victims.

Here the predication is one where the central participants in the granting are the granter, the receiver of the grant and the thing granted: thus *the committee*, *Portugal* and *100 000 EAUs* are complements to *grant*. Their roles are directly pertinent to the predicate *grant*. The remaining elements all provide the context for the whole predication: it is not merely the act of granting that goes on on behalf of the Commission, but the act of granting a particular sum to a particular country by a particular body; it is the whole event that is placed in the time by the adverbial *yesterday*; and again the disaster victims benefit not simply from a granting, but from a granting by the committee to Portugal of 100 000 EAUS.

The notion of central and peripheral participants is well established in linguistics literature outside the field of Valency grammar: Longacre (1973:35) distinguishes 'nuclear' and 'peripheral' elements, while Cook (1972*a*), Dik (1978) and Halliday (1970) have similar concepts. These have been discussed by me previously (Somers and Johnson, 1979:87; Somers, 1980*a*:10; 1980*b*:18; 1982*c*:240), and are also treated in later chapters (see Chapters 4, 6 and 9). In each of these discussions I made a three-way distinction between what I called 'obligatory', 'expected' and 'optional' roles; the terminology may be confusing, but these correspond for the most part to obligatory complements, optional complements and adjuncts respectively of standard Valency grammar. But the rider 'for the most part' is important, because it is not clear that all 'expected' roles are complements. I have noted that there are different degrees of expectation of these roles that are neither obligatory complements nor adjuncts. For example, the optional complement *Steve* in (3a), filling a role that is otherwise implicit – in (3b) we assume the recipient is unknown or unimportant – is more strongly 'expected' than the *hammer* in (4a), whose role is certainly not implicit if not realised, as in (4b).

(3a) Debbie gave Steve a book.
(3b) Debbie gave a book.
(4a) Nick smashed the vase with a hammer.
(4b) Nick smashed the vase.

So here already we have a possible subdivision, and while *with a hammer* in (4a) may not obviously be a complement at all, it is certainly somehow more central to the predicate *smash* than *yesterday* is in (4c).

(4c) Nick smashed the vase yesterday.

We can see from these examples then that there seems to be a type of relationship between the predicate and some elements that lies between complement and adjunct. The point is that while *Steve* in (3a) clearly 'pertains to the predicate itself' (cf. above), and *yesterday* in (4c) equally clearly 'pertains to the predication as a whole', no such clear-cut distinction can be made about *with a hammer* in (4a). Further examples fairly abound (5)-(8), and the difficulty is accentuated if the sentence includes a clearly peripheral element: in (8b) the adjunct *this morning* sets the time context for the entire predication (8a), including the non-valency-bound element *the squire*.

(5) Jock speaks French *with a Scottish accent.*
(6) Liz hid the keys *for a joke.*
(7) The monkey ate the banana *with obvious enjoyment.*
(8a) The gamekeeper shot *the squire* a rabbit.
(8b) The gamekeeper shot the squire a rabbit this morning.

Matthews seems to have recognised the same phenomenon, as Figure 1 shows:

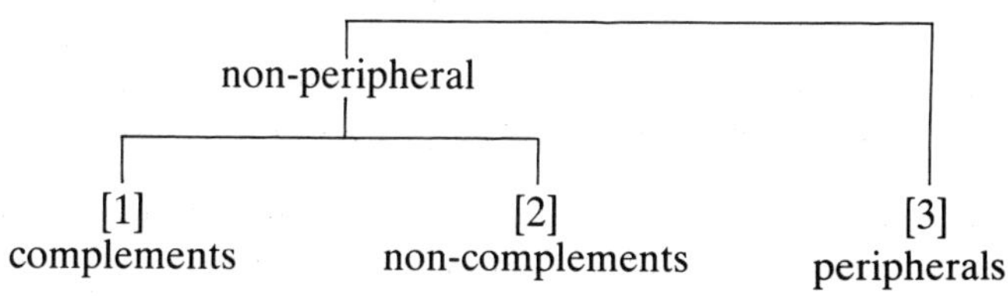

Figure 1: From Matthews (1981:140)

Note however that 'non-peripheral non-complements' [2] and 'peripherals' [3] can logically be grouped together as non-valency-bound elements, as in Figure 2:

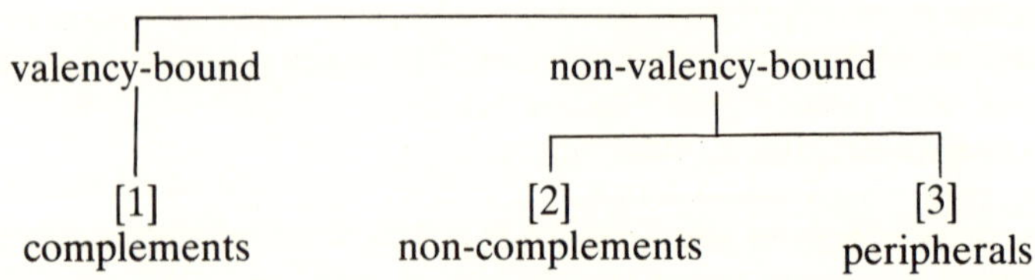

Figure 2

The particular usefulness of this approach to Valency in natural language processing will be expanded in Chapter 12 Section 1. Suffice to say that, far from undermining the theory as a whole, it gives it a certain flexibility without which it might be too rigid a formalism for the kind of task envisaged. Nor does the introduction of the concept of a middle term between complement and adjunct in any way devalue previous work in Valency. Dictionaries of verb valencies still reflect correctly the valency patterns of particular verbs: the introduction of 'middle' elements in sentences is a general feature of language, largely independent of the individual valency patterns of verbs, just as adjuncts form no part of the dictionary entry (even though they are not so freely insertable as some authors suggest). Indeed, with this new Valency framework in mind, we can review some of the tests described in Section 3, and note that perhaps in some cases where the tests seemed to fail or be difficult to apply, this may be precisely because the element being tested is in fact 'middle', i.e. neither complement nor adjunct, but a bit of both. For example, we might have suggested some correspondence between the ease of application of the backformation test and valency-binding; in addition to the correspondence suggested above, we could consider that if the test was difficult to apply for syntactic reasons (for example, difficulty in constructing a plausible subordinate clause), this might be a pointer to just this 'middle' type of valency-binding.

The next addition we wish to make is to distinguish a further more closely bound type of complement which, following Weissgerber (1983:24) we shall call an 'integral complement'. We have already seen that the term 'obligatory complement' is badly chosen, because these so-called obligatory elements can in fact be omitted in a fairly wide range of constructions – notably passives, infinitivals, nominalisations – and under certain contextual conditions. There are however some complements that are quite resistent even to these omission possibilities, because the complement is such an integral part of the predicate. Examples of this are the nominals in *pave the way*, *keep pace*, *have a chance*, *put at risk*, etc. In Somers (1984) this new distinction is discussed in more detail, but notice the key difference that integral complements are lexically determined, whereas obligatory complements are generally only restricted to a more or less general semantic class. One essential benefit of this analysis is that it relieves many verb-plus-integral constructions of their status as 'idioms', integrating them more systematically into the scheme of description.

To complete the picture, we may briefly mention 'extra-peripheral modifiers', which are, as their name suggests, more 'peripheral' than the outermost elements so far suggested. These are elements which modify an entire proposition, adjuncts included, and are typically logical or discursive modifiers like *usually*, or *as you know*. Figure 3 then represents the whole range from those elements most closely bound to the verb at the top to those most distant at the bottom: we have expanded the traditional two-value scale to six distinct degrees of valency binding.

integral complements
|
'obligatory' complements
|
optional complements
|
middles
|
adjuncts
|
extra-peripherals

Figure 3: Range of valency-binding

It remains of course to demonstrate what effects this new set-up has on the framework as a whole. In Somers (1984) a number of criteria are suggested for distinguishing the new values based on the syntactic and semantic properties associated with the various degrees of valency binding. These can be summarised as follows: (i) Integral complements are lexically determined; no substitution by close synonyms is permitted; modification within the complement (e.g. with adjectives) is severely restricted; they cannot be omitted; they do not enter syntagmatic substitution paradigms (e.g. pronominalisation).

(ii) 'Obligatory' and optional complements are strictly subcategorised by the predicate for semantic class, syntactic function (especially when prepositional) and often syntactic form (e.g. noun phrase, subordinate clause with *that*, etc.).

(iii) Middle elements are broadly determined by the general semantic class of the predicate; they have characteristics of both complements and adjuncts; thus they behave erratically in distinction texts.

(iv) Adjuncts are subject to more general semantic/pragmatic restrictions (i.e. the need to 'make sense'); they are less restricted as regards word order; they are more or less completely unpredictable from the predicate or predicate class; they can co-occur with complements of the same semantic type.

(v) Extra-peripherals are amost entirely unrestricted both semantically and as regards word-order; the only constraints are pragmatic, and therefore difficult to generalise.

7. *Dependency grammar*

Some of the notions of Valency theory have been strictly formalised in the writings on dependency theory of authors such as Hays (1960*a*, *b*, 1964), Gaifman (1965), Robinson (1970) and Mel'čuk (1979). In each case the writers have principally been concerned with describing the formal properties of dependency relations and the dependency trees which are used to represent them, and of establishing a notation for the theory. In the case of Gaifman and Robinson, the dependency model is compared with the phrase-structure grammar approach of Transformational Generative grammar. Heringer (1970*a*, *b*) is notable among Valency grammarians for establishing the link between Valency and Dependency theories. All these accounts tend to be highly rigorous and abstract, and although the mathematical properties were of interest in early computational Information Theory, the essential aspects of Dependency theory as far as the present work is concerned are adequately captured by Herbst *et al.* (1979:32-46) and by Matthews (1981:78-84), who describes the essential notions of the model and considers the extent to which a dependency grammar and a phrase-structure grammar are weakly and/or strongly equivalent (pp. 83ff). The interested reader is referred to these primary and secondary sources.

8. *Closing remarks*

In conclusion, we may consider to what extent the basic notions of Valency grammar are intuitively appealing. In particular the subdivision of elements into those more or less closely bound to the verb seems to reflect some linguistically correct notion, and if the additions proposed, especially the middle value between complement and adjunct, improve the formalisation, then so much the better. There is certainly a use for Valency-like grammars in computational linguistics, especially in connection with some notions taken from Case grammar, and in Part III we shall see how these diverse elements can be brought together in a computational model of natural language processing.

TWO

FILLMORE

1. *Introduction*

There can be absolutely no doubt that Charles Fillmore is regarded as the originator of the modern school of Case grammar. In this chapter, we shall look at the series of articles in which he expounded and developed the theory, and at some of the reactions to those papers. The most important problems of Case grammar (including the definition of some of the cases themselves) are treated elsewhere in this work (Part II), in keeping with the general theme here of a quest for a version of Case grammar which retains its benefits while trying to minimise its major deficiencies. We shall therefore limit ourselves in the present chapter to giving a brief résumé of what Fillmore has said. Such summaries are to be found in most major works on Case. We will assume in the reader a general familiarity with Fillmore's major works, and summarise in detail only those parts that we wish to make particular comment on, or to which attention is not otherwise generally drawn.

We may divide Fillmore's work on Case into three phases: in phase I, we see the development of the theory based, as the title of his (1966*a*) paper suggests, on a proposal for the treatment of prepositions in a Transformational Generative (TG) framework. In the two other articles during this period (1966*b*, 1968*a*), the TG version of Case grammar was consolidated. The latter of these two, 'The case for Case', was of course the one which attracted most attention, but already by this time it seems that Fillmore was entering into his second phase, with the publication of (1968*b*), the first of several papers in which the model became much more oriented towards describing in the lexicon the syntactic and semantic behaviour of verbs (1970, 1971*a*). During this period, Fillmore also published his first major revision of the model (1971*b*) in response to criticisms of (1968*a*), while his (1971*c*) article on 'verbs of judging', barely Case-like at all, indicated the new direction his thoughts would take. The third phase of Fillmorean Case saw him becoming more interested in discourse (1972) and lexical semantics (1977*a*), with standard TG considerations largely disappearing. The Case model itself did not undergo any more significant alterations – Fillmore left this to his disciples and imitators – though in his (1977*b*) article he attempted again to answer some of his critics. For a concise overview of this development of the model, see Platt (1972:33f).

2. *Phase 1. Up to and including 'The case for Case'*

While 'The case for Case' (1968*a*) is generally cited as the key reference for Case, it is interesting to see how the grammar was developed from his earlier paper, 'A proposal concerning English prepositions' (1966*a*).

In this paper, Fillmore presents his proposal in the light of the questioned validity of the relational notions 'subject' and 'object' as found in Chomsky's *Aspects* (1965:63-73), and, using the now familiar examples with *open*, suggests that the distinction between the categorial labels 'noun phrase' and 'preposition phrase' is not found in the deep structure, but is introduced by transformations and deletion of the preposition (which is part of every noun phrase) after the noun phrase which is to be subject has been chosen. The significant differences between this proposal and the better-known later model (1968*a*) are in two respects.

First, the set of cases suggested differs, though only slightly. Indeed Fillmore does not yet use the term 'case', but talks of '. . . nominal elements which are relevant to the subclassification of verbs' (1966*a*:22) which he calls 'actants', citing Tesnière (1959) as his source.

The second significant difference is his treatment of the prepositions themselves. We do not have the 'Kasus' function of (1968*a*:33), but a set of rules (renumbered here) as follows:

(1) Prop → V (Erg) (Dat) (Loc) (Inst) (Ag)

$$(2)\quad \left\{ \begin{array}{l} \text{Erg} \\ \text{Dat} \\ \text{Loc} \\ \ldots \end{array} \right\} \rightarrow \text{NP}$$

(3) NP → P (Det) (S) N

Fillmore notes the unusual 'unary and many-to-one' expansion of these elements, which distinguishes them from 'true grammatical categories' (p. 22). But most notably, Fillmore suggests three ways in which the surface forms of the prepositions can be chosen:

(i) 'Some prepositions are filled in from the Lexicon. Location prepositions (*over, under, on, in,* etc.) are introduced in this way, with some constraints. These prepositions bring with them semantic information'.

(ii) 'Some prepositions are assigned by inherent syntactic features of specific verbs. Thus *blame* requires the ergative preposition to be *for*, the dative preposition to be *on* . . .'

(iii) 'The remaining prepositions are filled in by rules which make use of information about the actants . . .' (1966*a*:23)

This approach contrasts with that in (1968*a*:32), where the third of these alternatives appears to be the norm, the second applying only to L]ocative] and T]ime] cases, and the first must be brought about by obligatory transformations associated with the particular verb (1968*a*:32*fn*). In retrospect, this innovation seems unfortunate, since his earlier position was rather more appealing intuitively and, incidentally, would have made Case appear more compatible with the Valency grammar view of prepositional complements.

A second paper 'Toward a modern theory of Case' (1966*b*) is almost identical to the first, at least in its interesting sections; indeed it is described as a 'longer version' of (1966*a*). However, there are some other points of interest. For example, the discussion of the syntactic behaviour of *open* is emphasised by a list (pp. 364f) of fifty-one similarly patterning verbs.

We move on now to the most important of the three articles of this period, and possibly Fillmore's best-known paper altogether: 'The case for Case' (1968*a*). The description of 'Case grammar', as it is called now for the first time, begins on p. 21 with, just as in the previous two versions, a replacement of the Chomskyan base rule (4) by (5), with the focus on the P element, expanded as in (6) (correcting the presumable misprint) (1968*a*:24):

(4) $S \rightarrow NP + VP$

(5) $S \rightarrow M + P$

(6) $P \rightarrow V + C_1 + \ldots + C_n$

It is at this point that occur the oft-cited definitions of the case notions as 'a set of universal, presumably innate, concepts . . . [etc.]', and the individual definitions of Agentive, Instrumental, Dative, Factitive, Locative and Objective. Fillmore continues: 'Additional cases will surely be needed. Suggestions for adding to this list will appear in various places below' (1968*a*:25) and indeed they do, though generally quite informally: on p. 32, the list of cases is repeated, though with Benefactive added, and Dative omitted. Does this imply one case or two? Presumably two, because lower down the page, the typical associated prepositions for both B and D are given. It is here also that another case, 'T (for time)', is introduced. The only other case we find is C[omitative], which comes in almost as an afterthought on p. 82.

This almost cavalier expansion of the set of cases has given rise to an amount of justified criticism: cf. Langacker (1970:171*fn*) and Chapin: 'For such a proposal to be of interest, it is essential that the inventory of cases be not just finite but quite small in number related to the number of predicates in the vocabulary of a single language. . . . Furthermore, it is essential that the cases postulated be precisely defined so as to force correct descriptive decisions. A case system which permits the postulation of a new case to handle every problematic instance is not a theory of substantive universals, but a notational system for ad hoc description' (Chapin, 1972:651).

The notion that the inventory of cases should form a closed set and that they should be well-defined is an important theoretical issue. If they do form a closed set, for example, then the use of one of them as a 'wastebasket', defined negatively in terms of the others, is quite acceptable, at least from a set theoretic point of view, even if it may not be intuitively very appealing. Mellema defends (perhaps unintentionally) this point: 'Since we already know how to recognise all the other cases, we can easily identify Objects as well. If an NP or S does not belong to any of the other cases, we know that it belongs in the "wastebasket" Objective case' (Mellema, 1974:49).

We shall consider in Chapter 7 in some detail the definitions of many of the individual cases, but we mention here three important constraints suggested by Fillmore as an aid to distinguishing and determining the cases. The first of these is the 'one-case-per-clause' constraint: '. . . only one representative of a given case relationship may appear in the same simple sentence' (1968*a*: 22). This constraint is discussed more fully in Chapter 9, but we may briefly note that apparent contraventions of this constraint may often be analysed as deriving from coordinations (7), subordinations (8), or some other dependency (9).

(7a) Harold went to the match with Nick. [two Agentives?]
(7b) Harold and Nick went to the match.
(8a) I sat on the bench in the park. [two Locatives?]
(8b) I sat on the bench which was in the park.
(9a) The car broke the window with its fender. [two Instruments?]
(9b) The car's fender broke the window.

The second constraint is that 'only noun phrases representing the same case can be conjoined' (1968*a*:22). This contraint is used to demonstrate that the surface subjects in (10a-b) are in different cases because of the unacceptability of (10c). This constraint is fairly straightforward, although reciprocal verbs like *fight* and *argue* cause some problems, since intuition tells us that the subjects and 'objects' in (11) are not playing the same roles, yet coordination is possible in each case (12).

(10a) John broke the window.
(10b) A hammer broke the window.
(10c) * John and a hammer broke the window.
(11a) The French fought the English.
(11b) Rod is arguing with Pete.
(12a) The French and the English fought.
(12b) Rod and Pete are arguing.

For many commentators, the combination of these two constraints is the strongest and most reliable tool Case grammar has.

The third constraint is in a sense the corollary of the one-case-per-clause principle, and that is that each argument is associated with one and only one case: 'one-case-per-argument'. As a result of these two 'unicity' principles, there should be a one-to-one mapping of cases and arguments. In fact this third constraint causes many problems, which we discuss in Chapter 8, when we consider the problem of 'dual roles'.

Independent of the definition of the set of cases, it will be remembered that Fillmore (1968*a*:24) claims, rather boldly, that his cases are both universal and innate. On the question of innateness, there have been a number of experiments aimed at testing the psychological reality of some of the case notions. The most interesting of these are those of Shafto (1973) and Braine and Wells (1978). In addition, Kintsch (1974) reports a large number of experiments which seem to support the general notion of a proposition consisting of a predicator plus cases as a plausible memory model for sentences. This finding is further supported by Abrahamson (1975) and Gentner (1975).

The next few pages of Fillmore (1968*a*) concern the lexical selection of nouns and verbs. In the former, selection is determined to some extent by rules relating features of nouns to the case they are dominated by – notably for example animacy for Agentive and Dative. More interesting though is the lexical selection of verbs: in this strictly TG-oriented version of Case grammar, note that 'The insertion of verbs . . . depends on the particular array of cases, the "case frame", provided by the sentence' (1968*a*:27). This contrasts with later, more Valency-like versions of Case grammar, where the case frame is given by the choice of the verb. Seyfert (1976:181ff) discusses this aspect in detail, and there does seem to be a certain incongruence in a verb-centred deep structure in which the verb is inserted last. The contrast with Chafe's (1970:97) approach, in which the case frame for the sentence is determined by the predicate, will be seen in a later chapter.

The next section of (1968*a*) concerns the conversion of the deep structures into surface strings, and includes the notions of prepositions associated with each case (p. 32), the 'Kasus' element (p. 33), subject selection and the associated transformations.

The association of a particular preposition with each case is, as mentioned above, a departure from the more attractive notion given in (1966*a*:23), in which there are three different ways in which prepositions are chosen, of which the one suggested here is the last choice, rather than the default, and the proposal is dropped by Fillmore in later reformulations: Dougherty (1970:524) is typical in noting that the preposition *by* is more obviously associated with whatever was the surface subject before passivisation (compare (13) and (14)) than with the Agentive.

(13) The book was seen by John. (Dative)

(14) The door was opened by the wind. (Instrumental)

Robinson on the other hand re-iterates the Valency-like notion of verbal government of prepositions: '. . . the prepositions often appear to have stronger selection ties with a particular preceding verb outside the prepositional phrase than with the following NP within the phrase' (Robinson, 1970:59).

Welin (1975:49) too notes the many-to-many correspondence between prepositions and cases, citing Walmsley's (1971) work on the Comitative case, Nilsen's (1973) study of the Instrumental (in which he illustrates pp. 32 62 the different cases with which the preposition *with* can be associated), and Brodda's (1973) work on Swedish (which has a relatively small number of prepositions at its disposal), and discussing the 'decidedly syntactic' use exemplified by the introduction of *by* by passivisation, and the 'inherent argument' use where the choice of preposition is governed by the verb. To these two uses already noted, Welin adds the 'independent lexical use' also noted by Fillmore (1968*a*:32), especially with Locatives (Fillmore calls them 'semantically nonempty' prepositions), and those choices of preposition for individual verbs which 'may imply small but regular differences in meaning' (p. 50), as exemplified by *smear with/on, read* (*from*), *climb* (*up*), *shoot* (*at*), etc. This final use comes under the 'holistic-partitive' distinction (terms coined by S.

Anderson, 1971:389). We shall return briefly to this topic in Chapter 7 Section 5.

A significant portion of (1968*a*) is concerned with illustrating the transformations involved in converting the underlying phrase-markers into surface strings, and it is in this respect that the TG orientation of the article is reinforced. A thorough and not uncritical résumé of this aspect of (1968*a*) can be found in Cook (1970). There seem to be two main respects in which the (1968*a*) model can be criticised as an alternative to the Standard Theory, along with a number of more minor criticisms concerning the particularities of some of Fillmore's rules (particularly (6) above) which we shall not go into in detail. The first of these major problems is that of regarding the cases themselves as categories in the way that NP and V clearly are; the second, related to the first, is that a tree with cases in it is really a dependency tree, not a phrase-structure tree.

That the cases might be intended to be seen as categories stems from their participation in rewrite rules and PS trees which is entirely analagous with that of more evident categories like NP, V, N, etc. Yet the descriptions of the cases are clearly relational, and even if they were to be regarded as labels rather than nodes *per se*, this would still be a departure from the standard TG notation: 'The rule schema . . . mixes categorial notions with relational (functional) ones in a way that Chomsky sought to avoid by defining functions in terms of configurations of categories, rather than by directly labelling them' (Robinson, 1970:65).

Certainly, there is evidence that Fillmore regarded the cases as relational rather than categorial entities, even if the following three extracts, juxtaposed by Falkenberg and Öhlschläger (1971:189; quoted by Emons, 1974:47f), seem to indicate that he was unclear as to what they related to:

(i) 'The sentence in its basic structure consists of a verb and one or more noun phrases, each associated *with the verb* in a particular case relationship.' (1968*a*:21)

(ii) '. . . the deep structure of (the propositional component of) every simple sentence is an array consisting of a V plus a number of NP's holding special labelled relations (cases) *to the sentence*.' (1968*a*:31f)

(iii) 'In their deep structure, the propositional nucleus of sentences in all languages consists of a V and one or more NP's, each having a separate case relationship *to the P* (and hence to the V).' (1968*a*:51) [emphases added by F & O]

Notice, in addition, that '. . . certain "cases" will be directly related to the modality constituent . . .' (1968*a*:23).

Once we accept the case labels as relational, the whole transformational setting for Case grammar is thrown into question. For example, there is a clear conflict between the status of the proposition (P) before and after the transformations take place. Fillmore defines it as 'a tenseless set of relations involving verbs and nouns . . .' (1968*a*:23), yet '. . . [transformational] rules like subject fronting are allowed to change its structure, removing arguments to other parts of the tree and leaving behind only a part of what was there before . . .' (Rosner and Somers, 1980:7).

Cook suggests that 'The development of phrase structure rules imposes a rigidity upon Case grammar which is not there in its deep structure. Although the rules are derived from trees, the trees are intended to be nonlinear representations, like a mobile, where none of the parts is in fixed order' (Cook, 1970: 14).

Chomsky (1972:100) comments that the rules described by Fillmore fall into two categories: those that 'map case systems into phrase-markers', and those 'which generate derivations in the usual way'. Cook's picture of trees as unordered nonlinear representations really underlines the fact that they are mis-shaped dependency trees, in which the governing nodes are identifiable either by their particularly different shape (as in (15)), or by some convention or labelling, though they appear at the same level as their dependents.

(15)

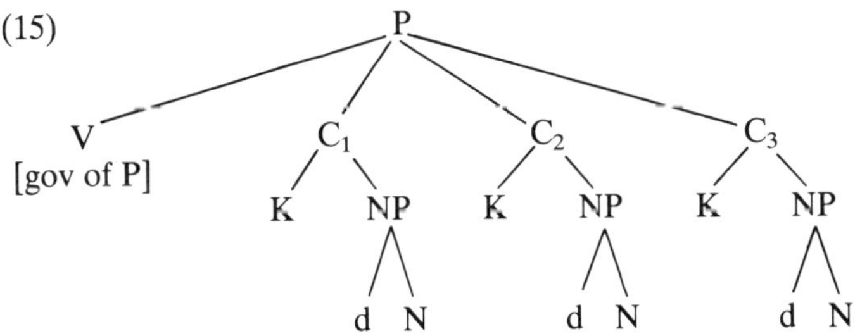

This notation is a useful way of simulating phrase-structure in a dependency framework (cf. Vauquois (1978:3) and King and Perschke (1982:29) for a computational exploitation of this), and it is perhaps interesting to speculate what might have been the reaction if Fillmore had recognised and promoted this concept.

In general however the intended TG framework of the model gave rise to much criticism, and is the source of negative reactions even by supporters of Case. Although many of these criticisms appeared much later, it is clear that as Fillmore entered what we are calling the 'second phase' in his development of Case grammar, he was beginning to concentrate less and less on the TG paradigm in which the theory had first been conceived, and to concentrate on the lexical-semantic aspects of the model.

3. *Phase II. Semantics and the lexicon*

As the subtitle of this section suggests, the second phase of Fillmore's development of Case grammar centres on the semantic side of the model, that is on the function of the cases as labels for roles of participants in events. At the same time, the emphasis on transformations and derivations gives way to discussions centring on some (rather abstract) notions of what information is contained in the lexicon.

This trend is already evident in 'Lexical entries for verbs' (1968*b*), which effectively leads us to a formulation of roughly the same Case model as in (1968*a*), but from a completely different direction. In this paper, Fillmore is concerned with showing how the notions and notations of predicate calculus can be adapted and applied to the description of verbs (as linguistic predicates).

What predicate calculus lacks, says Fillmore, is the ability to capture in a systematic way certain similarities and differences between the arguments of different predicates. Here a 'new order of concepts' is required to enable the argument places in related predicates to be equated or differentiated.

Fillmore goes on to restate the goals of Case theory using the example of the transitive versus intransitive uses of *break*. The following extracts seem quite familiar: '. . . it must be assumed that there is some fixed collection of role types to draw from, and that these recur in different expressions. . . . A part of the description of a verb, then, is a list of the various distinct roles which entities may assume in the expressions containing it' (1968*b*:382) and 'I believe that these roles types can be identified with certain quite elementary judgements about the things that go on around us: [. . . etc.]' (*idem*). Now the key difference between this article and (1968*a*) is that the exposition seems to be very much based on conceptualisations. For example, the notation given for the verb *hit* (1),

(1) HIT (place, instrument, [agent])

is meant to represent the observation that 'The basic concept requires an understanding of an object coming into contact with something, but it happens also to be true that simple expressions using this verb may contain mention of an animate being that is responsible for an act of hitting' (1968*b*:384). That it is the role that is optional, and not the expression of the role, is clear from this comment: 'To say that the Agent role is not an obligatory component of the meaning of expressions with *hit* is to agree that in a sentence like [(2)] one may quite well be referring to what happened when a rock rolled down a hill, completely without any implication of outside agency' (*idem*).

(2) The rock hit the tree.

Yet from the next quotation it can be seen that the possible omission of the Place does not make it optional: 'If a place is "understood", from the context, the verb *hit* may be used with the Instrument alone. Thus a sentence like [(3)] is usable whenever it is not necessary to indicate the Place' (1968*b*:385).

(3) The bullet hit.

But between these two extracts, Fillmore has given us details, not unlike those of (1968*a*:31ff), of the surface realisations of various combinations of the roles. This mixture of pragmatic and syntactic notions continues in the next two pages, where the difference between *break* and *hit* – notably as exemplified in (4) – is discussed.

(4a) The window broke.
(4b) * The window hit.

Fillmore states: 'We can summarise these facts by saying that the verb *break* is inherently a one-place predicate, that the role which is obligatorily expressed with it is one that can be given the label Object (. . .), and that expressions containing this verb assert of the noun identified as Object a certain kind of change of state from a whole to a damaged condition. The verb can be used with an Instrument or an Agent, under the restriction that an Agent is tolerated only if there is conceptually an Instrument present. The formula given in [(5)] summarises these observations' (1968*b*:386f).

(5) BREAK (object, [instrument, [agent]])

Notice how we have both pragmatic observations – 'inherently a one-place predicate', 'assert . . . a certain kind of change of state', 'conceptually an Instrument present' – completely intermingled with and undistinguished from syntactic ones – 'the role which is obligatorily expressed', 'The verb can be used . . .'. This distinction between the conceptual and syntactic levels is better recognised in 'Types of lexical information' (1971*a*), and in particular in the section subtitled 'Predicate structure': 'I have referred in this section to the *conceptually required* number of arguments. I am distinguishing this from the number of arguments that must be *explicitly identified* in English sentences. The various ways in which English grammar provides for the omission or suppression of conceptully required arguments is the subject of [another] section . . .' (1971*a*:375) [emphases mine]. The relationship between the conceptual roles and the syntactic arguments is made quite clear in the first indication that Fillmore gives of what his cases really are: '. . . what we need are *abstractions* from these specific role descriptions, abstractions which will allow us to recognise that certain *elementary role notions* recur in many situations, and which will allow us to acknowledge that differences in detail between partly similar roles are due to differences in the meaning of the associated verbs' (1971*a*:376) [emphases mine]. Another significant modification in (1971*a*) is in the set of cases Fillmore gives. Apart from more or less trivial name changes, there are a number of innovations which are more fully explored in Fillmore (1971*b*).

It is to this, the most significant of Fillmore's writings during this second phase, that we now turn, namely his (1971*b*) revision of the (1968*a*) model, 'Some problems for Case grammar'. Again we shall assume here some familiarity on the part of the reader with this article (though perhaps not so much as with (1968*a*)), and attempt to avoid a simple résumé of its contents. In some respects, (1971*b*) includes responses of various natures to the criticisms levelled at his earlier work, though interestingly the paper is not presented as such (in the way that (1977*b*) for example is).

The first two sections are largely introductory, and in fact Section 2 and the first part of Section 3 (pp. 37f) consist of a very precise and concise statement of the basic assumptions underlying Case theory. Of interest are some admissions and caveats that Fillmore makes (p. 36), notably that 'I now know what "ergative" means', and his introduction to Pāṇini's *kāraka* theory 'from a number of extremely polite colleagues'. The similarities between Case and *kāraka* theories are indeed striking, though the correspondence suggested by some writers (notably Ananthanarayana, 1970; Singh, 1974) is not as straightforward as they claim, and in fact the set of cases presented in (1971*b*) is – coincidentally or not – rather closer to Pāṇini's collection of *kāraka* than that of (1968*a*).

The most significant changes between (1968*a*) and (1971*b*) then are in the set of cases proposed, and in the move from a lexicalist-syntactic toward a more semantics-based approach.

Fillmore lists on p. 42 the cases that he has 'lately become comfortable with'. The most notable change is the disappearance of the Dative: 'I have reanalysed the old Dative by spreading it around among the other cases. Where there is a genuine psychological event or mental state verb, we have the Experiencer; where there is a non-psychological verb which indicates a change of state, such as one of dying or growing, we have the Object; where there is a transfer or movement of something to a person, the receiver or destination is taken as the Goal. I no longer confuse selection restrictions to animates with true case-like notions' (1971*b*:42). The new Source case is also introduced, though without much comment and explanation.

The full set of cases now is as follows: Agent, Experiencer, Instrument, Object, Source, Goal, Location and Time, plus 'one more, but I'm saving that till later'. It is only on close inspection that one can discover which of several candidates this 'one more' is: a possible Force case is discussed (p. 44), but rejected as being in complementary distribution with Agent or Instrument, and which for various reasons is absorbed into the latter. The Path case is introduced on p. 50 to complete, with Source and Goal, 'the complement possibilities for verbs of motion'. Finally on p. 52 the possible case Benefactive is discussed, but rejected in favour of an analysis in terms of an abstract embedded sentence.

This treatment of Benefactive is archetypical of the lexical-decompositionist generative-semanticist trend to be noted in this version of Case. The first example of this comes as part of Fillmore's discussion of the case assignment for the arguments in sentences like (6a) as compared to those like (6b), involving the same verb.

(6a) John pushed against the wall with his cane.
Agent Goal Object

(6b) I pushed the table into the corner.

The problem is that while in (6a) the 'impinged upon thing' – *the wall* – is Goal, he considers *into the corner* as an obvious Goal in (6b), so that this time the thing impinged upon is Object, resulting in the necessity to give the verb *push* a different analysis depending on the context. The solution offered is to analyse (7), which has a parallel case structure to (6b), as having the underlying structure of '. . . two clauses embedded to a higher predicate that has a meaning suggested by the word *cause*' (1971*b*:46).

(7) I hit the ball over the fence.

We can illustrate this as in (8) (cf. text, 1971*b*:46), though Fillmore does not himself introduce diagrams of this nature.

(8)

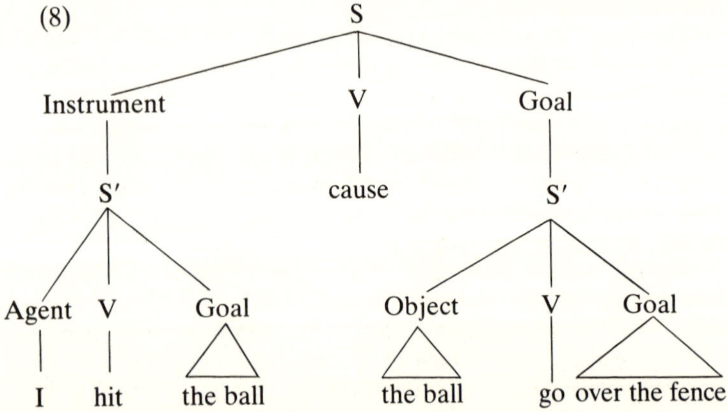

Another way of describing this situation is to say that *hit* is a possible lexicalisation of an underlying predicate 'by hitting cause to move', a conflation process 'governed by specific lexical items' (p. 47), amongst which is also *push*, but not for example *lean*, witness (9).

(9) * He leaned the table into the corner.

A similar analysis is proposed for verbs of motion like *swim* which incorporate some manner aspect and which may be regarded as being substitutions for the lexical construct 'move by swimming'. This provides a means of obtaining for English '. . . underlying structures which look something like what we will need for languages which do not allow conflation in these situations but which require surface sentences to keep the verbs separated' (1971*b*:49). Although this generative semantics approach has now become disfavoured, from the point of view of natural language processing with the emphasis on translation, this approach does in some instances have some attractions. Compare the following 'underlying predicates' (10) in which for English the manner aspect gives the surface verb, while in French it is the directional aspect that is lexicalised:

(10a) go across by swimming
= En. *swim across*
= Fr. *traverser à la nage*

(10b) go in by riding
= En. *ride in*
= Fr. *entrer à cheval*

(10c) go away by driving
= En. *drive off*
= Fr. *partir en voiture*

Fillmore's generative semantics approach continues in his discussion of the Locative and Time cases. While some verbs like *live* and *spend* take these cases directly, Fillmore proposes for other instances of the cases an analysis in terms of the underlying predicate *occur* or *happen*, justifying this by suggesting that '. . . its presence can serve to explain conditions under which the conflation process is blocked' (1971*b*:50) and exemplifying this with a rather tortuous example involving the killing of a cougar in which the time and/or place coordinates of the action performed do not correspond to those of the cougar's dying. For this reason, Fillmore proposes an analysis of *kill* not as 'cause to die', as proposed by McCawley (1968), but as 'by doing something cause to die'. It is not our intention to discuss in detail here the fairly considerable literature on this subject. The interested reader is referred to the lengthy discussions for and against such an analysis of causatives in Fodor (1970), Kastovsky (1973) and Wierzbicka (1975), and the wealth of related articles cited in these papers.

A further example of lexical decomposition is in Fillmore's treatment of the Benefactive case. Since 'Benefactive constructions only occur in sentences with Agents', Fillmore notes that to treat Benefactive as a case would involve 'a system of redundancy principles regarding the selection of cases', a possibility he does not want (p. 52). The alternative analysis is in terms of a 'higher sentence', the predicate of which is 'an abstract verb of giving', the beneficiary being Goal, and the deed performed being expressed as a sentence embedded in the Object case, perhaps something like (11):

(11a) John did it for me

(11b)

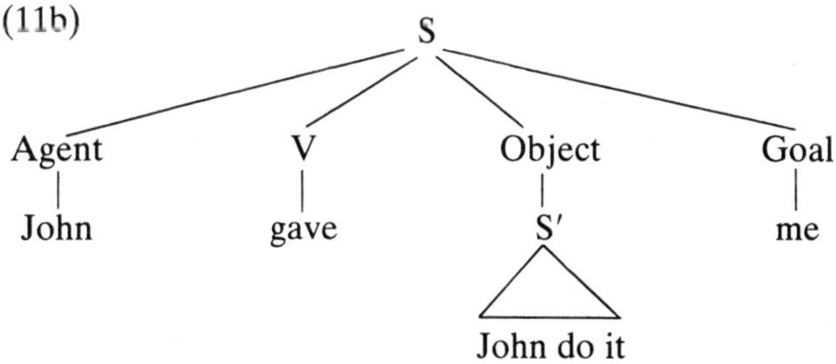

In the concluding paragraphs of (1971*b*) Fillmore addresses the problems concerning the relational rather than categorial nature of the cases, as discussed in the previous section. Considering the general question of how the cases fit into the framework of a grammar – and here he is once again overtly transformationist – Fillmore rejects the idea that the cases are features of the noun-phrases, and the idea that verbs have case features assigned to them as a kind of 'valence'. His rejection of this second proposal is based on the difficulty of '. . . keeping track of the case-identity of noun-phrases . . . after movement transformations are applied' (1971*b*:54) and a second complication regarding 'valence information associated in the dictionary with the lexical items' as distinct from 'valence features occurring with those lexical items in individual sentences' (*idem*). It is quite difficult to see just what he means by either of these difficulties, and it is arguable that in fact the most acceptable face of Case is as an extension to Valency theory, where the arrays of cases for a given sentence are seen as precisely verb features, or else at least directly derivable from such (cf. Chapter 4).

The third notation that he rejects is the one where '. . . case roles . . . are indicated by means of labeled nodes dominating the associated sentence or noun-phrase. The cases are clearly not categories, though in this notation they are treated just like grammatical categories' (1971*b*:54). Instead, Fillmore proposes 'a kind of dependency notion which makes use of kernel trees or "stemmas" which identify the "semantic interpretation of the sentence". This enters the transformational component of the grammar together with a ". . . composition plan" . . . by which the various stemmas are to be incorporated into each other to construct the surface sentence . . .' (1971*b*:55). Here at last we see a clearcut distinction being made by Fillmore between the semantic information which he wants to represent in a dependency-like formalism, and the syntactic information which he sees must be represented fairly independently. In fact Fillmore never got round to developing this version further, despite his claim (p. 56) to have 'a few proposals abrewing': no doubt the problems that seemed then 'fairly overwhelming' remained so, in spite of the appeal to Californian 'magic and witchcraft' with which he ends the article.

4. *Phase* III. *Recent extensions*

In this last phase of Fillmorean Case we see him expand his area of interest even more, taking note of work in disciplines on the fringe of 'classical' linguistics, including discourse analysis, speech-act theory and even Artificial Intelligence.

In his (1972) article 'Subjects, speakers and roles', Fillmore explores the connections between the abstract relational categories of Case grammar, and the mechanisms that determine the choice of surface subject, and more specifically, surface lexical items from the choice of items which are synonymous in terms of deep cases. Discourse questions such as thematisation play a part here. Fillmore also investigates the relationship between case labels at one level and more specific semantic labels at another. This is exemplified by the 'commercial event' involving a buyer, a seller, the thing bought and the price paid, the expression of which – and therefore the deep and surface cases that each role assumes – being determined by the focus the speaker chooses, that is in the choice of the surface verbs *buy*, *sell*, *cost*, *pay*, etc. The interest in this paper as far as Case is concerned is really only general, though we do find a particularly interesting passage (pp. 14ff) where the two levels mentioned above are discussed, and the problem of 'dual case roles' (see Chapter 8) are touched upon.

The first of the two more substantial writings of this phase is 'Topics in lexical semantics' (1977*a*), a collection of four 'lectures' on lexical semantics, of which only the first and second are of substantial interest from the Case point of view. The first of these (pp. 76-91) concerns the 'relativisation' of meanings of both words and sentences to 'scenes' (in roughly the Artificial Intelligence sense), and sets the background for his description of his latest view of Case. The section ends, significantly, with a description of how the lexicon specifies for each verb its 'valence' (here Fillmore cites both Tesnière (1959), and Helbig and Schenkel (1973)), consisting not only of references to surface syntagms, but also to '. . . the elements and aspects of the associated scenes' (p. 90).

In the second section (or 'lecture'), Fillmore talks more obviously in Case terms, including (p. 93) a very brief overview of the theory. Most interesting here though is his integration of the Valency-like notions of nuclear and peripheral elements and what he wants to say about the different 'perspectives' that are possible for a given scene. Note however that Fillmore's use here of these terms is very close to Tesnière's actants and circumstantials, since the nuclear elements in the expression of any given scene are those that are chosen as subject and object, '. . . the leftover element becoming a peripheral element, expressible in a preposition phrase' (1977*a*:95).

The different ways that elements defined by the valence of the verb can co-occur are described in four different scenarios. In the first, we have a direct choice between two elements for nuclear status, as with *blame* (1) (nucleus in italics).

(1a) *He blamed the accident* on me
(1b) *He blamed me* for the accident.

In the second, the choice of one element as nuclear may put constraints on the periphery. Thus both (2a) and (2b) with no periphery are possible, but only (2a) admits a peripheral element (cf. (2c) and (2d)).

(2a) He signed his name
(2b) He signed the contract.
(2c) He signed his name on the contract.
(2d) * He signed the contract with his name. [F's grammaticality judgment, p. 96].

The third scenario is where an element may be nuclear or peripheral, with a subsequent slight change in interpretation, as in (3).

(3a) She shot him.
(3b) She shot at him.

The fourth scenario is like the first, except that the different choices are reflected in different surface verbs being used. Fillmore describes this as '. . . pairs of verbs that have related meanings but differ from each other in the choice of what is in the nucleus and what is in the periphery' (1977*a*:96) and exemplifies it as in (4).

(4a) He put a towel over the alarm clock.
(4b) He covered the alarm clock with a towel.

We should stress again that Fillmore's use of the terms 'nucleus' and 'periphery' does not correspond to the use of similar terms that we evolved in our discussion of Valency grammar.

Where Case comes in is in Fillmore's attempt in the subsequent pages to investigate the relationship between various case relationships and their likelihood to be favoured for inclusion in the nucleus. Various such conditions are suggested, though it is not always clear whether they are general conditions, or apply to particular verbs. For example, the following statement is made with the verb *hit* in mind, though it may be meant to be taken as a general truth: '. . . one of the conditions favoring inclusion within the nucleus is the condition in which an element is a sentient being who is affected, in the event that it is being depicted, in ways we can empathize with' (1977*a*:98). The next example is more obviously a general remark: 'For situations in which a given noun can be either in the nucleus or in the periphery, one condition favoring inclusion in the nucleus is that of the affected object's undergoing some kind of change' (*idem*). When we consider that 'nucleus' is defined as a verb plus subject and object, these descriptions of guidelines for 'relative saliency' of cases do not seem very distant from the subject (and object) selection hierarchies offered in (1968*a*:35). It is in this way, incidentally, that Fillmore proposes to deal with the 'holistic-partitive' problem, discussed in Chapter 7 Section 5.

In fact Fillmore makes this comparison with his earlier case hierarchy overt, and his first approximation to a 'saliency hierarchy' (1977*a*:102) to replace the case hierarchy is clearly in terms not of cases, but something like case features:

1. An active element outranks an inactive element.
2. A causal element outranks a noncausal element.
3. A human (or animate) causal experiencer outranks other elements.
4. A changed element outranks a nonchanged element.
5. A complete or individuated element outranks a part of an element.
6. A 'figure' outranks a 'ground'.
7. A 'definite' element outranks an 'indefinite' element.

We come now to Fillmore's last significant work on Case up to the present time: 'The case for Case reopened' (1977*b*). In fact, this work is only his 'last' in the sense that this section terminates this chapter; and that what Fillmore says here has an air of conclusion about it. Actually, the two articles (1977*a*, *b*) were written and published at about the same time, and (1977*b*) is referred to informally in (1977*a*). Nevertheless for us there is a keen sense of finality about (1977*b*), in which Fillmore is principally concerned with answering his critics – in a much more direct way than in (1971*b*) – and offers little of significant novelty that is not also expressed in (1977*a*).

Fillmore begins by attempting to clarify what his theory of Case is or is not. The following extracts provide a good summary of the general picture: 'Within grammatical theory the concept of deep cases can be thought of as a contribution to the theory of grammatical levels, to the theory of grammatical relations, to the description of valences and collocations, and to the general theory of the functions of sentence constituents. The proposal is that there is a general level of structural organisation for a sentence which is distinct from what is usually thought of as a semantic representation and which is distinct likewise from the familiar notions of deep and surface structure representations' (1977*b*:60) and 'The theory of cases can also be seen as offering at least part of the *semantic valence* descriptions of verbs and adjectives, comparable to the syntactic valence descriptions given by [Tesnière, 1959; Helbig and Schenkel, 1973; etc.]' (*idem*) [emphasis his]. Fillmore then begins to concentrate on specific aspects of his theory, clarifying or emphasising the point of view intended in the earlier works.

The first such aspect is the question of subject selection, which he describes as a set of principles that may variously be language-universal, language-specific, or word-specific. It is slightly unnerving that his example of Agent as a universally preferred subject implies the notion that 'subject' is itself a universal syntactic relation, while his later reference to Cruse's (1973) finding that the notion of agentivity is by no means clearly established must cast a shadow of doubt over this suggestion. The notion of language-specific selection principles seems well founded however. His example is that the choice of 'certain enabling or occasioning causes' as surface subject tolerated in English, as in (5), is not permitted in Japanese or German.

(5a) Fifty dollars will buy you a second-hand car.
(5b) The smell sickened me.
(5c) The accident killed the woman.

The suggestion that some subject selection principles are due to individual words is entirely uncontentious, and this notion might be said to be at the very heart of any Case-oriented Valency descripton of language.

The next major aspect of Case theory that Fillmore discusses is the means by which different cases can be distinguished. Fillmore recapitulates three fairly well-known devices: the first is where the ambiguity of a sentence can be attributed to the assumption that there are several possible case roles assigned to one of its nominals.

The second device is where '. . . a single verb collocating with two seemingly disparate classes of nominals in a given grammatical relation, with the nominals from the two classes seeming to exemplify different semantic roles . . .' (1977*b*:63) suggests different cases – compare (6a) and (6b) – especially if the two roles can co-occur in a single sentence (6c).

(6a) My foot hurts.
(6b) My shoe hurts.
(6c) This shoe hurts my foot.

This argument seems slightly circular, especially given the second half of the above quotation, which seems to say 'different roles imply different cases' – something of a tautology if cases are what we think they are – but it is the notion of disparate classes in a given relation which is important, and the point might have been made better by the familiar examples (7).

(7a) John opened the door.

(7b) The key opened the door.
(7c) John opened the door with the key.

The third device for delimiting cases is to look at pairs or sets of surface verbs that express a similar predication, but assign different grammatical relations to the arguments or participants: *buy/sell* and *rob/steal* are familiar examples. Again the roles of the participants in the event underlying the verbs are said to correspond in each of the different surface realisations to the same deep case.

In the next paragraph (p. 64), Fillmore briefly clarifies the means by which Case theory is able to account for various types of optionality of constituents in a sentence. It seems to be important to distinguish two types of optionality: some roles are conceptually present – i.e. 'part of the speaker's and hearer's understanding of the sentence' (p. 64) – but may or must be absent from the surface sentence according to the operation of deletion transformations which remove such cases which are nevertheless stipulated in the case frame features of the verb. Where the absence of a constituent in the surface sentence is due to the absence of optionality is captured by the fact that the constituent's absence need not be accounted for by such transformations. Thus is Fillmore able to conclude '. . . that in principle my proposals take care of optionality sufficiently well' (1977*b*:64).

The next few pages of the article contain brief rejoinders to several more or less unimportant criticisms, including a restatement by Fillmore that he had abandoned his (1968*a*) position on prepositions (already in (1971*a*)), and that he acknowledged his confusion of relational and categorial notions (as in animacy restrictions for Agents and Datives; likewise already found in (1971*a*)).

Fillmore argues briefly against the criticism of 'mere notational variance' found in several authors, and against Dougherty's (1974:273) view that the proposal is a theoretically unimportant taxonomy of verb types. Fillmore's joint reply to both these charges is interesting: '. . . I see the notational and taxonomic possibilities of case theory as standing or falling together. A taxonomy is to be valued if it provides a convenient and revealing conceptual organisation of the entries in its realm, in our case something in terms of which grammatical and semantic generalisations can be easily formulated; a notation is to be valued if it allows the formation of such a taxonomy in a simple and straightforward way' (1977*b*:68).

The remainder of this article comprises a brief section on the problems of defining the cases – a major question which we shall consider at length in Part II – and then a lengthier statement of his current view of Case, which is much along the same lines as Fillmore (1977*a*). The key notions are once again that there are distinct levels of description of events etc., of which the Case level is in one sense the more abstract (compare the notion of 'Agent' to that of 'purchaser' in a commercial event expressed by the verb *buy*), yet in another sense are closer to the (more concrete) expression level. This apparent paradox is clarified by the following two extracts: '. . . the repertory of case is *not* identical to the full set of notions that would be needed to make an analysis of any state or event' (1977*b*:72) [emphasis his] and '. . . a case frame need not comprise a description of all the relevant aspects of a situation, but only a particular piece or section of a situation' (*idem*). The point is that the cases now provide a link between the participants in the underlying scenes and the arguments in the predications used to express some view of that scene. The cases are abstract in the sense that the 'same' cases are used for participants in different scenes, and it is only the vague similarity between the Agent of a commerical event expressed by *buy* and, say, the activity event expressed by *dance* that is perhaps at the heart of the sort of problems that we shall discuss in Part II, where we consider some problems in the definition of certain cases. Yet these cases interact in a significant way with surface structures, and it is this function of providing the bridge between sentences and the events they describe that seems to be the attraction of Case that we shall discuss in more detail in Chapter 11, on Case in Artificial Intelligence (etc.), a relationship that Fillmore hints at in his later articles (especially (1976:5) and in (1977*c*) for example).

THREE

ANDERSON: LOCALIST CASE

1. *Introduction*

In this chapter we shall consider the version of Case grammar proposed and expounded in a large number of publications by John Anderson. The first versions of his 'localist' Case theory, which differs quite radically from the Fillmorean concept, was presented as early as 1968 and 1969, though his main works are the two books published in 1971 and 1977, and it is on these works that we shall concentrate. Both books have fairly misleading main titles, their subtitles better reflecting their contents. *The grammar of Case* (1971) is entirely concerned with Anderson's own theory, while *On Case grammar* (1977) is partly an overview of Case in general, including a well-documented résumé (pp. 29-55) of some of the 'classical' problems for Case, partly a recapitulation and development of localist Case theory, and finally a treatise on grammatical relations.

2. *Localism*

The 'localist' view of Case on which Anderson bases his grammar dates back to the earliest grammarians' treatment of surface case, and in particular to the Byzantine scholar Maximus Planudes (see Anderson (1973) in particular). More 'modern' localist grammarians (i.e. nineteenth and twentieth century, with Hjelmslev (1935/7) the most recent) are listed by J. Anderson (1971:6); henceforth in this chapter, 'Anderson (1971)' will be taken to mean John (i.e. J.M.) Anderson's *The grammar of Case*. The basic philosophy underlying localism is to relate the 'concrete' uses of locational and directional (surface) cases to their 'abstract' uses, and to hypothesise that '. . . the underlying case relations of a language, and possibly all the relationships of a language, are seen as being basically derived from the notions of location and direction . . .' (Bauer and Boagey, 1977:123). Evidence to support this notion is offered in Anderson (1971:100ff), where stress is laid on the syncretisms of spatial and non-spatial case uses exemplified by the Finnish adessive (1), and in many other languages such as Latin, Russian, Swahili, etc. (see Chapter 7, Section 3).

(1a) Kirja on pöydällä.
BOOK IS TABLE-ON
'The book is on the table'.

(1b) Minulla on kirja.
ME-ON IS BOOK
'I have a book'

The localist basis to Anderson's grammar is its least contentious element, and it is interesting to note that in fact two of the four cases which he proposes do not seem to be localist at all.

3. *Formalism*

Anderson's theory is firmly couched in a transformational framework, and much of his work revolves around formalising his proposals. Langacker notes that '. . . it is unfortunate . . . that he must deal simultaneously with two issues that are conceptually distinct, however closely they may be associated in practice or in his own mind – the correctness of the localist hypothesis, and the adequacy of the theory of grammar in terms of which the hypothesis is discussed' (Langacker, 1973:320). This comment on the (1971) book is also true, though to a lesser extent, of the (1977) work, which in its middle section is essentially a summary of the original proposal with little new data. Several other reviewers of Anderson (1971) – Sampson (1972), Ebert (1974) and Bauer and Boagey (1977) – join Langacker in criticising Anderson's style and presentation, and in particular his method of 'showing his working'. The theory is presented as a successive revision of ideas and formalisms which only obscure the point he is making, and lead to apparent contradictions: since a claim made on one page may be refuted or revised later, one is never sure of the status of any of his pronouncements. For our purposes, we will be less interested in the formalistic aspect of his theory than in seeing what it has to offer in a more general sense. If by ignoring these we are disregarding half the theory, then so be it: a version of Case that is inextricably tied to a specific theoretical framework will be of relatively little value in our search for a more general concept of Case.

4. *Essential features of the theory*

Anderson is strictly dependency- rather than constituency-oriented. This however is no great radicalism, as we have seen in the previous two chapters on Valency and Fillmore. For the transformational framework this is quite a significant point however, and Anderson takes care in his tree diagrams to reflect this. As in Valency, the verb is the overall governor, its immediate dependents being the cases, and in some instances, a copula. The cases in turn govern the nominals. The prepositions and other surface markers of case appear to be the surface 'realisations' of the cases, as represented by the vertical dotted lines in, for example, (1) (1971:43).

(1)

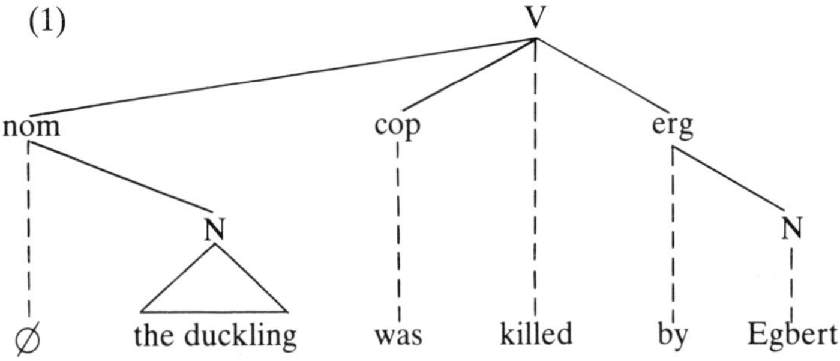

Anderson's case-set is limited to four cases, which he terms *nom*inative (later *abs*olutive), *erg*ative, *loc*ative, and *abl*ative. It is tempting to equate Anderson's four cases with more familiar names, and we shall do this here, though with the strong warning that we shall see below that there are several crucial differences between Anderson's and Fillmore's (etc.) Case theories. The nom (renamed later presumably so as to avoid confusion with the similarly named surface case) is the case found in a 'process' with a single nonagentive 'participant' (1971:37), as in (2) and (3):

(2) John died.
(3) John sneezed.

Nom is 'notionally the most neutral case' and is more or less equivalent to the traditional Object(ive) or Patient case: the choice of the name 'nom' is therefore quite misleading.

The erg, as the 'initiator of the action' (1971:40) associated with transitive verbs, clearly parallels the familiar Agent, though not as directly as Starosta (1981:727) seems to imply. Various syntactic tests are suggested (1971:41) to distinguish erg and non-erg subjects: only verbs taking erg subjects can form an imperative (4); clauses with erg subjects are suitable answers to questions phrased with *do* (5) while nom subjects require a question with *happen* (6).

(4a) Read the book!
(4b) Kill the duckling!
(4c) * Sneeze!
(4d) * Die!
(5) What did Egbert do? {(a) He killed the duckling.
{(b) * He died.
(6) What happened to Egbert? {(a) * He killed the duckling.
{(b) He died.

An important concept, treated lightly in (1971:50), but stressed in later works (e.g. 1977:81ff), is that nom (or abs) is regarded as compulsory for all verbs. Hence the rules in (7) are postulated, giving [nom] as the case frame for non-ergative verbs, [[erg] [nom]] for ergatives.

(7) V → nom // – V
+ ergative → erg // V –

Note that '→' is to be read as 'introduces' (rather than 'rewrites as'), and that '//' gives the context for the introduced element and '–' its position. For typographical reasons, some of Anderson's 'complex symbols' (in square brackets) are linearised.

Ergative and non-ergative verbs often form pairs distinguished only by whether or not they take erg. In some cases, these verb-pairs are morphemically identical, as with *open*, *move*, and *grow*, though this is not always the case (e.g. *kill/die*). Some verbs, however, have no +ergative counterpart (e.g. *sneeze*), and some have no −ergative counterpart (Anderson gives *read* as an example, though in (8) the verb appears to be used non-ergatively).

(8) This book reads well.

The concept of the obligatoriness of nom leads us to an important difference between Anderson's and Fillmore's conceptions of Case, when we consider what Anderson (1971:49) terms 'reflexive ergative clauses'. For verbs like *work* and *leave* (intransitive), Anderson proposes that the obligatory nom be attached to the erg: this clearly departs from the Fillmorean convention whereby each argument in a predication is assigned to one case and one case only. Reflexive ergative verbs can be recognised as those intransitive verbs which nevertheless conform to the syntactic tests for ergatives (compare (4) and (5) with (9) and (10), so that the structural representation for *work*, for example, is as in (11) (1971:49).

(9) Work!

(10a) What did Egbert do? He worked.

(10b) What happened to Egbert? * He worked.

(11)

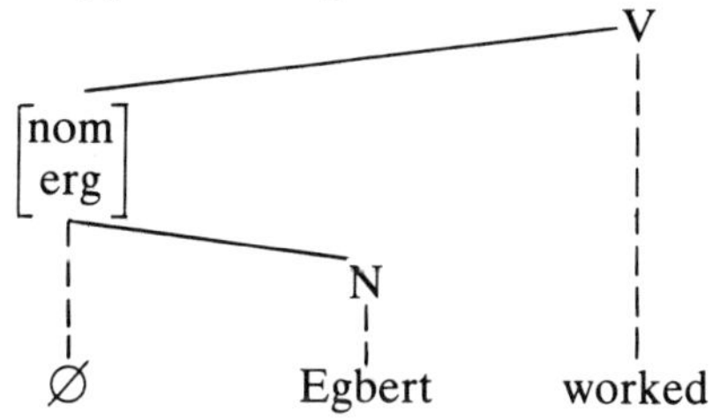

We quickly discover that a second fundamental tenet of Fillmorean Case is abandoned by Anderson: the one-case-per-clause principle. In his treatment of causatives, we find that Anderson (1971:75f) regards the case introduced by the feature +resultative as a second nom, so we have (12) for *elect*:

(12a)

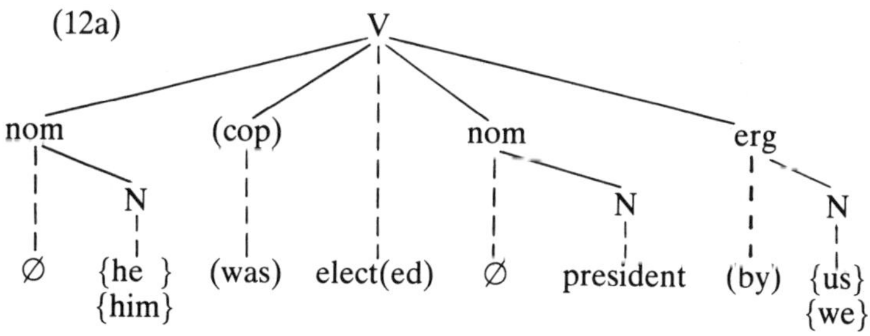

(12b) We elected him president.

(12c) He was elected president by us.

We shall return to this question below.

The loc case is introduced in Chapter 6 of Anderson (1971:81ff) for spatial locatives, and is in this respect very similar to Fillmore's (1968*a*) Locative. In Chapter 7 (pp. 100ff) its use is extended to 'abstract locatives', the justification being principally on the grounds of parallelisms in the use of surface 'cases', as mentioned in Section 2 above. Thus the subject of possessive verbs like *have* is regarded as loc. These two chapters of (1971) are principally concerned with elaborating rules accounting for the choice of loc as surface subject, or not, as appropriate, and we shall not dwell on details here.

Abl is similarly introduced (Chapter 8, 1971:119ff), with its use as the case representing spatial source (in roughly the Fillmore (1971*b*) sense), and in Chapter 9 (pp. 128ff) for more abstract uses, as exemplified in particular for the verbs *buy* and *sell*. Here again we see that cases can be combined, in rather more convincing fashion this time, since the simultaneous distinction and similarity of *buy* and *sell* is captured by the attachment of erg to the abl for *sell*, but to the loc for *buy*, roughly as in (13) and (14).

(13)

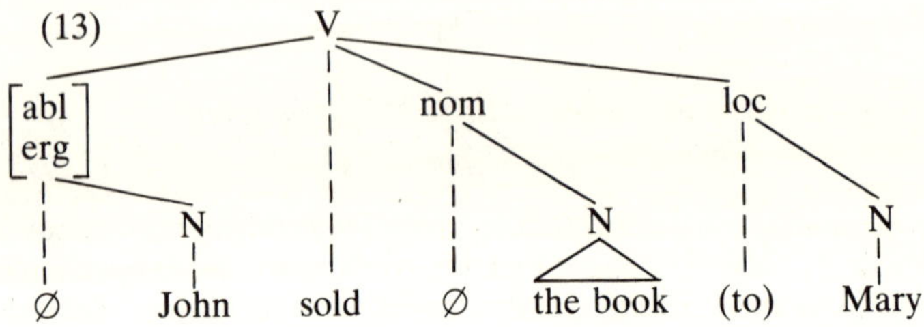

(14)

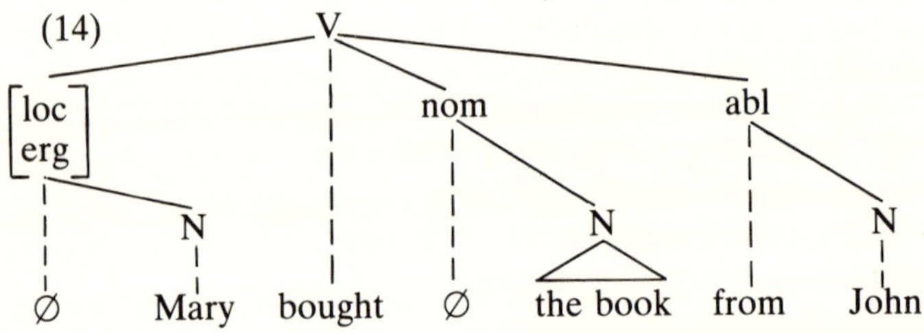

Verb pairs like *lend/borrow*, *teach/learn* are treated in a similar manner, and Anderson notes (1971:137) certain cases of lexical identity, where the two case configurations and associated meanings are available with a single verb. He illustrates this from Icelandic (15), noting also that for some English dialects, *learn* is used for both 'teach' and 'learn'. Other examples are fairly common, including English *hire* and *rent* and French *louer* ('hire', 'rent'). German has many morphologically related verbs, e.g. *kaufen* ('buy')/*verkaufen* ('sell'), *mieten* ('hire')/*vermieten* ('hire out'), etc.

(15a) Hann *fekk* mér bókina.
'He gave me the book'
(15b) Eg *fekk* bókina frá honum.
'I got the book from him'

We saw above how combinations of cases are permitted, both in the analysis of *buy* versus *sell*, and in treatment of 'reflexive ergatives'. By the same token, loc and abl combine to give the 'Path' locational. The corresponding 'abstract' is considered to be the relation usually called 'Instrumental', though the morphological evidence of syncretisms is much less convincing here.

Having introduced his four cases, Anderson draws attention to the parallel distribution of nom/erg and loc/abl:

(a) nom (b) nom erg (c) [nom, erg]
(a) loc (b) loc abl (c) [loc, abl]

'That is, nom and loc either appear alone (as in (a)) or together with erg and abl as a separate category (as in (b)) or as a feature in the C[omplex] S[ymbol] initiated by nom or loc (as in (c))' (1971:173). This parallel distribution together with the evidence of semantic parallels and morphological syncretisms leads Anderson to argue for a merger of the local and non-local cases, so that a four-term system is reduced to a two-term system, the terms additionally being marked ±locative. In fact, the four cases can be represented as a combination of two binary features, since the abl/erg versus loc-nom distinction can be read as ±direction (Anderson, 1971:120, 173; Bauer and Boagey, 1977:129), giving us Figure 1.

		locative +	locative −
directional	+	abl	erg
		loc	nom

Figure 1: Representation of cases as binary-feature combination

There is some question as to what is to be gained by reducing the already small number of case relations recognised. Indeed, as Bauer and Boagey (1977:129) note, Anderson reinstates erg as a separate case later in the (1971) book, and states specifically in a subsequent paper (1975:49) that there is insufficient evidence for a merger of this kind.

5. *Discussion*

In this section we will attempt to evaluate Anderson's approach as a general theory of Case. This is slightly difficult for two reasons. First, it is not easy to separate Anderson's theory from his grammar. Many of the analyses he proposes are justified by the exigences of the particular grammatical framework in which they are framed. Although Eisenberg's comment that '. . . case grammar is a transformational grammar and you cannot buy the form of its deep structures without buying its transformations' (Eisenberg, 1977:173) does not seem to be a reasonable general criticism of Case grammarians, it may be quite valid in the case of Anderson, for without the framework of the context-sensitive grammar in which his derivations are stated, it is not clear what Anderson had to offer. The second difficulty in evaluating Anderson is purely tactical: since we have not yet established general criteria for what we require of Case, we shall make some general criticisms (which will be damaging enough), without previewing too extensively our later discussion.

The most important thing to realise about Anderson is that his theory is radically different from the Fillmorean concept of Case. Notwithstanding the preference of dependency over phrase-structure as a representational device (Anderson, 1971:29), which Fillmore soon takes on too (1971*b*), there are several key differences.

The importance of morphosyntactic evidence as a basis for Anderson's cases contrasts sharply with Fillmore, where cases are based on 'a set of universal, presumably innate, concepts . . .' (Fillmore, 1968*a*:24). Anderson repeatedly invokes the evidence of identical or parallel case forms, historical syncretisms and comparable paraphrase relations. The main result of this is that Anderson's cases are spectacularly lacking in any intuitive cognitive appeal in the way that the case sets of Fillmore (1968*a*, 1971*b*) and his many imitators are, for all their faults. As Kilby says of the combination of formally coincident surface cases, 'There is clearly a place for such suggestions, as the boundaries of a single deep case relationship are extremely fuzzy, but there is a danger in too wide a postulation of such identities. . . . The most obvious danger is that they lead in many cases to particularly unrevealing semantic bases' (Kilby, 1978:67). Anderson also differs from other Case grammarians in his view of Case and the lexicon.

Although Fillmore originally (1968*a*:27) talked in terms of verbs being inserted as appropriate into case arrays already generated, his later view, and the more popular conception, is that it is the verbs themselves that determine the case frame of the sentence. This is particularly the view taken by writers such as Longacre, Chafe and Cook, as we shall see in Chapter 4. Fillmore, then, hints quite strongly at a notion of the lexicon containing entries for verbs in which their 'case frame features' are quite explicitly given.

The cases are thus markers of some sort of 'valency' for the verb, and although the valency-marking function may be complicated by both the individual character of certain cases, and the possibility of various types of optionality of cases, they nevertheless function as a bridge between the abstractions of the lexicon, and the actualisations of the sentence containing that verb.

Anderson's cases on the other hand are introduced in a much more indirect way, and although we do find things that look like lexical entries (1) (Anderson, 1977:56,81ff),

(1a) smear + [– [abs] [loc (abs)] [erg]]
cover + [– [abs] [loc, abs] [erg]]
throw + [– [abs] [loc] [erg]]
(1b) move + [– [abs (erg)] [(erg)]
(1c) occupy + [– [loc, abs] [abs, erg]]

these seem more likely to be simply formalised descriptions of contexts in which the verbs occur, derivable from the application of the grammar to the lexicon. From Anderson's various 'fragments of grammar' (which are not easily or usefully reproducible here), especially his final one (1971:211), it can be seen that it is as a result of feature combinations that the cases are actually introduced: it is the features like ±locative, ±directional, ±stative that are stored in the lexicon, and in this respect Anderson's theory shows a slight affinity with the Chafe/Cook model discussed in Chapter 4.

Finally, it is never very clear whether Anderson intends to treat both complements and adjuncts via this Case theory, or only the former. All the examples in Anderson (1971) involve complements only. In Anderson (1977) the topic is introduced in several places (Anderson uses Halliday's (1967/8) terminology: 'participants' versus 'circumstantials'), first in a discussion (pp. 126ff) of Stockwell *et al.* (1973), but thereafter mostly for circumstantial locatives. These present few difficulties, though the formalism has no way of distinguishing inner and outer locatives. There is the slightest hint otherwise that the treatment of circumstantials is not envisaged by Anderson: time-phrases are shrugged off (1977:126, 168) as being always circumstantial and their appropriate case designation is (therefore?) not demonstrated. As for other 'outer' roles, such as the Benefactive in (2), we cannot even guess at what Anderson would have proposed, since the topic is never broached.

(2) The gamekeeper shot *the squire* a rabbit.

Perhaps the most striking difference between Anderson and other Case grammarians is his disregard of the most solid of the basic tenets of Case, which is the one-to-one relationship between cases and arguments. The principle is seen both in the well-known 'one-case-per-clause' and in the 'one-case-per-argument' conventions (cf. Chapter 2 Section 2).

Neither of these conventions hold for Anderson, as we have seen. But it is arguable that without these Case grammar loses any attraction it might otherwise have. Since more than one instance of each case is allowed, the cases are no longer unique selectors defining a unique predicate-argument relation (notwithstanding the 'inner' versus 'outer' participant distinction – cf. Chapter 9). Since they do not appear to have a great intuitive appeal, it is hard to see what sort of relational labels they are at all.

The problems that arise from the convention allowing more than one case-label per argument are more serious yet. At first sight Anderson's cases appear to be not cases at all, but simple features, especially when we see that they can combine with (other) features like stat(ive), subj(ect), obj(ect) etc. But if they are features, then it is not clear how the distinction between [loc, nom] and [nom, loc] (e.g. 1971:156) could be explained. If it is the case that the first 'feature' has a special significance, then some notation distinguishing it should be introduced (but see Anderson, 1971:22f), though this would still leave us with the problem that these labels have a dual function of case categories on the one hand and case features on the other, whatever the difference between those might be. Bauer and Boagey (1977:139f) note that four cases should give twelve possible couplings, though only six are actually used. Furthermore, there are examples of doubling of the same label, as in the representation of (3), where *Egbert* has the label [nom, nom] (1971:193).

(3) They caused Egbert to fall through the window.

It is not clear whether examples of the other uses are just not shown, or whether the unused combinations must in some way be blocked.

The circumstances under which the cases combine seem to differ significantly too. Sometimes cases combine because the role they express is in some sense a combination of two (semantic) functions. Thus it is that in (4), *Egbert* is both erg and nom, the former as the initiator of the action, the latter as the entity undergoing the action.

(4) Egbert moved.

Sometimes though, cases combine by some convention, usually motivated, though rarely convincingly so: for example, we have abl corresponding to Source, and loc to Goal, with, by convention, Path represented as simultaneous abl and loc.

But a third way in which complex case assignments can be arrived at is the purely grammatical devices introduced in the later chapters of Anderson (1971), where derivations involving what Anderson calls 'raising', 'nom-copying' and 'conflation' are given for certain types of sentence. Consider for example (5) (Anderson, 1971:190f):

(5) Mary was sold a hat.

In the underlying structure, before sequencing rules (etc.) have introduced the necessary labels and nodes to give us the surface string, *Mary* is a simple loc (6):

(6)

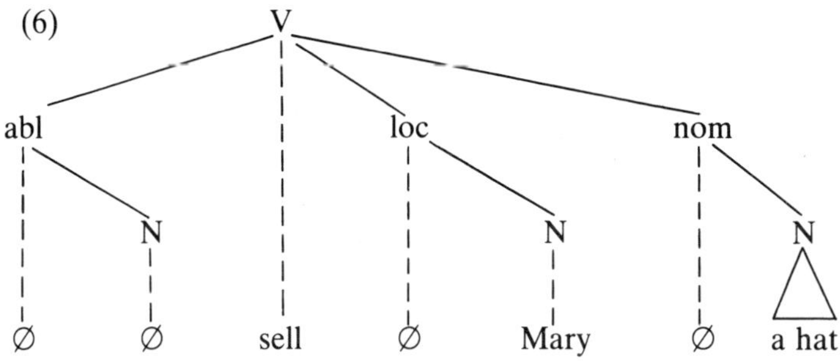

Yet as *Mary* is 'raised' to the passive subject position, the governing node acquires a nom (and, incidentally, the deep subject acquires another abl label), so the final picture is as in (7).

(7)

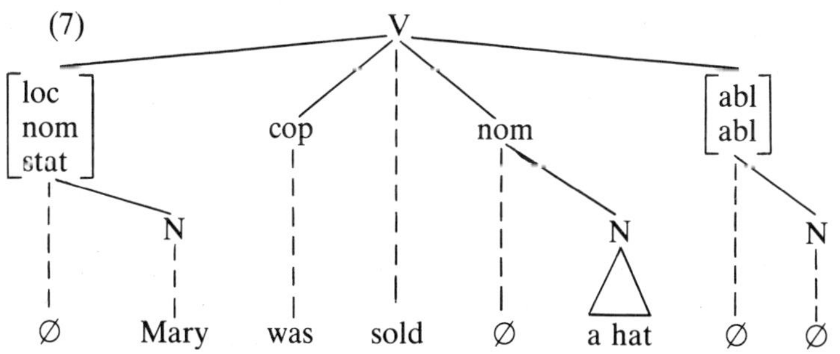

One thing that this last point demonstrates is the close relationship between Anderson's cases and surface grammatical functions, as compared to Fillmore's cases. It is not surprising then that much of Anderson's later work is more oriented towards this topic. In conclusion, it must be said that whatever attractions Anderson's work has as regards formal completeness are far outweighed by the lack of intuitive appeal of this version of Case.

FOUR

CHAFE, COOK, LONGACRE: VERB FEATURES

1. *Introduction*

In this chapter we shall look at a number of general linguistic models of a similar nature, which represent a rather more meaning-oriented view of Case than those we have so far seen. Wallace Chafe's original proposals were elaborated as a reaction against the Chomskyan revolution (cf. Chafe, 1970:2f; Akhmanova, 1973) and the particular aspects of Chafe's work that we shall be concentrating on form part of a much larger work. Chafe's ideas about verb features and case frames were taken up and elaborated by Walter Cook in a series of articles eventually published in a single volume (Cook, 1979), while the work of Longacre (1976) can also be regarded as a Chafe-derivative. Finally we shall consider the extent to which these linguistic theories can be related to the development by Dowty (1979) of Zeno Vendler's categorisation of event types.

2. *Chafe's basic verb features*

It is in Chapter 9 of his book *Meaning and the structure of language* (1970) that Chafe introduces his analysis of verb types which forms the basis of his model. Starting from the position of regarding sentences as being built up of a predicative element (the 'verb') plus (usually) one or more nominal arguments ('nouns'), Chafe shows that there are a number of basic verb types which dictate the number and type of nouns in the sentence as well as their relations to the verb.

Chafe first distinguishes state and non-state verbs. State verbs (p. 98) describe the state or condition of a single argument, and the examples given (1) are all predicative adjectives.

(1a) The wood is dry.
(1b) The rope is tight.
(1c) The dish is broken.
(1d) The elephant is dead.

As a 'rough practical guide' (p. 99), two tests are proposed to enable states and non-states to be distinguished. First, states are not suitable answers to a question formed with the verb *happen*, as in (2). And second, states cannot normally occur in the progressive form (3).

(2) * What happened? The wood was dry.
(3) * The wood was being dry.

Non-states can be subdivided into processes, where the verb expresses a change of condition or state in its argument, as in (4), and actions, where the verb describes something that its argument does or performs, as in (5) (p. 100).

(4a) The wood dried.
(4b) The rope tightened.
(4c) The dish broke.
(4d) The elephant died.
(5a) Michael ran.
(5b) The men laughed.
(5c) Harriet sang.
(5d) The tiger pounced.

Certain verbs express both an action and a process simultaneously, these having two arguments: the performer of the action and the thing undergoing the process, as in (6).

(6a) Michael dried the wood.
(6b) The men tightened the rope.
(6c) Harriet broke the dish.
(6d) The tiger killed the elephant.

Processes can be distinguished from actions as being suitable answers to questions formed using the frame (7a), as in (7b), while a similar test with the verb *do* (8a) gives the complementary distinction, as in (8b).

(7a) What happened to N?
(7b) What happened to Harriet? { She died.
{ *She sang.

(8a) What did N do?
(8b) What did Harriet do? { She sang.
{ *She died.

Chafe assigns the relational role (he avoids the term 'case') of Patient to the element whose state is described by a state verb, or which undergoes the change of state in a process, and the role of

Agent to the performer of an action, and notes that in an action-process, the frames (7a) and (8a) can be used to distinguish these two roles, as in (7c) and (8c).

(7c) What happened to the dish? Harriet broke it.
(8c) What did Harriet do? She broke the dish.

Chafe notes (pp. 101f) the existence of two further verb types: certain verbs do not need to be accompanied by any noun at all, and these are termed 'ambient'. Examples given are (9a-c), and applications of the tests described above indicate that they are state verbs (10). The parallel with Tesnière's (1959:239) 'avalent' verbs is obvious. (cf. Chapter 1 Section 2).

(9a) It's hot.
(9b) It's late.
(9c) It's Tuesday.
(10a) * What happened? It was hot.
(10b) * It is being hot.

A final class of ambient verbs exemplified in (11) appear to be non-states (11c), and the 'do'-test (11d) seems to indicate that these are ambient actions.

(11a) It's raining.
(11b) It's snowing.
(11c) *What's happening? It's raining.
(11d) What's it doing? It's raining.

The *it* in these ambients and ambient actions 'does not reflect any item in the semantic structure' (p. 102).

3. *Derivational features*

Having distinguished the various verb types, Chafe notes (pp. 122ff) that verbs of one type may be obviously related to verbs of other types, and he proposes a system of derivational features which enable these to be established. For each set of derivations, a basic or intrinsic form is postulated. Furthermore, these derivational features often (though not always) correspond to quite systematic surface phenomena such as morphological inflexions or the use of certain syntactic devices. Thus, for example, the feature 'inchoative', which, when added to a state gives a process, corresponds to the suffix which differentiates (*be*) *wide* (state) from *widen* (process), as in (1).

(1a) The road is wide.
(1b) The road widened.

The reverse derivation can be obtained by adding the feature 'resultative' to a process to give a state, which is exemplified with the intrinsic process *break* from which the state (*be*) *broken* is derived.

Action-processes can be derived from processes via the feature 'causative', giving us the transitive *break* and *open* (2)-(3), while example (4) shows the possibility of a complex derivation from the state (*be*) *hot* to the action-process *heat*.

(2a) The dish broke.
(2b) Linda broke the dish.
(3a) The door opened.
(3b) Linda opened the door.
(4a) The soup is hot. (state)
(4b) The soup is heating. (state + inchoative)
(4c) Linda is heating the soup. (state + inchoative + causative)

The opposite derivation of process from action-process is given by the feature 'deactivative', and is exemplified in (5), where *cut* is considered to be intrinscially action-process:

(5a) Roger is cutting paper.
(5b) The paper cuts easily.

Again with a concatenation of features – in this case deactivative and resultative – a state can be derived from an action-process (5c).

(5c) The paper is cut.

Finally, actions can be derived from action-processes via the feature 'deprocessive', as in (5d).

(5d) Roger is cutting.

We should at this point stress the relationship between these verb features and the associated case frames that can be inferred from them. These are summarised in Figure 1. Notice that some of the derivational features can be interpreted as causing the addition or removal of a case from the associated frame, as summarised in Figure 2. Notice also that there does not appear to be a feature with the capability of adding Patient. This implies that action-processes cannot be derived from intrinsic action verbs. We shall see below that there is a further feature 'completable' that fills this gap.

verb type	case frame
state	Patient
process	Patient
action	Agent
action-process	Agent Patient

Figure 1: Verb features and associated case frames

feature	case added	case removed
causative	Agent	
deactivative		Agent
deprocessive		Patient

Figure 2: Features affecting the associated case frame

Cook (1972*b*:69) gives a diagrammatic summary of Chafe's derivational features, though his representation omits the deprocessive feature which he shows elsewhere (1972*b*:70) along with the 'opposite' feature completable. Figure 3 combines these two Cook diagrams.

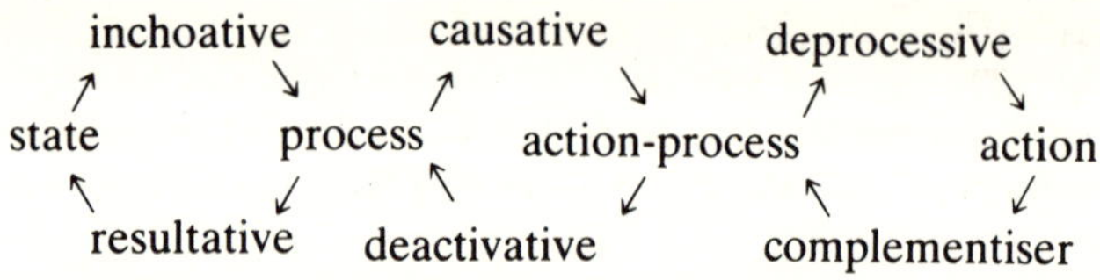

Figure 3: Summary of derivational features (after Cook, 1972*b*)

4. *Further relations and features*

Taking the specification of a verb as a state, process, action or action-process as basic, Chafe notes (pp. 144ff) that the role relations introduced by these verb features are not the only relations to be found. He points out first that there is the relation Experiencer, which is introduced by the feature 'experiential'. This feature can be found with states and processes, though not with actions (neither simple actions nor action-processes), giving us experiential state verbs *want*, *know* and *like* and experiential processes such as *see*, *hear*, *feel*, *learn* and *remember*. As states or processes, these verbs take a Patient as one of their arguments, while the feature experiential accounts for the other argument, Experiencer.

Chafe rejects the analysis of verbs like *show*, *teach* and *remind* as experiential action-processes, suggesting (p. 146) that they can be 'generated' via the causative derivation (presumably from the experiential processes *see*, *learn* and *remember*). The fact that these verb pairs are not morphologically related makes this analysis rather suspect, suggesting as it does that *show*, *teach*, and *remind* are not full lexical verbs.

The feature experiential may also combine with ambient states like *(be) hot*, as in the normal reading of (1). Note that as ambient states have no associated argument role, experiential ambient states have only one (viz. Experiencer).

(1) Tom is hot.

In a similar manner, the verb feature 'benefactive' and its associated role Beneficiary are introduced and exemplified by benefactive state verbs such as *have* and *own*. Benefactive processes are also possible, and these are exemplified not only with verbs like *find*, *win*, and *acquire*, but also *lose*. There is some discussion (p. 149) of whether these are intrinsic types or derived via the feature inchoative from benefactive states. In contrast to his treatment of experiential action-processes seen above, Chafe decides that they are intrinsic types, precisely because they 'remain simple verb roots', a criterion that might easily have been also applicable above. The benefactive action-process verbs *buy*, *sell*, *send* and *give* are posited, but *sell* and *give* are analysed as derivations, ultimately from a benefactive state which Chafe glosses as 'be in the (transitory or non-transitory) possession of'. This preference for deriving simple verb roots from non-lexicalised stative roots is difficult to understand, especially as there does not appear to be any underlying motive of defining all benefactive action-processes as derived, since at least *buy* and *sell* are admitted as basic verbs.

Chafe admits that '. . . there are no benefactive verbs which are simple actions rather than action-processes' (Chafe, 1970:150) but points out that sentence pairs like (2) and (3) seem to indicate that a Beneficiary can be optionally attached to any action verb (whether a simple action or an action-process).

(2a) Mary knitted a sweater.
(2b) Mary knitted Tom a sweater.
(3a) Mary sang.
(3b) Mary sang for Tom.

Just as the relation Beneficiary can be introduced with any action or action-process verb, there is the relation Instrument, which can be introduced with any action-process verb. However, Instrument '. . . differs noticeably from the relations Experiencer and Beneficiary in not being associated with a particular selectional unit within the verb' (Chafe, 1970:152). That is to say that there is no verb feature with which Instrument is associated, nor is there any intrinsic verb type which requires an Instrument.

The reader will recall that in the preceding section it was suggested that there was a missing derivation that would derive an action-process from an action. The corresponding feature, completable, is now introduced (p. 156) together with its associated relation Complement. This is the relation found with simple action verbs for the thing that comes into being as a result of the action (Chafe equates this, in a footnote, with Fillmore's (1968*a*) Factitive), as in (4), but also for the argument which 'specifies more narrowly the meaning of the verb' (p. 156), as in (5).

(4a) Mary sang a song.
(4b) The children played a game.
(4c) Tom ran a race.
(4d) The Infantry fought the war.
(5a) Tom sang "The Star-Spangled Banner".
(5b) The children played touch-football.

Completable states are also exemplified for *weigh* and *cost* (6), and the observation that the feature completable is possible with any non-process verb underlines the parallel between the relations Complement and (non-stative) Patient, which have similar syntactic distribution and realisation.

(6a) The book weighs a pound.
(6b) The candy costs ten cents.

The final relation that Chafe introduces is Locative, with which he associates a verb feature of the same name. Chafe exemplifies (pp. 106f) locational states (all his examples are of the copular with a locative phrase), processes (e.g. *fall*), actions (*sit, crawl*) and action-processes (*throw*, *put*). He suggests (p. 161) that in all his non-stative examples the verb can occur without the Locative: he concludes: '. . . that there are no nonstative verb roots which are intrinsically locative' (Chafe, 1970:161) and that therefore the verb feature locative is always optional.

To summarise then, we have in Figure 4 Chafe's verb features and their associated relations, and in Figure 5 an indication of the possible combinations of the basic verb features, according to Chafe. The two dimensional aspect of Figure 5 does not permit us to include ambient experiential states in the picture. Notice also the distinction between derivable feature configurations like experiential action-process (= experiential process + causative) and impossible combinations (marked as ×). It might be added that not all examples of a given feature combination necessarily represent an intrinsic type: for instance, Chafe (p. 149) regards the benefactive process *acquire* as derived from some benefactive state plus inchoative, whereas *win* is an intrinsic benefactive process.

Feature	Relation
state	Patient
process	Patient
action	Agent
ambient	—
experiential	Experiencer
benefactive	Beneficiary
completable	Complement
locative	Locative
—	Instrument

Figure 4: Features and associated relations

	ambient	experiential	benefactive	completable	locative
state	√	√	√	√	√
process	×	√	√	×	derived
action	√	derived?	×	√	derived
action-process	×	derived	√	×	derived

Figure 5: Possible feature combinations

5. *Cook's case frame matrix*

In a series of articles eventually published together in a single volume (Cook, 1979), Chafe's model of Case grammar has been described and developed by Walter Cook. Originally a Tagmemicist, Cook saw Case as a possible 'Deep structure' to complement the surface-form and -function descriptions provided by classical Tagmemic analysis (Cook, 1971). However, in what amounts to an in-depth review of Chafe's work, Cook (1972*a*) sets up a basic theory from which he develops his 'case frame matrix' model (1972*b*).

Cook first stresses (1972*b*:50) that of the cases proposed by Chafe, five can be considered 'propositional', because they, and only they, are introduced via verb features. In fact, Chafe described seven case relationships, but Cook omits Instrument as not being associated with any specific single verb feature and as not being required by any intrinsic verb type (cf. the previous Section), and conflates Patient and Complement under the 'more general' name Object.

Cook recapitulates how the four basic verb types state, process, action and action-process might each combine with either no case, or with one of Experiencer, Beneficiary or Locative. Ignoring ambients, this gives sixteen possible case frames in a four-by-four matrix, though, as Cook notes (p. 53) Chafe develops only fourteen of these, four of which are supposed to be derived from other frames (Figure 6).

	Basic type	+Experiential	+Benefactive	+Locative
State	O_S dry, adj. dead, adj. tight, adj.	E - O_S know like want	B - O_S have have got own	O_S - L (be) in (be) on (be) under
Process	O break, iv. die tighten, iv.	E - O feel hear	B - O find lose	O - L (derived) fall off
Action	A laugh pounce run sing	A - E (no frame)	A - B (no frame)	A - L (derived) sit in crawl under
Action-Process	A - O break, tv. dry, tv. kill tighten, tv.	A - E - O (derived) show teach remind	A - B - O buy give sell send	A - O - L (derived) throw x into place x next to

Figure 6: Cook's illustration of Chafe's verb classification (Cook, 1972*b*:56)

Cook proceeds to try and fill in the gaps to complete the full sixteen-frame matrix. He first looks at the class of experiential verbs and suggests two possible derivations of experiential action verbs to fill one of the empty slots. Cook notes (p. 57) that with experiential process verbs expressing 'psych movement', such as *amuse*, *frighten* and *please*, the notion of agentivity can be introduced, whereupon the Agent and the Object become coreferential.

Another class of experiential action verbs is derived from experiential action-process verbs via the lexicalisation of the Object into the verb. This is the case with *ask* in (1a) from which *question* can be derived, as in (1b).

(1a) The police asked the suspect a question. [A,E,O]

(1b) The police questioned the suspect. [A,E]/O–lex

Other verbs of saying seem to belong to this class, for example *answer*, *congratulate*, *greet*, *praise*, *salute*, *thank*.

Cook makes one further revision to the data for experiential verbs according to Chafe, in rejecting, as we did in Section 4 above, the status of verbs like *show*, *teach* and *remind* as being derived from *see*, *learn* and *remember* respectively, and adds to this list of intrinsic experiential action-process verbs of saying like *ask*, *say*, *speak*, *tell*, for which no causative derivation from some experiential process verb seems plausible (p. 58).

In a similar manner, Cook provides examples of a lexicalisation derivation of benefactive actions from benefactive action-processes to fill the other empty slot in Figure 6. The example used is *give* with the Object *bribe* from which benefactive action the verb *bribe* is derived. Further examples are *arm*, *equip*, *supply*, *support*, *help*, and *tip* (p. 59).

Turning now to locative verb types, Cook counters Chafe's claim that '. . . there are no nonstative verb roots which are intrinsically locative' (Chafe, 1970:161) and demonstrates that verbs of motion provide intrinsic locative processes and locative action-processes, while adding a further class of locative action verbs.

The locative processes are provided by those '. . . verbs of motion in English and other languages which specify the change of location of an Object without implying any Agentive causality' (Cook, 1972*b*:59). Examples given are *come* (2), *go*, *move* and other motion verbs incorporating lexicalised manner, direction or source-goal notions.

(2) A letter came to Washington.

Where these verbs of motion are used with animate subjects, and the element undergoing the change of location is also the instigator of the action, we have a locative action. Some motion verbs, such as *walk*, *run*, and *fly*, where the manner is lexicalised, have no locative process equivalent and so are unambiguously instrinsic locative actions.

Finally, Cook lists a number of non-derived locative action-processes with distinct Agent and Object, such as *take*, *bring*, *put* and *place*. This, with some other minor amendments listed by Cook (p. 61) completes his revision of Chafe's classification, as in Figure 7.

	Basic type	+Experiential	+Benefactive	+Locative
State	O_S	E - O_S	B - O_S	O_S - L
	broken, adj.	doubt	have	(be) in
	dry, adj.	know	have got	(be) at
	dead, adj.	like	own	dwell
	tight, adj.	want	belong to	stay
Process	O	E - O	B - O	O - L
	break, iv.	amuse	acquire	come
	die	annoy	find	go
	dry, iv.	enjoy	lose	move
	tighten, iv.	feel	win	shift
Action	A	A - E	A - B	A - L
	dance	(derived)	(derived)	(derived)
	laugh	answer	arm	come
	play	frighten	bribe	go
	sing	please	help	run
		question	supply	walk
Action-Process	A - O	A - E - O	A - B - O	A - O - L
	break, tv.	ask	accept	bring
	dry, tv.	say	buy	place
	kill	speak	give	put
	tighten, tv.	tell	sell	take

Figure 7: Cook's case frame matrix (Cook, 1972*b*:61)

Although Cook's case frame matrix is clearly an improvement on Chafe's original classification, there are a number of criticisms to be made. Notably the notion 'derived' seems intrusive, and it would be agreeable if we could fill all sixteen slots with intrinsic verb types. But note that in the Cookian matrix, this term now has three distinct meanings. In one case, the locative actions *come* and *go* are derived from locative process, that is from verbs appearing in another slot, via the insertion of a case-role (Agent, coreferential with Object); in another, the experiential actions *frighten* and *please* are derived, again from verbs which (ought to) appear in another slot, but this time by the simple fact of 'coreferentiality' of two of the roles; the third type of derivation we find stems from Cook's more or less Generative Semantics approach in that one of the roles is lexicalised: in a non-generative approach we might not wish to regard regular surface verbs like *arm* or *walk* as derived at all.

Notice further that the notation 'derived' in the three slots where it occurs covers any or all of these three possibilities: the benefactive actions *arm*, *bribe* and *help* are lexical derivations, while *supply* is a role-deletion derivation; the locative actions *come* and *go* are coreferentiality derivations, while *run* and *walk* are again lexicalisation derivations; and note, what is more, that these latter two are derived from verbs for which no slot is provided in the frame (i.e. verbs taking the Manner case). Notwithstanding the fact that it might be more intuitively appealing to regard *come* and *go* when used as locative processes to be derived in some way from locative actions, rather than vice versa, since the use exemplified in (2) above seems almost metaphorical, there seem to be good reasons for removing the epithet 'derived' from each of the three slots in Figure 7, leaving only *question* as an intrinsic experiential action, adding *congratulate*, *greet*, and *praise* to make up the numbers; *arm*, *bribe* and *help* remain as intrinsic benefactive actions; *supply* is a benefactive action-process, which like many other action-processes – including basic ones – can occur with one or other of Agent or Object deleted – cf. Somers and Johnson (1979:89); *come*, *go*, *walk*, and *run* are all intrinsic locative actions, while better examples of intrinsic locative processes are verbs like *fall* which cannot be used as an action-process, or *slide* and *roll* which are locative equivalents of ergative verbs like *break* and *open* – cf. (3)-(4).

(3a) Geoff slid the table into the corner.
(3b) The table slid into the corner.
(4a) Herbert rolled the stone down the hill.
(4b) The stone rolled down the hill.

Coreferential and lexicalised roles are treated further in Cook (1973), where they are termed 'covert roles'. A third type of covert role is also introduced: so-called 'deletable' roles are those which are introduced into the deep structure by the case-frame implication mechanism of the verb-features, but which happen not to appear in some particular surface structure. Thus for example the

Experiencer is deletable with the experiential action-process verb *say*, so that both (5a) and (5b) are possible:

(5a) Doris said a few words to me.
(5b) Doris said a few words.

Likewise, the Benefactive with the A-B-O verb *steal* (6a) and the Locative with the A-O-L verb *pour* (6b). Similarly, the Object role is deletable with A-E-O *tell* (6c), A-B-O *rob* (6d) and A-O-L *fill* (6e) (cf. Cook, 1973:105f):

(6a) The robber stole the money (from the bank).
(6b) He poured the milk (into the glass).
(6c) She told me (an interesting story).
(6d) The villain robbed the bank (of a lot of money).
(6e) He filled the glass (with milk).

This treatment of what seem to correspond to the Valency grammarians' 'optional complements' as being in some way present in the deep structure and subsequently deleted – and hence 'covert' – is again redolent of a deeper semantics-oriented approach. But in any case it may be considered a slight over-generalisation to regard 'deletable' roles as the same kind of phenomenon as lexicalised and coreferential roles. The notion of covert roles seems to be a useful one in explaining the possible case configurations of certain verbs, and particularly certain paraphrase relations, e.g. (7) and (8).

(7a) He bottled the wine. (covert L)
(7b) He poured the wine into bottles.
(8a) The police questioned the suspect. (covert O)
(8b) The police asked the suspect some questions.

The treatment of coreferential roles as resulting from covert roles again stems from a rather deep view of case role structure, but is quite compatible with other approaches to this problem (cf. Chapter 9).

If case structure is to be regarded as a level of description fairly near surface structure (or at least canonical form), then it would seem more appropriate to separate to a certain extent these three types of 'covert' roles, though in Cook's own rather deeper conception their parallel treatment does not seem totally unwarranted.

6. *Longacre's case frame scheme*

In this section we wish to look at the case frame scheme proposed by Longacre (1976), which represents a considerable development of Chafe's ideas. Longacre contrasts his 'scheme of case frames' with that of Cook in being 'more detailed and more irregular' (p. 40). Longacre first however introduces a set of ten nuclear cases which he has come to 'find useful' (p. 27), and which are worth reproducing here.

Experiencer (E): An animate entity whose registering nervous system is relevant to the predication (p. 27).

Patient (P): The inanimate entity of which a state or location is predicated or which undergoes change of state or location; the animate entity which undergoes change of (physical) state or location (p. 28).

Agent (A): The animate entity which instigates a process or which acts; an inanimate entity which acts (p. 28).

Range (R): The role assigned to any surface structure nominal that completes or further specifies the predicate; the product of the activity of a predicate (p. 29) [Chafe's Complement]

Measure (M): The role assigned to any surface nominal which completes a predicate by quantifying it; the price in a transfer (p. 30).

Instrument (I): An inanimate entity or body part which an (animate) agent intentionally uses to accomplish an action or to instigate a process; any entity (unintentional with animate) which conditions an (emotional) state or which triggers a change in emotional or physical state (p. 31).

Locative (L): The locale of a predication (p. 32).

Source (S): The locale which a predication assumes as place of origin; the entity from which physical sensation emanates; the animate entity who is the original owner in a transfer (p. 32).

Goal (G): The locale which is the point of termination for a predication; the entity towards which a predication is directed without any necessary change of state in that entity; the animate entity who is the non-transitory or terminal owner (p. 33).

Path (PA): The locale or locales transversed in motion etc. predications; the transitory owner (p. 34).

In addition to these nuclear cases, which are 'diagnostic of some case frames as opposed to others' (p. 35), Longacre recognises the existence of some essentially peripheral roles, amongst which he cites Time, Manner, and Accompaniment. Cause and Purpose are not to be regarded as part of clause structure, but belong to the sentence level.

We are now in a position to look at Longacre's case frame scheme, which, like those of Chafe and Cook, is based on the notion that groups of verbs characteristically occur with specific case frames, and that these groups can be delimited by a set of verb features. Longacre's 'case frame scheme' consists essentially of a twelve-by-four matrix, the four 'columns' corresponding to the familiar state/process/action-process/action subdivision, while the twelve 'rows', like Cook's second dimension of verb-features, represent a set of interacting verb features. Longacre's twelve rows are characterised as follows:

Row A: Ambient case frames. Longacre's 'ambient' corresponds to Chafe's feature of the same name, though the former's treatment differs from the latter's in that ambients are not restricted to states and actions: the progressive aspect gives us ambient processes as in (1), though Longacre's ambient action-processes, with metaphysical Agents, are rather unconvincing.

(1a) It's warming up.
(1b) It's cooling off.

Row B: Ambient experiential case frames. This row gives instances of ambient verbs used with a sentient subject, the verbs found here being essentially the same as in Row A. The action ambient experiential case frame is regarded as 'marginal in English', though (2) is suggested as a possibility.

(2) It hailed on me.

Candidates for action-process ambient experientials are process ambient experiential verbs which (in context?) imply a notion of activity, though again Longacre's tentative examples are unconvincing.

Row C: Experiential case frames. In this row are grouped 'emotive, psych, affective and impingement' verbs, all of which are characterised by the possibility of a nuclear Instrumental role being filled corresponding to the condition, trigger or stimulus of the emotion or whatever. This possibility seems to be behind Longacre's decision to distinguish between ambient and ordinary experiential verbs, though the parallels between these ambient experientials (Row B) and their impersonal counterparts in Row A would seem to be another factor motivating what might otherwise seem a bizarre subdivision of experiential verbs (i.e. between Rows B and C).

Row C′: Factual knowledge case frames. A further type of experiential verb is recognised and given its own row: verbs referring to factual knowledge, recognised by both Chafe and Cook as essentially experiential, are separated from those verbs in Row (s B and) C since associated verb features (and hence case frames) differ. Rather than admitting an optional Instrument like the verbs in Row C, factual knowledge verbs rather tend to be characterised by the feature 'completable' (and hence the role Range), as can be seen in (3) (Notice the slash notation A/E to indicate coreferential roles).

(3a) Susan knows algebra. (state: E R)
(3b) Susan has learned (a lot of) algebra. (process: E R)
(3c) Mr Smith taught Susan algebra. (action-process: A E R)
(3d) Susan is studying algebra. (action: A/E R)

Notice that in each of the non-states the Range case filler *algebra* is more or less optional.

Row D: Desire/cognition. This row consists of experiential 'directed' verbs, implying case frames with Experiencer and Goal (among others), and is differentiated from other experiential rows by the notion that there is a role which represents the entity towards which the desire or cognition is directed. The verb *know* appears again in this row, reflecting a differentiation apparent in many languages (though not English) between factual knowledge (state experiential completable: German *wissen*, French *savoir*) and cognitive knowledge (state experiential directed: German *kennen*, French *connaître*). Examples of experiential directed verbs from each column are given in (4).

(4a) Mary wants a Cadillac. (state: E G)
(4b) Mary fell in love with Tom. (process: E G)
(4c) I introduced Mary to Tom. (action-process: A E G)
(4d) John scorned Mary. (action: A E/G or A G)
(4e) John praised himself. (action reflexive: A/E/G)

Row D′: Sensation, speech and attention. Case frames in this row typically refer to a Source, and are completable (associated role, Range). While the state cell in this row is not filled, the process, action-process and action cells are filled by verbs of sensation, speech and attention respectively. Examples of experiential directed completable verbs are given in (5) together with their associated case frames.

(5a) I saw a strange sight (on Boston Common this morning). (process: E (R) S)
(5b) The mother told her child a story. (action-process: A/S E R)
(5c) Tom listened to the owl. (action: A/E (R) S)

Row E: Physical verbs. The remaining rows E to H′ contrast with the preceding rows A to D′ in allowing a Patient but no Experiencer, while for the rows already seen the opposite was true. Verbs in Row E correspond to Chafe's and Cook's basic verb types, and it seems that Longacre has some difficulty in characterising the row: he wishes to correlate the verb feature 'physical' with the role Patient, although the action slot in this row lacks both the feature physical and the corresponding role Patient. Longacre further notes that Instrument is an optional nuclear role for process and action-processes on this row, while the action cell in this row, which seems to be rather misplaced, can be optionally further specified as completable or directed. Completable actions are those that take a 'tautological accusative' complement such as *run* (*a race*) or take a factitive object, e.g. *build*. Directed actions seem to be distinguished from physical action-processes according to whether or not the direct object undergoes a change of state, corresponding to the choice of Goal (directed) or Patient (physical) – compare *kick* and *break*. In view of Longacre's apparent willingness to admit empty cells in certain rows (as we have already seen with experiential directed completable state), and with a certain degree of 'irregularity' (cf. p. 40), it seems strange that he should force action into this row, which as a result is somewhat heterogeneous.

Row F: Measure. In Row F we have verbs including the role Measure in their case frames. These verbs are a notable omission from the Cookian case frame matrix model. Again, each of the cells is marked as physical, except the action cell. Examples of measurable verbs are given in (6) together with their associated case frames.

(6a) The statue weighs one ton. (state: P M)
(6b) My bonds went down 10%. (process: P M)
(6c) I shortened it two inches. (action-process: A P M)
(6d) The Cowboys gained five yards. (action: A M)

Rows G: Locative and G′: Motion, propulsion, locomotion. Longacre makes a clear distinction between the static roles Locative – implying simple location – and the dynamic roles Source, Path and Goal – having to do with motion etc. Since the Locative role is essentially static, there is no locative process case frame, due to some 'obscure conflict of features' (p. 71). By the same token, there is an empty cell for statives in Row G′, since the notions of stativity and motion are contradictory. Longacre regards all the (filled) cells in these two rows as physical verbs (hence taking Patient) with the exception of action locative. In addition, he regards action locatives as able to be subdivided according to the presence of a feature 'posture', with the nonposture action locatives being optionally completable. Posture locatives are verbs like *stand*, *sit*, and *lie*; nonposture locatives include *spin*, *rotate*, and *revolve*. Case frames in Row G′ are notable for allowing various combinations of Source, Path and Goal, a state of affairs which underlines the problems in regarding these three roles as unrelated separate cases, which they clearly sometimes are not.

Row H: Property. The final row is again classified as physical, and contains verbs of possession and transfer of possession. Examples of each type, together with their associated case-frames, are given in (7).

(7a) Dick has a new book. (state: G P)
(7b) Mary obtained her visa. (process: G P)
(7c) Tom gave Bill a book. (action-process: A/S G P)
(7d) George grabbed the book from John. (action: A/G P S)

While it is certainly clear that Longacre's case frame scheme is indeed more detailed and further elaborated than Chafe's or Cook's schemes, it is not entirely certain that Longacre's scheme should be regarded as an unqualified improvement. The irregularity that Longacre introduces detracts from the neatness of the twelve-by-four matrix, especially when one considers that some of the cells are empty, while several of them are divided. Furthermore, there are several instances of verbs appearing in more than one cell, so that it is difficult to relate Longacre's subdivision of predicate types to a practical scheme in which information in dictionary entries can be used to guide a case-based parser, for example. Nevertheless, Longacre's version of the case frame matrix contains some important observations which might usefully be incorporated into a scheme that more closely resembles Cook's rather tighter framework, and this has been put into effect in the PTOSYS system (Somers and Johnson, 1979; Somers, 1980*a*), a computer program which performs case analyses of a small range of English sentence types (see Chapter 11 Section 3).

7. *Vendler/Dowty event classification*

In a series of studies quite independent of Chafe's verb features or indeed Case grammar in general, a number of linguistic philosophers have proposed schemes of event classification which, when compared to the types of schemes we have been investigating in this chapter, reveal some rather interesting parallels.

I have tended – in Somers (1982*b*) and my (1982*c*) article, completed some time earlier – to refer to these schemes as the 'Vendler/Dowty' system, after Vendler's (1967) work and development thereof by Dowty (1979), though the scheme dates back to Aristotle's distinction in *Metaphysics* (θ 6.1048*b* 28) between 'movements' (*kineseis*) and 'actualities' (*energeiai*) (cf. Apostle, 1966), and was originally developed to a certain extent by, notably, Ryle (1949) and Kenny (1963): see particularly Mourelatos (1978) for discussion. We shall consider here for the most part however the system described by Dowty (1979:37-132).

The basic system is a classification of event types, or more precisely of propositions (Steedman, 1977:218) and consists of the basic terms state, activity, achievement and accomplishment, defined as follows (cf. Steedman, 1977:21f; Mourelatos, 1978). States are propositions denoting states of affairs which may endure or persist over stretches of time. Activities denote happenings occupying a period of time, this time stretch being inherently indefinite; what is more, activities are essentially homogeneous, that is, '. . . any part of the [activity] is of the same nature as the whole' (Vendler, 1967:101). Achievements denote propositions having an instantaneous character: '[They] capture either the inception or climax of an act, they can be dated, or they can be indefinitely placed within a temporal stretch, but they cannot in themselves occur *over* or *throughout* a temporal stretch' (Mourelatos, 1978). Finally, accomplishments denote '. . . happenings which occupy a period, like activities, but which, unlike activities, involve some intrinsic end or conclusion' (Steedman, 1977:217). Lists of examples of each of these categories are given by both Mourelatos and Dowty, the two being combined in Figure 8.

States	Activities	Achievements	Accomplishments
know	run	recognise	paint a picture
believe	walk	spot	make a chair
have	swim	find	deliver a sermon
desire	push a cart	lose	draw a circle
love	drive a car	reach	push a cart
want		die	recover from illness
hate		win	run a mile
dominate		start	grow up
		stop	
		resume	
		be born	

Figure 8: Examples of Vendler's four categories (Mourelatos, 1978; Dowty, 1979:54)

Two things to be noticed immediately from this list of examples are that a given 'verb' may appear in more than one category (e.g.

run and *run a mile*), and that by no means all the examples are pure syntactic verbs as in classifications based on Chafe's work. Indeed an important distinction, as Steedman (1977:217) emphasises, is that we are not discussing here verbs or verb groups, nor even things that exist in the world, but rather descriptions of the world. Hence the preference of the term 'proposition', suggested above.

Dowty proposes various tests and criteria by which these four types can be distinguished. Several of these are purely syntactic, and it is the similarity of these syntactic tests to those proposed by Chafe and his followers that suggests comparison of the two systems. Thus, Dowty notes that only non-states occur in the progressive (1), occur as complements of *force* and *persuade* (2), occur as imperatives (3), co-occur with the adverbs *deliberately* and *carefully* (4), or appear in pseudo-cleft constructions (5) (Dowty, 1979:55). It is interesting that Dowty does not include examples of achievement verbs, perhaps because their behaviour with regard to these syntactic tests for stativity is not so stable (6).

(1a) * John is knowing the answer.
(1b) John is running.
(1c) John is building a house.
(2a) * John forced Harry to know the answer.
(2b) John persuaded Harry to run.
(2c) John forced Harry to build a house.
(3a) * Know the answer!
(3b) Run!
(3c) Build a house!
(4a) * John deliberately knew the answer.
(4b) John deliberately ran.
(4c) John carefully built a house.
(5a) * What John did was know the answer.
(5b) What John did was run.
(5c) What John did was build a house.
(6a) ? John is recognising the picture.
(6b) ? John forced Harry to recognise the picture.
(6c) ? Recognise the picture!
(6d) * John carefully recognised the picture.
(6e) What John did was recognise the picture.

Of rather more interest are the distinctions between these types based on co-occurrence possibilities with certain time adverbials and tenses, and especially the different entailments that result.

In the simple present tense, states do not have a habitual or frequentative interpretation, while activities and accomplishments do (7). (The position with achievements is rather complicated.)

(7a) John knows the answer.
(7b) John runs.
(7c) John recites poems.

Co-occurrence with time adverbials with *for* and entailments thereof distinguish the types. Accomplishments are marginal in this frame, and sentences like (8) usually imply an unfinished activity.

(8) John painted a picture for an hour.

The difference in entailment between activities and accomplishments with *for* adverbials is captured as follows: 'If ϕ is an activity verb, then *x ϕed for y time* entails that at any time during *y, x ϕed* was true. If ϕ is an accomplishment verb, then *x ϕed for y time* does not entail that *x ϕed* was true during any time within *y* at all' (Dowty, 1979:57). Achievements are generally quite strange with *for* phrases (9).

(9) * John noticed the painting for a few minutes.

Tests involving *for* phrases can be verified by transformation into a sentence with the verb *spend* (10)-(12), though accomplishments are less marginal in this frame (10).

(10) John spent an hour painting a picture. (cf. (8))
(11a) John walked for an hour.
(11b) John spent an hour walking.
(12) * John spent a few minutes noticing the painting. (cf. (9))

In a parallel manner, states and activities cannot co-occur with time adverbials with *in*, or related sentences with the verb *take* (13)-(14).

(13a) * John knew the answer in an hour.
(13b) * It took John an hour to know the answer.
(14a) * John walked in an hour.
(14b) * It took John an hour to walk.

Note that (13b) and (14b) are acceptable if *know* and *walk* are understood to mean 'learn' (or 'come to know') (an achievement) and 'walk a specific distance' (an accomplishment). Sentences with *in* or *take* also serve to distinguish accomplishments and achievements, which have different entailments: 'If ϕ is an accomplishment verb, then *x ϕed in y time* entails *x was ϕing during y time.* If ϕ is an achievment verb, then *x ϕed in y time* does not entail *x was ϕing during y time*' (Dowty, 1979:59). Entailments from the progressive to the non-progressive tenses serve to distinguish activities from accomplishments (states and achievements do not occur in the progressive tense): 'If ϕ is an activity verb, then *x is (now) ϕing* entails that *x has ϕed*. If ϕ is an accomplishment verb, then *x is (now) ϕing* entails that *x has not yet ϕed*' (Dowty, 1979:57). Compare (15) and (16), where in each case the (a) sentence has the entailment expressed in (b).

(15a) John is walking.
(15b) John has walked.
(16a) John is building the house.
(16b) John has not yet built the house.

Accomplishments and activities can also be distinguished in the entailments that apply when they are used as complements of the verb *stop*. Whereas (17a) does not necessarily entail the accomplishment (17b) (though it is possible), (18a) necessarily entails the activity (18b).

(17a) John stopped painting the picture.
(17b) John painted the picture.
(18a) John stopped walking.
(18b) John walked.

Achievements cannot occur as complements of *stop* (19), though states apparently can (20a), and have the same entailment as activities (cf. (20a) and (20b)).

(19) * John stopped noticing the painting.
(20a) John stopped believing his teacher.
(20b) John believed his teacher.

The verb *finish*, a near synonym of *stop*, serves to distinguish accomplishments from the other types in taking only these as possible complements (21).

(21a) * John finished knowing the answer.
(21b) * John finished walking.
(21c) John finished painting the picture.
(21d) * John finished noticing the picture.

Accomplishments also differ from the other types in forming ambiguous sentences with the adverb *almost*. While (22a-c) are unambiguous, (22d) does not make clear whether or not John actually ever started painting a picture.

(22a) John almost believed his friend.
(22b) John almost walked.
(22c) John almost noticed the painting.
(22d) John almost painted a picture.

Dowty's final criterion for distinguishing the types is to note that there is a class of adverbs, including *attentively*, *studiously*, *vigilantly*, *conscientiously*, *obediently* and *carefully*, which are semantically anomalous with achievement verbs. These 'agentive' adverbs are also unacceptable with states (cf. above).

To these tests of Dowty's we can add a number of additional

criteria. Potts (1965) for example distinguished Aristotle's 'actions without a limit', corresponding to our activities, and 'actions with a limit' (accomplishments) as follows:

Actions without a limit (=activities)
  ϕing inconsistent with not having ϕed
  ϕing entails having ϕed
  not having ϕed entails not ϕing
Actions with a limit (=accomplishments)
  ϕing inconsistent with having ϕed
  ϕing entails not having ϕed
  having ϕed entails not ϕing (Potts, 1965:67)

Mittwoch (1982:117) looked at the denotation of the present perfect simple, and noted that only with achievements and accomplishments was a single recent past occurrence implied (23). Activity verbs in this frame are understood as achievements (24). State verbs do not occur with this meaning (25a), though this tense is available, as in (25b), with the implication of past activity continuing up to the present. This interpretation of the present perfect tense can be underlined by the inclusion of the adverbial *just*.

(23a) I've (just) found my watch. (achievement)
(23b) I've (just) painted a picture. (accomplishment)
(24) I've (just) run.
(25a) * I've just known the answer.
(25b) I've known the answer (for three days).

Mittwoch also mentions some of the tests already discussed above, and adds, in a way clearly reminiscent of Chafe's test for processes, that 'The question *What happened?*, which picks out accomplishments and achievements, can be answered by [(26a)] but not by [(26b)]' (Mittwoch, 1982:118).

(26a) John typed some letters.
(26b) John typed.

Vlach (1981) mentions some further tense relationships for the four categories. States are distinguished thus: 'A sentence ϕ is stative if and only if the truth of (Past ϕ) *when I arrived* requires that ϕ was true for some period leading up to the time of my arrival' (Vlach, 1981:273). Accomplishments are characterised by the relationship between the perfect tense and the truth value of the associated 'tenseless' expression, as follows: '*Mary has run a mile* is true at an instant *t* if and only if *Mary run a mile* is true at some interval previous to *t*' (*ibid*, p. 277). For achievements, Vlach comments that '[The] property of being true at isolated instants only is the defining property of achievement sentences' (*idem*). Vlach's defining property for activities, which he confusingly terms 'processes', mirrors Dowty's observations, seen above, concerning the relationship between sentences with *for* time adverbials and their entailments.

Although there have been some further extensions to this Vendler/Dowty categorisation of events – notably by Steedman (1977), who introduces a distinction between 'actions' and 'activities', the former being activities that refer to an instantaneous event, are expressed by verbs like *bounce* and *tap*, and have slightly different entailments (especially with *for* time adverbials), and by both Steedman and Mourelatos (1978), who impose a hierarchy over these categorisations – and despite some serious flaws in the general scheme, especially due to interference of tense and aspect, and where indefinite plural or mass nouns occur as arguments to verbs, the Vendler/Dowty classification offers some interesting parallels to the Chafe/Cook scheme that suggest that the chiefly syntactic criteria suggested for the latter and the more epistemic criteria suggested for the former may be combined to give a wide range of properties for four distinct verb-event types. The idea that these parallels, namely state=state, activity=action, achievement=process and accomplishment=action-process, are valid is encouraged by Dowty's extensive list of examples of his four categories (1979:66-71), subdivided into syntactic verb-types. Dowty's list of examples is too long to be reproduced here, but the correspondences between the two systems are quite remarkable. There are however some differences, which are quite enlightening.

Statives include symmetric predicates like *resemble*, which are not accommodated in the Chafe/Cook scheme, and physical perception verbs, which can also be activities or achievements. In the Chafe/Cook scheme, such verbs are classed as processes, actions or action-processes, so there is at least an overlap here (process/achievement, action/activity), but the fact that this predicate type appears in (between the two systems) all four categories suggests either that this is a problem area that needs further investigation, or that these verbs can for some reason function in any of the predicate types.

Among Dowty's activities are included some adjectival predicates like *be brave*, *be rude*, and some nominal predicates like *be a clown*. Chafe seems to be mistaken in assuming that all predicate adjectives are stative, since predicates like *be rude* clearly pass syntactic tests for non-statives (27), but Dowty too seems to be guilty of overgeneralising in excluding predicate nominals from his list of statives. The predicate *be a clown* for example can clearly be used as both an activity (28a) or a state (28b).

(27a) Paul is being rude.
(27b) Don't be rude! Be brave!
(27c) What did he do? He was rude.
(28a) Fred was a clown today. (='acted like a clown')
(28b) Coco is a clown. (i.e. professionally)

Transitive verbs of movement like *drive*, *carry*, and *push* are classed as activities by Dowty, though for Chafe/Cook these would be action-processes, because of their associated Patient role. All the other activity verb types exemplified by Dowty would be actions in the Chafe/Cook scheme.

The only discrepancy between Dowty's set of achievement verbs and Chafe/Cook processes is in the inclusion in this category of verbs of motion like *reach* and *leave* which for Cook are action locatives. This discrepancy is quite understandable however since verbs of motion are semantically only vaguely distinguishable as actions, processes or action-processes because the Agent and Patient are coreferential.

By the same token, the two-place phrasal locatives like *walk to* NP which Dowty classes as accomplishments but which for Cook are again action locatives involve the coreferentiality of Agent and Patient which is unimportant for Dowty, but decisive for Chafe/Cook. A further difference is in the classification of intransitives like *grow up* as accomplishments by Dowty but as processes (not action-processes) by Chafe. It is in the list of accomplishment verbs that the biggest differences between the two systems can be seen, and this stems from the underlying difference in motivation for the schemes. The key notion for accomplishments is that of completion, whereas for action-processes it is the presence of two participants Agent and Patient. The conflict so caused can sometimes be explained away in terms of semantic action-processes which are syntactically one or the other (as with verbs of motion), but crucially it is the fact that notions such as agentivity are simply not relevant for Dowty. Yet although certain differences underline the different aims of the two systems, viz. case frame orientation versus event classification, the overwhelming impact is provided by the similarity of the two classifications, a similarity not fully brought out here, where for the sake of brevity we have concentrated on the differences and problems without emphasising the degree to which the correspondences do hold.

If the two systems are sufficiently comparable to allow their conflation in some way, what benefits accrue? First, the literature of the Kenny/Vendler/Dowty systems emphasises the extent to which aspect must be taken into account: verbs classified in one category can appear in others simply via a change of morphological tense. This is an observation that linguistic studies of verb types could profit from, as is hinted in Somers (1982*c*:285ff), where the need to distinguish between verb classification and sentence classification is pointed out. Second, if some criteria can be found for deciding the conflicts between the two systems, of which there are only a few after all, it seems that the criteria developed for distinguishing between the types in each system could be used in the other. The Chafe/Cook syntactic tests can be (and already are) used in the Vendler/Dowty model. More importantly, implication and entailment tests described in this section could be used to supplement the syntactic tests used to distinguish Chafe's four categories.

A final remark we might make on the two systems is this: since the two systems are so similar, does this mean that they are really the same thing, with only different terminology? If the answer to that question is yes, then it is surprising that writers in each of the fields have ignored each other's works and findings: none of the discussions of the Vendler system mention Chafe's or Longacre's linguistic work, nor vice versa. If the answer is no, then it must be that while the work of Chafe and Cook is about syntax and shallow semantics, the Vendler/Dowty classification has to do with the way we view the world as reflected in our language. If this is correct, then it is interesting (to say the least) that the correlation between the two (deep and surface) is so strong.

FIVE

STAROSTA'S LEXICASE

In this chapter we shall discuss the use of Case as part of a theory of grammar developed over the last decade by Stanley Starosta and colleagues at the University of Hawaii. 'Lexicase' has been described in a series of articles and working papers for the most part fairly inaccessible (Starosta, 1972, 1973, 1976, 1977, 1979, 1982), and is for this reason perhaps a rather little-known grammatical theory. The most easily available of these articles is Starosta (1977), though this paper concentrates almost entirely (as we shall do) on the Case-like aspect of the theory. In fact, however, there is a lot more to Lexicase than those aspects we shall cover here, and Starosta's (1979) article perhaps gives the best general overview of the theory. It is some measure of the isolation of Lexicase that there are effectively no discussions of the theory other than by Starosta or his colleagues, except for two general reviews (Swiggers, 1979; van Valin, 1980) of the Abraham (1977) volume containing one of Starosta's publications, and the more substantial (but unpublished) work of Kilby (1982).

Starosta describes Lexicase as a strictly formal and explicit 'hypothetico-deductive' theory of grammar (1977:463), generative but non-transformational (since transformations provide an unconstrainable power that renders grammars unfalsifiable and therefore lacking in empirical content (1978:464)), shunning the notion of deep structure, and considering the lexicon as the sole repository for grammatical rules, of which there are several types. The representation of syntactic structure is essentially a dependency representation, in which case relations (CR's) and associated case forms and case markers '. . . account for the internal structure of clauses and the syntactic relations obtaining between clauses' (1977:465). The set of CR's posited by Starosta (1977:471) are as follows:

AGT Agent
COR Correspondent; formerly Dative or Experiencer
INS Instrument
LOC Locus; formerly (Inner) Locative
MAN Manner
PAT Patient; formerly Object
PLC Place; formerly Outer Locative
REF Reference; formerly Benefactive
TIM Time

Starosta is keen to underline the reasons behind his rejection of certain 'traditional' names like Experiencer and Benefactive because of their association with semantic features. As we shall see, an important difference between Lexicase and more traditional Case grammars is in the primacy of syntactic criteria over semantic or situational criteria in determining CR's.

When we compare this list to Starosta's later (1982:4f) inventory, we find that several CR's appear to have been dropped, though in fact the (1977) list of nine CR's has rather been conflated into six: INS and MAN have come together under MNS (Means), LOC includes PLC, and REF is included in COR. This conflation is partly made possible by the notion of 'inner' versus 'outer' CR's, which we consider later, and also '. . . because many semantic distinctions can be captured separately in terms of independently needed localistic features of verbs, prepositions, and case inflections' (1982:5).

PAT is the 'fundamental' CR, and is defined as '(a) the entity which is viewed as affected by the action of the verb, (b) the entity which is viewed as moving or as being located in (abstract or concrete) space, or (c) the entity which is viewed as existing in a state, or whose state is changing' (1977:472). Although this definition appears to include semantic criteria, we find that there is an important axiom in Lexicase which overrules semantic intuitions captured here, namely that 'Patient is obligatorily present in the case frames of all verbs, and is the case relation of the grammatical subject for all intransitive verbs' (1977:4). This axiom, which Starosta claims (1977:473) to have found also in the work of several notable Case grammarians (though he is probably confusing primacy with obligatoriness) means that '. . . subjects of grammatically identical pairs of sentences such as [(1)-(3)] are given identical case relations' (1982:5).

(1a) John smiled.
PAT

(1b) The ice cube shattered.
PAT

(2a) Max rolled to the bottom of the hill.
PAT LOC

(2b) The rock rolled to the bottom of the hill.
PAT LOC

(3a) Sue deliberately fell out of bed.
PAT LOC

(3b) Sue accidentally fell out of bed.
PAT LOC

More unexpectedly, from a traditional Case point of view, the 'obligatory Patient' rule means that the subjects of intransitive verbs like *walk* and *swim* (Chafe's (1970) 'action' verbs – see Chapter 4) are also automatically assigned the PAT role, even though the 'semantic' definition of AGT – 'The perceived external instigator, initiator, experiencer, or (volitional or non-volitional) controller of an event or state' (1984:4) – makes it seem more appropriate for the subjects of (1a) and both sentences in (3). AGT, it seems, is only available when there is a better candidate for PAT, as in (4), and this means further that for the large class of English verbs which can function both transitively and intransitively (other than as 'ergative' verbs), as in (5), separate entries in the lexicon are required, each corresponding to the distinct caseframe.

(4) Vic hit Clint with a plank.
AGT PAT MNS

(5a) Horses eat grass.
AGT PAT

(5b) Horses eat.
PAT

As van Valin notes, 'This analysis has [the result that] the lexicon is virtually flooded with homophonous verb forms; one of the original positive features of Fillmore's model was that it allowed a unified treatment of verbs with both transitive and intransitive forms, and this is lost in the lexicase account' (van Valin, 1980:302).

For the most part, CR's are defined as relating not to the verb, but to the PAT. This can be seen in Starosta's definitions for COR: 'i) the entity perceived as being in correspondence with the Patient (inner Correspondent; formerly Dative or Experiencer); or ii) the perceived external frame of reference or standard for the state or action (outer Correspondent; formerly Benefactive)' (1982:5) and MNS: 'i) the perceived immediate effector of an event or state; the external entity which impinges most directly and immediately on the Patient (inner Means; formerly mostly Instrument); or ii) the abstract path by way of which an external influence impinges on the situation (outer Means; formerly Manner)' (*idem*).

This approach is reminiscent of Pāṇini where too there was a primary obligatory case or *kāraka* (the *kartā* – cf. '. . . there can be no sentence in Sanskrit without one' (Ananthanarayana, 1970:19)) which figured in the descriptions of the other *kāraka* (e.g. *karma*: 'that which is desired by the *karā* (*ibid.*, p. 1)). An interesting difference however is that for Pāṇini the obligatory *kāraka* was the Agent.

The thing to notice about Starosta's definitions is that they appear to be of an essentially semantic character, though the overwhelming vagueness of the definitions is their most striking characteristic. Things are not helped by the fact that correspondences between the (1982:4f) definitions and those found in the (1977) work are not always straightforward, but more problematic is the fact that they are so vague as to be of little genuine guidance in determining the assignment of CR's. This problem is exacerbated by the fact that, in any case, '. . . the ultimate choice [of CR assignment] is contrained by *syntactic* criteria' (1977:465) [emphasis mine], though Starosta rarely, if ever, gives an explanation of what exactly these syntactic criteria are, beyond the two fundamental constraints of 'obligatory Patient' and the 'one-case-per-clause' principle willingly adopted from Fillmorean (etc.) Case.

In connection with this second constraint, which he calls the 'one per sent' (*sic*) constraint, Starosta incorporates the notion of 'inner' and 'outer' CR's (cf. Chapter 8) extended to enable the reduction of his (1977) nine-case set to six in (1982).

Returning to the question of primacy of syntactic criteria over semantic criteria for the assignment of CR's, we can see here the main difference between Starosta's Lexicase and other Case grammars. Fillmorean Case grammarians seek to represent the situational perspective of a sentence by ensuring matching case assignments in logically equivalent sentence pairs as for example in (6) or (7).

(6a)	Lindsey gave	Doris	the book.	
	Agent	Dative	Object	
(6b)	Lindsey gave	the book	to Doris.	
	Agent	Object	Dative	
(7a)	Peter leapt	the chasm.		
	Agent	Locative		
(7b)	Peter leapt	over the chasm.		
	Agent	Locative		

However, as Starosta points out, the positing of identical underlying structures for different surface sentences requires the grammar to incorporate '. . . a powerful transformational framework to ignore the surface evidence and take one of the structures as reflecting the deep structure and derive the other from it. However there is no non-arbitrary way to decide which of the structures is the basic one and which the derived one' (1982:8).

In Starosta's view, it is not the task of the CR labels to reflect paraphrase relationships between sentences having different surface structures: this task is dealt with '. . . by Semantic Interpretation Rules, rules which operate outside the grammar proper, but take Lexicase syntactic-semantic representations as one of their inputs' (1977:464).

Paraphrase relations are certainly not captured by Lexicase CR assignments, as can be seen in (8)-(9), corresponding to (6)-(7) above.

(8a) Lindsey gave Doris the book.
AGT PAT MNS

(8b) Lindsey gave the book to Doris.
AGT PAT COR (cf. 1982:19)

(9a) Peter leapt the chasm.
AGT PAT

(9b) Peter leapt over the chasm.
PAT LOC (cf. 1977:524)

Notice in (9b) that a combination of syntactic criteria for assigning LOC and the obligatory Patient rule give an entirely different case frame compared to the almost synonymous (9a), while in (8) the preference of 'direct object' position (loosely defined in terms of position with regard to the verb and lack of preposition) for PAT forces us to stretch our imagination in interpreting *the book* as MNS in (8a), as well as the resulting conflicting case frames.

One may well ask what functions the CR's have in this grammar. The correspondence with syntactic function is fairly strong at first sight (AGT=subject, PAT=direct object), but on closer inspection it turns out that the relationship is not so straightforward. Although there are some very general correspondences, for example of LOC and COR to prepositional phrases (in English at least) as against AGT and PAT to subject or object, this may be just the kind of information that CR's are required to capture (cf. Starosta, 1973, 1976). Starosta bears out this notion, as noted above.

It has been pointed out by Kilby (1982:55) that Case grammars in general tend to be set up to bridge the gap between syntax and semantics, and that most of the better known systems tend towards the situational or cognitive side. This is true of Fillmore's later work (particularly as seen in Fillmore (1972): see Chapter 2), and an extreme example in Schank's (1975) Conceptual Dependency framework (see Chapter 11 Section 6). Lexicase (and to some extent J. Anderson's (1971) localist Case grammar (see Chapter 3)) tends more towards identifying CR's with syntactic relations. Whether this is a function that is particularly useful in the context of natural language processing will be discussed in Part III, but Starosta's (1979*a*:59) claim to have applied the model successfully to the description of several (chiefly Asian and Pacific) languages suggests that the theory at least merits more serious attention than it has so far received, at least to iron out some of its more important flaws, especially in other parts – not discussed here – which are not directly relevant to the Case-like aspect of Lexicase.

It might also be added that some of the problems mentioned here have been clarified or improved in publications which have appeared since this Chapter was first drafted (Starosta, personal communications).

SIX

DIK'S FUNCTIONAL GRAMMAR

1. *Introduction*

It is appropriate that in this last Chapter of Part I we should consider the Dutch linguist Simon Dik's Functional Grammar (FG), since there are several respects in which it represents a consolidation of some of the ideas discussed in the preceding sections. The theory is outlined in Dik (1978), and is applied, without substantial revisions, to several problems in Dik (1980). These two publications have been followed by three collections of essays within this framework (Bolkenstein *et al.* 1981; Hoekstra *et al.* 1981; Dik, 1983*a*), and with an active forum in existence, FG is more or less established as an important theoretical school.

The core of the theory is that as a grammar it is able to relate a category analysis of syntax to the functional roles of the categories, and in particular to their functions at three levels, syntactic, semantic and pragmatic. At the syntactic level there are functions such as Subject and Object; semantic functions are the Case-like notions of Agent, Goal, Recipient etc.; the pragmatic level is concerned with the functions Topic and Focus. In this chapter we shall be concerned primarily with the relationship between the first two of these levels. An explicit comparison of semantic functions in FG and cases in Case grammar is to be found in Mackenzie (1981).

Comparison of FG with Transformation Generative grammar (TG) on the one hand and Relational Grammar (RG) on the other are more or less appropriate and are highlighted in Comrie's (1979) review of Dik (1978). Unlike TG, FG has no transformations, filtering devices or lexical decomposition. Relationships like active-passive are described in terms of differing interactions between pragmatic functions and semantic and syntactic functions. Comrie contrasts the use of semantic functions in FG with the RG approach, noting that 'Within Relational Grammar, the main concentration of effort has been towards the role of syntactic functions in syntactic rules' (Comrie, 1979:271). Our main interest in FG is in its ability to relate semantic and syntactic structure. In the sections that follow we shall look at the way the semantic functions are related to the verbs via the notion of 'predicate frames' (in a manner highly reminiscent of Chafe (1970) – cf. Chapter 4), at the range of semantic functions Dik actually proposes, and at the ways in which semantic functions map onto syntactic functions via the 'semantic function hierarchy', for which Dik claims a degree of universality.

2. *Predications*

Dik's theory revolves around the familiar notion of a verb-centred structural description. He talks in terms of 'predicates', 'predicate-frames' and 'predications', involving concepts found in Valency theory and in the Chafian verb-feature system discussed in preceding chapters. The predication consists of a predicate (typically a verb) and an array of constituents made up of 'terms' filling slots of two main types: '(nuclear) arguments' and 'satellites'. A 'nuclear predication' is made up of the predicate together with its arguments. An 'extended predication' is a nuclear predication with satellites. The correspondence between these notions and those of Valency theory (argument = complement; satellite = adjunct) is very clear: 'The nuclear predication defines a state of affairs. . . . Satellites are constituents which do not function in the definition of the state of affairs as such, but give further information pertaining to the state of affairs as a whole, by specifying the time or the location of the state of affairs, giving the reason or cause of its obtaining, and providing other additional information. Satellites provide optional additions to the information contained in the nuclear predication. Nuclear arguments, on the other hand, are necessary for the definition of the state of affairs, although they may be left unspecified under certain contextual or situational circumstances' (Dik, 1978:25).

Mackenzie (1981:304) reviews the problems that both Case grammar and FG have in providing reliable criteria for distinguishing between arguments and satellites: it is not clear whether the distinction is essentially semantic, with syntactic repercussions, or vice versa, or indeed a combination. That the question is not straightforward is reflected by the extensive discussion of essentially the same problem within the framework of Valency grammar in Chapter 1 above.

Dik notes that the range of semantic functions for arguments and satellites overlaps: some semantic functions more typically attach to satellites, but '. . . some of these satellite functions [or all of them? - HS] can also characterise the arguments of certain predicates' (Dik 1978:26). He suggests that there are various degrees by which a term can be related to a predicate. We have already seen satellites and nuclear arguments. To these he then adds terms which are incorporated into a 'complex' predicate, and terms which are 'semantically incorporated into the meaning of some basic lexical predicate'. This latter relation, which Dik illustrates with the verb *kick* and its lexicalised Instrument *foot* (or whatever), seems to correspond to our own notion of 'integral complements' (cf. Chapter 1 Section 6), or to Cook's (1973) notion of 'covert case roles' (cf. Chapter 4 Section 5). What Dik has in mind with his complex predicate is not quite so clear. The English examples to be found (Dik, 1980:39,42) are not all convincing, though it appears that some of these might be simulations of constructions found in other languages. This phenomenon of argument incorporation, and in particular the differences in meaning between ordinary and complex predicates, is treated at some length in Dik (1980:39–43).

The predicate-frames are found in the lexicon, and specify the following information (Dik, 1978:29):

(i) the form of the predicate
(ii) the syntactic category to which the predicate belongs . . .
(iii) the number of arguments that the predicate requires . . .
(iv) the selection restrictions which hold for the terms which are to fill the argument slots . . .
(v) the semantic functions of the arguments.

Dik's predicate-frame concept is clearly quite like the Valency dictionary entry format proposed by Helbig and Schenkel (1973) (cf. Chapter 1 Section 2), except that it contains no information about the syntactic functions of the arguments: as we shall see below, these are given by general rule. In addition, Dik gives the arguments semantic function labels, showing clearly how Case and Valency can be brought together. In comparison with Fillmore's concept of case frame features (cf. Chapter 2 Section 2), the important difference is in (iv): for Dik, semantic restrictions on arguments are associated with individual predicates; for Fillmore, at least in the (1968*a*) version of Case, these restrictions are inherent in the cases themselves.

Dik puts an important, though informal, constraint on predications, limiting them other than exceptionally to four argument slots: 'It is an empirical fact that nuclear predications in natural languages hardly ever have more than four different argument positions. Even predicates [*sic*] with four nuclear arguments are rare in any language. This puts interesting constraints on the variety of predicate-frames to be found in the lexicon of any language' (Dik 1978:30).

Dik introduces a further notion concerning the relationship between predicate-frames and particular predications, suggesting that a partly-filled predication be termed an 'open predication'. Although at first sight this seems to correspond to the Valency notion of a predication with optional complement slots left unfilled (Tesnière's (1959:239) 'free valencies' – cf. Chapter 1 Section 2), this is in fact not the case. An open predication is rather a partially specified predication into which only some terms have been inserted. It is simply a name for a certain stage in the derivation (cf. Dik, 1978:31). This is an important point, since Dik does not otherwise seem to have any notion corresponding to optional complement (Valency) or frame feature incorporating optional case (Fillmore, 1968*a*). The derivations of transitive and intransitive sentence pairs are presumably from quite distinct underlying predicate-frames, since there is no indication anywhere in Dik (1978) that in an open predication any of the arguments can remain unfilled.

It is not clear whether this is a fair inference to make given Dik's failure to discuss this question at all; but if it is a correct analysis, then FG is clearly missing out on one of the main benefits of a Case-like approach in the possibility of connecting in the lexicon the two uses of such verbs. The above analysis implies two entries in the lexicon each generating its own predicate-frame with the attendant redundancy in, for example, expressing selection restrictions on the argument positions. Taken to its extreme, we can see that the different nuclear predications in (1) imply seven distinct lexical entries for *pay*.

(1a) Jeanette paid the waiter five pounds for the meal.
(1b) Jeanette paid five pounds for the meal.
(1c) Jeanette paid the waiter for the meal.
(1d) Jeanette paid the waiter five pounds.
(1e) Jeanette paid for the meal.
(1f) Jeanette paid five pounds.
(1g) Jeanette paid the waiter.

Dick also develops (1978:32ff) a 'typology of states of affairs' which is rather reminiscent of Chafe's (1970) and Longacre's

(1976) basic verb typology (cf. Chapter 4). Unlike Chafe, and Cook after him, however, Dik does not explicitly link the generation of predicate-frames to this typology. Dik distinguishes four types of states of affairs determined by the two binary parameters Control and Dynamic. Note that it is nuclear predications as a whole that Dik is classifying here, not predicates *per se*, an important distinction (cf. Chapter 4 Section 7) which explains why the typology cannot necessarily be used to imply predicate-frames, since a given predicate may be used to express a predication of more than one of these predication types depending on many factors including tense and mood of the verb, and how the argument slots are filled. The four states of affairs that Dik distinguishes are States, Processes, Positions and Actions as shown in Figure 1. There is a degree of similarity between Dik's classification and Chafe's, although the terminology is slightly different. States and Processes are the same in the two systems. Dik's Positions are controlled situations, and correspond to states in Chafe's model: the difference is that the principle argument in a Position is said to be in control of the situation. There is a distinction therefore between (2a) and (2b):

(2a) John stood on the table (Position)
(2b) The table stood in the corner (State)

Actions are controlled events, and as such correspond both to Chafe's actions and to action-processes.

	+dynamic EVENT	−dynamic SITUATION
+controlled	Action	Position
−controlled	Process	State

Figure 1: Dik's four states of affairs (1978:34)

Dik stresses that this categorisation applies to predications rather than predicates since these are '. . . distinctions in the designations of nuclear predications. The differences involved may be (but are not necessarily) determined by properties of the predicate as such. They may also arise from the interaction between the predicate and the terms to which it is applied' (1978:34). Many predicates may figure in more than one predication type, as Dik amply illustrates (3)-(4); cf. also (2).

(3a) Mary cooked the potatoes. (Action)
(3b) The potatoes are cooking. (Process)
(4a) John tasted the soup. (Action)
(4b) John tasted the wine in the soup. (State)

Dik catalogues (1978:35f) some restrictions that can be generalised using this classification. Of interest, in comparison with Chafe's syntactic tests for his verb types (Chapter 4 Section 2), is the fact that many of these restrictions can be stated in terms of one or other of the two parameters Controlled and Dynamic. Thus, for example, the imperative mood and parallel constructions are only available for controlled states of affairs (Actions or Positions); likewise, Beneficiary and Instrument can only attach to Controlled predications.

For each of the four states of affairs, some typical predicate-frames with examples are given (1978:38f): we need not repeat the details here, though of interest is Dik's introduction of the $\emptyset$ (Zero) function in state predications such as (5).

(5a) $\text{Roses}_{\emptyset}$ are red.
(5b) The $\text{cup}_{\emptyset}$ is on the $\text{table}_{\text{Loc}}$.

It is not clear whether Dik regards his list of predicate frames as exhaustive, either generally or for English. In either case, one can find gaps. Dik mentions (1978:30) the possibility of four-place predicates, though none are included in his list. One can imagine that the verb *pay* may be one such (cf. (1) above), though it is not clear what semantic function Dik would assign either to the price paid or to the commodity bought in such a predication. Dik also has no state of affairs corresponding to the 'ambient' types found in Chafe (1970) (cf. Chapter 4 Section 2), and in this respect we shall criticise Dik's notion of Zero function below. Finally, no examples are given of nuclear predications involving semantic functions more normally associated with satellites (e.g. *last* taking Time) other than Locative.

3. *The semantic functions*

Interestingly, Dik gives no explicit definitions for most of the semantic functions he introduces: only briefly (1978:39–43) does he compare a small number of them with the cases found in Fillmore's model: for a more explicit comparison, see Mackenzie (1981). In a later article, Dik clarifies rather more fully the roles that semantic functions play in FG, as follows: '(a) they characterise the fundamental semantic relations within the predication, (b) they co-define the typology of states of affairs, (c) they co-determine Subject and Object assignment possibilities, (d) they co-determine the formal expression of terms, (e) they indirectly play a role in patterns of constituent ordering, (f) they may take part in cross-reference and agreement relations, (g) they serve to differentiate Subjects and Objects in terms of their underlying semantic functions' (Dik, 1983*b*:13).

Lists of semantic functions are given in each of the publications as lists of abbreviations outside the main body of the texts. These lists are inconsistent as some functions are added in the later lists, in some instances only to disappear again. What is more significant is that only some of these are introduced, discussed and explained within the works themselves. The full list from Dik (1978:xi) is as follows:

Ag = Agent	Inst = Instrument	Proc = Processed
Go = Goal	Loc = Location	Fo = Force
Rec = Recipient	Temp = Time	Po = Positioner
Ben = Beneficiary	Dir = Direction	So = Source

In addition there is the Zero function and, added in Dik (1980:x) Exp[eriencer] (though see below) and Poss[essor]. The list is extended in a more or less principled way in the later publications as a result of analyses of various phenomena in a wide variety of languages, though it should be stressed that the set of semantic functions is nevertheless intended to be a closed set (cf. criticisms of Case grammar by Langacker (1970:171*fn*) and Chapin (1972:651) above – Chapter 2 Section 2). The semantic functions are closely related to the classification of states of affairs discussed above.

Dik distinguishes between the semantic function Agent and Force for the contrasting elements *John* and *the wind* in the familiar examples in (1):

(1a) John_{Ag} opened the door.
(1b) The wind_{Fo} opened the door.

This distinction is not, as in Fillmore, based on inherent semantic features of the participants (animate versus inanimate), but on the question of 'control', since in (1b) *the wind* '. . . though it does not control the Process, is nevertheless presented as an autonomous cause or instigator of it' (Dik, 1978:37). Note that (1a) is an Action while (1b) is a Process.

Positioner is the semantic function assigned to the controlling entity in a Position state of affairs. On the distinction between Positioner and Agent, Dik comments 'Notice that both Agents and Positioners are Controllers. The difference lies in whether they control a dynamic or a non-dynamic state of affairs' (1978:37). In a similar manner, Instrument and Force are distinguished on the Controlled parameter (1978:39f). Contrasting the function of *the key* in (2a)-(2b),

(2a) John opened the door with a key.
(2b) The key opened the door.

Dik suggests that the appropriate function in (2a) is Instrument, conforming to his definition as follows: '. . . entity used by a Controller in performing an Action or maintaining a Position' (1978:40), whereas (2b) '. . . does not designate an Action or a Position, but a Process in which *the key* is presented as an autonomous, non-controlling and non-controlled cause of the event. This, however, is precisely the sort of constituent to which the semantic function Force applies' (*idem*).

In comparing his approach with Fillmore's where *the key* is Instrument in both cases, Dik suggests that '. . . Fillmore's assignment of semantic function to constituents in certain respects unduly overgeneralises their common properties and neglects their differences' (Dik, 1978:39). Mackenzie (1981:306ff) regrets these distinctions, suggesting that they make Dik's taxonomy of semantic functions inconsistent, unclear, and, more seriously, unable to generalise. For example, he suggests that since the distinction between Agents and Positioners is captured by the dynamic nature of the predication, the distinction need not be recapitulated in the semantic functions. Furthermore, notice that because *remain* in (3a) is nondynamic whereas *leave* in (3b) is dynamic, *John* counterintuitively has differing semantic functions in (3a-b):

(3a) John_{Po} remained in Africa.
(3b) John_{Ag} did not leave Africa.

A notable apparent absentee from Dik's range of semantic functions is a Patient or Object function. Dik draws attention to this (1978:41), but points out that he does not wish to overgeneralise the Goal function (not to be confused with Direction – cf (4) and (5)) which is '. . . restricted to those entities which are affected (or effected) by the operation of some Controller (Agent [(4)] or Positioner [(6)]) or a Force [(7)]' (Dik, 1978:41), to entities in a certain State (Zero function) (8) or to entities undergoing non-Forced Processes (Processed) (9).

(4) John_{Ag} read a book_{Go}.
(5) John_{Ag} sent a book_{Go} to $\text{London}_{\text{Dir}}$.
(6) John_{Po} kept the $\text{present}_{\text{Go}}$.
(7) The wind_{Fo} opened the door_{Go}.
(8) The $\text{cup}_{\emptyset}$ is on the $\text{table}_{\text{Loc}}$.
(9) $\text{John}_{\text{Proc}}$ fell down.

It is interesting to contrast Dik's recognition of essential differences here, even when semantic functions are in complementary distribution, with other authors' desires to keep the number of relations small. Cook for example makes only a partial distinction between Objects in a State (o_s) and in a Process or Action-Process (o), whereas Chafe and Longacre use the umbrella term Patient (cf. Chapter 4). On the other hand, Dik's system leads again to loss of generalisation between sentence pairs like (7) versus (10), where *the door* is assigned a different semantic function in each.

(10) The door$_{\text{Proc}}$ opened.

Mackenzie (1981:307) criticises this distinction strongly, as does Watters: '. . . the two different roles for *the door* seem entirely unmotivated. In both sentences *the door* stands in the same relationship to the predicate *open*' (Watters, 1980:166). As regards the notion of a Zero function in States (cf. (8), (11) and (12)), this seems to be something of an avoidance of the rather difficult issue of the treatment of predications involving the copular.

(11) Roses$_{\emptyset}$ are red.

(12) That man$_{\emptyset}$ is the killer$_{\emptyset}$.

While (11) seems to imply that adjectives are to be treated as one-argument predicates, (12) suggests that Dik does not recognise the possibility of nominal predications. In addition (12) entails a rather uneasy contravention of the principle whereby there can be only one instance of any given function in a simple predication, otherwise apparently adhered to by Dik. On the subject of cases like 'Essive', see further Chapter 7 Section 6. But a more serious problem with the Zero function is its connotation of semantic vacuity, perhaps more appropriate for the (here missing) state of affairs termed 'ambient' by Chafe (1970) (Chapter 4 Section 2). Chafe assigns no semantic value at all to the formal subject of predicates like *rain* and this seems to be a quite different type of nullity compared to the relations in (11) and (12). While none of Dik's current semantic functions seems particularly appropriate, we could postulate a non-dynamic counterpart of Processed given the close relationship between certain States and Processes (13).

(13a) The wood dried. (Process)

(13b) The wood is dry. (State)

Dik's original (1978) set of semantic functions excluded Experiencer. Dik explains at some length (1978:42f) why he feels that there is no need for an Experiencer semantic function in his model. Certain states of affairs which can be designated in general as 'experiences' are expressed in a number of ways: as a State (14a), as a kind of possession relation (14b), or as a Process involving some Force (14c).

(14a) John was afraid of the dog.
(14b) John had a great fear of the dog.
(14c) The dog frightened John.

Dik concluded that '. . . it would be an oversimplification to assume that there is just one underlying structure for experiences and that such expressions as [(14a-c)] are simply alternative manifestations of this underlying structure. Rather, I believe that the various expression types found in natural languages reflect different conceptualisations of the notion of experience and that these conceptualisations follow the model of types of states of affairs which are not experiences' (1978:43).

Dik once again is taking a stand which simplifies the relation of syntactic and (shallow) semantic functions at the cost of losing the ability to capture approximate paraphrase relationships, since the semantic function assignments for *John* and *the dog* in the three sentences in (14) do not match up. Dik contrasts *John* in Zero function to the State caused by *the dog* (Source) in (14a) with *the dog* as a Force exerting a certain influence on *John* (Goal) in (14c). No analysis of (14b) is given. In Dik (1980:75) however, the semantic functions listed as associated with the Dutch verb *zien* ('see') are Experiencer and Goal, and in Dik (1981:33) he again uses the function for the subject of *see*, but with an excusing footnote (p. 38); various adherents of FG give arguments for including this semantic function (e.g. Bolkestein, 1983; Itagaki and Prideaux, 1983).

4. *Syntactic function assignment and the Semantic Function Hierarchy*

Since the main novelty of FG is its mechanisms for relating functions at different levels, it is proper that assignment of syntactic and pragmatic functions should be given the most thorough discussion in Dik's (1978) book. In fact we shall not look at the overlay of pragmatic functions, but concentrate on Dik's conception of syntactic functions, subject and object assignment, and his 'semantic function hierarchy' (SFH).

It is quite important to see where semantic and syntactic function assignment figure in the overall concept of the grammar. Nuclear predicate frames are derived from the lexicon and extended with satellites. Syntactic function assignment follows term insertion. Notice that semantic function assignments are expressed in terms of interactions between predicates and predicate-frames.

But first we should note that by 'syntactic functions', Dik is not referring simply or wholly to surface syntactic structure, since he considers the only relevant syntactic functions to be Subj[ect] and Obj[ect], these being '. . . sufficient to take care of the relevant differences between linguistic expressions which express the same predication' (1978:18). In fact the syntactic functions do not correspond at all to traditional notions, whence we might have expected (for English) a three- or four-member set including perhaps Indirect-object and certainly Prepositional-object (German, for example, might have five syntactic functions: four surface cases plus prepositional-object; etc.). Rather it is the case that '. . . although the term "syntactic function" is used (mainly for traditional reasons), FG gives a *semantic* interpretation to the functions Subject and Object. The semantic value of these functions is not judged to contribute to the definition of the state of affairs designated by the predication as such, but to the particular way in which the state of affairs is presented, i.e. to the point of view from which it is described' (Dik 1980:13) [emphasis mine]. Under these circumstances, it is questionable whether the term is well-chosen at all. First, Dik's syntactic functions correspond rather poorly to the traditional concept. Second, given their 'semantic' interpretation – though note that this is a different 'semantics' from that of the semantic functions already discussed – the term wrongly suggests to the reader a hierarchy of functions from surface structure via Case-like shallow semantics to the deeper level of thematic relations as captured by Dik's pragmatic functions.

Nevertheless, Dik's syntactic functions are used to a certain extent to relate the underlying predication to its surface expression, at least as far as the selection of surface subject and object are concerned. What Dik simply ignores is the generation of the appropriate surface forms for the other arguments, once the Subject and Object functions have been assigned. For English, this means the choice of preposition for nuclear arguments (and sometimes for satellites) where it is semantically empty (otherwise it is generated by term insertion rules). For languages with surface case this means also the choice of case. In spite of this failing, Dik's proposals for the assignment of these two major syntactic functions are of sufficient interest to merit closer attention, especially since they involve the perhaps controversial SFH.

Essentially Dik regards syntactic function assignment as the selection of the two arguments which will figure at a fairly superficial level in two key functions; in this respect FG is rather close to Fillmore's (1968*a*) conception of subject and object selection rules, especially when one considers that arguments not assigned one of the two syntactic functions remain unspecified as to syntactic function, and their surface form is determined by rules which operate on semantic function labels. To put it another way, Dik supposes that there are typical surface realisations for each of the semantic functions which may however get 'masked' by the assignment of the Subj or Obj function. These functions, meanwhile, determine certain aspects of surface structure (Dik, 1978:74f):

(a) . . . the way the constituent is marked by case or adpositions.

(b) . . . the positions the constituent[s] will take in the final linear structure of the clause. . . . Constituents which only have semantic function, however, are not normally tied to specified positions in the clause . . .

(c) . . . agreement between the verb and any other constituent in the clause . . .

(d) . . . different voices of the verb correlating with different choices of Subj and Obj.

Syntactic function assignment interacts significantly with semantic function, in that the possibilities of Subj and Obj assignment are constrained by a hierarchy which can be defined language independently over the semantic functions. This hierarchy (the SFH) is given in (1).

(1) Ag>Go>Rec>Ben>Instr>Loc>Temp

The schema is interpreted as follows: 'In principle, Subj function can be assigned to any semantic function in SFH, and Obj function to any semantic function except Ag. In both cases, however, these assignments become more and more "difficult" as we advance through the SFH' (1978:76). The SFH is claimed as a language universal, with, for different languages, a different cut-off point beyond which Subj or Obj assignment is more difficult. What is more, the SFH also defines markedness of constructions, since the 'normality' of the construction, the freedom from constraints and conditions on the function assignments, and the frequency of the resulting constructions all diminish as the Subj choice is made later in the SFH.

As regards the Object function, we find that there are parallels between Subj and Obj assignment, with the same SFH operating. One thing to note is that Dik's Obj does not correspond especially to direct rather than indirect objects, but is rather simply the function which is realised (in English) as a non-prepositional nominal coming immediately after the verb. Thus the choice of

Rec rather than Go as Obj in a predication like (2a) gives the resulting sentence (2b) as opposed to (2c). Note the semantic-syntactic function labelling, and in particular that in (2b) the Go has no syntactic function. The choice of surface form is dictated by general rule operating on semantic and syntactic function, including specification for a Goal with no associated syntactic function.

(2a) give $(\text{John})_{Ag}$ $(\text{the books})_{Go}$ $(\text{my brother})_{Rec}$
(2b) John_{AgSubj} gives my brother_{RecObj} the books_{Go}.
(2c) John_{AgSubj} gives the books_{GoObj} to my brother_{Rec}.

Kanno (1983) argues for the introduction of a third syntactic function Obj2 for this type of construction, especially with regard to accounting for various restrictions on passivisation.

One thing to notice about the SFH is that it defines only a preferred order for Subj and Obj assignment: given a predicate frame with Ag, Go and Rec, the SFH tells us only that the least marked selection will be AgSubj and GoObj. English however allows any of these three semantic functions to be assigned the Subj function and either of Go and Rec as Obj: the SFH predicts only the relative markedness of sentences reflecting Subj and Obj assignment ranging from the least marked (3a) through to the most 'unusual' (3e), and not that any of (3b)-(3e) are somehow impossible.

(3a) Rod_{AgSubj} gave the diskette_{GoObj} to Jock_{Rec}.
(3b) Rod_{AgSubj} gave Jock_{RecObj} the diskette_{Go}.
(3c) The diskette_{GoSubj} was given to Jock_{Rec} by Rod_{Ag}.
(3d) $\text{Jock}_{RecSubj}$ was given the diskette_{GoObj} by Rod_{Ag}.
(3e) The diskette_{GoSubj} was given Jock_{RecObj} by Rod_{Ag}.

There are nevertheless some problems with the general concepts at work here. In the first place, the SFH does not specify all the semantic functions introduced by Dik. This is a particularly significant omission in the case of Force, Processed, Positioner and Zero, which clearly appear to be argument functions, and whose interaction with the syntactic functions Subject and Object it is rarely necessary to capture. But by the same token, notice that while it seems to be acceptable to introduce new semantic functions – as discussed above – these are never accompanied by a corresponding revision of the SFH. Returning to the four functions singled out above, two solutions seem possible.

Bauer (1980:52) suggests that, in order to capture certain generalisations, '. . . it seems likely that syntactic and pragmatic functions will need to treat Agent, Positioner, Processed and Force as alike in certain respects . . .' (Bauer, 1980:52). If Bauer's suggestion seems to imply some sort of collapsing of the four roles, then it must be said that the original decision to distinguish the roles in the first instance now seems questionable, and indeed this was Mackenzie's (1981:306ff) view, as we pointed out above. A second, less radical solution is proposed by Okoth Okombo, who suggests that '. . . the SFH must be formulated in a way that allows some positions to be occupied not by single semantic functions but by sets of mutually exclusive semantic functions' (Okoth Okombo, 1983:151).

A more serious problem though is the possibility that the SFH is not as universal as Dik would claim. Even in Dik's own exemplification (1978:80) there are breakdowns: in Sre, a BenSubj assignment is questionable while InstrSubj is acceptable, and in Maguindanao RecSubj is not possible although Ben, Instr and Loc all allow Subj assignment. And Watters (1980:167) suggests that the hierarchy might differ between different predication types. He claims that this is 'obvious', his example being a verb like *elapse* which has as unmarked Subj the semantic function Temp at the bottom of the SFH and way beyond the cut-off point for English. Watters' point would be made all the more strongly by pointing to predicates whose unmarked realisations seemed to contradict the SFH, and indeed there are such predicates: *receive* introduces a Rec and a Go, but 'prefers' a RecSubj (4); and there are predicates where alternative realisations are equally unmarked (5), though the SFH would predict (5b) as being more marked than (5a).

(4a) $\text{Lindsey}_{\text{RecSubj}}$ received good $\text{news}_{\text{GoObj}}$.
(4b) Good $\text{news}_{\text{GoSubj}}$ was received by $\text{Lindsey}_{\text{Rec}}$.
(5a) $\text{Steve}_{\text{AgSubj}}$ supplies $\text{micros}_{\text{GoObj}}$ to CCL_{Rec}.
(5b) $\text{Steve}_{\text{AgSubj}}$ supplies $\text{CCL}_{\text{RecObj}}$ with $\text{micros}_{\text{Go}}$.

A final problem for the SFH is that it is not clear to what extent it cuts across the argument-satellite distinction. Little is said in any of the published works with regard to syntactic function assignment to satellites: presumably they normally have no syntactic function as such – cf. comments above on the 'automatic' assignment of surface form for elements other than Subject and Object – or else choice of a satellite as Subject or Object results in a highly marked sentence pattern, since the typical satellite semantic functions are all low on the SFH.

There appear then to be some problems with the SFH concept, both in the incompleteness of Dik's elaboration of it, and in his claims for its universality. My own feeling is that FG would be an attractive model (especially with a more surface-oriented approach to syntactic functions) without the SFH, though for Dik the generalisability of his model to a large number of languages seems to be important. Certainly the range of languages treated by FG devotees is impressive: in the first two works alone (Dik, 1978 and 1980) no less than 113 different languages are mentioned, though of course few of these get extensive treatment. Certainly reviewers of Dik's work suggest that FG is an important approach, but for our purposes we might find that his elaboration of certain instantly appealing notions – in particular the interrelationship between predicate-frames, semantic functions and surface structure – diminish the overall attraction of the model.

PART II: SOME CLASSICAL PROBLEMS FOR CASE

In this part we shall take a 'horizontal' view of Case in contrast to the 'vertical' view in Part I. Here we wish to discuss a number of specific issues that recur in Case grammar, to an extent comparing the way different grammarians have approached them, but also seeing how much the problems are themselves artefacts of ill-conceived formulations of the theory. To a greater degree than in Part I we shall also discuss the relevance of these 'classical' problems to multilingual language processing, for it is clear that if a theoretical problem has no consequences for this particular application, then it is only of academic interest. We follow Anderson's (1977:29–55) review of Case in focusing on three particular problem areas.

We begin however with the cases themselves, and in Chapter 7 discuss in four separate sections the questions of agentivity and causality, the distinction of roles termed Experiencer, Beneficiary, Recipient and/or Dative, various types of Object/Patient, the localist roles of Source, Path and Goal, and the two 'questionable' cases Comitative and Essive. Running through this chapter are the related problems of 'specificity' and 'multiplicity' which we discuss, along with a number of 'Case hierarchy' proposals, by way of introduction to Chapter 7.

In Chapter 8 we consider the 'one-case-per argument' restriction, and the ensuing problem of 'dual roles'. The problems that this restriction throws up are discussed, in particular, the problem caused by the desire to have some correspondence between cases in related predicates and sentences. The significance of this problem is heightened in a multilingual application, where we desire not only to relate near synonyms and paraphrasing sentence-pairs, but also translational equivalents.

A sort of corollary to the 'one-case-per-argument' principle is the principle of 'one-case-per predication' and the related proposal of 'inner' and 'outer' roles. We shall see in Chapter 9 that the distinction made by Valency grammarians between complements and adjuncts offers a straightforward answer to this problem, and we shall consider the effect on this solution of our own contention that the inner/outer distinction is a multiple- rather than dual-value scale.

The discussions in these last two chapters are of particular relevance to my own 'case grid' proposal, an outline of which is given in Chapter 10 and brings Part II to a close.

SEVEN

DEFINING THE CASES: SPECIFICITY AND MULTIPLICITY

1. *Introduction*

A recurring problem for Case grammarians has always been the definition of a 'comfortable' set of cases. Whether or not a given case-set is intended, following Fillmore's (1968*a*:24) original notion, as a 'set of universal, presumably innate, concepts', there has always been a tendency, criticised strongly for example by Langacker (1970:171*fn*) and Chapin (1972:651), to allow the number and nature of the cases to grow, in particular by introducing new case notions or distinctions to cater for particular problem sentences. This unfortunate lack of formality has been discussed above (Chapter 2 Section 2). However, it is not clear that, from author to author, there is any particular need for consistency. Although Nilsen states accusingly '. . . unless there is a tight and consistent system for identification of deep cases, there will continue to be widely divergent opinions about the number, *and even the nature*, of deep cases' (Nilsen, 1972:47) [emphasis mine], I have argued elsewhere (Rosner and Somers, 1980:20f) that different applications of Case theory should indeed – even inevitably – result in different case systems. I criticised comparisons of inventories of cases made by Samlowski (1976:67ff) and Longacre (1976:23ff) for not taking into account theoretical differences underlying their conception, and attempted to illustrate the point by contrasting environments where the affected and effected objects (Objective and Factitive in Fillmore, 1968*a*) may or may not need to be distinguished (Rosner and Somers, 1980:21-3).

In general however almost all case sets are a mixture of what I wish to term 'specificity' and 'multiplicity'. Neither of these must be considered objectionable if they can be justified in terms of a given application, but in fact there is very little evidence of authors explicitly tailoring their case systems to a particular need, other than by describing their lists of cases as those which seem 'necessary', 'useful' or 'comfortable'. In Chapter 11 we shall see the other side of the coin where a case system often taken directly from Fillmore (1968*a*) or Fillmore (1971*b*) without modification is applied to very specific problems quite different from the domains envisaged by Fillmore.

By 'specificity', I mean the distinction of a general case notion into more specific ones: examples might be the subdivision of an Objective case into affected (1a), effected (1b) and neutral (1c), the distinction between animate and inanimate Agents (2) as Agent versus Causal Potency, dynamic and non-dynamic Recipient/Possessor (3), or volitive and non-volitive Experiencer (4).

(1a) Toni broke *her pencil.*
(1b) Juan built *a model theatre.*
(1c) Karen opened *the door.*
(2a) *The workmen* demolished the house.
(2b) *The tornado* demolished the house.
(3a) *Jeanette* has a book.
(3b) *Jeanette* received a book.
(4a) *Pete* listened to the talk.
(4b) *Pete* heard the talk.

The problem with specific case distinctions is that these are often difficult assignments. In the case of the three types of Objective, we can easily distinguish effected versus affected in (5a) and (5b), but (5c) is ambiguous as regards these two (and a third reading, perhaps more apparent than the one matching (5a), with the bedroom as a model for the painting!).

(5a) Leonardo painted *the Mona Lisa.*
(5b) He painted *the window frame.*
(5c) Van Gogh painted *his bedroom.*

The converse of specificity is 'multiplicity' where a variety of intuitively differentiable relations are grouped together under one case name. In an earlier work I defined Patient as '. . . the entity that undergoes the action of the verb; the entity whose state is described by a stative verb; the entity which undergoes a change of state or location; the entity which specifies the content (. . .) of an experience' (Somers, 1980*a*:7).

In both specificity and multiplicity the overriding criterion should be the application for which the case-set is designed. We do not wish to criticise any case systems for having either of these traits for that reason alone. It is important however that these two tendencies be recognised and reconciled. Certainly, from the point of view of the general user, a severe mixture of specificity and multiplicity can be disconcerting and even misleading, as might be the case with the set of 'semantic relations' used in the METAL Machine Translation system (Lehmann *et al.*, 1980) – cf. Chapter 12 Section 3. Here the danger is that the relations that are very generally defined (showing multiplicity) often coincide with the more specific relations, of which there are many in this system, so that one cannot always be sure which to choose in the case of overlap.

One approach to the problem is to arrange the cases hierarchically, defining 'supercases' which are further specified as and when necessary. Examples of this approach are the systems of Brodda (1973) (and after him Ruus, 1979), Grimes (1975), and more recently, Paterson (1983), though even Fillmore (1971*b*:52) talks of the possibility of a 'hypercase', e.g. for Agent and Instrument.

Brodda's (1973:21) case system has seven supercases (*huvudkasus*) which are subdivided into thirteen subcases (*underkasus*). The cases are given English names (the text is in Swedish), most of which have the expected meaning, and are as follows: Cause, Source, Goal, Patient, Object, Space, Time. Cause and Source are respectively distinguished as the direct origin or cause as against the phenomenon 'which conditions (e.g. facilitates or is a precondition for)' the state of affairs denoted by the verb. Patient and Object are respectively the 'being' (*varelse*) and 'phenomenon' (*företeelse*) affected by or participating in the state of affairs, and are therefore, parallel cases distinguished only by animacy.

The definitions of the subcases are rather more specific. Cause is divided into Intentional Cause and Unintentional Cause, the former being further subdivided between Agent and Instrument. Source is not subdivided, while Goal divides between Aim and Result. Patient breaks down into Receiver, which is defined as 'Being towards which (the verb expresses that) the activity contained in s(v) [The state of affairs which a verb, v denotes] is intentionally directed.' All other Patients are Experiencer. Objects can be Affected or Unaffected. Space is subdivided into Location and Direktion (*sic*), and in a parallel fashion Time can be Moment or Duration.

It is interesting to note the different criteria Brodda uses to subdivide his supercases. One criterion is animacy, which partially distinguishes Agent and Instrument, though which also distinguishes the supercases Patient and Object. Another is volition which distinguishes Intentional and Unintentional Cause and perhaps also Aim and Result. It is also interesting to see many of the cases defined negatively in terms of their 'sister' subcases: Unintentional Cause, Result, Experiencer and Unaffected are all simply 'other instances of' their respective supercases.

Ruus (1979) took Brodda's case system and adapted it for the specific purpose of text analysis. The differences between Brodda's and Ruus's systems are that Instrument is no longer a subcase of Cause, but of a new supercase Means, along with Material. Cause is now simply therefore Unintentional versus Agent. Patient and Object are still supercases, but rather more distinct: Patient/Receiver is like Brodda's subcase of the same name, while Patient/Experiencer is no longer negatively defined, and seems to correspond to Experiencer in other (non-hierarchised) systems. Ruus's Object is divided not between Affected and Unaffected, but between Concrete and Abstract, these names having the expected connotations. The supercases and subcases in general are delimited on a practical rather than a simply intuitive basis, each pair of subcases being in complementary distribution, (Ruus, 1979:164). This principle explains the reorganisation of Brodda's system, and in particular the move of Instrument from Cause to Means and the introduction of Material. Ruus found this arrangement highly satisfactory for her particular purpose, since some generalisations could be made in terms of supercases. For example, the surface realisations for Unintentional Cause and Agent were essentially the same; on the other hand some selection restrictions and surface realisation tendencies could be distinguished on a subcase basis.

In his work on discourse structure, Grimes (1975) distinguished three subsystems of semantic role structure, which he then found could be conflated into a 'combined role scheme'. In this inverse manner, Grimes arrives at a case system which can be compared with the Brodda/Ruus system as a supercase-subcase system.

Grimes first (pp. 119ff) discusses 'orientation roles' which go with verbs expressing motion or position. There are five orientation roles, Object, Source, Goal, Range and Vehicle, as follows:

> 'Object identifies the thing that is moving . . . , or the thing that is in a particular position. . . .'
>
> 'Source . . . identifies the location of the object at the start of the motion . . .'
>
> 'Goal . . . identifies the location of the object at the end of the motion.' (p. 120)
>
> 'In an expression of motion, range indicates the path or area

traversed . . . With position, range indicates static location . . .' (p. 121)

'Vehicle . . . refers to something that conveys the object and moves along with it.' (p. 122)

Grimes's second set of roles are termed 'process roles', and have to do with changes of state or stable states. There are four process roles, Patient, Material, Result and Referent, as follows:

'Patient . . . is the relation between a thing that gets changed and the process that changes it, or . . . between a thing that is in some state and the state it is in.' (p. 123)

'Material and result identify the state of something before and after it undergoes a process.' (p. 125)

'Referent distinguishes the limitation of a process to a certain field or object from the actual application of a process to a patient.' (p. 125)

Finally, Grimes introduces the 'agentive complex' which subsists alongside processes and orientations, and introduces the roles Agent, Instrument, and Force, these having their expected 'meanings'. The roles in the agentive complex, plus the Benefactive role 'stand outside both the orientation and the process role systems' (p. 132), so it is the other roles that we are interested in in terms of some kind of supercase system. Grimes notes that 'The roles set up for orientation have counterparts on the process side, and vice versa. Both kinds could be considered complementary variants of a single set of roles' (p. 133). And so it is that Grimes sets up a 'combined role scheme' with a 'unified set of role labels', as in Figure 1. Grimes captures in a nutshell the advantages of this dual system: 'The exact meaning of those roles that combine is then dependent on a characteristic of the predicate with which they are used. . . . We have a more compact system. At the same time, it may be useful for some things to retain the orientation and process role labels as distinct' (p. 134). This second point is illustrated with examples from some Melanesian languages.

Orientation	→	Combined	←	Process
		Agent Instrument		Force
Vehicle	→	Vehicle		
Object	→	Patient	←	Patient
Source	→	Former	←	Material
Goal	→	Latter	←	Result
Range	→	Range	←	Referent

Figure 1: Combined role scheme (Grimes, 1975:134)

Peterson's (1983) approach is to break down the case roles into their component features. The reasons Peterson gives for this outlook are as follows: '. . . rather than define the cases monolithically in the traditional fashion (Fillmore, 1968*a*:24), we choose to describe them as bundles of features in the manner of sound segments in phonological theory. This proves to be a convenient method because it allows interesting generalizations about the relationship of deep case to lexical verbs and prepositions . . .' (Peterson, 1983:84). Peterson recognises that some cases share certain attributes – for example causation in Agents and Instruments – while at the same time individual cases could sometimes be subdivided into different types – as with the Agents of *carry* and *throw*, where the motional relationship of the Agent to the Patient differs. Peterson lists a set of case-defining features, stressing that they define functional rather than inherent properties of the role fillers. Thus, when Instrument is defined as – sentient, this implies not that an animate entity cannot be an Instrument, but that when it is, it functions as if it was not sentient. Peterson's eight case-defining features are as follows:

Originator
Sentient
Purposive
Sourcive
Recipient
Motional
Locational
End

These eight features serve to distinguish nine cases variously subdivided to give twenty-three separate case types, as follows:

Agent	Recipient, Sourcive, Motional, ±Purposive	
Instrument	Recipient, Sourcive, Locational, Motional	
Patient	Purposive, Motional, simple	[Situational]
Goal	[no subtypes]	
Benefactive	±Recipient	
End	±Situational	
Source	[no subtypes]	
Locative	[no subtypes]	
Neutral	Motional, Situational, simple	

Peterson gives (p. 88) an impressive array of examples for each of these subcases, but we may briefly attempt to clarify some of the less obvious distinctions without reproducing some fifty sentences.

The recipient and sourcive Agents are found with verbs like *catch* and *buy* (A^R) and *throw* and *sell* (A^S), though interestingly, the 'indirect object' with *sell* is also regarded as agentive, so that the case configuration for *sell* has two Agents, subcategorised as sourcive and recipient. The motional Agent is found with verbs of motion like *walk*, but also with verbs like *carry* where the Agent has a motional relation to the Patient.

Of the Instruments, the most usual is motional, which 'usually involves the motion of some implement applied to some other entity' (p. 87). Locational Instruments are physical media, natural, accidental or staged events, or vehicles. The sourcive Instrument is the stimulus or cause of some non-agentive event. The recipient Instrument is defined as '. . . a stationary object which affects some other motional participant by receiving the force of its action' (p. 89) though of the three examples given on p. 88 (6) only (6c) seems to fit this definition.

(6a) We laughed *at his foolishness*.
(6b) I was amazed *at its size*.
(6c) The glass broke *on the floor*.

Of the three types of Patient, one is defined neutrally with respect to the others, which indicate 'a recipient in a rôle of volitional compliance' (purposive) or Patient moving in a location (7a), or the direct object of a motional verb used transitively (7b).

(7a) The garden is swarming *with bees*.
(7b) The guard marched *the prisoner* into the cell.

Benefactives are distinguished between those actual recipients

(8a) and general beneficiaries (9a), a distinction which Peterson (wrongly) equates with the possibility of dative movement (8b, 9b): the * on (9b) is Peterson's, though compare the Benefactives in (10) which are presumably all $B^{\varnothing}$.

(8a) Pierre baked a cake *for Alice.*
(8b) Pierre baked *Alice* a cake.
(9a) Alphonse opened the door *for Marie.*
(9b) * Alphonse opened *Marie* the door.
(10a) Sing *me* a song.
(10b) Can you buy *me* some flowers for my wife?
(10c) I asked Liz to photocopy *me* that article.

Situational and simple Ends are apparently distinguished by their syntactic form, the E^{Si} being a sentential complement: in (11a) we have an E^{Si} but with the same verb in (11b) an $E^{\varnothing}$.

(11a) I want *Joe to stay.*
(11b) I want *some beer.*

The same syntactic distinction is used for the situational and simple Neutrals, while the motional Neutral is the object that undergoes a change of location with verbs like *throw*.

We can contrast the Brodda-Ruus system with Grimes's system on one very clear point, namely the criteria by which the supercases can be related to the subcases. With Grimes, this is the strict division of predication types into orientations and processes, and it is this distinction that applies to each and every one of the five or so 'supercases'. In stark contrast is the Brodda/ Ruus system, where all manner of distinctions are used: inherent features in the role-filler distinguish Agent and Unintentional Cause (animacy) and Concrete and Abstract Object (tangibility). Time and Space are both divided between punctual and relational subcases, while Aim and Result could be said to differ in terms of intentionality. Depending on the particular supercase, the nature of any of the role-filler itself, the predicate, or the filler of some other role could determine the choice of subcase. And yet other supercases seem to have no greater raison d'être than the accident of complementary distribution of two particular roles (e.g. Instrument and Material). From a practical point of view, the Brodda/Ruus system may have validity, but compared to the Grimes system it lacks the underlying uniformity which at least gives the latter some theoretical interest which the former somehow lacks. Peterson's system seems to come between these two positions: while the distinctions are more systematic than in Brodda/Ruus, there is an overall lack of symmetry which makes the supercase-subcase relationship slightly arbitrary.

These three particular approaches notwithstanding, what can be said in general about this approach? We have seen that the possibility of making significant generalisations about supercases seems to be a strong motivation, though we should not confuse these generalisations with others that are about. Two general examples serve to make this point: first, available syntactic functions sometimes trigger general rules, so that (for example) it is not very enlightening to try to put together Agent, Instrument and Recipient in one supercase because of possibilities they have in common in passives – this stems more simply from their availability for deep subject and has nothing to do with their case identity; second, there are many generalisations that are statable in terms of inherent features in the role-fillers, and the confusion of this with relational notions was one of the criticisms of the Fillmore (1968*a*) model, and an obvious weakness in the Brodda/Ruus system too. The important point is that the notion of supercase-subcase merely reflects the point that Case is altogether a question of making significant generalisations, and in the discussions of particular case notions that follow, this idea will recur. For example, although 'Agent' is taken by many to be a basic relation, there is a sense in which this is already a generalisation, since the activities involved in, say, dancing as compared to eating or walking are clearly different in at least some sense, yet this difference does not seem to play an important role at the level of description aimed at in Case analysis. The combination of, for example, Grimes's Material and Source is merely an abstraction at the 'next' level, and the logical conclusion can be seen in Anderson's minimal case-system (cf. Chapter 3). The aim must be to arrive at a level of abstraction and generalisation that serves the purpose to which the model is to be put.

2. *Agentivity and causation*

Of all the case relations proposed in all the 'mainstream' Case systems (i.e. not including fringe systems like those of Anderson or Starosta, outlined in Chapters 3 and 5), it would seem that 'Agent' is the most common, and, at first sight even one of the least controversial. A large corpus of example sentences can be built up which, it would generally be agreed, illustrate this role. However, the question of agentivity is not as straightforward as this. The mythical large corpus would probably turn out to contain chiefly animate entities performing willingly or intentionally an act, most often on some other entity. We can see the root of this archetypical Agent in Fillmore's original conception of '. . . the typically animate perceived instigator of the action identified by the verb' (Fillmore, 1968*a*:24).

The association of animacy with the notion of Agenthood was quickly attacked. Various critics led Fillmore (1971*b*:42) to retract the strong association of inherent features of typical role-fillers with the role itself, and that removed for some the problems associated with inanimate Agents like anthropomorphised machines (1a) or institutions with animate connections (1b). There still remained a grey area for instances like (1c), where some grounds for distinguishing Agents and Instruments would have to be found, and we shall return to this later.

(1a) *The computer* calculated the wages.
(1b) *The bank* will give free gifts to new customers.
(1c) *The car* smashed the window.

For some authors, animacy is a typical though not necessary feature of Agents, inanimate Agents being metaphorically attributed some kind of animacy. Platt (1971:73) takes this view, listing 'natural forces' and 'mechanical devices' as possible inanimate Agents. Animacy is taken as one of the distinctive differences between Agents and Instruments by Nilsen (1973:65), but this view is only partially backed up by the psycholinguistic experiments of Braine and Wells (1978), who reported that children seemed to 'prefer' Agents to be animate, but would nevertheless recognise inanimate Agents. Pleines (1976:19) notes that at least one consequence of distinguishing between Agents and Instruments as animate and inanimate respectively would be that verbs thereby have associated with them more case frames, and thus more and bigger entries in the lexicon.

An alternative view, reflecting the underlying notion that Agents are typically animate, comes with the suggestion of a feature marking 'potency'. This is the approach taken by Chafe (1970:109), who suggests that only entities that have, or can be conceived to have, their own internal power can function as Agents. This clearly includes natural forces like *wind* and *heat*, as well as machines. Cruse takes the notion of 'potency' a step further by noting that 'it seems, therefore, that inanimate objects can, as it were, acquire a temporary "agentivity" by virtue of their kinetic (or other) energy' (Cruse, 1973:16). The idea is supported by the evidence of sentences like (2a), for which syntactic tests for Agents proposed by Cruse (2b-c) are positive.

(2a) The bullet smashed John's collar-bone.
(2b) What the bullet did was smash John's collar-bone.

(2c) * What happened to the bullet was that it smashed John's collar-bone.

Huddleston's (1970:504) treatment of inanimate instigators is to introduce a third case 'Force', distinguished from Agent(ive) by animacy, and distinguished from Instrumental subjects, as in (3), by the lack of an easily understood (unexpressed) Agent.

(3a) *The wind* opened the door. (Force)
(3b) *The key* opened the door. (Instrument)

Huddleston goes on however to note that Agent(ive) and Force '. . . cannot occur in the same proposition, which suggests they may be complementary variants of a single case, say Causer' (Huddleston, 1970:505). He correctly states that if the only distinction between Agent(ive) and Force was animacy, then this subcategorisation would be redundant, being predictable from the filler of the Causer case.

Zoeppritz (1971) looks at the intransitive use of verbs like *creak* and *rustle* and contrasts them with other 'ergative' verbs like *move*, *break* and *tear*, in that even when used transitively (4)-(5), the source or cause of the action identified by the verb remains constant.

(4a) John creaked his boots.
(4b) The boots creaked.
(5a) Mary rustled her dress.
(5b) The dress rustled.

That the boots or the dress are not like Patients (or whatever) in ordinary ergative verbs (cf. (6)) is evidenced by the 'happen'-test for Patients (7).

(6a) Martin broke the computer.
(6b) The computer broke.
(7a) What happened to the computer? It broke.
(7b) * What happened to the boots? They creaked.
(7c) * What happened to the dress? It rustled.

Zoeppritz calls the subject in (4b) and (5b) 'inanimate Agent'; the flaw in this proposal is in the case assignments for sentences (4a) and (5a): either there are two Agents (contravening a basic principle of Case grammar – see Chapter 3), or the Agents in the (b) sentences are assigned some other case in the (a) sentences, with the resultant loss of parallelism between the (a) and (b) sentences, and the increased complexity in the lexical entries for these verbs (different selection restrictions on Agents dependent on whether other cases are realized).

For many authors, intention is taken to be the criterion for Agents. This is the view taken explicitly by Jackendoff (1972:32) and Quirk *et al.* (1972:353*fn*) for example, and implicitly by others who give tests for Agents based on the possibility of forming an imperative (e.g. Platt, 1971:73f), co-occurrence with adverbials like *deliberately, intentionally* (Nilson 1973:92; Talmy, 1976:87), as complement of verbs like *forget*, *remember* (Teng, 1975:57), or *force* and *persuade* (Talmy, 1976:87).

Yet the problems with this approach are clear. If intentionality (also termed 'volition') is crucial, then the simple addition of an adverb like *accidentally* to (8a) implies a different case assignment for *Karen* in (8b), even though the underlying action is – at all but the deepest levels of representation – the same.

(8a) Karen kicked her horse.
(8b) Karen accidentally kicked her horse.

Furthermore, sentences like (8a) become ambiguous if we accept that the non-volitional reading implies a different case, and the lexical entries for a great many action verbs become complex, having to specify in each instance alternative case-frame freatures. Huddleston remarks that 'It is very difficult to determine whether sentences like these are genuinely ambiguous rather than simply vague, i.e. non-specific as to intentionality' (Huddleston, 1970:505). Various tests for intentionality are proposed. If a sentence contains an Instrument, then a paraphrase with *use* is only possible for the volitional reading (Nilsen, 1973:91) (9); clearly adverbs like *deliberately* and *accidentally* serve, but also *masterfully*, *carefully* (and others) for intentional and *reluctantly* for unintentional bring out the distinction (Nilsen, *idem*); other tests have been mentioned above.

(9a) Dave broke the egg with his foot. (±Intent)
(9b) Dave used his foot to break the egg. (+Intent)

Teng (1975:56) notes an interesting feature of some dialects of Mandarin Chinese, where non-volition on the part of the Agent is reflected in a verb suffix *-dao*, as in (10) and (11).

(10a) Ta qie-le cai le
HE CUT-asp VEGETABLE asp
'He cut the vegetables.'

(10b) Ta qie-dao zijide shou.
HE CUT OWN HAND
'He (accidentally) cut his hand.'

(11a) Ta ti xiao meimei.
HE KICK LITTLE SISTER
'He kicked his little sister.'

(11b) Ta ti-dao xiao meimei.
HE KICK LITTLE SISTER
'He accidentally kicked his little sister.'

This is apparently a quite productive morpheme, as is the suffix *-jian* which in standard Mandarin distinguishes verb pairs like *kan* ('look') and *kan-jian* ('see'), or *ting* ('listen') and *ting-jian* ('hear').

Talmy (1976:86f) distinguishes volitional and non-volitional causer as Agent and 'Author' respectively, noting several syntactic correlations of this distinction. Some of them have already been mentioned, but the choice of subordinating conjunctions for an instrumental adverbial clause (*in* versus *by* (12)), and the different imperative forms (13) for the two roles are interesting.

(12a) I killed the snail in hitting it with my hand. (Author)
(12b) I killed the snail by hitting it with my hand. (Agent)
(13a) May you mislay your pen and never find it again. (Author)
(13b) Hide the pen somewhere in the kitchen! (Agent)

Although again the Author/Agent distinction involves us in the problem of multiple entries for certain verbs, Talmy does note that there are some verbs which form pairs differentiated principally by taking an Agent or Author. One such pair is *hide* versus *mislay* seen in (13); others are *pour/spill*, *listen/overhear* and *jump/fall*.

An interesting angle on the question of intentionality is found in van Oosten's (1977) treatment of 'patient-subject' sentences, as in (14).

(14a) This wine drinks like it was water.
(14b) The trailer pulls easily.
(14c) A good tent puts up in about two minutes.

Although, clearly, none of the subjects in (14) is an Agent, van Oosten notes that '. . . when the patient is made the subject of the sentence it, or a property it has, is understood to be responsible for the action of the verb' (van Oosten, 1977:461). This argument is presented quite convincingly and at length, and one example will suffice to give its flavour (15):

(15) The clothes wash with no trouble because . . .
(a) . . . they are machine-washable.
(b) . . . * I have plenty of time.

The relevance of this to the question of intentionality in Agents is reflected in her comment that '. . . the patient-subject construction . . . is used when we want to say that the patient of the action is to some extent acting as an agent' (*idem*). The point to be made is that on the one hand van Oosten clearly associates 'responsibility' with Agenthood. But another conclusion is possible: that perhaps intentionality has more to do with the syntactic role of the subject with certain verbs, and that close association for many authors between Agenthood and intention stems perhaps from the fact that Agents typically occur as subjects.

Something approaching a solution to these problems is offered by Cruse (1973) and by Nilsen (1973), who both suggest that 'Agent' is not a semantic primitive, but can be analysed into a number of components. For Nilsen, in fact, none of the semantic roles is atomic, all of them being defined in terms of a matrix of semantic features (p. 121), different combinations of these being definitional, though a weakness in Nilsen's system is the possibility of some roles being marked '±' for some features, Agent for example being ±Intent.

Cruse argues that the presence of any one of four features will suggest Agenthood, these features being volitive, effective, initiative, and agentive. The first of these has already been discussed at length.

The second is contrasted with the notion of inherent 'potency' discussed earlier, and is the 'temporary agentivity' in the Cruse quote given above. He elaborates: 'This feature is present in a sentence which refers to something which exerts a force (literally or metaphorically), not by virtue of an internal energy source but because of its position, motion, etc.' (Cruse, 1973:19). The third feature, 'initiative', is based on Halliday's (1967/8:42) notion of the 'initiator' of an action, and is used to distinguish the two candidates for Agenthood in sentences like (16), where the role associated with the direct object is clearly agentive in some sense, in relation to the action of the verb.

(16) The warder marched the soldiers across the yard.

In general terms, it is *the soldiers* who are performing the action of the verb, and who are therefore Agent, while *the warder* is Fillmore's (1968*a*:24) 'perceived instigator of the action'. Cruse's final feature, 'agentive', corresponds to Chafe's (1970:109) 'potent', and is applicable to an entity 'which is regarded as using its own energy in carrying out the action' (p. 21).

Dillon seems to agree with this analysis of Agenthood as an uncertain complex: 'It is conceivable that there is no right or wrong definition of an Agent, particularly if one is trying to capture the conceptualizations people actually make and use, but rather that Agent is vague. . . . One might also speculate . . . that children only gradually abstract the more general characterization from [various specific characterizations]. The refinements would come in the direction of including some inanimates, recognizing limits of intention and voluntary control, and the like . . .' (Dillon, 1977:72).

Ever since Fillmore's original (1968*a*:24) conception of Instrument as the 'force or object causally involved in the action', it became clear that the notions of Agent and Instrument are somehow closely related. Although the tendency to assign to Instrument any inanimate that otherwise looks like an Agent has been somewhat superceded, on the understanding that animacy is not a defining feature of Agent, there are still some problem cases. Since Agent and Instrument are both causal roles, there sometimes arises conflict as to which to choose.

For Nilsen (1973:121) the two roles can be distinguished in three features: intent, controlled and animate, as in Figure 2. Note that animacy is a defining criterion for Nilson, who does not discuss problem sentences like (17) in which case the italicised element is an obvious Instrument, so that one wonders what case Nilsen would assign to *program*.

	Intent	Controlled	Animate
Agent	±	–	±
Instrument	–	±	±

Figure 2: Distinction of Agent and Instrument
(after Nilsen, 1973:121)

(17) This program calculates integrals *using Taylor's expansion*.

But more important to note in Nilsen's feature matrix is that the two cases are not uniquely distinguishable, since the feature combination –Intent, –Controlled, +Animate could be either Agent or Instrument. It is not at all clear why Nilsen admits the possibility of a –Controlled Instrument, since he prefers (p. 109) the case Force for *fire* in (18a) which he contrasts with (18b) in which the implicit Agent makes *fire* +Controlled.

(18a) The rats were killed *by fire*.
(18b) The rats were killed *with fire*.

Pleines (1976:57ff) follows Fillmore (1971*b*) in looking at chains of causality and notes that generally only the original cause and the immediate cause can be expressed as subject of a sentence. Thus for example, if someone makes a hole in a wall with a hammer and chisel, the possibilities for describing the events are as in (19):

(19a) He made a hole in the wall.
(19b) * His hand made a hole in the wall.
(19c) * The hammer made a hole in the wall.
(19d) The chisel made a hole in the wall.

It is on this basis that Agent and Instrument can be differentiated as 'original' and 'immediate' cause respectively, with the notion of Agenthood taking precedence if these are coincident. The essential element for both roles is 'causativity'.

Willis and Jeffreys (1982) take this approach a step further. Noting that a 'prototypical' Agent is animate, volitional, has self-energy and is remote (i.e. not immediate cause), and that a 'prototypical' Instrument is negative in these four features, there are nevertheless instances where the feature configurations for Agents and Instruments are mixed up. They propose a 'cline' from Agent to Instrument, with participant roles (cases) plotted at intermediate points along it. Thus for example *John* in (20) is more like an Agent than an Instrument, *despite* being −Volitional; in (21) *the machine* is seen as 'less' Instrumental in (21b) than *the spike* in (21a) in being +Self-energy, and in (21c) *the machine* is even more Agent-like with *the spike* introduced as −Remote.

(20) John sneezed.
(21a) John pierced the paper with a spike.
(21b) The machine pierced the paper.
(21c) The machine pierced the paper with a spike.

This notion of the possibility of 'relative Agenthood' seems to be useful, especially if verb-senses can be adequately characterized with regard to the cline, as the authors suggest. One minor problem though is whether it is really a cline: given that there are four defining features, a lattice may be a more suitable representation, for we are given no indication which of (22a) and (22b), for example is 'more' Agent-like.

(22a) +Animate +Volitional −Self-energy +Remote
(22b) +Animate −Volitional +Self-energy +Remote

If the features are ordered in some sense, so that, say, volition is a more salient feature of Agenthood than self-energy, then it is clear that we could differentiate even instances like in (22), and score (22a) as 'more' Agent-like than (22b). What seems likely however is that this ordering of features might differ from verb to verb, so that for example volition is highly salient for correctly assigning roles with a verb like *hide* (23), but less for *open* (24), where self-energy may be more important.

(23a) *The boy* hid his school report, (Agent)
(23b) *The police* hid the view of the procession (Instrument)
(24a) *Peter* accidentally opened the door. (Agent)
(24b) *This key* ought to open the door. (Instrument)

3. *Dative/Experiencer/Benefactive/Recipient*

In this section we wish to discuss a group of cases that have tended to cause some critics and students problems, due to the difficulty in distinguishing between them. These are cases that might loosely be termed 'dative' cases, principally because of their realisation (often) in Indo-European languages in the (surface) dative case, or as indirect object. In fact, we shall argue that there are at least two distinct roles (Experiencer versus Beneficiary), with the status of Recipient depending on whether Goal is included in the case-set.

Let us start however with the 'Dative' case, introduced in Fillmore's (1968*a*) case set, and perhaps the root of some of the problems. In Fillmore (1968*a*), Dative is defined as 'The case of the animate being affected by the state or action identified by the verb' (p. 24) and examples of it include the sentences as in (1).

(1a) *John* believed that he would win.
(1b) We persuaded *John* that he would win.
(1c) It was apparent *to John* that he would win.

A number of other verbs are designated as having Dative in their case-frame features: *kill*, *murder*, *want*, *expect*; *force*, *persuade* (p. 28); *die* (p. 30); *see*, *hear*, *know* (pp. 30f); *give* (pp. 35ff); the case also underlies the possessor in noun phrases like *John's books* (pp. 49ff).

There are several things to note about this fairly wide range of roles designated as Dative. For some, there is a clear sense in which Dative corresponds to Objective, the two cases being differentiated only in the feature animate: so with *kill*, *murder* and *die*, and perhaps also *force* and *persuade*. Critics were quick to point out the parallel between Dative and Objective on the one hand and Agentive and Instrumental on the other, suggesting that these four cases could be reduced to two, as in Figure 3.

	+Animate	−Animate
Cause	Agentive	Instrumental
Affected	Dative	Objective

Figure 3: Parallels between two case-pairs in Fillmore (1968*a*)

Dative was also being used for two other slightly different case roles however: with *see*, *hear* and *know* we have verbs of perception and cognition. Here the notion of 'affected' is more metaphorical, and furthermore, unlike with *kill* etc., the other role in the case-frame features would have to be ±animate Objective – witness (2)-(4).

(2a) Lindsey saw Brian.
(2b) Lindsey saw the book.
(3a) Pete heard Kieran.
(3b) Pete heard a noise.
(4a) David knows Karen.
(4b) David knows New York.

Finally, co-occurring with both an Agentive and an Objective is the Dative with *give*. A problem with this use of the Dative is that it seems to clash with another of Fillmore's (1968*a*) cases, Benefactive, introduced though not elaborated upon on p. 32. We have already noted (Chapter 2 Section 2) that it is not clear whether Benefactive is introduced to replace or complement Dative (we assume the latter): no 'definition' of Benefactive is offered – only that its associated preposition is *for* – so must we take it that its name is self-explanatory? If so, then is the role of *Daniele* in (5a) Dative by analogy with (5b), or Benefactive, after (5c)?

(5a) Nick bought Daniele a birthday present.
(5b) Nick gave Daniele a birthday present.
(5c) Nick bought a birthday present for Daniele.

Faced with this diversity of characterisations for his Dative, plus the undesired connotations with indirect objects and/or the (surface) dative case (see Platt, 1971:59), which sometimes are used to realise other (deep) cases, Fillmore abandoned the case in 1971*b* (though several major users of Case persisted with it – notably, e.g. Stockwell *et al.*, 1973; see also Chapter 11): 'I have reanalyzed the old Dative by spreading it around among the other cases. Where there is a genuine psychological event or mental state verb, we have the Experiencer; where there is a non-psychological verb which indicates a change of state, such as one of dying or growing, we have the Object; where there is a transfer or movement of something to a person, the receiver or destination is taken as the Goal' (Fillmore, 1971*b*:42). Although this reappraisal alleviated some of the problems associated with 'Dative', the new concept Experiencer is no less problematic. As far as psychological-event and mental-state verbs are concerned, several authors have suggested that the new case is unnecessary. Grimes (1975:124) for example notes that if some other case can be found for the stimulus of the psychological event, then the Patient role adequately captures the relationship between the event and the affected entity, the fact that this is someone's psyche being insufficient grounds for positing a new case. Teng (1975:66) similarly notes that if *Sam* in (6) is Patient, but Experiencer in (7), with *Jane* Patient in (7), this implies a false correspondence of roles (*Sam* to *Jane*), whereas *Sam* would be expected to have the same role in all four predications. (Teng's point is equally valid for English; I have therefore replaced the original (Chinese) names.)

(6a) Sam is happy.
(6b) Sam is scared.
(7a) Sam likes Jane.
(7b) Sam is scared of Jane.

'This treatment leaves the fact unexplained that [Sam] throughout all the sentences in [(6)-(7)] is the one whose mental disposition is affected, not [Jane]' (Teng, 1975:66).

Of course Teng's observation could be taken as an argument in favour of analysing predicates like *be happy, be scared* as 'experiential' state verbs, i.e. verbs taking an Experiencer, and this is indeed the approach found in Chafe (1970:147) and Longacre (1976:54). This analysis is further supported by the fact that comparisons and conjunctions as in (8) are unacceptable, which might be explained as contravening the well-known constraint that 'only noun phrases representing the same case may be conjoined' (Fillmore, 1968*a*:22).

(8a) * Graham is sadder than the book he is reading.
(8b) * Graham and the book are sad.

In this case one would have to say that *be sad* is a polysemous predicate having two interpretations, 'be likely to cause sadness' (9a) and 'suffer from sadness' (9b), with associated different case-frame features. This seems quite appealing intuitively, since there is a related two-place predicate *sadden* which combines the two meanings (9c).

(9a) The book is sad.
(9b) Graham is sad.
(9c) The book saddened Graham.

Platt (1971:59f) includes 'emotional' predicates among those taking his equivalent case (which he calls 'Participative'), and gives examples *like*, *irritate*, *fear* and *hate* which demonstrate a range of syntactic functions for the Experiencer. Similar verbs are listed by Chafe (1970:144ff), Cook (1972*b*:58) and Longacre (1976:59f). The last of these authors also includes under Experiencer '. . . one thus [i.e. psychologically] affected by someone else's activities as in [(10a)], or he may be the object of an activity . . . in which he experiences somebody else's violence, affection, notice, etc. as in [(10b, c)]' (Longacre, 1976:27) though this is no longer very far from the original Dative (=animate Objective) of Fillmore (1968*a*).

(10a) I cheered *her* up.
(10b) John hit *Bill*.
(10c) John kissed *his wife*.

Several other groups of predicates are associated with the Experiencer case. One such is verbs of perception and sensation like *see*, *hear*, *feel* (Chafe, Longacre, Cook, Platt, *cit*.). These experiential verbs generally form pairs with agentive counterparts – *look*, *listen*, *feel* – a relation which for some throws more doubt on the necessity of the case. Teng (1975:67) for example regards these verbs of (non-volitional) perception as taking an Agent rather than an Experiencer, an analysis perhaps encouraged by his Chinese data, where verbs meaning 'see' and 'hear' are not lexical verbs, but are realised by the affixation of *-jian* to the agentive verb (cf. Section 2) (11):

(11a) Zhang San ting-le niao jiao.
ZHANG SAN LISTEN-asp BIRD CALL
'Zhang San listened to the birds singing.'
(11b) Zhang San ting-jian niao jiao.
'Zhang San heard the birds singing.'

For Platt, though not for the other authors mentioned above, verbs like *die* simply denote mental or sensual movement, and are therefore also classed as experiential.

Continuing the association of Experiencer with 'mental state' or 'mental event' verbs, we have verbs of cognition (*know*, *believe*) and desire (*want*, *hope*), the normal subjects of which are taken to be Experiencer by Chafe, Platt, Cook and Longacre (as above). Various tests for Agent (cf. Section 2) seem to support this analysis: adverbs implying volition or non-volition (12) are equally odd; these verbs cannot always form the complement of verbs like *force* or *persuade* (13) and if they occur acceptably in the imperative, they tend to take on a meaning-shift towards an agentive counterpart (14).

(12a) * Rod deliberately knew about my situation.
(12b) * Pete carefully believed he would get the top score.
(12c) * Paul accidentally wanted Arsenal to win.
(12d) * Jock masterfully hoped his program would compile.
(13a) * Sandra forced Rod to know her plans.
(13b) * Doris persuaded Pete to hope for fine weather.
(14a) Know the answer by tomorrow! (= learn)
(14b) Believe you can win! (= convince yourself)
(14c) * Want a Guinness!
(14d) Hope for world peace! (= change your attitude)

Considering the role of Experiencer with the verbs of cognition, Anderson (1977:150) suggests that it is difficult to relate verbs like *know* to verbs like *teach* and *learn* (15), since Experiencer does not seem appropriate for these dynamic situations. Certainly the tests for Agent demonstrated in (12)-(14) would suggest that *the professor* in (15c) is Agent (15d-f), while the equivalent role in (15b) is open to debate (cf. Section 5 on 'Goal').

(15a) The professor knows demotic Greek.
(15b) The secretary has taught the professor demotic Greek.
(15c) The professor has learnt demotic Greek from the secretary.
(15d) The professor carefully learnt demotic Greek.
(15e) The secretary forced the professor to learn demotic Greek.
(15f) Learn demotic Greek!

Nevertheless, Chafe (1970:145f) and Longacre (1975:58) both regard *learn* and *teach* as experiential verbs, while Cook (1979:210f) has Experiencer in the case-frame (features) for *teach*, but not *learn*, where it is rather a secondary role for the Agent.

So far we have mostly looked at verbs whose surface subject is a candidate for Experiencer. There are a number of verb types however where Experiencer might seem an appropriate case for some other argument. Clearly causative verbs related to the verbs we have already discussed may be such candidates: mental state verbs like *fear* and *be happy* have causative counterparts *frighten* and *please*, and these indeed are proposed (e.g. by Cook, 1972*b*:57 and Longacre, 1975:55); causative verbs of perception might include *show* and the whole range of verbs of communication (*tell*, *address*, *ask*) (cf. Cook, 1972*b*:58; Nilsen, 1973:154); we have already seen the causative verb of cognition *teach*, to which Cook (*idem*) adds *remind*.

Fillmore offers a test for Experiencer based on the observation by Postal (1968) that '. . . the adverb *personally* occurs only in sentences with subjective experience verbs and in connection with the NP identified as the Experiencer' (Fillmore, 1972:10). Four examples are given, as in (16):

(16a) Personally, I don't like roses.
(16b) Your proposal doesn't interest me, personally.
(16c) * Personally, you hit me.
(16d) * Personally, ontogeny recapitulates philogeny.

Anderson (1977:26f) takes up the discussion, noting that the adverb must have the interpretation 'as far as I am concerned' as implied by the punctuation (cf. the interpretation 'in person' when there is no comma (17), the usage of which is relatively unrestricted).

(17a) I wrote to the director personally.

(17b) The director personally took charge of the project.

Anderson suggests that the test does not work, since the adverb can attach to other cases, though in fact his examples (18) are not very convincing.

(18a) Personally, that doesn't give me a kick.
(*Me* is 'allative' [?])

(18b) Personally, I gave it up years ago. (*I* is agentive; 'action is linked to some inferred later state')

A more important point is that the adverb attaches only to a first-person pronoun, which is why (16c-d) are unacceptable. Other than that, it is an extra-peripheral element (see Chapter 1 Section 6) that can attach to any statement involving a first person which in a specific context in informal discourse can be interpreted as an expression of opinion (19). The test therefore can be discarded, though not for the reasons Anderson gives.

(19a) Personally, I always vote for Plaid Cymru.

(19b) Venezia Trattoria is my favourite restaurant, personally.

(19c) Personally, I will claim both extensions are necessary.

We end this discussion of Experiencer with a selection of brief characterisations of this role, which together seem to give a consensus view of what Experiencer is, omitting ones which I feel to be untypical. In doing so we should not however lose sight of the problems and inconsistencies uncovered here, the major one being perhaps the conflict between the aptness of Experiencer and some other case: the general problem of 'dual roles' is treated at length in Chapter 9.

'. . . one who [is] mentally disposed in some way, one with respect to whose mental experience [something happens].' (Chafe, 1970:145)

'. . . one whose mental disposition or mental processes [are] affected.' (*idem*)

'. . . emotionally . . . , mentally . . . , or sensually . . . involved in the state or action indicated by the verb.' (Platt, 1971:60)

'. . . the undergoer of a psychological event of sensation, emotion or cognition.' (Cook, 1972*b*401:52)

'An entity . . . which is internally affected by the action of the verb.' (Somers, 1980*a*:7)

'An animate entity whose registering nervous system is relevant to the predication.' (Longacre, 1975:27)

'. . . the one to whom an emotional state is ascribed . . . , or who is undergoing a psychological process . . . Similarly, the experiencer may be one who knows, or learns, or who studies. With verbs of teaching, the experiencer is the one who is taught. Again, the experiencer may be one who undergoes desire, love, appreciation, . . . The experiencer is the subject of sensation verbs . . . Finally, the experiencer is the recipient of verbs of speech . . . and in such kindred verbs as *show* . . .' (*ibid.*, pp. 27f)

As mentioned above, the 'Benefactive' case is partially introduced by Fillmore (1978*a*:32), though without any clear indication of its characterisation, other than its association with the preposition *for*. The case as used by other authors seems to have two distinct meanings, one having to do with possession, and the other in instances where the paraphrase *on behalf of* is appropriate.

As the case for the entity gaining possession of something, Benefactive or Beneficiary is suggested by Chafe (1970:148f), Platt (1971:48f) and Halliday (1970:147), with verbs like *win*, *find*, where the Benefactive is expressed as the surface subject, and *sell*, *send*, *give*, where it is indirect object. As with experiential verbs, the problem of 'dual roles' arises again. This is so with verbs like *buy* and *get*. Chafe includes in his list of benefactive verbs *lose*, demonstrating that we should not confuse the linguistic semantic notion of Benefactive with any 'real' notion: because the 'benefit' of a loser is negative is no reason to introduce a new role, just as we still have Agents in sentences expressing inaction or failure to act. Grimes (1975:132) makes a similar point, and indicates that in some languages where Benefactive is expressed by a form of the verb meaning 'give', this form is still found even for 'malefactives', as in the Saramaccan pidgin example (20) quoted from Grimes and Glock (1970).

(20) Hén fufuu-man ko fufuu da-een suni fu-en
THEN STEAL-MAN COME STEAL GIVE-HIM THING FOR-HIM
'Then a thief came and stole his things from him.'

If the person who loses something is as equally Benefactive as the gainer, then presumably there is an argument for assigning the role of Benefactive to the giver in *give*, the seller with *buy*, or the person taken from with *take*. This however, causes a clear conflict, because we obviously want to say that the receiver, buyer and taker respectively are Benefactive. This conflict is exemplified in Cook's (1972*b*:61) case frame matrix, where *accept*, *buy*, *give* and *sell* are all classed as verbs having the case frame features [A-B-O], i.e. taking Agent, Benefactive and Object. If we consider the obvious candidate for Agent in each of those verbs, then we get a clear clash between a receiving Benefactive with *give* and *sell*, and a giving Benefactive with *accept* and *buy*. (Note that no 'dual roles' are implied here: Cook's formalism is quite distinctive in this regard.)

Given the use of Benefactive to indicate gain or loss of possession, it is a short step to propose this case also for non-dynamic possession, as do Chafe (1970:148), Platt (1979:49) and Cook (1972*b*:61) with their benefactive state verbs *have* and *own* (where the Benefactive is subject) and *belong to* (where it is prepositional object). Platt is keen to distinguish alienable and inalienable possession, suggesting (pp. 59f) that for the latter the sensual involvement implies his Participative (Experiencer) role. Several authors have argued, on the grounds of surface structure evidence in a wide variety of languages, for the equation of possessives and locatives. In Finnish, for example, there is a parallel between (21a) and (21b) (J. Anderson, 1971:107) which we also find in possessive expressions in Latin (21c), Russian (21d) (Lyons, 1967:392, 394), Swahili (21e) (Christie, 1970:170), and at least fourteen other languages from a wide spread of language families (Clark, 1970:31).

(21a) Kirja on pöydällä.
BOOK IS TABLE-ON
'The book is on the table.'

(21b) Minulla on kirja.
ME-ON IS BOOK
'I have a book.'

(21c) Est mihi liber.
IS TO-ME BOOK

(21d) U mena kniga.
AT ME BOOK

(21e) Mtu ana kitabu.
MAN HIM-TO BOOK

Apart from its use to indicate receipt or possession the Benefactive case is often put to a clearly distinct use best characterised as 'on whose behalf . . .', Chafe (1970:151) and Platt (1971:30, 50f) suggest that this Benefactive can accompany any action, as in (22), though for Grimes (1975:166) the Benefactive 'can be added to almost anything' (23a), while Teng (1975:21) gives examples of Benefactives with states (23b) and processes (23c).

(22a) Mary knitted *Tom* a sweater.

(22b) Mary sang *for Tom*.

(22c) I'll walk the dog *for you.*
(23a) The grass is green *for me.*
(23b) I feel really happy *for you.*
(23c) He died *for his country.*

Certainly Grimes's example (23a) is a little dubious, and the paraphrase possibilities as in (24) make this look more like an Experiencer (see Chapter 9).

(24) I consider the grass to be green.

Further examples (25) from Teng (p. 151) demonstrate two distinct types of 'on behalf of', which have corresponding realisations in Chinese, and point out an ambiguity in the English (25a). The one, meaning 'intended recipient', is translated by the Chinese *gei* ('give') (25b), while the other, meaning 'in place of' has *ti* ('substitute') (25c).

(25a) I'll write a letter for him.
(25b) Wo gei ta xie xin.
I GIVE HE WRITE LETTER
(25c) Wo ti ta xie xin.

Notice that one can easily construct sentences where these two roles co-occur, as in (26a), which, following the one-case-per-sentence constraint and the co-ordination principle (Fillmore, 1968*a*:22, 24; cf. Chapter 2 Section 2) (26b) suggests that these may be two distinct cases.

(26a) I will write him a letter for you.
(26b) I will write a letter for him and you. [≠ (26a)]

An alternative analysis is suggested by Platt (1971:50) who distinguishes between 'inner Benefactives' for recipients and possessors, and 'outer Benefactives' for persons who benefit generally from the action of the verb. This is an attractive solution, recalling the Valency grammar distinction between complements and adjuncts (cf. Chapter 1), and one to which we shall return in Chapter 9. Importantly, with the 'outer Benefactive', there is no necessary notion of eventual possession or receipt, since the italicised elements of the sentences in (27) can be understood as outer Benefactives, either in the 'substitute for' sense (27a), or as persons generally benefiting from (27b) or getting pleasure from (27c) the events described.

(27a) A twelfth man is allowed to field *for an injured player.*
(27b) He got the spider out of the bath *for me.*
(27c) The patient swallowed the pills *for the doctor.*

It is not entirely clear whether these three notions of Benefactive are mutually exclusive, since sentences like (28b) in the context of (28a), incorporating, besides the inner Benefactive (the recipient *the newspaper*), two outer Benefactives (the general beneficiary, *Mr Smith*, and the substitute *Mr Jones*), are marginal (though perhaps only due to human parsing limitations), rather than unacceptable. It seems likely that outer Benefactives (and other 'outer' roles) can 'stack up' as far as processing limitations allow, each one relating to the proposition as a whole including the previous Benefactive, so that (28b) has the dependency structure shown in (28c).

(28a) Mr Jones asked me to write a letter to the newspaper for Mr Smith.

(28b) I'm writing the newspaper a letter for Mr Smith for Mr Jones.

(28c)

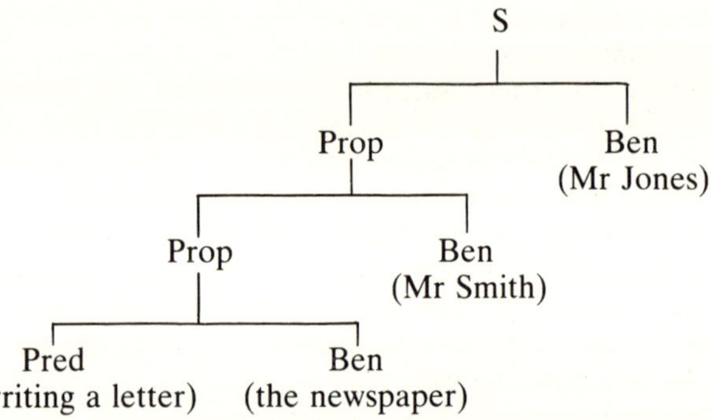

Compare the parallel stacking possibilities of 'outer Agents' in (admittedly improbable, but quite understandable) sentences like (29).

(29) Harry had Rod have Paul have Pete have Liz make coffee.

See also section 5 below and Chapter 9. I am grateful to Pete Whitelock for the 'stacking up' observation. Compare also Panevová's remark: 'Certainly, it is not difficult in some cases to find an occurrence of a verb with two (not to speak about three or more) adverbials of the same type, to find an acceptable lexical setting and a stylistically plausible combination of morphemic means. This, however, is connected with the recursive properties of the language as a whole and with its potential infiniteness, which contrasts with the restricted and finite character of performance' (Panevová, 1977:232).

Note that in English, the 'double object' construction is equally available for inner and outer Benefactives (30), and in sentences with both there is no special preference for the outer Benefactive to be a prepositional object (31).

(30a) The man gave *his wife* a present. [inner]
(30b) The gamekeeper shot *the squire* a rabbit. [outer]
(31a) Can you write me a letter to the headmaster?
(31b) Can you write the headmaster a letter for me?

4. *Objects, Patients, etc.*

In this section we shall look at a fairly heterogeneous group of semantic roles that it is appropriate to treat together, since a number of different Case users tend to regard at least some of them as one and the same case. A reasonable general name for these roles seems to be Patient or Object(ive), which we shall use indiscriminately, with a preference for the first, but included are distinctions reflected in terms such as 'affected' versus 'effected', 'complementiser', and some other more idiosyncratic terms.

Because of this heterogeneity, it is difficult to find a suitable starting point. Even Fillmore's (1968*a*) original 'Objective' case contrasts with 'Factitive', a distinction we shall discuss below. Dillon (1977:74f) begins his discussion by comparing the Case grammar model, in which direct objects of transitive verbs and subjects of (some) intransitive verbs are assigned the same case, with the surface syntax of so-called 'ergative' languages. These are languages where the nominative-accusative distinction familiar in Indo-European languages is replaced by a distinction between the ergative and absolutive cases. Basque (1) is a frequently cited example of an ergative language, and although the list of such languages ranges over a number of 'exotic' languages, such as Tongan (2), Yucatec (3), Eskimo, Tibetan, Chinook, Punjabi and Georgian, both nominative-accusative and ergative-absolutive languages are 'very widespread among the languages of the world' (Comrie, 1975:112). Basque examples are from J. Anderson (1971:52), adapted from Lafitte (1962), Tongan and Yucatec from Edmonson (1977:636).

(1a) Gizonak ogia jan du.
MAN-erg BREAD-abs EATEN aux
'The man has eaten some bread.'

(1b) Gizona ethorri da.
MAN-abs COME aux
'The man has come.'

(1c) Ogia ona da.
BREAD-abs GOOD aux
'The bread is good.'

(2a) Na'e taak'i 'e Sione 'a e puaka.
past HIT erg JOHN abs def PIG
'John hit the pig.'

(2b) 'Oku lahi 'a Sione.
pres BIG abs JOHN
'John is big.'

(3a) Bin in kins oobe.
fut I-erg KILL THEY-abs
'I will kill them.'

(3b) Bin kink oobe.
fut DIE THEY-abs
'They will die.'

Anderson (*cit.*) gives an extensive list of primary references and Comrie's (1973) discussion is an important contribution on this subject. Data from ergative languages have been used by some authors to lend credibility to Case grammar (note that for these languages there is an obvious correspondence between surface and deep cases: Agent/ergative, Patient/absolutive), and the alternation possible in the North-East Caucasian language Bats quoted by Comrie (1973:241) from Meščaninov (1967:82) (4) reinforces this, introducing a semantic element into the surface-case distinction.

(4a) So wože
I-abs FELL
'I fell (accidentally).'

(4b) As wože.
I-erg FELL
'I fell (through my own fault).'

Interest in ergative languages is focused not so much on the question of 'deep case' assignment but on the question of grammatical relations, which will not concern us here.

One of the problems with the Objective case stems from its rather 'negative' description, compared to the other cases, in Fillmore (1968*a*) as '. . . the semantically most neutral case . . . whose role in the action or state identified by the verb is identified by the semantic interpretation of the verb itself' (Fillmore, 1968*a*:25). This led to criticism from a number of authors (e.g. Mellema, 1974:49) that Objective was a 'wastebasket' case, the case to be chosen when no other case seems appropriate. In fact, as was pointed out in Chapter 2 Section 2, this approach is quite reasonable from the point of view of set theory, as long as the set of cases is a closed set. However, given the position of Case as a semantics-based syntactic model, the wastebasket approach is relatively unattractive, and is a prime motivator to those responsible for the wanton proliferation of new cases to handle every problematic instance, criticised so strongly by Langacker (1970:171*fn*) and Chapin (1972:651).

The especially close association of the Objective and the meaning of the verb is perhaps less controversial. Chafe (1970) regards the Patient-verb relation as more 'internal' than the Agent-verb relation, noting that when a verb proform is found it is understood in place of the entire verb-plus-Patient configuration (5).

(5a) Harriet broke the dish.
(5b) She did it (that is, broke the dish) accidentally.

'This observation suggests that the verb plus patient configuration behaves as a unit in a way that the verb plus agent configuration does not, for there is no "proverb" form analagous to *do it* which substitutes for the verb plus agent as a unit' (Chafe, 1970:103). This argument whereby the precise 'meaning' of the Patient role stems from the verb to which it attaches or from other cases present (cf. Halliday, 1967/8:195; Bennett, 1975:14f) is one frequently used in various debates, as in the distinction of stative and non-stative Patients, or affected versus effected objects. Yet it is a dangerous argument if followed too far, since its logical conclusion is a minimalist Case theory like those of J. Anderson (1971) or Marino (1972), where it is felt that the number of cases need not exceed the highest valency found for any one verb (probably four), these cases being interpretable on a verb-by-verb basis. As Kilby points out, 'The most obvious danger is that [the widespread merger of cases in complementary distribution] lead in many cases to particularly unrevealing semantic bases' (Kilby, 1978:67). The same can be said if the close connection between Patient and verb is overstated. For Starosta (see Chapter 5), the Patient is an obligatory case for all verbs, even monovalent verbs of motion which for most other Case grammarians take an Agent (or equivalent).

Regarding the close association of verb and Object, Lehrer (1970) has distinguished four degrees of cohesion with verbs whose Objects are deletable, to which we can add a fifth degree where the Object is non-deletable. (We should note that Lehrer is looking at surface (direct) objects rather than the deep case 'Object'. However, I feel that her observations are largely transferable.) The tightest cohesion is where verbs take what Warnock (1953) termed 'tautologous accusatives' – these are Objects which add little or nothing to the understanding of the verb, and are often morphologically cognate, as in (6). We shall have more to say on these 'complementisers' below.

(6a) I dreamed a dream.
(6b) He yelled a yell.
(6c) They danced a dance.

Cognate objects can be deleted without altering the meaning of the sentence, and indeed are understood as such. Thus, in a context like (7), the deleted object is any dance, not necessarily *the tango*.

(7) Mary dances the tango badly. Can you dance?

The second degree of cohesion is where verbs take a limited range of Objects. Deletion implies some unspecified member of this range, but specification of the Object particularises an instance of the verb. In the first sentence of (7), *dance* is of this type (cf. (8a)). Other examples are *sew* (8b) and *borrow* (8c).

(8a) I can dance the tango. What can you dance?
(8b) I like to sew clothes. What do you like to sew?
(8c) I don't approve of borrowing money. What do you approve of borrowing?

With the third degree of cohesion, pronominalised Objects in a discourse can be deleted without loss of meaning, as in (9).

(9a) I tried to learn to play the piano, but I can't play (it) well yet.
(9b) John didn't want to continue the bridge game, but Henry wanted to continue (it).

These verbs are characterised by the fact that '. . . selection restrictions and likely objects . . . are so vague or ambiguous that they provide little semantic information, and so context takes over to provide clues to the meaning. Thus speakers would not use sentences without the object unless it is clear what is meant' (Lehrer, 1970:243). The fourth degree of cohesion is with verbs where the range of possible Objects is so vast that deletion alters the overall meaning. This can be seen in discourses like (10), where the omission of the pronominal reference to the Object gives a different understanding of the verb.

(10) John drinks only gin, but I don't drink (it).

Returning to the cognate objects mentioned above, it is interesting to note that several authors want to distinguish the case appropriate for such elements from the regular Patient. Chafe (1970:156f) has the case Complement for this role which attaches to essentially action verbs, as long as they are specified as 'completable'. Examples given are *sing*, *play*, *run* and (more dubiously) *fight*, for some of which (but not all) the Complement is morphologically cognate (11) (in (11d) *fight* would seem a more appropriate cognate object than *war*).

(11a) May sang *a song*.
(11b) The children played *a game*.
(11c) Tom ran *a race*.
(11d) The infantry fought *a war*.

Complements can also be specified more narrowly, as in (12), and the sentences in (13) are given as marginal examples of Complement.

(12a) Tom sang '*The Star Spangled Banner*'
(12b) The children played *touch-football*.
(13a) Tom won *a television set*.
(13b) Tom read '*War and Peace*'.

Cook (1972*b*:70) introduces the verb-feature complementiser to account for the derivation of an (apparent) action-process verb from an action, but justifies the separation of the case associated therewith from other Patients by noting that action-processes derived from intrinsic action verbs cannot undergo the further derivation deactivative (other than by passivisation). Although he gives no examples, we can imagine that this ruling would account for the marginality of sentences like (14), where the deactivative derivation is applied to such verbs. Despite this, however, Cook eventually combines Patients and Complements into a single Object role.

(14a) ? 'Rule Britannia' sang well tonight.
(14b) ? Tennis plays a lot in this country.

Chafe suggests that there are also completable states such as *weigh* and *cost*, as in (15).

(15a) The book weighs *a pound*.
(15b) The candy costs *ten cents*.

For these verbs the Complement appears to be obligatory (16a-b), though some such sentences may be acceptable in informal discourse (16c), especially when a 'dative' is introduced (16d).

(16a) * The book weighs.
(16b) * The candy costs.
(16c) ? That wheelbarrow full of bricks will weigh!
(16d) That lost library book will cost you.

There are clear differences between Complements in completable states and those in completable actions that make Cook's decision to group them under the same case name seem quite odd. Firstly, these Complements regularly co-occur with Patients, as in (17a) without the possibility of coordination (17b) which would suggest that they are not the same case. Second, there seems to be a role available to action verbs that parallels this stative Complement, as in (18), which differs significantly from the 'cognate object' Complement in behaviour: the latter can be passivised, but cannot be ergativised (19); for the former both these 'deactivisations' are possible (20).

(17a) This elephant weighs ten tons.
(17b) * This elephant and ten tons weigh.

(18) Bannister ran *a mile*.
(19a) Tennis is played from April to September.
(19b) * Tennis plays from April to September.
(20a) A mile was run in under four minutes.
(20b) A mile runs in under four minutes.

This clear necessity to distinguish two roles with verbs like *weigh* and *cost* led Longacre (1976:30) to introduce a Measure case which serves not only for the element which 'completes a predication by quantifying it' but also is the case for the price in a transfer. Pam (1971) too suggests an independent case is needed for this role. Longacre differs from Chafe however in separating Measure from other complements, which he groups together with objects of result (see below), on the grounds that although *The Star Spangled Banner* in (12a) was in existence before Tom sang it, Tom's particular rendition of it did not exist beforehand, and so there is a parallel between (12a) and (21).

(21) Tom built *a table*.

Many case systems distinguish between the object coming into being as a result of an action or process ('effected object') as in (21) and the object simply impinged upon ('affected object'). This was the distinction made by Fillmore (1968*a*) between his Objective and Factitive (though he later (1971*b*) merged the Factitive into his new Goal case), is reflected in the usage by Teng (1975) and Longacre (1976) of the Range case, and is one of the uses of Chafe's (1970) Complement (as we have just seen). Other Case grammarians on the other hand make no such distinction (e.g. Cook, 1972*b*; Stockwell *et al.*, 1973; Grimes, 1975). The range of verbs taking this case is fairly easy to typify (22), with the Object having some sense of 'being brought into existence'.

(22a) Jack built *the house*.
(22b) Tolstoy wrote *a book*.
(22c) Warhol painted *a picture*.

If we accept this distinction as a case difference, then we must accept for some verbs the possibility of alternative case frames (23a-b), and in some instances a possible ambiguity (23c).

(23a) Van Gogh painted *the canvas*. (affected)
(23b) Van Gogh painted '*Starry Night*'. (effected)
(23c) Van Gogh painted *his bedroom*. (either?)

I have tried to show elsewhere (Rosner and Somers, 1980:22f) that the necessity to make this distinction depends on the use to which a case analysis will be put. For example the distinction enables the blocking of verbs taking a Factitive combining with the verb *to do* (24); or the correct inference of (possible) truth values for sentences like (25b-c) from the premise (25a).

(24a) What did Bev do to the dinner?
(24b) What Bev did to the dinner was ruin it.
(24c) * What Bev did to the dinner was make it.
(25a) Chomsky wrote 'Syntactic Structures' in 1957.
(25b) I read 'Syntactic Structures' in 1963. [possible]
(25c) I read 'Syntactic Structures' in 1955. [impossible]

But most important of all, especially in a multilingual language processing environment, are examples where the distinction between a Factitive and an Object show up in the translations of verbs which are neutral in this respect in the source language; or in the monolingual situation, where we wish to distinguish two verb senses on this basis, for whatever reason (e.g. different selection restrictions of various case-slot fillers). In German, for example, the English verb *paint* will be rendered by *streichen* or *bemalen* if its direct object is Objective, but by *malen* if Factitive (26).

(26a) Hans *strich* ein Haus.
'Hans painted a house.' [Hans is decorating]
(26b) Hans *bemalte* die Leinwand.
'Hans painted the canvas.'
(26c) Hans *malte* ein Haus.
'Hans painted a house.' [Hans is an artist]

Becker (1971) suggests that the use of the prefix *be-* in German is highly productive in making this distinction (27)-(28).

(27a) Der Dichter schrieb ein schönes Sonett.
'The poet wrote a beautiful sonett.'
(27b) Der Dichter *be*schrieb das Pergamentstück.
'The poet wrote on the parchment.'
(28a) Der Bauunternehmer baut ein Hochhaus.
'The contractor is building a high-rise.'
(28b) Der Bauunternehmer *be*baut das Grundstück.
'The contractor is building on the site.'

In Finnish, the distinction between (26a) and (26c) is captured in the choice of surface case, with the accusative for the affected and the partitive for the effected object (29) (Rosner and Somers, *cit.*)

(29a) John maaloi talon.
JOHN PAINTED HOUSE-acc [Objective]
(29b) John maaloi taloa.
JOHN PAINTED HOUSE-ptv [Factitive]

Although the tradition has been to make just this two-way distinction, it seems to me that a third value is needed, since the Object or Patient may be neither affected nor effected. This appears to be the case for the Patient with verbs of perception (30a) and cognition (30b), and related verbs, and with Patients in stative predications (30c).

(30a) I saw *the house*.

(30b) I know *the answer*.

(30c) *The door* is open.

For this role I would coin the term 'neutral', and depend on the same criteria as used in deciding whether to distinguish formally between Objective and Factitive to determine whether this third case is to be posited. The point is that given the choice between characterisations of affected and effected objects, neither seems particularly appropriate for the Patients in (30), and so this third term should be introduced, whether at the level of a new case in contrast to Objective and Factitive, or whether as a third possible sub-case of general Patient.

This solution may not be completely satisfactory however, because further subdivisions can be made. For example, Martinet (1972) draws attention to the different roles that the Objective plays with *remove* and *open*: 'In any case, *remove a can* means to displace the entire can, whereas *open a can* means to cut off its lid. If one were to look hard enough, one should be able to find a paraphrase that will demonstrate that the two operations are of fundamentally different types' (Martinet, 1972:19*fn*). One might argue that this distinction can be captured, if necessary, by specifying the distinction in the semantic characterisation of the verb, except that exactly the same argument can be used to eliminate the Objective-Factitive distinction.

It is clear from the foregoing discussion that the notion of Object/Patient is perhaps one of the loosest in Case grammar. A wide range of criteria is used to distinguish or to decide not to distinguish different types of Patient, including, importantly, syntactic and 'semantic' correlation, and better suitability of other cases in the system for a given role. For some, the need for a given notion to be homogeneous is a crucial factor. For others, complementary distribution of cases is seen as a sufficient motive for grouping a number of roles into one heterogeneous collection. Blansitt (1977:314f) makes a similar point, taking 'grammatical form' and '[grammatical?] meaning' to be the contrasting and contradictory bases for the determination of cases. For our own purposes, purely pragmatic criteria will prevail, though our 'case grid' proposal (Chapter 10) will permit some compromise between the two approaches.

Let us conclude this section, however, by reproducing Cook's

(1972*b*) characterisation of his Object case. This is an appropriate way to summarise, since Cook's Object is something of a conglomeration of the sorts of roles that others have variously incorporated under the heading. Note that Cook's lack of a Source or Goal case avoids any conflict in the assignment to Object of stimulus in experiential verbs and result of factitive verbs respectively.

> '(a) The case required by a "stative" verb, which specifies the object that is in that state, or,
> (b) the case required by a "process" verb, which specifies the object which undergoes a change of state.
> With Experiencer verbs, the Object specifies the content of the experience, or the stimulus for the experience.
> With Benefactive verbs, the Object specifies the thing possessed, or the thing which is transferred.
> With Locative verbs, the Object specifies the object in a location, or undergoing change of position.' (Cook, 1972*b*:52)
> '. . . complement [cf. Section 4.3] and patient nouns have been subsumed under the Object case.' (*ibid*, p. 70)

5. *Locative/Source/Path/Goal*

Nearly all Case grammarians have recognised the general need for a case for the 'adverbs of place' in (1), and by extension for various locational expressions as in (2).

(1a) We saw the play *at the theatre.*
(1b) It is windy *in Chicago.*
(1c) We played cricket *on the beach.*
(2a) He put the book *on the table.*
(2b) He walked *past the station.*
(2c) I sent a telex *to Pisa.*
(2d) She got her hoover *from Rumbelows.*

In this section we shall discuss a number of problems and developments of this seemingly straightforward case assignment. The Locative for example seems at first sight to be able to contravene the one-case-per-clause principle (3). Under certain circumstances it is a candidate for promotion to subject or object (4). The behaviour of the Locative is closely associated with a putative Temporal case – do we have one or two cases here (5)? More significantly, there seems to be a distinction between Locatives describing static locations (1) and aspects of direction (2).

(3) *In Geneva* I often stay *at Mike's house.*
(4a) *Chicago* is windy.

(4b) They filled *the swimming pool* with water.
(5a) We saw the play *at 9 o'clock.*
(5b) It is windy *in April.*
(5c) We play cricket *on Wednesdays.*

Let us consider first those instances where two Locatives co-occur in a sentence as in (3), though without the possibility of coordination, as in (6).

(6) I often stay in Geneva and at Mike's house. [≠ (3)]

The non-equivalence of (3) and (6) would seem to suggest two separate cases here, but closer examination of tendencies suggests that it is more useful to distinguish between 'optional' and 'obligatory' Locatives: many authors have noted a fundamentally different relationship between the Locatives and verbs in (7a-b), and have been able to identify a range of verbs that require a Locative element, whereas Locatives of the type seen in (7b) seem to be able to be attached to almost any predication, including those of the type illustrated in (7a), cf. (7c).

(7a) He keeps his car *in the garage.*
(7b) He washes his car *in the garage.*
(7c) *In Manchester*, he keeps his car *in the garage.*

Various terms have been suggested for this distinction. Fillmore (1968*a*:26*fn*) contrasts elements 'inside the vp' and 'outside the vp', Halliday (1970:149) and Platt (1970:30) suggest 'inner' and 'outer', Cook (1972*a*:42) 'propositional' and 'modal', Longacre (1976:35) 'nuclear' and 'peripheral', Dik (1978:25f) 'argument' and 'satellite'. Whatever terminology is chosen, it should be fairly clear that the notion corresponds to the Valency distinction of complements and adjuncts, and we shall discuss at more length in Chapter 9 the application of this distinction to Case grammar in general. Note that inner Locatives are characterised by the fact that they cannot be omitted without changing the meaning of the verb (compare (8a) and (7a)), and for some verbs cannot be omitted at all (8b-c).

(8a) He keeps his car.
(8b) He put the flowers *in the vase.*
(8c) * He put the flowers.

It is sufficient to note at this point however that whatever we have to say about Locatives in general, we should bear in mind possible differences in behaviour between inner Locatives, which enter into the case frame features for particular verbs, and outer Locatives, which can effectively accompany any predication.

This last remark is actually slightly controversial, since Fillmore (1968*a*:26*fn*) and following him Platt (1971:30) suggest that outer Locatives can only attach to predications involving an Agent.

Counterexamples are found in Anderson (1977:28) (9a-b) and are also admitted by Platt (p. 33) (9c-e) who resolves this dilemma by positing a more freely occurring 'far-outer Locative'. This three-way distinction is reminiscent of our own extended view of Valency binding discussed in Chapter 1 Section 6.

(9a) Fred died *in his bed.*
(9b) The butter in this dish has melted *in the cupboard.*
(9c) *In that town*, people know their neighbours.
(9d) *In that country*, people believe their politicians.
(9e) *In that region*, people want a new dam.

That the distinction between outer and far-outer Locatives is anything more than a question of the presence or absence of an Agent is not easily demonstrable, even though intuitively at least the relationship between the Locatives and the predicate in (9c-e) does seem to be more distant than in (9a-b). But in a sentence like (10a), which contains an Agent, who is to say whether the phrase *in Italy* is outer or far-outer? The only proof would be to construct a sentence containing all three types, which (without the bracketed afterthought) is a bit strained.

(10a) In Italy, people eat a lot of spaghetti.
(10b) In Italy, at home people keep their cars in garages (but at the seaside they keep their cars on the street).

Notice that in (10b) we used the verb *keep* which requires an inner Locative. We could just as easily have formed a sentence with *park* which does not. The result (11) with a series of outer Locatives in a succession of increasing 'outer-ness' suggests that, just like the outer Benefactives in Section 3 (and the outer Agents there), outer Locatives can stack up as far as processing or plausibility limitations allow.

(11) In Italy, at home people park their cars in garages . . .

The position of the Locative *at home* in (10b) and (11) is also important: for the sake of the example it was necessary to separate the two Locatives *at home* and *in garages*, since juxtaposed Locatives often form not a series of stacked outer Locatives, but a subordinated (12a) or coordinated (12b) single Locative, whether inner or outer (cf. Bennett, 1975:30). These form a single phrase-structure constituent, a fact that can be demonstrated in surface structure with subordinated Locatives by inserting the ellipsed relative pronouns (12c) and with coordinated Locatives by the fact that the repeated prepositions can be omitted (12d).

(12a) I was sitting on a bench by a tree in a park in London.
(12b) Birds build their nests in trees, in hedges, in fields, in the open countryside or on buildings.

(12c) I was sitting on a bench which was by a tree which was in a park which was in London.

(12d) Birds build their nests in trees, hedges, fields, the open countryside or on buildings.

Locatives – both inner and outer – are most commonly realised as prepositional phrases. They are distinguished from other cases so realised by the fact that the preposition used is often not semantically void. Although Fillmore's (1968*a*:32) claim that each case is primarily associated with a given preposition is overstated (cf. Chapter 2 Section 2) it is nevertheless true that for most of the other cases, when realised as a prepositional phrase, the preposition has no lexical content of its own. Van Langendonck (1974:1) distinguishes in this sense between 'internally referring' (semantically void) and 'externally referring' (semantically valid) prepositions. In many instances of Locatives, the preposition is meaningful, though van Langendonck does point out (p. 3) that for certain Locative expressions, the preposition is internally referring. He gives examples in Dutch where, when neutral location is indicated, the choice of preposition *in*, *op*, *te* and *aan* is determined by the type of noun phrase to which it is attached (13). Dirven (1981:105) makes similar remarks concerning English.

(13a) Het is warm in de kamer.
'It is warm in the room.'

(13b) Het is fris op de berg.
'It is cool on the mountain.'

(13c) Het is vandaag koud te Gent.
'It is cold today in Ghent.'

(13d) Het is gevaarlijk aan de Halve Steen.
'It is dangerous at the Halve Steen.'

Van Langendonck attempts to characterise via semantic features in the head noun the choice of such prepositions (pp. 17ff), and although his analysis happens to work for both English and Dutch, he is mistaken in assuming such characterisations are generalisable. For while in English specifying type of location is sufficient to predict the correct preposition (14), the rules for French, for example, are on quite different (and varied) bases (15).

(14) *in* – cities, countries, enclosed spaces, streets, buildings
on – islands, mountains, streets
at – buildings

(15)	cities: *à Paris* but *en Avignon*	(phonetic)
	countries: *en France* but *au Japon*	(gender)
	islands: *en Corse* but *sur l'Ile d'Elbe*	(political status)

The distinction between internally and externally referring prepositions with Locatives is nevertheless a valid one. For example, as van Langendonck (p. 3) correctly points out, only Locatives expressed with internally referring pronouns can be transformed into surface subjects (compare (13) and (16); also (4a)). Although Locatives with externally referring prepositions can be moved into thematic position (17a-b), the elimination of the preposition changes the meaning (17c).

(16a) De kamer is warm.
'The room is warm.'
(16b) De berg is fris.
'The mountain is cool.'
(16c) Gent is vandaag koud.
'Ghent is cold today.'
(16d) De Halve Steen is gevaarlijk.
'The Halve Steen is dangerous.'
(17a) It is dangerous beyond the forest.
(17b) Beyond the forest is dangerous.
(17c) The forest is dangerous.

Locatives can be 'promoted' to both subject and object position, and this transposition often entails a change in meaning: in the following examples (18-21) the italicised elements are understood to have a 'partitive' reading in the (a) sentences, but a 'holistic' reading in the (b) sentences.

(18a) John smeared paint *on the wall.*
(18b) John smeared *the wall* with paint.
(19a) Bees are swarming *in the garden.*
(19b) *The garden* is swarming with bees.
(20a) John loaded hay *onto the wagon.*
(20b) John loaded *the wagon* with hay.
(21a) The press secretary read *from his prepared speech.*
(21b) The press secretary read *his prepared speech.*

The terms 'partitive' and 'holistic' were coined by S. Anderson (1971), and the problem has been discussed at some length in Fraser (1971), Chomsky (1972:102), Mellema (1974:50f), Pak (1974:46f), van Langendonck (1974:6), Welin (1975:50f), Anderson (1977:48ff) and Fillmore (1977*b*:70), to which the interested reader is referred.

Besides these special cases of Locative 'promotion', there are a number of verbs which require a Locative which is expressed as subject or object. Stockwell *et al.* (1973:60) suggest that *contain* has a Locative subject, to which (following Cook, 1979:216) we can add *empty* and *fill* (intransitive). Verbs with Locative objects are more numerous and include *descend*, *enter* and related verbs, and – perhaps more controversially – *paint* ('apply paint to'), *skin* ('remove skin from'), and so on.

It is perhaps one of the few universals of linguistics that many of the means used for expressions of location are also used in temporal expressions. For Case grammarians, this parallelism – reflected in the use of the same prepositions or case forms for locative and temporal adverbials – has led to many discussions as to whether Locative and Temporal should be considered to be a single case, subcategorised for the two orientations.

Those authors who argue that there should be only one case point to the essential similarities in behaviour between the two types of expression. There is the question of prepositions, both 'internally referring' (22) and 'externally referring' (23).

(22)	in London	in June
	on the mountain	on December 11th
	by land	by night
	at sea	at 5 o'clock
(23)	before the bank	before daybreak
	from Liverpool	from morning
	through the countryside	through the night

Next there is the fact that conditions under which temporal prepositional phrases can be promoted to subject or object are very similar (van Langendonck, 1974:11), as in (24)-(26),

(24a) It is warm in June.
(24b) June is warm. [cf. (13) and (16)]
(25a) It is dangerous before daybreak.
(25b) Daybreak is dangerous. [a ≠ b; cf. (17b-c)]
(26a) They danced together during the evening.
(26b) They danced the evening together. [cf. (18-21)]

though there seem to be a much smaller number of verbs, in English at least, regularly requiring a Temporal direct object (e.g. *last*, *take*), and none requiring a Temporal subject spring to mind.

Like Locatives, Temporals seem to divide into inner and outer instances, with similar co-occurrence (27a) and stacking (27b) possibilities.

(27a) *In winter* it takes *two hours* to get to work.
(27b) *Last year* the sports news lasted twenty minutes *on some occasions*.

All these similarities seem to suggest to many authors that Locative and Temporal can be considered to be a single case. Van Langendonck states '. . . the history of language shows that the abstract category "time" has borrowed many elements from the concrete "place" (or more widely "space"). Such facts at any rate plead for an identical or at least similar treatment of place and time adverbials . . .' (van Langendonck, 1974:10). Bennett puts the point more strongly: '[One possible] analysis involves ascribing a purely spatial meaning to the "locative" case, and then evoking in addition a "time" case . . . The disadvantage of such an analysis is that it implies that the occurrence of the same preposition in *at the supermarket* and *at 10 o'clock* is merely a coincidence. This follows from the fact that *at* would be attributed a different meaning in these two phrases. According to the analysis adopted here, on the other hand, it is certainly not coincidental that *at* occurs in these two phrases, since it is regarded as expressing the same notion in each instance. From the present standpoint, the "locative" and "time" cases of Fillmore [(1971*b*)] are semantically complex. Each contains a general notion of location combined with either "place" or "time"' (Bennett, 1975:16). The general notion, then, is that we have here a single case, subcategorised for place or time. As Anderson has it, '. . . temporal adverbs do not involve a distinct type of predication from those including spatial locatives; they are locative phrases in which the N is temporal rather than spatial' (Anderson, 1972:194). The unicity of space and time adverbials is underlined by Miller's (1970:496) analysis of adverbials like *in Moscow* in (28a) not as adverbials of place, but as adverbials of time, due to the possibility of the paraphrase in (28b), and the fact that (28a) would be more likely to answer (28c) than (28d).

(28) In Moscow he believed in Communism.
(28b) He believed in Communism when he was in Moscow.
(28c) Where was he *when* he believed in Communism?
(28d) Where did he believe in Communism?

There are problems with this analysis however. If Locatives are subcategorised as 'time' and 'space', where does this feature come from? Anderson's comment suggests that the feature resides in the noun head, but as van Langendonck (1974:14) points out the Locative does not necessarily have to coincide with any feature 'place', and he gives examples of objects and animals as Locatives (29); likewise Temporals can be made up with nouns not especially associated with the notion 'time' (30).

(29a) A fly is sitting *on the window*.
(29b) The rider is sitting *on the horse*.
(30a) My father was injured *during the war*.
(30b) Their marriage broke up *after his illness*.

If the time or place subcategorisation does not reside in the noun then does it stem from the preposition? Clearly not, since we have already seen that a number of prepositions serve for both Locatives and Temporals. Perhaps then the distinction stems from the verb: this is clearly a possibility, and in such instances the criteria for distinguishing two cases would be much like those discussed in Section 4 for separating Objective and Factitive. But notice that a rather large proportion of Locatives and Temporals are (in Cook's terms) modal rather than propositional cases (i.e. 'adjuncts' rather than 'complements'), and features in the verb therefore cannot be invoked. And there is even more persuasive evidence that we must treat these as two separate cases, albeit closely related.

First, Locatives and Temporals can co-occur in a single sentence, though without the possibility of coordination: if they are a single case, then it is a case that is exempt from the one-case-per-predication constraint (31). Apparent contradictions to this coordination constraint can be found where Locatives can be interpreted as Temporals (cf. (32), the acceptability of which – assuming knowledge about Igor's defection to Canada in the sixties – is explained by Miller's (1970) analysis of sentences like those in (28)).

(31a) I met him in Liverpool in September.
(31b) * I met him in Liverpool and in September.
(32) Igor was less productive in 1959 than in Montreal.

This picture of free co-occurrence is slightly blurred by the fact, noted by Fillmore (1971*b*:41), that directional time and space Locatives cannot be combined (33).

(33a) He walked from the top of the hill to the cemetery gate.
(33b) He walked from noon until sundown.
(33c) * He walked from the top of the hill until sundown.

Bennett (1975:96) also points out that while for Locatives there is a distinction between directional Locatives as in (34a), where 'something moves through a particular stretch of space', and 'extent' Locatives (34b), where 'the whole of a particular stretch of space is occupied at the same time', this distinction is more or less neutralised for Temporals (34c).

(34a) Trevor walked from Buckingham Palace to Trafalgar Square.
(34b) The Mall goes from Buckingham Palace to Trafalgar Square.
(34c) The film lasted from seven o'clock to nine o'clock.

Grimes (1975:122) is quite clear that Temporals are distinct from Locatives (his Range case), from the point of view of co-occurrence in a simple sentence (35a) – cf. (31a) – but more importantly from the restrictions on the possibility of forming 'thematically reduced' expressions involving Range (35b-c).

(35a) It is sizzling in January in Brisbane.
(35b) When it is January, it is sizzling in Brisbane.
(35c) * Where it is Brisbane, it is sizzling in January.

We should not however confuse evidence like this, which supports a complement-adjunct distinction rather than shedding much light on the necessity to distinguish temporal and spatial locatives. In fact, Grimes's observations suggest that there might be an argument for regarding Locatives and Temporals as a single case when they are complements, where the time/space subcategorisation is given by the verb, but acknowledging two separate adjunct cases.

In his overview, Dillon (1977:76) mentions the conflict as to whether a separate case should be set up for the 'place to which something goes', perhaps based on the surface evidence that 'locational' and 'directional' roles are differentiated by surface case (e.g. German and Latin dative versus accusative) or by preposition (e.g. English *at* versus *to*) – though see below. Some Case grammarians choose to do so, while '. . . others rely on the semantic characterization of the verb as a verb of motion to predict this reinterpretation of Location' (Dillon, 1977:76). Fillmore variously takes both approaches. In (1968*a*) he states that '. . . locational and spatial elements do not contrast but are superficial differences determined either by the constituent structure or by the character of the associated verb' (Fillmore, 1968*a*:25). In (1971*b*) however, he introduces the directional cases Source and Goal, though principally to enable him to capture essential similarities between '. . . earlier and later locations, earlier and later states, or earlier and later time points' (Fillmore, 1971*b*:41). Nevertheless, these directional cases do now contrast with Locative and Time (1971*b*:42), though these latter, except with verbs like *be* (in one of its uses), *live* and *spend*, occur chiefly as 'optional complements of essentially any predicator', and may even be analysed as being '. . . embedded into higher sentences containing as their main verb something like *occur* or *happen*' (*ibid*., p. 49).

Frajzyngier's (1975) analysis of Awutu very strongly supports the non-distinction of stative and directional Locatives, assigning 'direction' as a verb feature. This preference seems to stem from the fact that in Awutu the case-markers for Source and Goal coincide with the surface verbs meaning 'leave' and 'go' – compare the use of *cú* and *yò* in (36).

(36a) ò sĩ mé né ò cú áwùsò yò s̀ìmpá.
YOU REACH WHAT conj YOU LEAVE AWUTU GO SIMPA
'How do you get from Awutu to Simpa?'

(36b) mò cú ǹklá
HE LEAVE ACCRA
'He came from Accra.'

(36c) mò yò ǹklá
HE GO ACCRA
'He went to Accra.'

However, a very similar situation arises in Chinese, where many of the case-markers are (synchronically or diachronically) also full verbs (37)-(40) – cf. Li and Thompson (1974) and Teng (1975:37).

(37) Ta xihuan *yong* maobi xie zi.
HE LIKE USE BRUSH-PEN WRITE WORD
'He likes to write with brush-pens.' (Instrumental)

(38) Ta *gei* mama mai zhe-jian yifu.
HE GIVE MOTHER BUY THIS-class DRESS
'He is buying this dress for his mother.' (Benefactive)

(39) Ta *zai* Zhongguo nian shu.
HE BE-IN CHINA READ BOOK
'He is studying in China.' (Locative)

(40) Ta zuotian *gen* ta baba yikuar shang-jie.
HE YESTERDAY FOLLOW HE FATHER TOGETHER GO-STREET
'Yesterday he went to town with his father.'
(Comitative)

Although this happens not to be the case with *cong* ('from') for Source, the Goal preposition *dao* is also the full verb 'reach', as in (41). Yet Teng's (1975) Case analysis includes these cases, the status of which, following Frajzyngier's conclusions, would be questionable.

(41a) Ta kai dao Beijing.
HE DRIVE REACH PEKING
'He drove to Peking.'

(41b) Ta zuotian dao-le Beijing
HE YESTERDAY REACH-asp PEKING
'He reached Peking yesterday.'

In J. Anderson's (1971) account, 'static' and 'dynamic' Locatives can be distinguished via a ±dynamic feature residing in the verb. But Anderson notes that dynamic Locatives have the possibility of occurring in pairs, which he labels 'allative' and 'ablative'. Because allatives and static Locatives share in some languages (e.g. English, French, Dutch) surface realisations (p. 119) (42)-(44), Anderson groups these two cases together, in contrast with the Ablative. We shall see below how the analysis of Locatives is extended by Anderson and others to cover a wider range of cases.

(42a) He dived in the water.
(42b) Fish live in the water.
(43a) Il entra dans la chambre.
'He entered the room.'
(43b) Il y avait un lit dans la chambre.
'There was a bed in the room.'
(44a) De jongen viel op de grond.
'The boy fell to the ground.'
(44b) De jongen zit op de grond.
'The boy is sitting on the ground.'

Bennett (1975:404f) notes that the static/dynamic distinction is not sufficient to distinguish Source and Goal locatives from positional locatives since Source and Goal can also be found in stative expressions such as (45), so that ±dynamic is inadequate to subcategorise Locatives fully.

(45) The Mall extends from Buckingham Palace to Trafalgar Square.

Chafe (1970:161f) avoids the problem altogether by associating the preposition with the verb via the introduction of a 'locativizer' feature, presumably then taking the Fillmore (1968*a*) view that any distinction resides in the verb. Chafe regards *sit in* and *crawl under* as derived predicates comparable to the basic (i.e. nonderived) verbs *occupy* and *enter*. He does not however mention verbs taking more than one Locative element, as in (45) and (46), and it is not clear how this approach could handle such sentences.

(46) Harry flew from Tunis to Luxembourg.

Arguments in favour of one or other approach seem indecisive. Anderson's recognition of not three but two cases seems something of a compromise, and his grouping of the allative rather than the ablative with the static is a rather arbitrary decision based on an almost coincidental feature of some languages that happen to have lost certain surface case distinctions: compare (42) and the German equivalents in (47).

(47a) Er tauchte ins Wasser. [Accusative]
(47b) Fische leben im Wasser. [Dative]

On the other hand, it is true that static Locatives do not co-occur with directional Locatives except in combinations of inner and outer cases, as in (48), which would not in itself be a strong argument for differentiating.

(48a) In Copenhagen you can go by bus from the airport to the city centre.

(48b) From London to Crewe I sat in the guard's van.

Once again, our approach would be to justify such a distinction on the grounds of the use to which the case analysis is being put. Certainly data from German (47) suggest that the distinction is necessary, and in fact the metaphorical extension of these locative notions to be discussed next will provide the basis of our own 'case grid' proposal in Chapter 10.

Note finally that, as before, some of these properties of Locatives also apply to Temporals, as suggested by Fillmore's (1971*b*:41) comment cited above, though in fact the degree of correspondence is relatively weak, and provides additional support to those arguing for their separation. But we do find temporal Source and Goal in both stative (49a) and dynamic (49b) expressions, and combination inner and outer Temporals (49c-d). Examples of coinciding allative and static Temporals in parallel with (42)-(44) do not however spring readily to mind.

(49a) The film lasts from 7 p.m. till 9 p.m.

(49b) I worked from midnight until three in the morning.

(49c) On Tuesdays I play cricket from five till eight.

(49d) From May to September parking restrictions start at lunchtime.

Often associated with the directional case Source and Goal is a case usually called Path. It seems that this case was first introduced in 1970 in an unpublished paper by David Bennett (cited by Fillmore, 1971*b*:50 and Stratton, 1971:221), and the most important discussions of Path are provided by Stratton and in Bennett (1975), who comments 'It is rather obvious that any change of position involves an earlier location and a later location, and not surprising therefore that a distinction between source and goal expressions has often been invoked in the past. On the other hand, the need to recognize path expressions in addition has frequently been overlooked' (Bennett, 1975:18). So it is for example that Grimes (1975:121) simply uses his Range case (equivalent to Locative in states) for the 'path or area traversed' with verbs of motion.

But Stratton is able to demonstrate that analysis in terms of only Source and Goal can lead to problems: while Goal seems a reasonable case assignment for *over the fence* in (50a), *Jim* is a more obvious candidate for Goal in (50b), while *over the fence* seems to characterise 'the space intervening between source and goal' (p. 222).

(50a) Sam threw the watermelon over the fence.

(50b) Sam threw the watermelon over the fence to Jim.

Having postulated a Path case and its characterisation, can we further specify its likely realisations? Not subscribing to the notion that cases and prepositions are in a one-to-one relationship, Bennett includes Path as one of the cases marked by a number of prepositions, as in (51a-h). Note that the 'archetypical' Path preposition *via* is only one of many available, and not even the most common of these. The status of Path as complement or adjunct with verbs of motion is unclear, but for some verbs where it appears as a direct object (51i-j) and by extension presumably as a subject (51k), it is clearly a complement (contradicting Anderson's claim that Path is always 'outer').

(51a) Pass that lamp *over the counter*.

(51b) The dog ran *under the table* to the door. [cf. also *in front of, behind*]

(51c) We drove *past the post-office*. [cf. also *by*]

(51d) The train went *through the tunnel*.

(51e) Columbus sailed *across the sea* to America.

(51f) You can get to Wales *along the A5* [cf. also *down, up*]

(51g) She walked *round the corner* to the bank.

(51h) I flew from Copenhagen to Manchester *via Amsterdam*.

(51i) Caesar crossed *the Rubicon*.

(51j) Alcock and Brown flew *the Atlantic* in 1919.

(51k) *The A580* connects Manchester with Liverpool.

Bennett (p. 18) notes that prepositional phrases with *behind*, *in front of*, *over* and *under* (51a-b) can be ambiguous between Goal and Path when no ultimate location is specified, as in (52): in (52a) it might mean that the dog stayed under the table, in which case it is Goal, or else it may be that the scene expressed in (51b) is described, though without mentioning the dog's destination; likewise with (52b).

(52a) The dog ran under the table.

(52b) The boy ran behind the tree.

Stratton (1971) attempts to show that Path has certain properties that set it apart from the other cases in general, and from Source and Goal in particular. However most of his claims are either insignificant (e.g. that Path can be direct object with most verbs of motion – cf. (51j) – whereas Source and Goal cannot) or wrong (e.g. 'Path is typically (always?) inanimate' (p. 225) – but cf. (53)).

(53) I got the book from Jock via Pete.

But the most serious mistake that Stratton makes, and which is replicated by Fillmore (1971*b*:50f) and Longacre (1976:34), is to suggest that Path is not subject to the one-case-per-clause constraint. Stratton gives (54a) as an example, Fillmore gives (54b).

(54a) Sam went from Chicago to San Francisco via Joliet, Bloomington, Springfield, St. Louis, Kansas City, Salina, Denver, . . .

(54b) He walked down the hill across the bridge through the pasture to the chapel.

We know that apparent contraventions of this principle can be explained either by analysing the multiple case fillers as being coordinated or subordinated (ignoring for a moment the third possibility of 'inner' versus 'outer'). Stratton rejects the idea that they are coordinated, because their sequence is significant (unlike the coordinated Locatives in (12b) above). Neither, clearly, are they subordinated, since the list of points traversed does not involve 'a successive narrowing down of the scope of location' (p. 226) (cf. (12a) above). On the next page however Stratton states that 'They *can* be thought of as coordinate elements under a single Path node, but it is difficult to think of them as a set of hierarchically related subordinate elements' (Stratton, 1971:227) [emphasis mine]. This statement effectively seems to disprove the point Stratton is trying to make. And even if he is (rightly) uneasy with the notion of a multiply specified Path as a 'vertical' (narrowing) hierarchy, could it not be thought of as a 'horizontal' hierarchy? What is perhaps pathological about the Path case (to use Stratton's pun) is that it is difficult to construct subordinated Paths that look like contraventions of the constraint. Compare the attempts in (55), and note that in (55a) only the location at the bottom of the hierarchy carries a typical Path preposition; (55b) on the other hand is deviant. Only in the sense of further specifying a Path in the special case where there is an ambiguity in the real world do we get the desired structure (55c).

(55a) I flew home via O'Hare in Chicago in Illinois in the U.S.A.

(55b) * I flew home via O'Hare via Chicago via Illinois via the U.S.A.

(55c) I went from Stockwell to Euston on the Northern Line via Charing Cross.

Concerning the co-occurrence of Source, Path and Goal, Bennett makes the interesting point that 'Very few sentences that are actually attested (as opposed to invented by a linguist) contain three directional prepositional phrases' (Bennett, 1975:20). He goes on to explain the reason behind this is that often one or two of the three elements may be considered unimportant, obvious, or unknown. More interesting though is the fact that one of the directional locatives may sometimes be partially lexicalised, as in (56), though the possibility of further specifying the implied case is usually available.

(56a) Trevor appeared from behind the desk. [*appear* implies Goal]

(56b) Jock has left for Copenhagen. [*leave* implies Source]

(56c) We crossed from Dover to Calais. [*cross* implies Path]

We have seen above the close relationship between Locatives and Temporals. We should now ask whether it is appropriate to posit a temporal Path case. Bennett argues as follows: 'With regard to "path", it would seem that there must be a fixed route between any pair of points in time, owing to the unidimensional nature of time . . . For instance, when it is a question of getting from seven o'clock to nine o'clock, there is hardly any choice of which way to go. Consequently, one might suppose that it would not be necessary to posit path expressions as far as time is concerned. However, prepositional phrases such as *throughout the evening* . . . force us to recognize temporal path expressions after all' (Bennett, 1975:94). Temporal Path then may be characterised as expressing duration, and just like locative Path can be captured either as a combination of Source and Goal, as in *from dawn till dusk* (cf. *from London to Birmingham*) or as a single nominal phrase as in *during the day* (cf. *along the M1*).

So far we have been concerned with Locative, Source, Path and Goal in their spatial and temporal uses. However, for many case users, these notions also have a metaphorical extension. J. Anderson (1971) contrasts the 'concrete' and 'abstract' uses of (surface) cases in general, while it is to be remembered that Fillmore's introduction of Source and Goal was in these terms: 'Depending on the type of predicator, the Source and Goal are interpreted as earlier and later locations, *earlier and later states*, or earlier and later time points' (Fillmore, 1971*b*:41) [emphasis mine]. The Source and Goal states are characterised in Fillmore's example (57),

(57) He changed from a 96-pound weakling into a famous football hero.

while he also associates his old Factitive case for the result of a process with Goal (p. 42), as well as one of the uses of his old Dative: 'Where there is a transfer or movement of something to a person, the receiver as destination is taken as the Goal' (*ibid.*, p. 42). This seems to be the goal he uses in (1971*a*:390) with verbs like *blame*, *accuse* and *criticise* where he assigns as Goal the entity to whom the judgment is directed and as Object the stimulus of the judgment. Source is for each verb the normal surface subject, though this novel use of Source (as opposed to Agent) is not discussed.

In Fillmore (1977*a*:98f) he contrasts Goal and Patient with the verb *shoot* as the case for *Harry* in (58a-b) respectively. Source is proposed as the case for *gun* in both sentences in (59).

(58a) I shot at Harry.
(58b) I shot Harry.
(59a) I shot a bullet from the gun.
(59b) I shot the gun.

However, in neither of these two articles (1971*a*, 1977*a*) is Fillmore's exact concept of Source and Goal clear. For example, in both the sentences in (60) it appears from his commentary (1971*a*:99) that he regards *hammer* as Patient, *vase* as Goal.

(60a) I broke the hammer on the vase.
(60b) I broke the vase with a hammer.

Anderson's version of Case is very much based on the idea that locational and spatial notions can be extended metaphorically. We have already discussed elsewhere (Chapter 3 Section 2, and this chapter Section 3) the possible parallels between locatives and possessives. Anderson's treatment (1971:100ff) of verbs like *know*, *like* and *want* draws similar evidence (from surface structures in other languages – e.g. Georgian (61), Latin, French and German (62) for verbs of liking, and on paraphrases (63) and residual forms like *methinks* or (German) *mich dünkt* for verbs of knowing) to suggest that Locative is the appropriate (deep) case for such roles.

(61) Svils deda uqvars.
SON-dat LOVE MOTHER-nom
'The son loves his mother.'
(62a) Mihi placet.
(62b) Il me plaît.
(62c) Er gefällt mir.
(Lit.: 'He pleases to me')
(63a) I know the answer.
(63b) The answer is known to me.

Directional or dynamic locatives 'ablative' and 'allative' (Source and Goal) are appropriate (1971:128ff) not only for verbs of motion, but also verbs of transfer like *buy* and *sell* (64), *lend* and *borrow*, *teach* and *learn*; verbs like *thank* (65) and *help* (66) with supporting evidence again from German (66b), and other verbs of non-physical transfer, e.g. *obey* (cf. Basque (67a) and French (67b)). Verbs of perception are also treated as 'locative' (68).

(64a) John sold the book to Mary.
(64b) Mary bought the book from John.
(65a) I thank you.
(65b) I give thanks to you.
(66a) He helps his mother.
(66b) Er hilft seiner Mutter.
(67a) Obeditzen dio aitari.
OBEY-HE aux TO-FATHER
'He obeys his father.'
(67b) Il obéit à son père.
(68a) The rose smells nice.
(68b) The rose gives off a nice smell.
(68c) It smells nice to me.

Grimes's (1975) treatment of metaphorical Source and Goal is quite explicit, since he first postulates four distinct cases – Source and Goal in verbs of motion (p. 120) as 'orientation roles', and Material and Result in states and processes (p. 125) as 'process roles' – and then noting that they form pairs of 'complementary variants of a single set of roles' (p. 133) which he terms Former and Latter. Grimes exemplifies Material and Result in (69).

(69a) She makes dresses from flour sacks.
(69b) She makes flour sacks into dresses.

Of all the treatments of Source and Goal in their metaphorical extension, Teng's (1975:126ff) is the most idiosyncratic. In fact Teng is mostly concerned with his Goal case. He notes that Halliday (1967/68), on whose work his overall thesis is loosely based, has a role named Goal, but that Halliday's Goal is most like the Patient or Object of mainstream Case grammar (cf. Halliday, 1970:147), and should therefore not concern us here. Teng proposes two distinct types of Goal: the Transitivity Goal (T-Goal) contrasts with his Patient and Range cases, the Circumstantial Goal (C-Goal) is in contrast with Source. The T-Goal is generally defined as the 'state a Patient changes into' or the 'location whereupon an activity is, in a loose sense, executed' (p. 131). Examples given show that this Goal is realised as the object of verbs such as *like*, *resemble*, *hit*, *look for*. In contrast with Anderson's analysis, with verbs like *know* T-Goal is the thing known rather than the possessor of knowledge. Teng's reasoning is that these verbs have in common the notion of the property expressed by the verb being directed towards something: in the case of *like* it is 'fondness', in the case of *know* it is 'knowledge'. Teng attempts to contrast his T-Goal and Patient by comparing the verbs *buy* and *sell*. With *sell*, the object sold is disposed of, and therefore Patient; with *buy* the object is sought after and acquired, and therefore T-Goal. Note that for Teng it is not the buyer who is T-Goal, but the thing bought, in parallel with the verbs *like*, *look for*, *want*. Although Teng does not admit any conflict here, there is clearly an area of doubt when this T-Goal is more or less glossed as 'recipient' (p. 130). Remember however that Teng has a Benefactive role (cf. Section 3.2) for the role of intended or actual recipient. Teng's T-Goal seems to have a lot in common with Pāṇini's *karma*, usually associated with Patient, but glossed as '. . . that which is primarily *desired* by the *kartā* [Agent]' (Ananthanarayana, 1970:16) [emphasis mine], '. . . that *kāraka* which the agent aims at above all' (Rocher, 1964:47), '. . . a goal, destination which is desired to be achieved through [the] activity by the agent' (Singh, 1974:288).

The treatment of verbs of cognition, perception and emotion in terms of metaphorical direction can be quite problematic. We want to characterise these verbs as expressing motion of something towards something else, but it is not always clear which direction is the obvious one. With verbs of perception it is perhaps more intuitive to think in terms of an object emitting something perceivable which is received by the perceiver. In the case of emotion, which way does the process apply? When I make a statement like (70a) do I imply that girls emit something likeable that I receive (cf. (70b)), or that I emit something towards them (cf. (70c))? Note that *like* is not simply commutative, which would otherwise explain the duality, since (70a) does not imply (70d)! The same problem arises with verbs of cognition (71).

(70a) I like girls.
(70b) Girls are likeable to me. [cf. Les filles me plaisent.]
(70c) From me fondness emanates towards girls.
(70d) Girls like me.
(71a) I know Clacton.
(71b) Clacton is known to me.
(71c) I am a source [*sic*] of knowledge with regard to Clacton.

Teng's concept of C-Goal is much less controversial, though the distinction between the two types (which does not correspond to our 'inner'/'outer' distinction) is not always obvious. For while verbs like *owe*, *give*, *loan* and *lose to* take a C-goal (p. 145), so do *be angry with*, *be interested in*. The difference seems to lie in whether the Goal is governed by a preposition (in Chinese) (p. 146), and this surface-structure oriented view seems to be a departure from normal practise in Case grammar. Nevertheless, there is at least some consistency in regarding *Bev* in (72a-b) as Goal in both cases, even if paraphrases like (72c) once again suggest that the emotion might just as well be regarded as being directed the other way round.

(72a) I am angry with Bev.
(72b) I like Bev.
(72c) Bev is the source of my (dis)pleasure.

Teng's treatment of Source, notwithstanding the problems already mentioned, is otherwise uncontroversial. One interesting point he makes is that Source (in his use) rarely if ever occurs in states: 'In a simple-verb [i.e. state] construction, the verb indicates either the State a Patient is in or the State a Patient enters (i.e. Goal). No [state] verb is observed to indicate the State a Patient departs from (i.e. Source)' (Teng, 1975:127). Teng concludes his chapter on Source and Goal by noting that there are many verb-pairs which contrast in focusing on Goal or Source, e.g. *buy/sell*, *request/give*, *beat/lose to*. Despite his idiosyncratic understanding of Goal, this is an important point (cf. also Fillmore, 1977*a*), especially when we find that some such verb pairs are not found in other languages as distinct verbs. For example 'borrow' and 'lend' are both *jie* in Chinese and *leihen* in German; 'rent' and 'let' are undistinguished in both Chinese *zu* and French *louer*; similarly, 'bring' and 'take' are in Chinese *na* and Icelandic *finga*; French *apprendre* and Danish *lære* can mean both 'teach' and 'learn' as can *lehren* in southern German variants; and so on. In children's or 'uneducated' language in English such contractions are also found (73).

(73a) That teacher never learns us anything.
(73b) Can I lend a quid off you?

In the discussion so far, we have said nothing of possible metaphorical extensions of Path, and little (besides Anderson's treatment of possessives) of non-directional Locatives. This lacuna in the literature might suggest that no metaphorical extension is possible, and this is the impression one gets, until one looks again at J. Anderson (1971) and Ostler (1980). Remembering that for Anderson, Path is defined as a combination of Loc and Abl, we do indeed find at least one metaphorical extension of Path to Instruments, so that the sentences in (74) are felt to have a parallel case structure (cf. also Anderson, 1977:123).

(74a) They travelled by way of Stirling.
(74b) They travelled by car.

Although Anderson does not take this any further, it is an interesting proposal, especially coupled with various possible extensions already discussed, and in our 'case grid' proposal (Chapter 10) we shall develop it further.

Ostler (1980), whose proposals are superficially similar to our 'case grid' and are considered further in Chapter 10, does include Path in his metaphorical extensions of locative roles. In predications involving descriptions of characteristics, Ostler has 'abstract' Source, Path and Goal, the Goal or 'tendency' being *Mary* in (75), the Source or 'point of reference' being *Birmingham* in (76) while '. . . the abstract path will denote the Respect or characteristic in which the predicate holds' (Ostler, 1980:35) as in (77).

(75a) John is similar to Mary.
(75b) John is getting used to Mary.
(76) London is larger than Birmingham.
(77a) David is long *in the leg*.
(77b) This store is unbeatable *for value*.

The locational cases also extend, as we have seen elsewhere, to possessional and cognitional predicates, and here Ostler proposes metaphorical extensions for Path as well as for others. For Ostler, the 'possessional Path' is '. . . the medium of exchange, the objection *in return for which* the theme [= Patient] passes from the source to the goal' (*ibid.*, p. 37) [emphasis mine] in a predicate of transfer. In a parallel fashion, in a cognitive predicate the Path is the 'medium of communication', as exemplified in (78).

(78a) I told him the news *over the phone*.
(78b) I heard it *with my own ears*.
(78c) Joan witnessed the spectacle *with unbelieving eyes*.

Finally, Ostler proposes a metaphorical Path in his subcategory of volitional predicates: 'The identity of the Path in this context is rather less clear. We shall tentatively identify it with the Stratagem, or means by which the theme's [i.e. wisher's] desires [= Goal] are to be fulfilled' (*ibid.*, p. 41).

6. *Other cases: Comitative and Essive*

In this chapter we have attempted to cover the most important issues in defining the cases, and in the course of our discussion a number of proposals have emerged, and a number of cases put forward. There remain however some small areas of lesser significance which we should briefly consider. Not including some highly idiosyncratic proposals, and also the fairly straightforward

Manner case, there remain two cases which are proposed relatively often which have so far not entered our discussion: Comitative and Essive.

There has been a considerable amount of debate concerning the status of a possible Comitative (or 'accompaniment') case. Included in Fillmore's earliest (1966*b*) case inventory, it has been the particular topic of a number of papers, notably Teng (1970), Walmsley (1971) and Buckingham (1973). Often implicated in discussions of the Instrumental, it also features in Nilsen's (1973) book and in Seiler's (1974) paper.

The main area of discussion seems to be whether Comitative is a true deep case, or merely a surface phenomenon, related to coordination (Teng). An alternative approach (that of Walmsley) is to attempt to combine it with some other case, typically Instrument, because they share the same surface form in almost all languages (Nilsen, 1973:71ff). A third approach is to treat it in deep structure as derived neither from a true case nor from coordination, but as an associated but separate predication (Seiler).

Let us consider first the arguments for treating Comitative as a 'true' case. For one thing, taking Fillmore's characterisation of what cases are, it does seem to correspond to a '. . . type of judgment human beings are capable of making about the events that are going on around them' (Fillmore, 1968*a*:24). If it is a case, then there are certainly some predicates for which it is a complement, notably *accompany*. Furthermore, there are a number of sentence patters containing elements for which no other case assignment is available or suitable. The coordination arguments that we shall consider shortly are said to fail here because of the non-equivalence of paraphrases as in (1)-(3).

(1a) Paul left with Lisa.
(1b) Paul and Lisa left.
(2a) Rod went to the Harwood Room with Jock.
(2b) Rod and Jock went to the Harwood Room.
(3a) Harry saw 'Tootsie' with Lindsey.
(3b) Harry and Lindsey saw 'Tootsie'.

None of the (b) sentences necessarily imply what Teng (1970) calls 'joint participation', i.e. that the coordinands performed the action of the verb together.

A class of verbs often termed 'reciprocal' introduce an interesting element into the Comitative discussion. The ambiguity of sentences like (4a) could be explained by the two possible cases available for one of the participants (cf. (4b-c)).

(4a) The English fought with the French.
(4b) The English fought with [against] the French at Waterloo.
(4c) The English fought with [alongside] the French at Dunkirk.

The whole question of case assignment for these verbs is complicated by the fact that they seem to permit contravention of either the constraint on coordinating different cases (5a) or the one-case-per-clause constraint (5b) (depending on whether the arguments are regarded as representing different cases or not), since (5a-b) are true paraphrases.

(5a) Harry and Yorick met in Aix-en-Provence.
(5b) Harry met Yorick in Aix-en-Provence.

In fact these reciprocal verbs provide fundamental evidence against Comitative as a true case, for these are verbs which happen to require a single plural argument which may be realised as just that (6a), as a coordinated noun-phrase (6b), or as a derived 'surface Comitative' (6c).

(6a) My neighbours are quarrelling.
(6b) Stan and Hilda are quarrelling.
(6c) Stan is quarrelling with Hilda.

Apparent contraventions of this plural-argument constraint (7) must be regarded as elliptical.

(7) Stan is quarrelling.

Before considering the coordination argument further, we should mention one more even more damning argument against Comitative as a true case: Comitatives are always associated with a second case. In (1a) and (2a), the 'Comitative' is also Agent; in (3a) and Experiencer. We can also contrive Patient-Comitatives (8).

(8a) You can pay my bill *with yours*.
(8b) Barbara took David to the zoo *with his friend*.

This is a very important point, stressed by Teng (1979:334) and Buckingham (1973:115), and underlined by Fillmore's (1968*a*:82) distinctive treatment of Comitative as being introduced not by a rewrite of VP like all the other cases, but of NP (9), and sharing the dominating NP's selection restrictions.

(9) N → NP + C

As Nilsen (1973:48) comments, the Comitative relation is between two NPs, not between an NP and the verb. Whatever Comitative is then, it cannot be a case *per se*.

Let us look now at the evidence concerning coordination. The relationship between *and* and *with* as in (1)-(3) was recognised as long ago as Jespersen (1924:90). Both Fillmore (1968*a*) and Lakoff and Peters (1969) attempt to derive both structures from a common underlying structure, the latter proposing that the coordinated structure is basic, the former – as we have seen – claiming the reverse. But we have already seen that sentences with *with* and *and* do not necessarily paraphrase each other. If this does not indicate a different underlying structure, then how can the difference in meaning be explained? Teng's (1970) solution is to admit an ambiguity in coordinated sentences like (10a) and to distinguish between sentential conjunction, where no 'joint participation' is implied (10b), and phrasal conjunction which, along with comitative structures, is subject to a number of identical constraints: we have already seen that the elements concerned must share the same role. Phrasal coordinands and comitatives will share a 'common goal': (10a) in its phrasal conjunction reading allows both (10c) and (10d), but in its sentential conjunction reading there is no comitative form (10e). Phrasal conjuncts are also subject to the same selection restrictions (11).

(10a) John and Ringo sang a song.
(10b) John and Ringo each sang a song.
(10c) John and Ringo sang 'I am the Greatest'.
(10d) John sang 'I am the Greatest' with Ringo.
(10e) * John sang a song with Ringo each.
(11a) * Rod and his cat wrote a letter yesterday.
(11b) * Rod wrote a letter with his cat yesterday.

The main difference, Teng claims, between phrasal conjunctions and comitatives is in the notion of 'principality'. For Teng, the comitative construction introduces a hierarchy among nouns in the same role. Two of his three examples (1970:333f) are fairly convincing (12)-(13). He explains (13) as follows: (13a) does not 'properly express the unfortunate situation of repression'. Perhaps our own example (14) makes the point more clearly: (14a) does not indicate who is the principle occupier of the house in the way that (14b) does.

(12a) Mr and Mrs Li want to go to Japan.
(12b) Mrs Li wants to go to Japan with Mr Li.
(13a) Black people and white people must not walk together.
(13b) Black people must not walk with white people.
(14a) Janet and John are going to live in London.
(14b) Janet is going to live in London with John.

Teng sees this 'principality' feature as the main difference between phrasal conjunctions and comitatives, from which other differences follow. The fact that for every comitative structure there is a phrasal conjunction counterpart but not vice versa suggests to Teng that it is the latter that is basic, with the generation of a comitative structure being enabled by the presence of the principality feature on one of the coordinands. This analysis accords with Jespersen's suggestion that *and* constructions imply coordination while *with* constructions imply subordination. For Teng, then, there is no Comitative case.

The approach of Walmsley (1971) is to show that Comitative can be subsumed under another case, the Instrument. His evidence for this is that first, Comitative cannot be a type of coordination because of the possible differences in meaning of sentence pairs like (1)-(3) above. He notes the possibility of paraphrase with either *accompany* or *assist/help* depending on whether a locative is present or not (15)-(16).

(15a) She went to the funeral with her brother.
(15b) Her brother accompanied her to the funeral.
(16a) The woman killed her husband with an accomplice.
(16b) An accomplice helped the woman to kill her husband.

This suggests to Walmsley a parallelism with the Instrument case, which has a similar paraphrase relationship with the surface verb *use*, as was pointed out in Lakoff's well-known (1968) article. Walmsley's conclusion to treat *accompany*-Comitative, *help*-Comitative and *use*-Instrument as a single deep case is based on the fact that Comitatives and Instruments cannot co-occur (17) (one-case-per-clause constraint),

(17) * She killed her husband with her sister with a hammer.

and that the three 'cases' can be characterised as being in complementary distribution, and marked by the features–animate corresponding to the *use*-variant, and ±locative for *accompany* and *help*. This evidence is further supported (in a weak way) by the range of languages in which Instrument and Comitative share the same realisation possibilities (cf. above and Nilson, 1973:71ff).

Buckingham responds to Walmsley's suggestion critically: '. . . if a linguist is going to propose a theory which seems counterintuitive, then it is his responsibility to provide strong structural evidence for support, but the evidence which Walmsley provides is quite weak' (Buckingham, 1973:116). In particular, the unacceptability of (17) is due to surface structure constraints, especially the contiguity of the two *with* phrases. Nilsen (1973:27) makes the same point with regard to (18). Both Nilsen and Buckingham suggest alternative ways of expressing the same information (19)-(20), showing that Instruments and Comitatives can co-occur.

(18) * The child pounded in the nail with a hammer with his father.
(19a) She, along with her sister, killed her husband with a hammer.
(19b) Together with her sister, she killed her husband with a hammer.
(20a) The child, in the company of his father, pounded in the nail with a hammer.
(20b) The child, accompanied by his father, pounded in the nail with a hammer.
(20c) The child, along with his father, pounded in the nail with a hammer.

Buckingham does not make the further damning point that, to take one of Walmsley's own example sentences (21), we have more evidence that Instrument and Comitative are not the same case, if (21) is regarded as negative evidence for the coordination test: elements in the same case can normally be conjoined.

(21) * She killed her husband with her sister and a hammer.

Walmsley's suggested paraphrases with *accompany* and *help*, and their parallel with *use*, do however suggest a fourth possible analysis, presented by Seiler (1974) and termed 'concomitant predication'. This is once again the view of Lakoff (1968), who suggested that Instrument was not a deep case but that sentences like (22a) and (22b) are derived from a common underlying deep structure, perhaps something like (22c).

(22a) Seymour sliced the salami with a knife.
(22b) Seymour used a knife to slice the salami.
(22c) Seymour used a knife + Seymour sliced the salami.

Seiler proposes the same kind of analysis for Comitatives, but Welin (1975:45) suggests that this analysis could be taken even further. While Seiler restricts the notion of concomitant predication to Instruments and Comitatives, or more precisely to prepositional phrases with *mit* ('with'), Welin suggests that Seiler's characterisation of the concomitant predication as relating to both the subject and the main verb simultaneously '. . . is in full accordance with the description in traditional Swedish grammar of the grammatical function "predikativt attribut" (predicative attribute). Most prepositional phrases, adjectival phrases, and participles can function as a predicative attribute of a sentence. This can relate either to the subject or to the object of the sentence, and simultaneously it relates to the main verb, or the entire sentence' (Welin, 1975:45). Welin goes on to describe the treatment of such phenomena in the framework of generative grammar, and concludes with the important principle that '. . . a main predication and a concomitant predication together describe something that the speaker (or writer) conceives of as *one unitary action, process, relation or state*. If such a description is paraphrased by means of a main clause and a subordinate clause, one will inevitably say something different. One will split up the unitary action etc. into two different actions, or an action and a state, and introduce some kind of mediating relationship between them' (*ibid*. pp. 46f) [emphasis mine]. The key notion, with which I agree, of the unitariness of the predications we have been considering seems to drive us back to the notion of Comitative as a true case (though this is not exactly Welin's conclusion).

In this respect, Seiler notes, most interestingly, that there seem to be different degrees of participation with Comitatives ranging from vague accompaniment or helping through to full partnership or reciprocity. It is my own feeling that some sort of answer lies in this distinction. Since the argument for regarding Comitative as a concomitant predication is not really an argument against regarding it as a case (merely a statement about some deeper representation of its origins, more divorced from surface structure than we might care to go – the same can be said of Lakoff's proposal for Instrument), we have now a counter-proposal to our strong conclusion that Comitative is not a true case. In the case of partnership or reciprocity, as exemplified by sentences like (4c) and (6c) above, as well as the joint-partnership readings of (1)-(3), there seem to be good reasons for regarding the Comitative as a form of coordination, the key factor being that the Comitative is 'governed' by another case cf. ((8)). But where simple accompaniment is meant, as in (19) and (20), and also in sentences like (23) – discussed by Buckingham (1973:115) – where Mary does not actually eat any of the pie, it is more difficult to think of the semantic structure as one of coordination.

(23) He ate the pie with Mary.

Notice too sentences like (24a), where analysis in terms of coordination is rather strained, since (24b) seems to miss something of the meaning of (24a) expressed by the preposition *without*. Indeed in (24a) there is no indication whether or not the girlfriend stayed at the party (or had already left), unlike in (24b). In terms of a Comitative deep case realised by a negative argument, this distinction could perhaps be better brought out.

(24a) He left the party without his girlfriend.

(24b) He left the party, but his girlfriend didn't.

Finally, if we do accept the Comitative as a deep case for

accompaniment, we do of course have a number of verbs for which it is a complement: if we do not posit such a case, then these arguments must presumably be analysed much more neutrally as a Patient. This then is a further factor in favour of positing a Comitative case, but for a more restricted range of roles than foreseen in some of the literature.

Let us now turn to the question of the 'Essive' case. Nominal predications like those in (25) have been seen as a problem for Case grammar, and have led some authors to introduce an Essive case.

(25a) John is an idiot.
(25b) A hammer is an important tool.
(25c) That man is a good teacher.

In most cases, Stockwell *et al.* (1973) being the prime example, Essive is proposed as the case of the complement of the copular. That the copular is not a special case of a predicate taking a deep coordination is reflected in the fact that (26a) is barely acceptable, and is certainly not a paraphrase of (25a); (26b) likewise does not mean the same as (25b). Also, structures such as (26c) are not possible.

(26a) ? An idiot is John.
(26b) An important tool is a hammer.
(26c) * John and an idiot are.

Stockwell *et al.* extend the range of the Essive case to cover prepositional complements of the copular, as in (27).

(27) That book is by Chomsky.

Nilsen sums up the dilemma facing us with this type of construction: 'The concept of Predicate Nominative is a concept of surface structure. It is therefore difficult to see how a deep case label (Essive) can be assigned to a surface phenomenon. On the other hand, if it is argued that Essive is not a deep case, then we must assign the correct deep case label . . .' (Nilsen, 1973:25f).

Anderson's (1977:127) criticism of the notion lies in the fact that it appears that there is only one verb in the lexicon which requires an Essive, namely *be*. Furthermore, to handle a sentence like (28) it would appear that Essives must be allowed to contravene the one-case-per-argument constraint, since *in Switzerland* is clearly a Locative, or else we must hypothesise two distinct verbs *to be*.

(28) That village is in Switzerland.

We might ask if *be* is indeed the only verb in the lexicon that requires an Essive. The process verb *become* is closely related to *be* in its distribution, but presumably takes a metaphorical Goal case for its complement. There are no parallels to look at since for other state/process verb pairs the state verb is either monovalent, or takes a Locative. However, a change in case frame feature resulting only from a modality feature like process (cf. Somers, 1982*c*:258) does not seem a particularly attractive solution.

A radically different approach is suggested by Fillmore's (1968*a*:84) treatment of nominal predicates. He notes that sentences of the type N *be* N are often actions rather than states: witness the possibility of imperativisation (29a) and occurrence in the progressive (29b).

(29a) Don't be a fool.

(29b) He's being a bastard again.

This suggests that the second noun phrase is in fact acting as a predicate, and the verb *be* is merely a surface element. Many languages (e.g. Russian, Hebrew) lack a copular (30), so the question of its case frame features never arises.

(30a) Ivan moj drug.
IVAN MY FRIEND
'Ivan is my friend.'

(30b) Av-ij m'lamer
FATHER-MY TEACHER
'My father is a teacher.'

Parallels between predicative nominals and adjectives (31) reinforce this interpretation, especially when adjectives occur as nominals, as in certain constructions in English (32), and more freely in, for example, German (33) and French (34).

(31a) He is blind.

(31b) He is a blind man.

(32) The blind suffer many hardships.

(33a) Er ist blind.

(33b) Er ist ein Blinder.

(34a) Il est aveugle.

(34b) C'est un aveugle.

Although this treatment of predicate nominals presents problems for the lexicon (should all nouns appear also as 'verbs' with associated case-frame features?), these can probably be overcome via some generalisation, and the case for an Essive case seems fairly weak.

EIGHT

ONE-CASE-PER-ARGUMENT: DUAL ROLES

In this chapter we shall discuss one of the major problems for Case grammar, that of 'dual roles': it will be remembered that one of the constraints proposed by Fillmore (1968*a*:24) is that each argument is associated with just one case, so that there is a one-to-one matching of cases and arguments in any proposition. The contravention of this constraint in certain circumstances has been recognised by many authors, and such examples have variously been termed dual, double, coreferential, covalent, conflicting or multiple roles. The problem arises in a number of verb classes which are fairly easy to characterise, and it can be broadly subdivided into cases involving the 'locational' relations Source and Goal, for which our 'case grid' proposal (Chapter 10) will offer a solution, and those which do not, which are more problematic.

1. *Dual roles involving Source and Goal*

Several classes of verbs take arguments where roles can be characterised both by one of the 'locative' cases of Source or Goal and another case, most often Agent. These classes include verbs of transfer, communication, propulsion, and (in Longacre's (1976) analysis) verbs of judging. Verb pairs denoting transfer either of goods (*buy/sell*) or some abstract entity (*teach/learn*) are often taken as classical instances of this problem. Fillmore discusses such verbs in both (1971*a*:378) and at length in (1972). As he states in this latter article: '[One of] The most serious difficulties [has] to do with . . . determining whether or not it would turn out to be necessary, at least for some verbs, to interpret certain arguments as serving two role functions simultaneously' (Fillmore, 1972:15). It is clear that verbs of transfer such as the pair *buy* and *sell* have in common a case structure involving the original possessor (Source), the subsequent possessor (Goal) as well as the item being transferred (Patient) and, sometimes, the price or whatever paid for the exchange (let us say Instrument for the sake of argument – this is not an issue here). Overlaid onto this scheme is the notion of instigator (Agent) as reflected in the choice of *buy* or *sell* as in (1):

(1) *buy* Agent = Goal
sell Agent = Source

If the notion of agency is regarded as primary, the obvious parallel between the two verbs is obscured (2). If on the other hand the Source or Goal specification is retained at the expense of specifying the Agent, the difference between the two is lost (3), or at least only captured in relating deep and surface case (i.e. choice of Source versus Goal as surface subject determines the choice of surface verb) as in Dik's Functional Grammar (Chapter 6). A third solution is to involve an additional level of labelling reflecting 'focus' or 'topicalisation', having obvious (but not trivial) correlations with syntactic functions, as in (4) (order of cases is significant). This is the approach hinted at in Fillmore's (1977*a*:104ff) treatment of *buy*, *sell*, *cost* and *pay*.

(2) *buy* [Agent Patient Source Instrument]
sell [Agent Patient Goal Instrument]
(3) *buy* [Source Goal Patient Instrument]
sell [Source Goal Patient Instrument]
(4) *buy* [Goal Patient Source Instrument]
sell [Source Patient Goal Instrument]
cost [Patient Instrument Goal]
pay [Goal Instrument Source Patient]

The alternative of attributing two roles to a single argument contravenes the principle of unicity of cases to arguments, a solution which undermines an otherwise useful constraint (useful in delimiting the range of cases necessary), and in any case regarded by some commentators (e.g. Niéger, 1973:44) as 'unnatural'.

Welin (1975) suggests that the conflict stems from the different levels of abstraction involved in the distinction of the Agent versus the Source/Goal distinction: 'If one wants the case frame to provide substantial information about the roles of the arguments, one is generally tempted to define the cases in referential terms, i.e. one invents criteria of case membership which specify features of typical referent situations and predicates. But the "typical referent situation" of a predicate can as a rule be described on several different levels and from several different points of view, and the nature of the participation of a given argument may change with the level or point of view. It follows that it will in many instances be quite difficult to decide which case role of an argument should be regarded as the "dominant", which of two conflicting criteria should be regarded as the stronger one . . .' (Welin, 1975:42f).

To illustrate this further, consider two examples. In his (1972) discussion of verbs of buying and selling, Fillmore introduces the notional roles of Merchant, Customer, Goods and Payment. Note that these are not cases as such, but 'map' (in some sense) onto more familiar cases. But now we have an even deeper level of abstraction (from surface form), there are even more complications. For the Merchant is the source of the Goods, but the goal of the Payment. So if we consider verbs like *pay* and *charge*, where the focus is on the transfer from Customer to Merchant of the Payment rather than of the Goods, we get yet another set of case configurations. Welin's own exemplification of this situation is with verbs of communication, where we have a Sender, a Receiver and a Message. The Sender is typically Agent, and as such is the Source of the Message. From the point of view of the Sender, the Message could be regarded as Goal in the sense of Factitive. From the point of view of the Receiver (Goal, in the sense of Recipient of the Message) the Message can be regarded as Source in the sense of Stimulus (Figure 1).

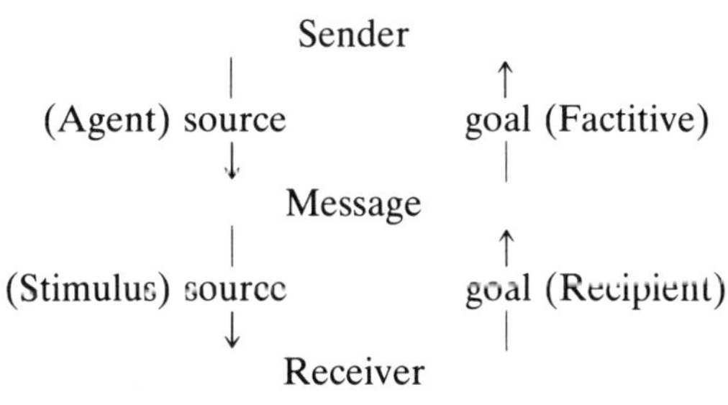

Figure 1.

Two solutions to this particular version of the 'dual roles' problem seem appropriate. With regard to the multiplicity of relations illustrated above, especially in *buy/sell* versus *charge/pay*, we must first fix a level of abstraction beyond which we will invoke other means to capture relationships if necessary. If we wish to keep Case at a relatively shallow level of semantics, it is probably desirable to stop at the level where only one range of roles is variable (e.g. Agent versus non-Agent), but where Source and

Goal remain constant. If we do not, we are forced to analyse such predicates as involving two primitive tranfers (as Welin suggests), which seems to involve us in semantics too far beyond the lexical level. The alternative is to recognise that we have two different systems at work here, one involving directionality and the other conveying notions of agency, and other elements. This is the basis of the proposal we shall present later. It is also seen in the recent work of Willis and Jeffreys (1983:16), who regard the directional 'cases' Source, Path and Goal as subcategorising (some of) their other cases; and it is also at the heart of J. Anderson's (1971) 'localistic' version of Case (cf. Chapter 3).

2. *Other instances of duality*

We now turn to the rather more problematic area of instances where cases other than directional ones appear to combine. Notably here we have verbs of motion, where Agent and Patient are sometimes coreferential, verbs of perception where the Experiencer can be ±agentive, and some other individual instances.

The conflict of Agent and Patient is most clearly seen in verbs of motion. Fillmore (1971*a*:376ff) compares verbs like *rise*, *arise*, *ascend* and *lift*, which entail combinations of A[gentive] and O[bjective], as illustrated in (1):

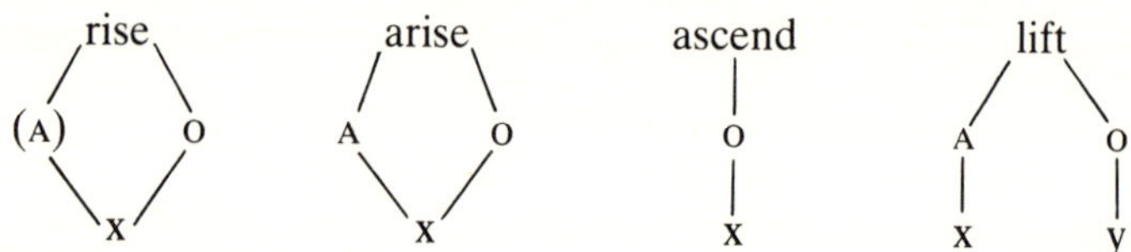

(1a) (1b) (1c) (1d)

For each of the verbs, the O case is for the entity which undergoes the change of position. With *rise*, this O may or may not be simultaneously A (2a-b) while with *arise* it is always A (2c-d). *Ascend* has no possible Agentive use (2e), while *lift* separates the two roles (2f). Missing from Fillmore's representation is the use of *lift* as an ergative verb, partially mirroring *ascend* (2g).

(2a) John rose.
(2b) The smoke rose.
(2c) John arose.
(2d) * The smoke arose.
(2e) * John ascended.
(2f) John lifted the lid.
(2g) The lid lifted (without any trouble).

The problem is a general one for verbs of motion like *rise*: if Patient is the appropriate case for the entity that undergoes a change of state in sentences like (3a-b), then so it should be too for *Dave* in (3c): but *Dave* in (3c) is at the same time the instigator of the movement, just as *Paul* is in (3a).

(3a) Paul moved the wardrobe.
(3b) The wardrobe moved.
(3c) Dave moved.

Cook (1972*b*:59f) discusses this problem briefly, pointing out the duality of the Agent/Object, but analyses these verbs of motion as 'action locatives', although giving no reason for considering the notion of agency as primary. Interestingly, he suggests different case assignments for the two readings of (4a) illustrated in (4b,c) where *John* is Object and Agent respectively.

(4a) John went to hospital.
(4b) John went to hospital in an ambulance.
(4c) John went to hospital on foot.

In my own earlier discussion of this problem (Somers, 1982*c*:249) I suggested three possible solutions with regard to locating verbs of motion in a Cookian case-frame matrix, one of which (not very helpfully) was to consider them as falling outside the system. The other two solutions seem more reasonable: one was to create a new case, say 'Moved', which, if agentive (on problems with this notion, see Chapter 7 Section 2), blocks the filling of both Agent and Patient slots by some other argument, but if not corresponds exactly to Patient. The alternative and I now think preferable solution was to regard verbs of motion as 'action-process-locational' verbs, i.e. taking the three cases Agent, Patient and Locative, noting that when Agent and Patient slots are not both filled, this is either because they are coreferential, or because the Agent is unknown or unstated. This seems attractive because it captures the three uses of *move* in (3) and reflects the inherent ambiguity in a sentence like (5a), where we do not know if the case assignments should parallel those of (5b) – *Rosie* having been pushed or having slipped – or of (5c), the roll being deliberate and therefore agentive.

(5a) Rosie rolled down the hill.
(5b) The boulder rolled down the hill.
(5c) Rosie ran down the hill.

Furthermore, it suggests a nice case assignment (to Patient) for the reflexive pronoun in languages like French, where some verbs of motion are not ambiguous as to agentivity (6a-d). Note that for *lever* ('raise') the Patient is obligatory (6c), and (6d-e) show that the Agent can only be omitted via passivisation, (though the possibility of passivisation via the use of the reflexive (6f) – cf. (6g) – clouds the issue slightly).

(6a) Dominique se leva.
'Dominique got up.'
(6b) Dominique leva le couvercle.
'Dominique lifted the lid.'
(6c) * Dominique leva.
(6d) * Le couvercle leva.
(6e) Le couvercle fut levé
'The lid was lifted.'
(6f) Le couvercle se leva.
'The lid rose.'
(6g) Les gâteaux se vendent ici.
'Cakes are sold here.'

Finally, verbs of motion behave like both action and process verbs in tests like the 'do'-test and 'happen'-test (7) (cf Chapter 4 Section 2), lending further support to this analysis.

(7a) What happened to Rosie? She rolled down the hill.
(7b) What did Rosie do? She rolled down the hill.

In fact, we can say that the only distinction between verbs of motion and other action-process verbs is that when they occur with only one argument (other than Locative) (so-called ergative use) there is a reasonable chance that the Agent will not have been omitted, as is the usual case, but may have been combined with the Object. Note however that with some motion verbs which are essentially intransitive (e.g. *travel*, *run*) though which are 'completable' (as in *run a mile*, with the complement not usually regarded as filling the Patient case slot), the Patient and Agent are obligatorily combined, and there is no true use parallel with (3a) above in which the two roles are separated. Note however, the apparent ergative use as in (8a) suggesting this possibility which one would expect to be expressed in (8b), but which for some reason is not found.

(8a) This wine travels well.
(8b) * You can travel this wine.

Other verbs for which the Agent and Patient are coreferential are suggested by Longacre (1976:47), and include verbs like *wash* and *shave*. Like verbs of motion, Agent and Patient can be coreferential (9a) or not (9b), but unlike verbs of motion, it is the Patient that is essentially optional: (9c) cannot be read as meaning the same as (9d) where it is clear that *Nick* is Patient, not Agent.

(9a) Nick shaved yesterday.
(9b) The barber shaved the customer.

(9c) Nick shaves quite often at the barber's.
(9d) Nick gets shaved quite often at the barber's.

Again, French typically requires both the Agent and the Patient to be expressed, the latter if necessary as a reflexive pronoun (10).

(10a) Le barbier rasa le client.
'The barber shaved the customer.'
(10b) Nick se rasa hier.
'Nick shaved yesterday.'

Unfortunately, this assignment of the reflexive pronoun as Patient looks a little more dubious in the face of sentences like (11a), where *visage* ('face') seems a more likely candidate (unless it is Locative?), with the reflexive *se* as Experiencer, especially considering (11b), where *barbe* ('beard') is an even clearer candidate for Patient, with the surface dative *lui* as Experiencer – cf. also (11c), where the surface case of reflexive *se* is shown to be dative rather than accusative by the lack of number concord with the past participle *rasé* ('shaved').

(11a) Daniele se lava le visage.
'Daniele washed her face.'
(11b) Le barbier lui rasa la barbe.
'The barber shaved his [someone else's] beard.'
(11c) Ils se sont rasé [*rasés].
'They shaved.'

In this case though we still have a dual role problem one way or the other (in comparing English (12) with French (11c)): Agent and Experiencer are combined, unless we choose to regard the reflexive as a purely surface phenomenon.

(12) They washed their hands.

Sentence pairs like (13) however suggest that the problem is rather more complex, and one recalls Fillmore's (1968*a*:23) treatment of sentence pairs like (14), where if *fender* is Instrument in (14a), it is presumably also there in (14b): similarly we must account for the fact that in (13b) the Experiencer ends up as a possessive adjective. (Actually Fillmore does it the other way round, suggesting that *with its fender* is derived from the possessive and is not a case-bearing argument at all; cf. on this subject Dougherty, 1970).

(13a) Claude m'a lavé les pieds.
(13b) Claude washed my feet.
(14a) The car broke the window with its fender.
(14b) The car's fender broke the window.

We shall return to the question of Agent/Experiencer duality shortly, but we should not leave the Agent/Patient conflict without briefly considering the special case of causative constructions. The problem here is that when action verbs occur in causative constructions the Patient undergoing the causation is also the Agent of the caused predication. This is especially complex when the 'causee' (to borrow Saksena's (1980) term) is being caused to move, because we already have an Agent/Patient conflict with verbs of motion. Thus in (15) the soldiers are the Patient of the sergeant's action, but simultaneously Agent/Patient of the verb *march*.

(15) The sergeant marched the soldiers across the parade ground.

Saksena's (1980) data from Hindi suggest that the concept of an 'affected agent' (i.e. an Agent having a Patient-like function) is recognised in surface syntax: the causee in a Hindi causative is differentially marked as (surface) dative or instrumental depending on whether it is affected by its own action or not (16). (Compare van Oosten's (1977) notion of 'responsible' Patient-subjects, discussed in Chapter 7 Section 2).

(16a) mãĩ-nee raam-koo khaanaa khil-aa-yaa.
I-agt RAM-dat FOOD EAT-cause-past
'I made Ram eat some food.'

(16b) mãĩ-nee raam-see peer kaṭ-aa-yaa
I-agt RAM-inst TREE CUT-cause-past
'I made Ram cut down the tree.'

Saksena enumerates the verb classes which take an affected Agent (at least according to Hindi data) and these include verbs of perception and motion, and also verbs like *drink* and *read*. She adduces (p. 822) independent evidence for this notion from languages like French and Spanish, where (some) verbs taking affected Agents are reflexive (e.g. French *se lever* ('get up'), *s'asseoir* ('sit down'), Spanish *acostarse* ('lie down') and *levarse* ('get up')). Saksena also suggests that in English verbs with non-affected Agents do not form lexical causatives; thus while the postverbal position with a verb like *bathe* is filled by the affected Agent (17) and likewise (in a child's utterance) with *dance* (18), this construction is not available for verbs taking non-affected Agents: (19b) is not a causativisation of (19a).

(17a) John bathed.
(17b) I bathed John.
(18) Mommy, please dance me again.
(19a) John cut down a tree.
(19b) I cut John down a tree.

However, Saksena's observation tells us little, for with transitive verbs the preferred role for this element is Benefactive (19b) and if that reading is unlikely, the sentence is ungrammatical (20). So the construction is only available for affected Agents in intrinsically 'intransitive' (i.e. action?) verbs like *feed* (21) or *get up* (22), and not by any means for all the sample verbs listed by Saksena (p. 821) as affected-Agent verbs (e.g. (23)-(25)).

(20) * The wicked witch ate Snowhite the poisoned apple.
(21a) The monkey fed.
(21b) I fed the monkey.
(22a) Karen got up early.
(22b) I got Karen up early.
(23a) The child ran away.
(23b) * The angry parent ran the child away.
(24a) The startled cat jumped.
(24b) I jumped the startled cat. [≮ (24a)]
(25a) I was reading.
(25b) * My mother read me.

Our final list of examples of dual role verbs are those verbs of agentive perception like *look*, *listen*, *feel*, *taste*, *smell*. We have noted elsewhere (e.g. Chapter 7 Section 3) that these verbs form (sometimes lexically identical) pairs with non-agentive *see*, *hear*, *touch*, *taste* and *smell*. Similarly we have cognition verb pairs like *learn* versus *know*, *invent* versus *discover*, and various experiential processes which can be expressed differently if intentionality is to be specified, e.g. *warm oneself* versus *become warm*, *cheer oneself up* versus *cheer up* (though in these cases the reflexive pronoun is again available to fill the non-agentive role).

The point about these verb pairs is that when they are lexically identical, we are faced with either positing two lexical entries – one with Agent and the other with Experiencer – and/or treating them as ambiguous. Huddleston points out the difficulty in making '. . . the analysis reflect both the common component here and also the differentiating one' (Huddleston, 1970:507), and the fact that separating the verb types 'shows only the difference, not the similarity' (p. 509). That the distinction is important can be seen when we consider translational equivalents, where the distinction not made in English is made in some other languages (e.g. *taste* = French *goûter* versus *sentir*) or vice versa (e.g. Japanese *miru* = *see/look*). Various devices are used to establish or demonstrate the Agent versus Experiencer uses. Clark (1971) points out that test frames used to distinguish states and non-states (notably actions) also serve this purpose, for example use of the command imperative (26), co-occurrence with *persuade* (27) and manner adverbials like *carefully*, and occurrence in the progressive (28).

(26a) * Smell onions!
(26b) Smell the rose!
(27a) * I persuaded Bev to know German.
(27b) I persuaded Bev to learn German.
(28a) * I am smelling something delicious.
(28b) I am smelling my uncle's prize tea rose.

Clark cites Boyd and Thorne's (1969) observation that expression of the progressive aspect with non-agentive verbs is achieved via the model *can* as in (29).

(29) I can see the blackboard.

The difference of use of *can* between agentive and non-agentive experiential verbs is important when we consider translation: with agentive verbs it has its 'permission' or 'ability' meaning (30), but with non-agentives a translation in this vein (in French) would be erroneous (31).

(30a) I can taste your apple-pie (now that my cold is better).
(30b) Je peux *goûter* votre tarte aux pommes (maintenant que je ne suis plus enrhûmé).
(31a) I can taste garlic in this omelette.
(31b) * Je peux goûter de l'ail dans cette omelette.
(31c) Je *sens* de l'ail dans cette omelette.

In some languages, the Agent/Experiencer distinction may not be lexicalised at all, but expressed by some regular morphosyntactic device. This is the case in Chinese (Teng, 1975:54) where we have *kan* ('look') versus *kan-jian* ('see'), *ting* ('listen') versus *ting-jian* or *ting-dao* ('hear'), and *wen* versus *wen-dao* (both 'smell'), the marked form in each case being non-agentive. The situation in German is similar where a number of separable prefixes perform this function: *hören* ('hear') versus *zuhören* ('listen'), *sehen* ('see') versus *ansehen* ('look'), *schmecken* versus *herausschmecken* (both 'taste').

3. *A valency solution?*

I want in this section to express briefly a view of this dual role problem that I find appealing, though I admit it might be rather difficult to put into practice. It is generally recognised that Case and Valency are closely related, especially in that the 'valency pattern' of the verb defines, like its 'case frame features', the number and type of arguments a verb takes. The notion of 'valency' is borrowed from Chemistry, where a certain value associated with each element determines the way in which it combines with other elements (or radicals). The most simplistic illustration (1), taken from Brown (1953), shows one atom of aluminium (A1) as having three 'arms' or 'hooks' all of which must be 'used up' when forming a compound: when aluminium oxide is formed, each oxygen (O) atom uses up two hooks, and so the 2:3 ratio of A1 to O atoms is arrived at.

(1) 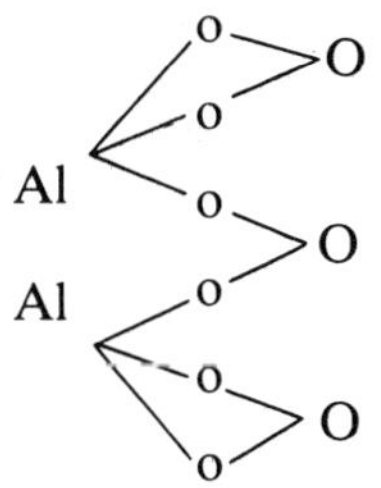

Russell's (1971) account of the development of this notion in Chemistry is very interesting, and shows that advances in the understanding of the electronic properties of elements have revealed that the traditional numerical notion is a vast oversimplification, but still has some value.

Let us consider how far the analogy between Chemistry and Linguistics goes. In fact Linguistic Valency (LV) is a fairly impoverished replica of Chemical Valency (CV), and it is in enriching the analogy that I hope to address the dual role problem. The main differences between CV and LV is that while in the former all elements have a valency, ranging usually from one to four, but variable for a number of elements, in the latter only a certain class of 'elements' (predicates) have a valency, though again in the same range (not including avalents), and only occasionally variable. Perhaps we should rather say that in LV, predicates have a range of possible valency values, but their arguments always have a valency value of one: this is a key issue. Consider a verb of motion, e.g. *roll*, as having valency three. If we take Brown's 'hooks' analogy, we can say that such a verb has three hooks that must be used up, and we can illustrate this as in (2).

(2) 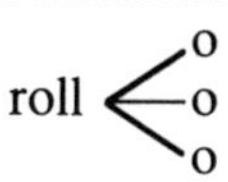

In LV these hooks are actually differentiated as to the type of thing they can be used by or hook onto: in this instance let us call the hooks Agent (A), Patient (P) and Locative (L) (3).

(3) roll < A / P / L

Now in a sentence like (4a), all three hooks are used up, each by monovalent arguments which, by dint of various combinations of syntactic and semantic properties (analogous to physical properties in elements) can be attributed to the appropriate 'hook feature', so that the predication is complete (4b).

(4a) Paul rolled the stone down the hill.

(4b) roll < A — Paul
P — stone
L — down the hill

In the case of a sentence like (5a), we want to say that one of the hooks is unused, but this is legitimate because this verb permits this structure. What we really want to say is that here *roll* is exhibiting its other valency value (5b).

(5a) The stone rolled down the hill.

(5b) roll < P — stone
L — down the hill

This is not however the case in the non-accidental reading of (6a), where we want to say that this is the trivalent *roll*, but that two of its hooks are being used up by a single argument (6b).

(6a) Paul rolled down the hill.

(6b) roll < A — Paul
P — Paul
L — down the hill

This is quite normal in CV: the compound-forming substances divide up into classes that are analagous to our predicates on the one hand (radicals such as SO_4, NO_3, etc., and certain key elements like carbon, hydrogen, oxygen, chlorine, etc.) and arguments on the other (the remaining elements), this division corresponding to a difference in ion charge. The crucial difference is that the 'arguments' in CV are not constrained to have a valency value of one. So for example the divalent 'predicate' carbonate (CO_3) can combine with two monovalent 'arguments' (e.g. sodium (Na)) (7a), but both its valences can be used up by a single divalent 'argument' (e.g. calcium (Ca)) (7b). Note that the two monovalent arguments can either be the same element, as in (7a), or two different elements (7c), giving a picture more like the LV analogy.

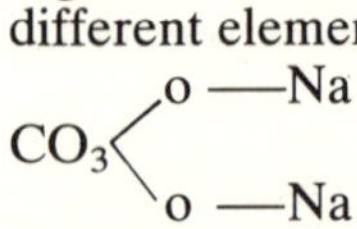

(7a) Na_2CO_3

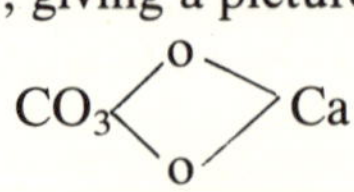

(7b) $CaCO_3$

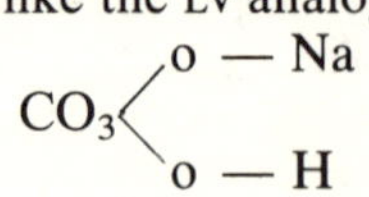

(7c) $NaHCO_3$

The required extension of the analogy to LV is to allow arguments sometimes to have a valency other than one, so that (6a) is represented as (8).

(8) roll 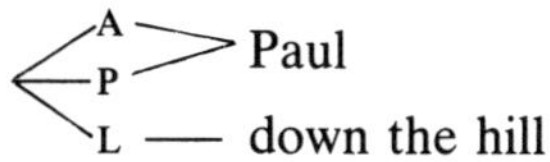

The types of elements that form arguments could be said to 'prefer' to be of valency one, but under certain circumstances can have a different valency value. The analogy with CV persists, since many of the multivalent elements have a 'preferred' valency: for example ferrous compounds (Fe^2) are easier to form than ferric ones (Fe^3), and carbon dioxide (with C^4) forms more spontaneously than carbon monoxide (with C^2). The only problem – and it is substantial – with the LV version is determining and describing the circumstances that invite an argument slot filler to change its valency. In a sense that is what we have done in describing verbs of motion above: put now into extended LV terms, we can say that verbs of motion (trivalent) may invoke a valency change (mono- to di-) in arguments having certain properties, and so on. I admit that I am unclear how useful this proposal could be, but I at least draw some satisfaction from improving the quality of the valency analogy, even if in Chemistry the numerical valency notion is now demoded.

NINE

ONE-CASE-PER-CLAUSE: 'INNER' VERSUS 'OUTER' ROLES

A mainstay of Case grammars is Fillmore's (1968*a*:21) proposal that 'each case relationship occurs only once in a simple sentence'. This constraint has come to be known mostly as the 'one-case-per-clause' constraint, and, as we have seen in Chapter 7, is often invoked, along with the 'coordination constraint', as a criterion for distinguishing different cases: if an apparent contravention of the 'one-case-per-clause' constraint cannot be analysed as an instance of coordination or as subordination then we must have two different cases.

The constraint is not without its detractors, and in particular 'minimalist' Case theories like that of J. Anderson strongly reject the principle. But we maintain that it is one of the few firm principles on which Case is based, and without which the notion of deep case is a relatively arbitrary labelling convention of little use. Certainly, at first sight, there seems to be no intuitive logical reasons why the constraint should apply: why should each semantic relation associated with a verb be realised by only one entity? But the important distinction to make is between a multiplicity of arguments filling the same role, and a semantically plural single argument filling the role. It should be clear that in (1a) we have two entities jointly filling the Agent role, but just as in (1b) this is a single role filled by a plural argument, not a contravention of the constraint.

(1a) *Rod and Sandra* invited me for dinner.
(1b) *They* invited me for dinner.

We shall not dwell here on Case theories like that of Anderson where this constraint appears to have been rejected, because Anderson's four 'cases' (see Chapter 3) are in reality case features which combine to define several discrete 'cases' in the traditional sense which, although Anderson does not stress this, do in fact conform to the principle.

More serious however are Nilsen's (1973:23ff) reasons for rejecting the principle, since Nilsen's Case grammar is essentially on traditional lines. Nilsen cites equational and symmetric predicates as contravening the constraint, rejecting the introduction of a case like Essive for one of the arguments (cf. Chapter 7 Section 6). His main reason for rejecting the Essive for equatives like (2) is that these are predicative nominals and should be considered to be the predicate themselves, with the apparent predicator *be* analysed as only a surface element. As we saw, there is some support for this approach from languages lacking a copular in such sentences.

(2) John is a lackey.

Nilsen's arguments regarding symmetric predicates like *resemble* are easier to refute. He suggests that the difference between (3a) and (3b) is only one of thematisation (cf. also Huddleston, 1970:510), but this is clearly false when we consider that (4a-b) and (5a-b) are not paraphrase pairs and the (b) sentences are not even wholly acceptable out of some special context: it seems that we must assign the two arguments of *resemble* to different cases, whatever they may be, as Fillmore (1971*b*:39) shows.

(3a) John resembles Peter.
(3b) Peter resembles John.
(4a) That donkey resembles a unicorn.
(4b) ? A unicorn resembles that donkey.
(5a) John resembles his famous ancestor.
(5b) ? His famous ancestor resembles John.

Nilsen's next counter-argument concerns Locatives and Temporals like those in (6a) and (7a), which proponents of the constraint want to analyse as subordinations (6b, 7b).

(6a) He sat on a bench under a tree in the park.
(6b) He sat on a bench which was under a tree which was in the park.
(7a) He came at 1.30 in the afternoon yesterday.
(7b) He came at 1.30 which was in the afternoon which was yesterday.

His argument is that the same kind of semantically possible subordination with other cases, for example Instrument (8a) does not lead to similar possible surface structures (8b).

(8a) He used a gun which was a Winchester to shoot the outlaw.
(8b) * He used a gun a Winchester to shoot the outlaw.

But this argument is surely fallacious. Why should some rule for associating a certain deep structure with a type of surface structure not be restricted in its availability to only certain cases?

Nilsen's next counter-argument concerns predicates where some case is lexicalised. These, as Nilsen points out, can occur with an additional surface realisation of the lexicalised case as in (9a) with Manner or (9b) (not Nilsen's example) with Instrument.

(9a) John hammered the window relentlessly.

(9b) Southall kicked the ball with his right foot.

Two answers seem possible here. One is to claim that lexicalised cases (Cook's (1973) 'covert roles') are not part of the case frame for a given sentence, and that to consider them as such is an application of Case too far removed from an essentially surface-oriented analysis, veering towards the deeper semantics of lexical decomposition. The more preferable answer is to accept that the covert role is relevant and to be recognised, and to treat this as a special kind of coordination in the case of (9a), or subordination (the implicit Instrument being further specified) in (9b).

It is strange that Nilsen did not consider a number of apparent contraventions of the constraint which are much harder to analyse in terms of subordinations. We have seen some of these in preceding discussions in Chapter 7, and have characterised them as 'inner' and 'outer' roles. This approach is a particular feature of Platt's (1971) version of Case. This can be seen with Locatives (10a) and Benefactives (10b), and as we shall see shortly, with most other roles.

(10a) In Paris, we stay at the Hôtel Place du Louvre.

(10b) I am writing a letter to the headmaster for you.

The key distinction here is that one of the instances of the given case is closely associated with the verb, but the other pertains to the predication as a whole. Clearly here the Valency distinction between complements and adjuncts is relevant, and we can recall here the way that various authors in both Case and Valency traditions have recognised this distinction (Figure 1).

We should note immediately that for some authors the distinction between inner and outer roles is a clearcut subdivision between two distinct sets of role types. In the Valency tradition, as was noted in Chapter 1 Section 3, some types of 'adverbial' are regarded as essentially 'freely insertable'. In Case, we see already in Fillmore (1968*a*:23) that some cases are introduced not in the rewrite of the 'proposition' element, but of the modality element, these being Time, Manner and so on. This is the case in Moskey's (1979:11) Case grammar for Dutch – based on Cook – where

author(s)	'inner'	'outer'
Tesnière, 1959	*actant*	*circonstant*
Brinkmann, 1962	*Mitspieler*	*Umstandsbestimmung*
Halliday, 1970	participant	circumstantial
Platt, 1971	inner	outer
Cook, 1972*b*	propositional	modal
Helbig & Schenkel, 1973	*Ergänzung*	*Angabe*
Vauquois, 1975	*ARGument*	*CIRConstant*
Longacre, 1976	nuclear	peripheral
Panevová, 1977	inner participant	free adverbial
Abraham, 1977; Matthews, 1981	complement	adjunct
Dik, 1978	argument	satellite
Ostler, 1980	internal	external
Somers, 1981	central	peripheral
Somers, 1982*c*	obligatory	optional

Figure 1: Terminology for 'inner' and 'outer' roles

Temporal, Source, Goal and Instrument are modal (outer), Agent, Object, Locative, Experiencer and Beneficiary propositional (inner). But just as the Valency notion of free insertability was shown to be wrong, so too the status of a given case depends on the particular predicate. For all the cases supposed essentially to apply to adjuncts we can suggest verbs for which they are complements – *wait* and *spend* require a Temporal, *behave* a Manner, and so on.

It is worthwhile recollecting and assembling some of the observations relevant to this question that we have made so far. In Chapter 1 we saw how the complement-adjunct distinction operates and the extent to which, at the syntactic level at least, the distinction can be recognised. In Section 6 of that chapter (and in Somers, 1984) we noted how inner elements divide between integral, 'obligatory', and optional complements, and how non-valency-bound arguments seemed to differ in their degree of centrality ranging from 'middle' elements, which are only marginally 'outer', through adjuncts, to extra-peripherals, which are 'far-outer'. An example incorporating some of these levels is (11a), the relative centrality of whose participants we could perhaps represent as a series of concentric orbits around the central predicator, where elements on successively more distant orbits could be said to be orbiting (i.e. modifying) not just the predicator but the more inner orbits as well (11b).

(11a) Nick unexpectedly smashed the vase with a hammer yesterday.

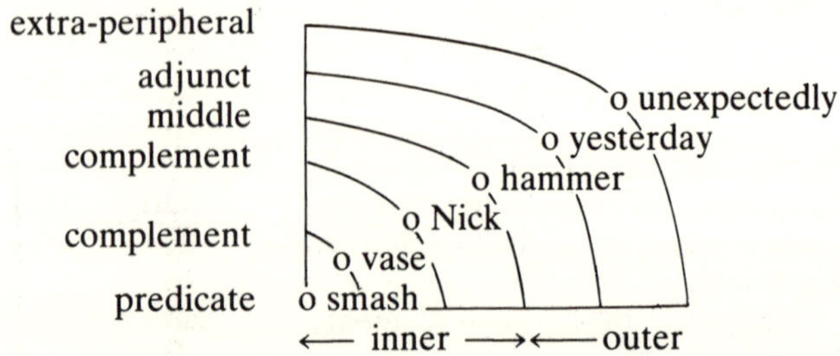

With regard to Case, and other phrase-structure models, the distinction comes into play in comparing the Locatives in (12).

(12a) John keeps his car in the garage.
(12b) John washes his car in the garage.

In recognising that the two Locatives attach at different levels in the underlying phrase-structure (13), Case grammarians reinforced, without acknowledging it, the complement-adjunct distinction of Valency grammar. This distinction was recognised too in earlier models, and Fillmore's (1968*a*:26) reference to elements 'inside the VP' or 'outside the VP' recalls a similar distinction in Chomsky (1965:101) (cf. Platt, 1971:30).

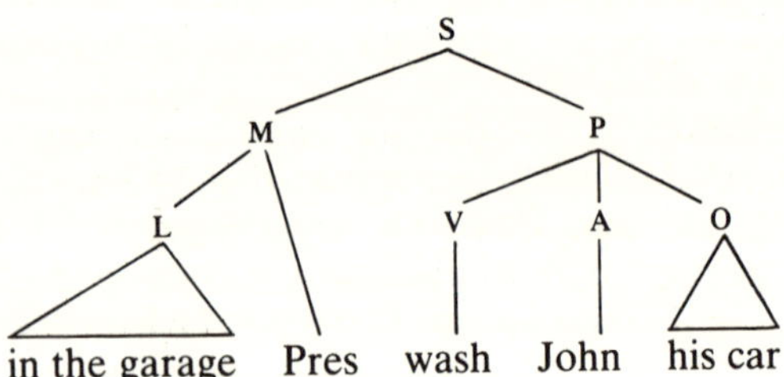

(13a)

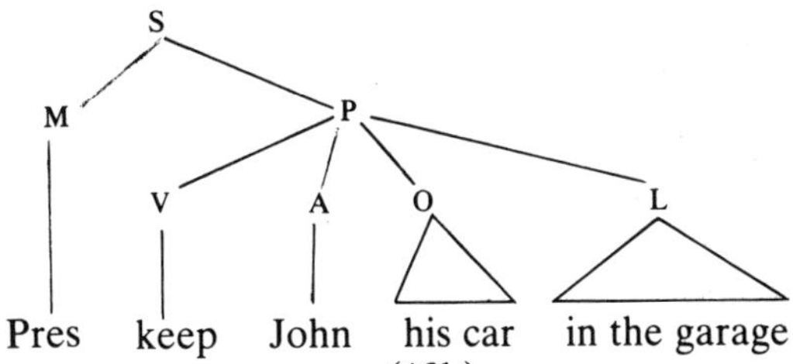

(13b)

In Chapter 7 Section 5 we noted that Locatives attaching to M can co-occur with Locatives attaching to P, as in (14), making the inner versus outer distinction crucial for explaining apparent contradictions of the one-case-per-clause constraint.

(14) In Geneva I stay at Mike's house.

We had already noted in Section 3 a similar possibility with Benefactives (cf. (10b) above), and remarked on the fact that they seemed to be able to 'stack up' as far as processing limitations would allow (15a). 'Outer Agents' seemed to have the same property (15b), and Locatives (15c) and Temporals (15d) can be stacked, as we noted in the appropriate place.

(15a) I am writing the newspaper a letter for Mr Smith for Mr Jones.

(15b) Harry had Rod have Paul have Pete have Liz make coffee.

(15c) In Italy, at home people park their cars in garages.

(15d) Last year the sports news lasted twenty minutes on some occasions.

Now let us see for what other cases the inner versus outer distinction is valid, whether they can occur in pairs, and whether they can stack up.

Experiencer is clearly an inner role for a large number of predicates. For some, especially 'action-process-experientials' like *ask*, *tell*, it is optional, but still intuitively part of the case frame (16).

(16a) The students often ask (me) questions.

(16b) Dave tells (us) tall stories.

The 'ethic dative' in German discussed by Abraham (1973) seems to be a good candidate for 'outer Experiencer' (17a). It is even more obviously modal in English (17b).

(17a) Du bist *mir* ein fauler Kerl.

(17b) *For me*, you're a lazy chap.

In English, such a direct means of expressing the outer Experiencer is not so common, and circumlocutions like *in my opinion* or *as far as I'm concerned* are preferred.

Another type of outer Experience is exemplified in Chinese by Teng (1975:78) who notes that *si* ('die') can occur in a sentence like (18a) with an outer Experiencer (cf. (18b)). A more literal translation (18c) than that given by Teng gives us an equivalent type of outer Experiencer for English.

(18a) Ta si-le fuqin.
HE DIE-asp FATHER
'He lost his father.'

(18b) Fuqin si-le
FATHER DIE-asp
'His father died.'

(18c) His father died on him.

Japanese has a similar construction with so-called 'double subject sentences' (Kuno, 1973:68f; 1978:74f): compare (19a) with the more neutral (19b):

(19a) Taroo *ga* otoosan ga sinde simatta.
TAROO nom FATHER nom DYING DO-past
'Taroo's father died on him.'

(19b) Taroo *no* otoosan ga sinde simatta.
gen
'Taroo's father died.'

In (19a), following Kuno (1978:75), *Taroo* can be described as 'subject of the whole sentence', while *otoosan* is subject of the verb. This analysis accords with our distinction (Chapter 1 Section 6) between elements pertaining to the predication as a whole ('outer') as against those pertaining to the predicate itself ('inner').

A further example of outer Experiencer is again found in Japanese in the form of the so-called 'adversity passive' (Kuno, 1973:22ff; Jacobsen, 1982:20). Morphological passives can be formed with intransitive verbs where the passive subject is understood to be adversely affected by the action of the verb, as in (20):

(20) Taroo wa tuma ni nigerareta.
TAROO subj WIFE BY RUN-AWAY-passive-past
Lit. 'Taroo was run away by his wife.'
i.e. 'Taroo's wife ran away on him.'

Adversity passives are also available with transitive verbs – cf. (21a) with outer experiencer and the more neutral (21b):

(21a) Ziroo wa kaizoku ni ie o yakareta.
JIROO subj PIRATE BY HOUSE obj BURN-passive-past
'Jiroo had his house burned down by pirates.'

(21b) Ziroo no ie wa kaizoku ni yakareta.
JIROO gen HOUSE subj PIRATE BY BURN-passive-past
'Jiroo's house was burned down by pirates.'

Can either of these outer Experiencers co-occur with experiential verbs, that is with an inner Experiencer? Clearly, if *in my opinion* is regarded as a means of expressing the first type, it can (22a). And in (22b) we have the experiential verb *forget* taking the inner Experiencer *he* and the outer *us*.

(22a) In my opinion, Dave tells us tall stories.
(22b) He forgot his lines on us.

It is difficult enough to give really convincing examples with a single outer Experiencer (though I feel we have enough evidence to confirm it as a possibility, even if rare). An example of stacked outer Experiencers is extremely hard to imagine. The indulgent reader might accept a sentence like (23a) as such, but the fact that it probably needs glossing (23b) demonstrates that English at least seems not to tolerate stacked outer Experiencers. Whether this is again a processing constraint or a real limitation on this particular relationship is unclear however.

(23a) For me, for you, I am an idiot.
(23b) I think you think I am an idiot.

Some of Laing's (1970) 'knots' are of this nature, but the fact that most people regard them as tricks, and not part of ordinary language at all does nothing to bring Experiencer into line with the outer cases seen so far.

Let us now turn to Source, Path and Goal. Discussion of these cases is made difficult by their hybrid nature in being subcategories of (or subcategorisable for) location, time and state. In addition, there is little or no consensus on their status, especially vis-à-vis other putative cases. For example Niéger (1973:45) cites (24) as an example of the two Goals, *un poème* ('a poem') and *pour sa soeur* ('for his sister'), co-occurring, whereas this example would be unproblematic for a system which distinguished Goal from either Factitive or Benefactive.

(24) Jean écrit un poème pour sa soeur.
'John wrote a poem for his sister.'

Beyond that kind of problem it is relatively easy to construct examples like (25) with, say, an inner locative Source (*Euston*) and an outer temporal Source (*from seven o'clock*) and so on.

(25) Trains leave Euston from seven o'clock.

We should therefore consider each of the subtypes of Source, Path and Goal as separate cases. First it is clear that they all occur as inner cases with verbs like *leave*, *cross* and *arrive* for the locatives and with *last* (*from/for/until*) for temporals. As outer cases, examples for them all can also be found (26).

(26a) From Birmingham to Liverpool we sang songs.
(26b) On the M1 we saw several breakdowns.
(26c) I work steadily from nine till five.
(26d) Throughout the day women have been phoning me.

We do appear also to be able to construct examples of co-occurring inner and outer Source, Path and Goal, though some of these look very similar to simple thematised subordinations (27).

(27a) From London the train leaves from Euston.
(27b) I crossed London on the Jubilee line.
(27c) I arrived in Paris at Roissy.
(27d) From 28th May flights will depart from 8 a.m.
(27e) During summer daylight lasts a long time.
(27f) Until August work lasts until 6 p.m.

It seems equally likely that, given appropriate circumstances, these outer cases will be able to be stacked up, though probably not to great degree, given the restricted nature of our conception of space and time.

Let us consider now Instrument. With verbs like *use* it is a complement. Most action-processes can take an Instrument adjunct. Do they co-occur however? Given the relatively small number of verbs which take an Instrument complement, examples may be difficult to find. A sentence like (28) seems to me fairly odd, though most of my colleagues find it quite acceptable.

(28) He used a fork with his left hand.

Does the same apply to other 'typically adjunct' cases for which there are a few verbs with which they are complements? An obvious test case is Manner, and again with (29) I have some difficulty which does not seem to be mirrored by my informants.

(29) He behaved well awkwardly.

The same is true of the problem case Comitative. Remembering that we restrict the use of Comitative to instances where paraphrases with *in the company of* or *together with* are available, (30) is another such example.

(30) Together with his father, he accompanied his mother to the zoo.

Let us turn finally to one clear-cut case. We have said nothing so far of Patients, and this is because the facts here are quite clear. It is perhaps not surprising, given the especially close connections between Patients and predicates, that we are not able to conceive of outer Patients at all. There is nothing in any of the typical characterisations of Patient, even those not stressing the neutral, predicate-dependent nature of this case, that suggests that Patients can ever be anything other than complement.

These facts taken together suggest a rather interesting possible hierarchisation of the cases in general, reflecting whether a case is more typically complement or adjunct (31).

(31) Patient
Experiencer
Agent
Benefactive, Locative, Source, Path, Goal
Manner
Instrument, Comitative

Notice that at either end of the scale, combinations of inner and outer cases are difficult or impossible to construct. In the very middle of the scale, such examples are extremely easy to find. It would be interesting to see (though we shall not attempt to do so here) if this hierarchy corresponded to some ordering of the cases according to some other criterion (for example, occurrence with or without prepositions or their equivalent in a number of languages; thematisation possibilities; etc.).

TEN

THE CASE-GRID PROPOSAL

1. *Introduction*

I conclude this Part II with some thoughts on a version of Case in which some of its problems may be answered. It should be pointed out that the ideas to be presented here are for the most part untested (though see Section 3 below). However I take some satisfaction in noting that the approach I am taking here is not dissimilar to a recent proposal by Ostler (1980), though his work is not as systematic as my own proposal, nor is it envisaged as applicable to the same range of problems as the current suggestion.

2. *Ostler*

Ostler's proposal is to represent semantic relations as bundles of features, with four basic roles which he calls Theme, Goal, Source, and Path, which are further subcategorised with various additional features to give a range of cases. In fact, these four basic relations can be identified as 'complexes of two binary features', namely ±Source and ±Goal (in a similar manner to J. Anderson, 1971), as in Figure 1. Predicates are divided between static and dynamic, a key difference being that roles associated with static predicates are always −Source, that is only Theme or Goal. Further role features are positional, identification, possession, and cognition, which again map onto a pair of binary features ±sentient and ±abstract (Figure 2).

	Goal	Source
Theme	–	–
Goal	+	–
Source	–	+
Path	+	+

Figure 1: Characterisation of basic cases (Ostler, 1980:32)

	Sentient	Abstract
Position	–	–
Identification	–	+
Possession	+	–
Cognition	+	+

Figure 2: Feature matrix for sentient and abstract

	Theme	Goal	Source	Path
Static				
Positional	Theme	Locus	—	—
Identification[1]	Theme	Attribute	—	—
Dynamic				
Positional	Theme	Goal	Source	Path
Identification[2]	Theme	Tendency	Point of Reference	Respect
Static				
Possession	Owned object	Owner	—	—
Cognition[3]	Mental object	Experiencer	—	—
Dynamic				
Possession	Transferred object	Recipient	Ex-owner	Medium of Exchange
Cognition[4]	Percept	Experiencer	Source of Cognition	Medium of Communication
Volition	Wisher	Aim	Aversion[5]	Stratagem[6]
Eventive[7]	Event	Patient	Cause	Circumstance
Agentive[8]	Action	Victim	Agent	Means/Recipient

Figure 3: Ostler's (1980:47) functional roles

Together with volition and two action types, eventive and agentive, which are not found as static, we have the complete set of cases, as in Figure 3 (roles which are felt to need explanation or exemplification are indicated by superscript number referring to an example sentence: examples are from Ostler, except where preceded by †). As we shall see, Ostler's classification of cases is superficially similar to our own, especially in having among the four basic roles the locationist Source, Path and Goal, and in one or two of the rows (notably his Agentive).

(1) † That man is a teacher.
Theme Attribute
(2a) John is similar to Mary.
Theme Tendency
(2b) London is larger than Birmingham.
Theme Point of Reference
(2c) This store is unbeatable for value.
Theme Respect
(3) † George knows about John's death.
Experiencer Mental object
(4a) I learnt of John's death through the obituary column.
ExperiencerPercept Source of Cognition
(4b) John witnessed the spectacle with unbelieving eyes.
Experiencer Percept Medium of communication
(5) '[We] identify the volitional source with the object which is avoided or abhorred, i.e. what the wisher-theme is trying to move away from in his quest for the volitional goal.' (Ostler, 1980:41)
(6) 'We shall tentatively identify [volitional Path] with the Strategem, or means by which the theme's desire are to be fulfilled.' (*idem.*)
(7) The dam-burst hit the village with a wall of water
Cause Patient Circumstance
in the worst disaster of the century.
Event
(8a) Helga hit Sigurd a hefty blow with the milking-pail.
Agent Victim Action Means
(8b) The president met with his ministers.
Agent Reciprocal

It should be noted that for the possessive and cognitional rows there are complementary rows with 'inverted values', where the Theme and Goal are in each case interchanged, and the Source (in the case of the dynamic) is the 'item lost' (possession) or 'item unknown' (cognition). In these inverted domains, no value is suggested for Path.

The roles we have seen so far are 'internal' roles. Ostler's distinction between internal and external roles is just like the traditional 'inner' versus 'outer' distinction seen in so many other Valency and Case grammars (cf. Chapter 9). But Ostler suggests that these too can be mapped onto his scheme, though with a number of gaps, as in Figure 4. It is interesting to note that Ostler excludes his Theme from this chart, and one is reminded of our finding (Chapter 9) that of all the traditional cases, only Patient cannot function as an outer role.

	Goal	Source	Path
Static			
Positional	Place	—	—
Identification	Time	—	—
Dynamic			
Positional	Limit	Point of Origin	Extent
Identification	*Until*	*Since*	Duration
Possession	Beneficiary	*Thanks to*	?
Cognition	Ethic dative?	Subject-matter?	Criterion?
Eventive	Affectee	Cause	Manner
Agentive	Affectee	Instigator	Accompaniment

Figure 4: External roles (Ostler, 1980:49)

Ostler's proposals for external roles are fairly sketchy, and he himself notes that the chart in Figure 4 is only a 'starting point'. Few comments are made, and even less exemplification is offered. The positional/identification distinction is used for space and time, though it is not clear why (except that both identification and time are –position!), while in the Affectee we see the 'outer Experiencer' recognised above (Chapter 9) for Chinese (9) and exemplified by Ostler in English (10).

(9a) Ta si-le fuqin.
HE DIE-asp FATHER
'He lost his father.'
(9b) His father died on him.
(10) They confiscated my licence on me!

We need not look in much further detail at Ostler's work. He uses this classification of cases to elaborate a set of rules based on feature combinations to account for 'case linking and agreement', i.e. the relation of deep and surface cases, particularly in Sanskrit. Where it is relevant to some of our own suggestions, we shall return to Ostler for clarification and explanation of the distribution of traditional case notions throughout his chart.

3. *The case grid*

The proposal that I wish to elaborate here is intended in response to what I see as the key problems for Case. The case-grid proposal does not solve all of Case's problems, but I believe it does go some way to alleviating several of them. The problems I hope to address can be summarised as follows:

1. Dual roles (cf. Chapter 8)
2. Some cases are more specific than others (cf. Chapter 7, and for example Chapter 12 Section 5)
3. The proliferation of cases for problem examples (cf. Chapter 7 Sections 1 and 6)
4. The opposite of 3: multiple uses for general cases (cf. Chapter 7 Section 1 again)
5. Non-correspondence of cases in related verbs (a specific problem related to 1: cf. Chapter 8).

We do not need to recapitulate here examples of each of these problems. What I hope the case-grid proposal offers is a systematic approach to Case which directly answers points 1 and 5, closes the door on 3, and reduces the arbitrariness introduced by 2 and 4.

In the case grid (I would have preferred a term like 'frame' or 'matrix', but both of these have been used for other concepts), cases are described in terms of values on two axes. I find the analogy of the International Phonetic Association's (1949) consonant chart useful: here phonetic units are characterised on two principle parameters (place and manner of articulation). For some of these units, further feature specifications are possible or desirable, or even implied, but generally (ignoring voicing) the two values are sufficient to specify a sound. In the same way, on the case grid we have a four-by-six matrix which gives us twenty-four distinct roles, some of which can, if necessary be further specified. Again, as in phonetics, certain generalisations can be stated about cases that appear in the same row or column, while at other times it is strictly necessary to specify both parameters. Finally, and perhaps most controversially, the two axes reflect what I hope are intuitively distinct and distinguishable parameters on which case relations can be defined.

The case grid is made up of four columns and six rows: we can alternatively describe the case grid as consisting of two axes, one with four values, the other with six. Either way we have twenty-four points or cells each representing a distinct case concept. The smaller axis is very easy to characterise, since it consists of the very familiar localist values used in many Case systems for both spatial and temporal orientation, and in many extended uses (cf. Chapter 7 Section 5). A number of names suggest themselves (1) – typically we have (1a), though this nomenclature should perhaps be avoided because of its already wide usage. I have discovered that people unfamiliar with Latin find the names in (1b) and (1c) fairly unuseful, and I dislike both (1c) and (1d) for their hint of association with surface case which I would like to avoid. So we shall chose (1a) after all, though with the strong warning against the association of (some) other linguists' uses of these terms with our own, and preferring 'Local' to 'Neutral' so as to avoid any hint of 'wastebasketry' (1e).

(1a)	Source	Path	Goal	Neutral
(1b)	UNDE	QUA	QUO	UBI
(1c)	Ablative	Translative	Allative	Locative
(1d)	From	Via	To	At
(1e)	Source	Path	Goal	Local

For the six values on the larger axis it is rather more difficult to characterise the general nature of the rows, even to the extent of finding names for (some of) them. I am happy with 'Locative', 'Temporal' and 'Ambient' for three of the rows, but for the other three I have considered at various times any of (2a-d). Again collocation with standard Case (2a), verbal voice (2b) or surface case (2c) is unfortunate. The names in (2d) are slightly preferable, since they fit well with the three I am happy with, and since they at least hint at a connection with verb types. But since none of the sets of names exactly conveys the nature of the row, the nomenclature is not likely to be very helpful, and so might as well be fairly arbitrarily chosen. For this reason, I have taken euphony as criterial, and use the six row names in (3).

(2a)	Agentive	Objective	Benefactive
(2b)	Active	Passive	Dative
(2c)	Nominative	Accusative	Dative
(2d)	Actional	Processive	Experiential

(3) Active Objective Dative Locative Temporal Ambient

Of the six rows, let us begin with the two that are easiest to understand and appreciate, and which can be used as models for the other more perhaps idiosyncratic distinctions.

On the Locative row we have the spatial start-point (Locative Source), end-point (Locative Goal) and transversal (Locative Path) specified for some event or action, and the stationary point (Locative Local) at which some event occurs. These are quite straightforward and correspond to the expected values as found in many other Case systems. We have the usual parallels on the Temporal row. For exemplification and discussion see Chapter 7 Section 5. We introduce here the 'arrow diagram' device, which we will find helpful in explaining later rows, the interpretation of which is very clear with the Temporals. In (4), the arrow represents the passage of time for some event or action: the points A and B represent the start and end time and are thus the Temporal Source and Temporal Goal. The duration of the event is represented by the line AB, and corresponds to the Temporal Path. Any point C on the line AB is a Temporal Local.

(4) 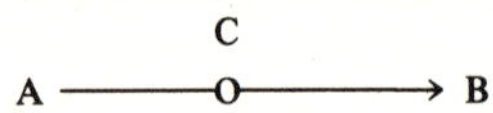

The Locative and Temporal rows are summarised in Figure 5.

	Source	Path	Goal	Local
Locative	place from where	space traversed	final destination	static position
Temporal	time since	duration	time until	time at which

Figure 5: Locative and temporal rows

We may now turn to the first of the three major rows, the Active (or Agentive or Actional). Again we may use the arrow diagram in (4), but this time the arrow represents an action. A is the instigator of the action, and so Active Source corresponds roughly to the traditional Agent or Causer. In this sense, further features volitive and animate may be appropriate to this cell. The Active Goal B represents the end point of the action and so can be interpreted either as the intended result of the action, that is, deliberate goal or purpose; or else with some predicates it can be interpreted as the active recipient of the action, as with verbs like *buy* and *get*. These two roles can be distinguished by the feature animate, which is loosely interpreted as 'functioning as if animate', and not in the narrow sense as an inherent defining feature (cf. Peterson, 1983:85). The Active Path AB can be understood as the traditional Instrument or means by which the action is carried out. This treatment of Instrument as some kind of Path is also found in J. Anderson (1971) and in Ostler: 'If we consider . . . what is likely to be the path of an action, i.e. that through or over which the actor inflicts the action on the [victim], the most natural identification is with the Means through which the action is completed. This will be the familiar role of Instrument . . .' (Ostler, 1980:44). This leaves only the Active Local on this row. If wc think of point C in our arrow diagram we have the point through which the action passes. This concept suggests the role of the thing undergoing the action, corresponding to one common use of Patient. But as we shall see shortly, we have a similar interpretation for the same column on the next row (Objective), so we can differentiate between these two by stressing the Active nature of roles in this row as compared to the more passive nature of roles in the Objective row: in this way we see that Active Local becomes appropriate for the reflexive sort of role, especially in verbs of motion where the Active Source instigating the motion also undergoes the change of location. So Active Local can be glossed as non-passive Patient, a characterisation which also incorporates Ostler's 'Reciprocal', as in (5), which he – lacking an equivalent of our Local – includes as a second type of agentive Path.

(5a) John talkcd *with Mary*.

(5b) The president met *with his ministers*.

The Active row is summarised in Figure 6.

	Source	Path	Goal	Local
Active	instigator of action	instrument or means	intended result active recipient	non-passive patient

Figure 6: Active row

In the sense that the Active row represents an action, the Objective row represents a process, and the two rows are differentiated in the sense that roles on the Objective row are generally more passive. The Objective Source can be the original state in a change-of-state, or can be the material out of which something is made. These two interpretations can if necessary be distinguished by the additional feature concrete. The Objective Goal can similarly be the final state in a change-of-state, or the physical result of some process (traditional Factitive), these two senses again differentiated as ±concrete. Note that the Objective Goal will tend to be accidental or coincidental, since we have the Active Goal for intended and aimed at results, though the distinction may become cloudy. The Objective Local is the element undergoing a change-of-state, or whose state is described in a stative predicate. Again Objective and Active locals will be differentiated by their degree of 'willing' participation. The Objective Path will represent rather rarely the intermediate state in a change-of-state: more commonly the Objective Path acts as a kind of 'counter-Instrument' to the Active Path, and will represent the passive means or 'enabler' in an action (i.e. noncontrolled non 'tool-like' Instrument), or the Instrument in an Agent-less process. The Objective row is summarised in Figure 7.

	Source	Path	Goal	Local
Objective	original state material	counter- instrument passive means	result state factitive	undergoing change-of -state

Figure 7: Objective row

The Dative row represents the roles in propositions that are neither true actions nor true processes in that they are typically predications of a psychological nature, or involve transfer of possession. Let us consider first psychological predicates, including perception and cognition. The Dative Goal corresponds fairly closely to the traditional Experiencer case. If we think of the arrow diagram again, this time the arrow represents some psychological 'experience' or the phenomenon of cognition, so the role of the Goal is fairly clear: the experience (perception, sensation, cognition) impinges on the entity at point B in the diagram. Note that the Dative Goal may be dynamic (as in the experiential process) or static (experiential state). The experience of course emanates from the Dative Source. In a psychological experience (perception, sensation) this will be the stimulus or cause of the experience; in cognition, it is difficult to separate the stimulus and the content, though where the source of knowledge is not agentive, the distinction may be clearer. The Dative Path along which the experience passes represents the medium of the experience, while the Dative Local represents any point along this path, and seems most appropriate for the content of the experience.

In transfer of possession predicates, the Source and Goal roles are fairly clear. Note however that typically one or other of these will be agentive, and therefore properly Active rather than Dative. Again the Path represents the medium of exchange, and may correspond to the thing given in return for the transferred object. Parallel to the 'content of the experience', the Local in a transfer of possession corresponds to the object transferred. There is some overlap between these roles on the Dative row in its possession reading, and similar roles on the Agentive and Objective roles, though note that the columns always correspond: the choice between the rows may reflect the perspective in which the proposition is viewed. The Dative row is summarised in Figure 8.

	Source	Path	Goal	Local
Dative				
psychological:	stimulus	medium	experiencer	content
possession:	original owner	medium/price	recipient	thing transferred

Figure 8: Dative row

The final row is Ambient. The roles along this row are typically abstract, and in a sense more peripheral than those in the other cells, though we shall have a little more to say about the central versus peripheral distinction below. The Ambient Source is the reason or abstract cause for the action or event. The Ambient Goal is the aim, result or consequence. This is distinct from the Objective Goal which is a concrete result; and aim and consequence may be distinguished by the same feature volitive we saw with the Active Source. The Ambient Path corresponds to the manner in which something happens, while the Ambient Local represents the conditions under which a predication occurs. The Ambient row is summarised in Figure 9.

	Source	Path	Goal	Local
Ambient	reason	manner	aim consequence	condition

Figure 9: Ambient row

The overall picture is given in Figure 10, which combines the previous figures, and also incorporates the optional secondary features.

	Source	Path	Goal	Local
Active	instigator of action ±volitive ±animate	instrument or means	intended result (−animate) active recipient (+animate)	non-passive patient
Objective	original state (−concrete)	counter-instrument	result state (−concrete)	undergoing
	material (+concrete)	passive means	factitive (+concrete)	change-of-state
Dative psychological:	stimulus	medium	experiencer ±dynamic	content
possessive:	original owner	medium/price	recipient	thing transferred
Locative	place from where	space traversed	final destination	static position
Temporal	time since	duration	time until	time at which
Ambient	reason	manner	aim (+volitive) consequence (−volitive)	condition

Figure 10: Completed case grid

We have seen throughout this work that an important distinction can be drawn between inner and outer roles and I have suggested in other chapters that this very distinction can serve to reduce the number of cases needed by allowing contraventions of the 'one-case-per-clause' principle where the case occurrences are distinguished by degree of valency binding. It also seems likely that the range of cases needed for inner roles may be significantly more general and therefore less numerous than those needed for outer roles. In view of these two statements, where does the case grid fit in? It is clear that the roles on the Ambient row for example are more often found as peripheral roles, so if the case grid were to be offered as a model for inner cases only, we might decide to do away with this row. Some of the other cells correspond quite clearly to traditional case roles like Instrument, Agent, Experiencer, and various types of Patient are spread out among the cells. I feel that the grid is probably not quite specific enough to handle all types of outer role, though it will certainly manage with those outer roles that correspond to inner roles, as discussed in Chapter 9. So we can probably view the grid as a slightly elaborate model for inner roles.

There are various ways of looking at the values on the axes, and at the rubrics that appear in the slots of the grid, and I am relatively neutral as to which of these is adopted. For example, the axes could be regarded as specifying non-binary features, so that the cases become bundles of distinctive features. I am not concerned either whether one arrives at the case specifications via the axes or vice versa: given some semantic role, does one look at the rubrics to find the nearest match, or does one attempt to calculate the appropriate value-pair according to some other criteria? In a computational environment, I can imagine the latter being the favoured approach: perhaps in some circumstances one or other of the two values can be straightforwardly computed – indeed the choice of which of the two is arrived at in this way might not even always be the same. I can also conceive of occasions when it might not be necessary to compute both values. In a more general environment the 'directionality' of the grid may not have any significance at all. Furthermore, it is not necessary to clarify whether these specifications are definitions of the content of the slot, guidelines as to which slot is appropriate for some application, or simply typifications of a most general nature. It seems quite acceptable, for example, to use some of the names found in the cells as a kind of shorthand, especially where these names are fairly well understood in the Case community: for example, 'Instrument' will probably remain as a mnemonic for 'Active Path' and 'Experiencer' for 'psychological Dative Goal'. All this vagueness may appear to be theoretical unsoundness, but my view is that it in fact reflects the general applicability of the proposal.

The proposal would certainly be easier to judge given some examples, particularly showing to what extent this proposal goes towards answering the problems mentioned above. The general problem of the arbitrary nature of the traditional cases (varying degrees of specificity, random introduction of new case distinctions for special problems) is avoided by the strictly symmetrical and systematic nature of the case grid. The number of roles is fixed at twenty-four, and there is no room for additional cases, unless a whole new row or column is introduced. For example, the two subrows of Dative could be explicitly distinguished as distinct rows, though the complementary distribution of roles on this row plus the traditional association of both reception and cognition with Experiencer/Dative (cf. Chapter 7 Section 3) motivated the decision to present them together.

It is a very important feature of the case grid that there are no empty cells. Admittedly, the device of secondary features compromises this symmetry a little, but I have tried to stress that the introduction of subcategorisations via secondary features is strictly optional, and does not constitute an extension of the grid in any dimension.

It is in the area of dual roles and correspondence of cases in related verbs that the grid comes into its own. The beauty of the bi-axial system is that any two roles can be simultaneously 'the same' and 'different': in this way, related verbs can be assigned cases that show both their similarities and their differences. For example, the verbs of perception form pairs like *look* and *see* which differ in the agentivity of the perceiver. In traditional Case we can capture this difference by saying that *look* takes an Agent while *see* takes the Experiencer. But we have no means of distinguishing this situation from the apparently parallel relationship between *dance* and *know*. But on the case grid we can capture the similarity between *look* and *see* by saying that both take a Goal, but that the difference is that *look* takes an Active Goal while *see* takes a Dative Goal. Consider now the verbs *buy* and *sell*, where again traditional Case is unable to capture at the same time the fact that they both express a transfer of goods from one person to another and the agentive perspective that choice of one surface verb over the other indicates. On the case grid, the buyer is Goal for both verbs, and the seller Source. Again we distinguish between Active and Dative to capture agentivity.

The case grid may also incorporate some happy side-effects: for example, following the localist theory (J. Anderson, 1971), we can expect cells in the same column to share some syntactic properties. If this is the case, then these can be used in a computational environment to calculate half the case value for the role. By the same token, the values on the other axis look like they might correspond in a vague sense to some semantic criteria. Notice that I am not claiming that this is how the grid works: if it were the case that deep case roles could be mapped trivially onto a matrix of surface case on one parameter and semantic features on the other, this would surely have been recognised and exploited a long time ago. It is clear that Case is rather more complex than that, but that this sort of consideration is occasionally of assistance.

It remains to put the case grid through its paces, and in particular to see how easy or difficult it is to arrive at the correct case assignments for a far-ranging set of examples both in computational and human terms. In the latter case, it is clear that the rubrics in the cells can be used as guidance, but I feel the validity of the grid would be better ascertained if the correct case assignments could be arrived at simply by independent choice of a value on each of the axes. Discussions with colleagues as well as a small pilot study (with Chris Lewis, a final-year Computational Linguistics student at UMIST) seem to indicate that the most difficult problem is in arriving at a clear understanding of the abstractions implied by the row distinctions (hence the importance of nomenclature), whereas the localist column distinctions seem universally quite intuitive. Ten subjects, mostly final-year Computational Linguistics students but including some members of staff, were asked to assign case labels to the verbal complements and adjuncts indicated in twenty-four sentences on the basis of the above description of the case grid. The sentences were a mixture of some closely corresponding to the types of predication hinted at in the description, and some expected to entail problematic assignments. Typically, subjects tended to select one of the values if this was clearcut (and it was not always the localist value that got chosen first), and then scan along the row or down the column for the most appropriate rubric. In most cases, even the 'problem sentences', there was a reasonable degree of consistency on at least one of the two values, and although a number of problems were highlighted, the informal results suggested that the case grid was at least as good as a traditional case set in terms of this type of test, and often superior. This was especially so where subjects disagreed in one of the two values but were consistent with the other: with a traditional case set this partial agreement would presumably not have shown up.

One thing that is clear from a number of recent sources (notably Ostler, 1980; Peterson, 1983; to a lesser extent Ruus, 1980 and Willis and Jeffreys, 1983) and a number of discussions with colleagues representing various outlooks on Case, is that the way forward for Case lies in the kind of componential analysis that the case grid exemplifies, at the expense of what Peterson calls the 'traditional monolithic definitions'.

PART III: CASE AND VALENCY IN LANGUAGE PROCESSING

Introduction

In this final part we move away from General Linguistics into the realm of Computational Linguistics, as we investigate the application of the theories and standpoints discussed in Parts I and II to the related areas of parsing, Artificial Intelligence (AI) and Machine Translation (MT).

In Chapter 11 we look at the general field of Computational Linguistics and AI and the widespread use in these fields of various versions of Case. We distinguish systems that use Case from those that are directed towards investigating Case, and as examples of the latter discuss three systems including our own PTOSYS. We then note the degree to which Case supplants the use of syntax in parsing, again looking at three representative systems, and investigating briefly the possibility of using Case to drive an ATN parser. In the next section, we consider some Case-like approaches to language processing which do not adopt a traditional view of Case, but which are interesting from the point of view of certain parallels between their approaches and the more standard Case-based systems. Amongst the approaches discussed here are the Knowledge Representation Language KRL, and Minsky's well-known 'frames' concept. Following this we look at the use of Case in cognitive rather than linguistic systems, with Schank's Conceptual Dependency representation an important example. The chapter ends with a general discussion of what constitutes Case and 'using Case' in the fields alluded to.

In Chapter 12 we concentrate on one specific area of Computational Linguistics: MT. The use of Valency as well as Case is discussed here, with reference to a number of systems, with particular regard to the problems that can be solved and those which are exacerbated by the use of Valency with or without Case. The Case-using MT system LRC-METAL receives particular attention as a model system, while in the final section I take the opportunity to express some personal views regarding the use of Case in transfer-based and interlingual MT.

ELEVEN

CASE IN COMPUTATIONAL LINGUISTICS AND ARTIFICIAL INTELLIGENCE

1. *Introduction*

First we shall outline some fundamental areas of interest in Computational Linguistics and AI, though without detailed discussion. We shall then consider some individual systems and some specific points of view on the issues raised. We shall conclude the chapter with some more general discussion of the use of Case in these domains. A similar, though necessarily narrower, survey was published by Bruce (1975). Although most of the systems described by Bruce were those of colleagues, and his extensive references are largely to unpublished technical reports, it is conceivable that Bruce was responsible for bringing Case to the attention of a large number of workers in the field lacking formal linguistic training.

2. *Fundamental issues*

The first distinction we wish to make is between computational language processing implementations that 'use' Case in some sense, and those which are directly concerned with investigating Case as a linguistic theory. In Rosner and Somers (1980:2) we listed a number of computational domains in which Case has been used as a component of some further aim. These include general-purpose language understanding systems, natural-language front-ends for question-answering and/or database development, inferencing, modelling memory, cognition, or belief systems, automatic abstracting and summarising, automatic programming and speech understanding. In contrast to these Case-using systems, we shall consider some examples of programs whose only aim is to generate Case-based representations of text, whether these representations are then to be used for purposes such as those listed above, or are simply demonstrations of the feasibility of the linguistic model, or even provide an environment for testing competing models of Case. Systems that enter this category include Marcus's (1980) PARSIFAL, Celce-Murcia's (1975) implementation of the UCLA/Air-Force grammar (Stockwell *et al.*, 1973), and our own PTOSYS (Somers and Johnson, 1979; Somers, 1980*a*). Three more similar systems which we shall not consider here are those of Friedman (1970), Binot *et al.*'s (1980) French parser SABA, and van Bakel and Hoogeboom's (1981) KASUS extension to their AMAZON syntactic parser for Dutch.

A large number of systems using Case depend on a prior essentially syntactic parse which typically aims at distinguishing the main verb and its 'arguments' (noun phrases and adverbials) to which case values are then assigned. In many of these, although not all, this syntactic phase is accomplished with an Augmented Transition Network (ATN) parser (Woods, 1970; cf. Bates, 1978; Johnson, 1983; Winograd, 1983:195-271). Of particular interest though are those systems where syntactic and Case-like semantic criteria are used in parallel, such as Nash-Webber's (1975) speech understanding system SPEECHLIS. In Taylor *et al.*'s (1977) parser, case assignment is used to distinguish alternative verb senses, following a preliminary ATN-drive parse. Some systems claim to dispense with syntax altogether, for example Wilks's (1973*a*, *b*) system, while Hendrix *et al.*'s (1973) question-answering system is of particular interest, since the parser appears to be Case-driven ATN. For a general discussion of the roles of syntax and semantics in parsing, see Ritchie (1983).

While a large number of language processing systems have adopted 'standard' Case systems – typically those of Fillmore (1971*b*) or even Fillmore (1968*a*) – there are some where a purpose-built set of cases have been introduced. This position is exemplified in Taylor and Rosenberg's (1975) parser, and especially in Martin's (1973) system where over thirty cases are used. But interesting and perhaps more controversial are systems which appear or claim to use Case, but where the cases are 'specialised' with regard to the general domain. Examples of this approach are CHRONOS (Kulikowski and Weiss, 1971; Chokhani, 1973), and PLANES (Waltz, 1978), in which there is an interesting mixture of specialised and general cases, as there is in PROLID (Harbusch and Rothkegel, 1984). The prime example of this phenomenon is however Bobrow and Winograd's (1977) KRL, which we shall discuss in some detail.

There is a significant contrast running through this entire area between systems which are essentially language-oriented, and those claiming to represent or capture some deeper cognitive aspect. The classic 'deep' system is Schank's (1972, 1973*a*,*b*, 1975, 1977) 'Conceptual Dependency' (CD), and the long-term memory model of Rumelhart *et al.* (1972), Rumelhart and Norman (1973), Norman *et al.* (1975). While not as deep as Schank's CD, this is still clearly cognitive rather than linguistic. Many of the systems already mentioned contrast with these two in this respect, but were not generally developed with psychological modelling in mind. In this respect, the work of Simmons (1972, 1973) and Simmons and Slocum (1972) makes an interesting comparison. In Rosner and Somers (1980) we considered this distinction in some depth, contrasting case frames for sentences and verbs with case frames for events and event types. We shall recapitulate some of the points in this discussion at the appropriate moment. We shall also consider just how appropriate Case is in fact for providing a mapping between these two levels, noting that Case is wholly ideal neither for Linguists wishing to describe the essentially syntactic behaviour of words, nor for Cognitive Psychologists wishing to model concepts and conceptualisations independent of the language used to express them: rather, Case provides us with an (albeit rickety) bridge between the two levels.

3. *Case parsers*

In this section we shall consider a number of computational systems in which a case analysis of some text is considered to be the central goal. Such systems are important, because they encourage us to look closely at how the various elements of Case grammar are best employed in a computational system. Other implications which we shall consider later are more concerned with end-goals, and so do not concentrate on more linguistic matters. In this section however we can dwell on the fundamentals for a while.

For most commentators (e.g. Tennant, 1981:91ff), PARSIFAL (Marcus, 1980) is significant for its syntactic approach: Tennant stresses that PARSIFAL is a primarily deterministic parser, having no backtracking facilities, while Winograd (1983:402) makes a similar point, also stressing the association with Transformational Grammar. Indeed these points are reflected in Marcus's introduction (p. 2), and most of his account is concerned with the mechanisms of deterministic parsing (cf. also Sampson, 1983). However, in an appendix to his book, Marcus introduces a 'case frame interpreter'. There are two important points about this additional module:

first it is explicitly not deterministic (p. 311), and second it is implemented not after the syntactic parse, but at least partly in parallel, '. . . monitor[ing] the construction of the annotated surface structures . . . and construct[ing] a predicate/argument representation of the utterance from the parser's output' (Marcus, 1980:311). The case frame representation is intended to be fairly shallow, aiming at 'word-sense disambiguation, but no deeper semantic generalizations' (p. 312). Marcus stresses this bridge-like function of case frames between syntax and semantics: 'Although the caseframe builder in a natural language system may interact with the semantic component to resolve word sense questions, case frames allow the semantic component to remain unaware of how predicate-argument relations *are expressed in the sentence*. The purpose of a case frame representation as *an intermediate step* in the mapping from a sentence to its semantic representation is similar to that of *functional* decomposition. The case frame component can use a limited number of cases, enough to capture the different behaviors present in English sentences. . . . Cases are not expected to reflect *semantic* roles . . .' (*idem*) [emphases mine]. The 'case frame interpreter' is taken from Levin (1977), whom Marcus quotes at length. The algorithm is summarised as follows: the case-frame filler proceeds by comparing the grammatical roles of the arguments with the grammatical roles associated with the cases given by the case frame for the predicate. During processing, there is an extra component attached to the case frame, listing hypotheses consisting of different case-grammatical role configurations. These hypotheses get modified as cases are assigned to arguments, until a point is reached where the hypothetical case frame is completely filled (success) or else either no cases remain for leftover arguments or vice versa, whereupon the hypothesis is discarded. Case slots are filled according to syntactic and semantic criteria, for example, the choice of Agent or Instrument for the surface subject depends on animacy. The cases used are those of Stockwell *et al.* (1973).

The remainder of Marcus's account describes how the caseframe builder interacts with the syntactic parser, running in parallel and 'monitoring' its decisions. Of interest is the fact that case frames attach not only to verbs, but also to modified noun phrases, so that adjectives and dependent prepositional phrases are assigned 'case relations' with regard to the head noun. Although Marcus does not stress this point, this homogeneous treatment of dependencies at all levels is very attractive from a theoretical point of view. Marcus does not discuss either how suitable the chosen case-set is for this task, though presumably at least for verb nominalisations there is little difference between the levels. Finally, the semantic tests that form part of the hypothesis confirmation are in terms of Katz and Fodor (1963) markers which are given in the lexicon for the nouns, and by general rule for the cases. Marcus notes (p. 320) that this approach is rather stark, and that the parser would have to be able to make judgments about comparative semantic 'goodness': results are marked as 'strongly' or 'mildly preferred', and obviously the combination of case assignments with the greatest number of strong preferences will be taken as correct.

In conclusion, Marcus's case-frame interpreter can be seen as a fairly straightforward implementation of the classical concept of Case: the case-set derives from earliest attempts at putting Fillmore's (1968*a*) proposals into practice, and the associated semantic theory is similarly relatively traditional in terms of the TG school.

Like Marcus's case frame interpreter, Celce-Murcia's (1975) seeks to find a representation for surface strings deep enough to 'permit semantic interpretation' (p. 2), and does so by assigning case roles to elements in a syntactic structure.

As above, a purely syntactic parse stage is assumed, which is '. . . capable of recognizing constituents such as noun phrases, prepositional phrases, finite verbs or verb phrases, and adverbs or adverb phrases in [the] surface string of words' (Celce-Murcia, 1975:104f). The cases ('functional relations') used are Theme (= Patient), Causal Actant (CA), Locus, Source and Goal. The one-case-per-clause principle is maintained, though CA is subdivided between 'direct' and 'indirect', corresponding to Agent and Instrument respectively, the distinction only being upheld when they co-occur (p. 16). Goal (and other roles?) is divided between 'immediate' and 'remote' – roughly the inner versus outer distinction seen in Chapter 9 above.

The most interesting feature of Celce-Murcia's approach is her recognition of different verb paradigms '. . . that summarize or recapitulate the functional relations and syntactic and semantic features of large classes of verbs. Then the only feature needed in the lexicon would be a specification of which paradigm(s) a given verb sense belongs to' (*ibid.*, p. 22).

This approach is clearly reminiscent of Chafe (1970), whom she cites (cf. Chapter 4), but in fact the paradigms that are proposed derive from the verbs' syntactic behaviour rather than from their semantic characterisation, as in Chafe. Several such paradigms are exemplified by Celce-Murcia, and are summarised in Figure 1. This is not, apparently, the complete list, however.

Paradigm	associated relations	example
intransitive	Theme	*walk*
transitive	CA, Theme	*kill*
ergative	CA, Theme	*open*
two-way transfer	CA, Theme, Source, Goal	*carry*
source-subject transfer	CA, Theme, Goal	*give*
goal-subject transfer	Goal, Theme, Source	*buy*
one-way *put/take*	CA, Theme, {Source, Goal}	*put, take*
two-way *put/take*	CA, Theme, Source, Goal	*lead*
have	Locus, Theme	*have*
have inverse	Theme, Locus	*occupy*

Figure 1: Examples of verb paradigms

Associated with each paradigm is not only a set of associated relations (= case frame features), but also a number of underlying transformations that can be taken into account. Note that these are not transformations that are applied as such, but rather they can be assumed to have applied. Thus, for example, verbs in the ergative paradigm, with which two relations are associated, are marked for a transformation which deletes the CA: this feature can be used to account for the occurrence of an ergative verb with a surface subject only, and correctly assign the Theme relation to that argument. In a similar way, 'virtually all motional verbs' (p. 30) will be said to have undergone a 'reflexive deletion', accounting for the dual-role (CA and Theme) of the surface subject. Another such transformation is 'accusative deletion' which accounts for the missing Theme (normally obligatory for all verbs) with verbs like *eat*. The system also includes 'real' transformations, i.e. those that rearrange the syntactic structure, such as 'passivisation reversal' which inserts a dummy CA when a passive is recognised.

Little is said in Celce-Murcia's account about the actual algorithms which implement this grammar. Nor is there mention of semantics. For example, it would appear that the assignment of relations to noun-phrases (etc.) is essentially a function of the syntactic role and the verb paradigm. This explains why there is no need to distinguish Agent and Instrument unless they co-occur, since there are no 'semantic' features associated with any of the relations.

The final system we wish to consider here is our own PTOSYS (Somers and Johnson, 1979; Somers, 1980*a*, 1982*c*,*d*) which is like the other two systems in having as its aim the mapping of '. . . surface strings of English onto a formalism representing a level of "deep" structure (a Case frame)' (Somers and Johnson, 1979:85). Like the other two systems, PTOSYS first subjects the text to a straightforward syntactic parse which identifies the main predicate and its 'arguments': noun phrases and adverbials.

The case-frame generator in PTOSYS relies on matching these arguments with the cases in the potential case-frame which is inferred from inherent features of the predicate. These are like Celce-Murcia's 'paradigms', except that they are essentially semantic in nature, the linguistic models of Chafe (1970) and Cook (1972*b*) forming the linguistic basis of the system. The case-slot filling algorithm is based on an interaction of four basic types of information available to the system:

(i) cases associated with syntactic functions such as subject, object or with the prepositions in prepositional-phrase arguments;

(ii) noun features (like those of Chafe) which limit the possible cases for each argument, e.g. animate cannot be Manner;

(iii) verb features which determine (a) the obligatory, optional, expected and prohibited cases, and (b) the likely syntactic functions that these cases will have;

(iv) various heuristics based on co-occurrence possibilities of certain syntactic functions and cases (e.g. when there are two non-prepositional objects, the first is likely to be Beneficiary), and of various verb features and cases (e.g. Beneficiary can only co-occur with an action or benefactive verb).

The general flavour of PTOSYS is clearly more semantic than either Marcus's or Celce-Murcia's systems, though the semantics are still fairly shallow: the representation is 'not independent of (some of) the lexical items' (Somers, 1982*c*:238).

PTOSYS is intended as a general-purpose natural-language front-end for various purposes, or even as a model for testing theories of Case; also of interest is the system's method of dealing with new lexical items (see especially Somers, 1982*d*): new dictionary entries are built up via a three-way interaction between the system, a human operator, and the text, in which the system asks questions, sometimes framed using other items from the sentence under analysis, to complete its knowledge about the syntactic and semantic properties of the new lexical items. In some instances, the system can infer some of the information it requires from the text alone, and then only seeks confirmation of hypotheses from the operator.

The most recent work on the system (Gormley, in prep.; Somers and Nomura, 1987) has involved a complete re-implementation in a more appropriate programming language (Lisp as opposed to Pascal), as well as a more explicit and direct relation of verb-features to case-frames: 'default frames' detailing case, syntactic function, syntactic form and semantic features are stored in a table, as in (1) for example.

(1) default frame for emotion verbs

```
(EMOTION-FRAME
  ((CASE EXP) (SYNTACTIC-FORM (NP))
              (SEMANTIC-FEATURES (HUMAN))
              (SYNTACTIC-FUNCTION (SUBJ))
              (OBLIG))
  ((CASE PAT) (SYNTACTIC-FORM (NP S))
              (SEMANTIC-FEATURES (ANY))
              (SYNTACTIC-FUNCTION (DIR-OBJ SCOMP))
              (S-TYPE (INFINITIVE GERUNDIVE))
              (OBLIG)))
```

Dictionary entries for verbs simply indicate the appropriate verb class (2), to which verb-specific information in the form of modifications to slots or additional slots can be added (3).

(2) dictionary entry for *love*

```
(LOVE (SYNTACTIC-FORM (V))
      (CLASS (EMOTION)))
```

(3) dictionary entry for *regard*

```
(REGARD (SYNTACTIC-FORM (V))
  (CLASS (EMOTION)
        ((CASE COMPL) (SYNTACTIC-FORM (PP))
                      (SEMANTIC-FEATURES (EMOTIVE))
                      (SYNTACTIC-FUNCTION (POBJ))
                      (PREPOSITION (WITH))
                      (OBLIG))))
```

In this way, the information required by the case-slot filling algorithm is now more centralised, allowing a more orderly procedure than in the original implementation, as described above.

4. *Case supplants syntactic parse*

In the next selection of systems we shall look at, Case plays an instrumental rather than target role, and in particular it is used to assist or replace a purely syntactic parse, the whole functioning to some purpose other than discovering case-frames *per se*. We shall look first at SPEECHLIS (Nash-Webber, 1975), where syntax and Case work hand in hand, and at two systems where it is claimed that syntax is dispensed with altogether in favour of Case (Wilks, 1976*a*; and Hendrix *et al.*, 1973).

SPEECHLIS (Nash-Webber, 1975) is a speech understanding system developed at Bolt, Beranek and Newman and applied experimentally to two domains: information retrieval from the lunar geology database, also used in the LUNAR system (Woods, 1977), and from a similar database concerned with travel budget management. SPEECHLIS is one of the systems included in Bruce's (1977) summary. The system 'understands' spoken requests for information by calculating a 'semantic representation' for the request in the form of a case-labelled syntactic structure. Predicates (which can be nouns or verbs) recognised by the system have associated with them case frames which '. . . are useful both in making local predications in the form of proposals and in checking the consistency of syntactic and semantic hypotheses' (Nash-Webber, 1975:372f). The case frames themselves contain a specification of the associated cases, and the likely realisation of the (filled) case frame (e.g. clause or noun phrase), information about 'intercase restrictions' (if any), as well as

> '. . . descriptive information about each case in the frame:
> a) its name, e.g. NP-OBJ, S-HEAD (The first part of the names gives redundant information about . . . syntactic realization. The second part is an abbreviated Fillmore-type (Fillmore, 1968[*a*]) case name . . .);
> b) the way it can be filled – whether by a word or phrase naming the concept (EQU) or an instantiation of it (MEM), . . . ;
> c) a list of prepositions which could signal the case when it is realized as a prepositional phrase . . . ;
> d) an indication of whether the case must be explicitly specified (OBL), whether it is optional and unnecessary (OPT), or whether, when absent, it must be derivable from the context (ELLIP). . . .' (*ibid.*, p. 372)

The case frames for the verb *contain* and the noun *analysis* are given (p. 370) as examples (1)-(2). Note that the predicate itself is treated as if it were a 'case' (HEAD) – a minor notational convention.

(1) Case frame for *contain*
(((REALIZES.CLAUSE))
(ACTIVSUBJ S-LOC)
(PASSIVSUBJ S-PAT)
(S-HEAD (EQU.CONTAIN) NIL OBL)
(S-LOC (MEM.SAMPLE) (IN) OBL)
(S.PAT (MEM.COMPONENT) NIL OBL))

(2) Case frame for *analysis*

```
(((REALIZES.NOUN-PHRASE))
 (NP-HEAD (EQU.ANALYSIS) NIL OBL)
 (NP-OBJ (MEM.COMPONENT) (OF FOR) ELLIP)
 (NP-LOC (MEM.SAMPLE) (IN FOR OF ON) ELLIP))
```

Nash-Webber stresses (p. 373) the use of the case frame to make local predictions about the syntactic structure, and to confirm syntactic hypotheses. The marking of cases as obligatory or optional clearly plays a part here, as does their association with certain prepositions. Note that, unlike in Fillmore (1968*a*), the association of prepositions with cases is done on a predicate-by-predicate basis, as we see in the two examples, where LOC is associated with *in* with *contain*, but with a range of prepositions with *analysis*.

One final remark concerns Nash-Webber's use of the term 'case frame' (cf. Rosner and Somers, 1980 and Section 6 below). Note that Nash-Webber's 'case frames' are like Fillmore's 'case frame features' and define the possible configurations for a given predicate. These contrast with what she calls 'case frame tokens' (p. 375) which express hypotheses about how a given occurrence is to be analysed, and which is exemplified in (3).

(3) Case frame token for *analyses of ferrous oxide*

```
[CFT #6
(((REALIZES.NOUN-PHRASE))
 (NP-HEAD (ANALYSES.ANALYSIS) NIL OBL)
 (NP-GOAL (CFT #5.COMPONENT) (OR FOR) ELLIP)
 (NP-LOC (MEM.SAMPLE) (IN FOR OF ON) ELLIP))]
[CFT # 5
(((REALIZES.NOUN-PHRASE)
  (CASEOF CFT #6))
  (NP-MOD (FERROUS.ELEMENT) NIL OBL)
  (NP-HEAD (OXIDE.RADICAL) NIL OBL))]
```

An approach to parsing in which conventional syntactic analysis is essentially eschewed in favour of a 'purely semantic' processing is exemplified in the Stanford Machine Translation project of Wilks (1973*a*, *b*). We consider this here rather than in the next chapter because the translation aspect of the system is only seen as a testing ground for the parser: 'This environment provides a pretty clear test of language understanding, because French translations for everyday prose are either right or wrong, and can be seen to be so, while, at the same time, the major difficulties of understanding programs . . . can all be represented within a machine translation environment. . . . In that way the French output makes quite clear whether or not the program has made the correct inferences in order to understand what it is translating' (Wilks, 1977:370). General descriptions of this system, and its underlying notion of 'preference semantics', are widely available (e.g. Wilks, 1975*a*, *b*; 1976*b*:158ff; 1977:369ff; 1978), so we need not recapitulate the details here, since we are principally interested only in how Case fits into the general scheme. Suffice it to say that Wilks's parser attempts to build a meaning representation made up of 'templates' having the basic form of 'agent-action-object', which are bound together by 'paraplates' and 'inference rules'. The templates are built up from 'formulas' which represent the individual word senses. Each of these structures is ultimately constructed from an inventory of eighty 'semantic primitive elements', and from functions and predicates 'ranging over' them (1976*b*:158; 1977:369f). An important and interesting point about these representations is that '. . . the basic representation is applied directly to the text and can then be "massaged" by various forms of inference to become as deep as is necessary for well defined tasks demonstrating understanding' (1977:369).

Our interest lies in Wilks's use of Case notions, a feature of his system on which he concentrates only in Wilks (1967*a*). The eighty primitive semantic elements mentioned above divide up into different types, one of which is 'case elements', which are enumerated in (1976*a*:8f) as follows:

DIRECtion (subdivided into TO, FROM, UP, THRU)
INSTrument
FOR [= Recipient]
IN [= Containment]
LOCAtion [spatial]
TLOCA [= Time LOCAtion]
GOAL [purpose]
SOURce [substance from which something comes]
WAY [= Manner]
OBJEct
SUBJ [= Agent: 'a semantic, rather than a surface subject']
WITH [accompaniment]
POSSessive

The preferred semantic values for fillers of these cases are given not by general rule, but in the formulas for individual words, as in (4) for *break*, which can be read as 'human Agent (SUBJ) strikes something (OBJE) which is a physical object using (INST) something with the purpose of causing the physical object to be not whole'.

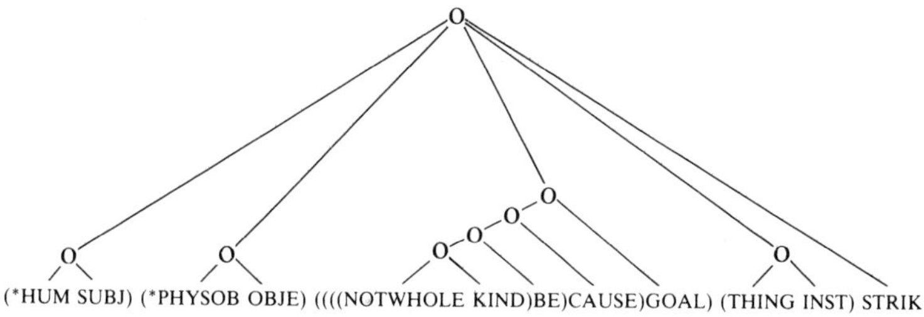

(4) Formula for *break* (Wilks, 1976*a*:11)

When the word *break* is encountered in a text, this formula is used to cause appropriate templates to be constructed, specifying slots and typical fillers. The formula can be regarded as a case frame (feature) for the surface verb, but it also specifies other aspects that can be used if necessary for later inferencing or untangling idiosyncratic ('Idiomatic', preference-breaking) uses of the verbs. Thus in (4) the cases SUBJ, OBJE and INST belong to the surface case-frame, while GOAL stipulates more precisely the 'meaning' (and differentiates, for example *hit* from *break*). However, Wilks stresses that '. . . the formula maker is concerned only with specifying, as best as he can, the *semantic preferences* of the particular word in question. If it were a verb he would semantically specify the preferred agent, say, of that action, *with no implicit reference to agenthood as such*' (1976*a*:23f) [emphases mine]. The question whether it means nothing *per se* to be an agent, or whatever, is an important one, to which we shall return in our general discussion.

Wilks further underlines the role of the formula in providing an interface between surface form and underlying meaning. Although there is nothing in the formula corresponding to the traditional notions of obligatory and optional cases, Wilks explains that these notions are less important in an analysis model (like his) than in generative model (like Fillmore, 1968*a*). The point is, presumably, that Wilks's system 'does not mind' if cases remain unfilled, and so the notion of optionality is redundant. Furthermore, the system does not seek to confirm wellformedness of input, and so the notion of obligatoriness is likewise unnecessary.

Note that formulas are not empty case-frames with slots to be filled in, but '. . . "blueprints" for how representations are to be assembled *elsewhere from whole formulas*' (p. 14) [emphasis mine]. Wilks takes great pains to stress the role of these formulas in his system, contrasting the surface-oriented view of Case represented by Fillmore and the very deep Case used by Schank (see Section 6). In Wilks's system Case plays both roles plus the intermediate role of connecting the two: 'Formulas are meaning structures for surface word senses. Formulas for surface verbs *can* be interpreted as case frames for the verbs, in that they contain case subparts . . . that the formula maker has considered necessary to express as part of the meaning of the verb' (p. 23) [emphasis original]. '. . . I have tried to justify the *intermediate* role of case descriptions in formulas: by claiming both that they give a meaning structure that, under inferences processes [*sic*], can provide a real underlying structure for text and that they must include enough of the surface case behaviour (of the verb meaning being expressed) to give procedural power in analyzing the input surface sentences' (p. 27) [emphasis original].

Let us look now more closely at how the formulas are used to assist in the computation of representations. Wilks stresses a second time that the formulas are more like lexical entries than completable frames: a good analogy might be in embroidery where you might copy some design (formula) as against the case where the pattern is printed onto the material to be embroidered over. The actual representation consists of 'templates': '. . . a network based on an agent formula, an action formula and an object formula (although any of these may be dummies)' (p. 28). Wilks explains the process as follows: 'Templates, matched onto sentences and clauses expressed as strings of formulas, try to pick up surface subjects and use the formulas as blueprints for selecting the best template, by trying to ensure that the surface subject is also the agent. In the initial matching of "The hammer broke the window" this will not be possible because the formula for "hammer", the surface object, will be placed at the first (or agent) node of the template. However, since the formula for "break" will be at the corresponding action node the system will know at any point in later processing that the surface subject is not the underlying (animate) agent as preferred by the "break" formula at the action node of the same template. This clash will . . . lead to later extraction inferencing that deals with the ergative paradigm in a uniform manner' (p. 29).

Whereas verbal and nominal elements have formulas associated with them, prepositions are dealt with by 'paraplates', which correspond to the cases in the system, though on a many-to-one basis. The paraplates are in fact principally associated with surface prepositions on the one hand and with pairs of 'template-skeletons' on the other. These template-skeletons are like real templates, except that instead of having their nodes associated with formulas, they define characteristics of formulas that could attach there. Thus for example one of the paraplates for the preposition *by*, applicable to its use in (5), would have at its three nodes (6) part of the formula for a MOVE verb, the semantic element corresponding to the case (TO), and a formula for its 'object'. We can see that prepositions are thus treated in a manner analagous to verbs.

(5) He left Lugano by the autostrada.

(6) ((*ANI)(MOVE)(WHERE POINT) TO→ □ □ (WHERE LINE)

The representation for the entire sentence is as in (7), with the tie between *left* and the *by*-template being established by dint of (i) the match between the formula in the first node of the *by*-paraplate (8a) and all three nodes in the *leave*-template (8b-d), and (ii) the match between the formula in the third node of the *by* template and the formula for *autostrada* (8e).

(7) [He left Lugano]

TO→ [□ by the+autostrada]

(8a) (*ANI)(MOVE)(WHERE POINT)

(8b) *he* has head MAN included by *ANI

(8c) *leave* has head MOVE

(8d) *Lugano* has head containing subpart (WHERE POINT)

(8e) *autostrada* has head containing subpart (WHERE LINE)

There are several paraplates associated with *by*, to cover all the possible uses in (9).

(9a) He left Lugano by courtesy of the police.

(9b) He left Lugano by Comano.

(9c) He left Lugano by car.

(9d) He left Lugano by stealth.

(9e) He left Lugano by Monday night.

(9f) He left Lugano by following the arrows.

(9g) He left Lugano by stealing a boat.

(9h) This painting is by Titian.

The different paraplates are stacked, this stack being ordered according to the primitive action (p. 34), though not necessarily straighforwardly (p. 35). But this ordering will pick out first the most likely case for a given preposition with a given action, and thus can partly capture the Valency grammar notion of 'strongly governed case' if necessary.

Wilks gives further details of 'case extraction' processes, which represent inferences that can be made from the case content of the formulas associated with input words. Thus, for example, since the formula for *fire+at* is as in (10), 'case specialists' appropriate to each case in (10) produce extracted templates which constitute possible but unstated inferences from the input sentence (11a). The case specialist for INST for example might yield the inference (11b).

(10) Formula for *fire+at*

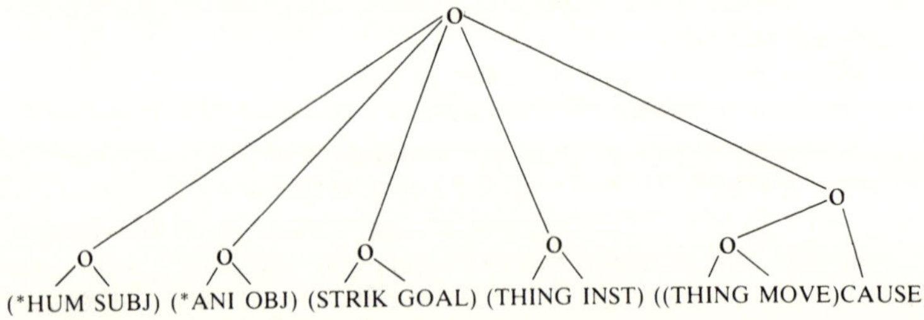

(11a) John fired at the stags.

(11b) John used a thing (= a shotgun).

We need not concern ourselves here with the mechanism by which this is done, but may note that this feature of the system gives it a power considerably beyond that normally needed for translation (other than of classical problem sentences as in (12), where the referent of the pronoun *them* must be identified for translation into French, which has gender concord in such constructions), and puts it on a par with other language understanding systems aiming at a deep level of knowledge representation.

(12a) The soldiers fired at the women and some of them fell.
Les soldats tirèrent sur les femmes et quelques *unes* tombèrent.

(12b) The soldiers fired at the women and some of them missed.
Les soldats tirèrent sur les femmes et quelques *uns* manquèrent.

The system of Hendrix *et al.* (1973) is a question-answering system for a small database with a natural-language analyser for requests and input of new information, and a generator for responses. Both these modules are driven by a 'variant' of a (Woods, 1970) ATN, while the form of the database or 'modelling system' is in terms of 'canonical structures' resembling case frames. I present the system here as a model of a simple and straightforward use of Case.

The parser, it is claimed, 'allows for direct translation into canonical structures' (Hendrix *et al.* 1973:262), and although, as we shall see, this is only partly true, there is nevertheless no syntactic analysis phase as such. Entries in the lexicon for (surface) verbs (e.g. the entry for *buy* (13)) specify, in the form of a property list, the canonical verb/event associated with the verb, its various surface forms (not shown here), and a list of 'P-RULES' relating to the surface noun phrases and prepositional phrases to the deep cases associated with the canonical verb. These P-RULE attributes are formed of triples indicating (i) surface form ('OK' means 'no preposition'), (ii) semantic features and (iii) the associated deep case. As can be seen in the example, the cases are slightly 'specialised' (see Section 5).

```
(13) L-BUY
        WORDCLASS VERB
        CANON-VB EXCHANGE
        [. . .]
        PRULES ((OK (HUMAN ORGANIZATION) BUYER)
                (OK (PHYSOBJ) THINGBT)
                (FROM (HUMAN ORGANIZATION) SELLER)
                (FOR (MONEY) THINGGIVEN)
                (AT (PLACE) LOC)
                (OK (DAYPART) TIME)
                (IN (DAYPART) TIME))
```

The application of the parser to a text gives two intermediate structures: the first acts as input to the 'case interpreter' and simply divides the text up into its major constituents – not a full-blown syntactic analysis, note. This structure consists of the verbal constituent, given its canonical form, together with modality information plus a list of the prepositional and noun phrases, given as, again, a triple indicating (i) the syntactic form, (ii) semantic features copied from the lexicon, and (iii) some morpho-syntactic feature information. This is illustrated in (14).

(14a) Who bought a cake at the new bakery from the baker?

(14b) Verbal constituent

```
        (CANON-VB EXCHANGE MODAL (TENSE PAST MOD
                                      INTERROG . . .))
    NP-PP constituents
        ((OK (PHYSOBJ)(TOK L-CAKE DET INDEF NBR S))
         (AT (PLACE)(TOK L-BAKERY DET DEF NBR S MOD (AGE
                                              L-NEW)))
         (FROM (HUMAN)(TOK L-BAKER DET DEF NBR S)))
    Q-word constituent
        (OK (HUM)(TOK L-WHO))
```

The case assigning stage is relatively straightforward: for each constituent an entry in the P-RULES of the verb is sought which matches for preposition. If the corresponding set of semantic features intersect and the given deep case has not already been assigned, then that case is associated with that element. This process gives a 'canonical structure' for our example sentence as in (15).

(15) (CANON-VB EXCHANGE MODAL (. . .)
SELLER (TOK L-BAKER . . .)
THINGBT (TOK L-CAKE . . .)
LOC (TOK L-BAKERY . . .)
Q (ARGS (BUYER) TOK L-WHO))

The case assignment to the Q-word element – if the sentence is a question – differs from the other elements in that all the cases remaining that are compatible with the features of the Q-word are assigned here.

So far, the system looks like the classical model in which the verb determines an array of case slots to be filled, their expected surface form, and associated selection restrictions in terms of broad semantic features. What is interesting at this point is the use of the ATN to effect the parse, though unfortunately more precise details than those reported above are not given. It is no doubt in part due to the use of this mechanism that the system achieves such favourable processing times, as the authors report (p. 269).

The 'modeling system' for the database is in terms of the same sorts of entities, which makes mapping from the parsed statements or requests relatively straightforward. For example, with a statement like (16a) which might be represented as (16b), the canonical verb EXCHANGE will trigger a set of deletions and additions to the database as shown.

(16a) John traded his car to Tom for Tom's boat.

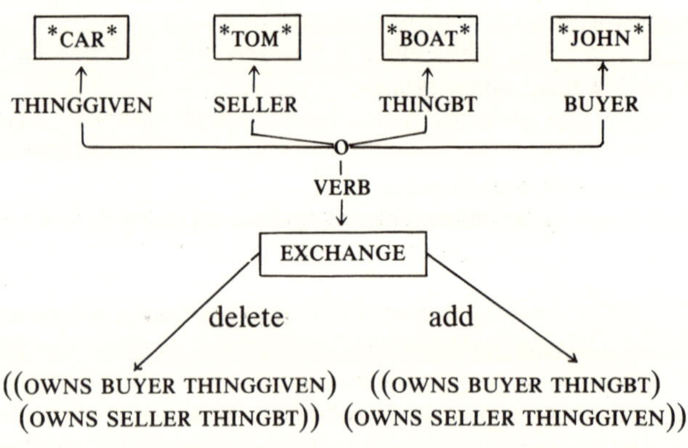

(16b) [after Hendrix *et al.*, 1973: 265]

Finally, the generation of responses from the database is also accomplished with a case-drive ATN. Lexical entries for canonical verbs specify surface verbs which in turn have – as well as the P-RULES seen in (13) – 'G-RULES' which give the possible surface configurations as exemplified in (17), again for *buy*.

(17) GRULES ((BUYER ACTIVE THINGBT (FROM SELLER)
(FOR THINGGIVEN))
(THINGBT PASSIVE (FROM SELLER) (FOR THINGGIVEN)))

It is fairly obvious how these G-RULES will be applied. Note that as we are now generating from deep structures, we are much closer to the original concept of Case as a component of a generative grammar: the case frames are 'given', the surface structures are what is aimed at. Here, as in Fillmore's (1968*a*) case-frame features, brackets indicate optionality. The generator must search the lexical entries of the verbs specified by the canonical verb for one where no non-optional cases are unspecified. Thus for example if the database stipulated only the thing bought and the seller, then obviously the active form of *buy* could not be chosen, since the buyer in this structure is obligatory. The parser would choose 'in any desired fashion (perhaps by random choice)' (p. 268) between the available structures: presumably *buy* in the passive or *sell* in the active.

Bruce (1975:346) comments on the directness of the link between surface expression and the chosen representation in this system. As we have seen, this allows a very direct parsing strategy, and as Bruce says, '. . . the structure used is not completely adequate for all the knowledge needed. Nevertheless it is valuable in showing what can be done with a transparent representation . . . , as opposed to the customary use of more general, but opaque procedures' (Bruce, 1975:346).

Before we leave this section on Case-drive ATNS, we should perhaps pick up on the fact that we have not been able to discuss in more detail the possible characteristics of an ATN based on Case. In Hendrix *et al.*'s description of their system, we are told that ATNS are used, and we are shown some of the linguistic details, but we do not see what the parser itself looks like.

I would like here to sketch a proposal for a Case-driven ATN parser, and put forward some ideas that, surprisingly, I have not come across in any of the literature on Case or on ATNS. Because this is only to be a sketch of a theory, I shall not deviate into an explanation of the working of an ATN. Three overviews cited above (Bates, 1978; Johnson, 1983; Winograd, 1983;195-271) cover this ground admirably.

It is noteworthy that ATNs are often used for syntactic parsing, and as such the calls to sub-processes (PUSH) and category tests (CAT) are typically in terms of syntactic elements. It seems at least conceivable to me that an ATN could be devised in which transitions represent tests for cases rather than syntactic categories.

The simplest scenario would be one like (18), where we have two stages each of which has a number of loops, one for each case (only four are actually shown).

(18)

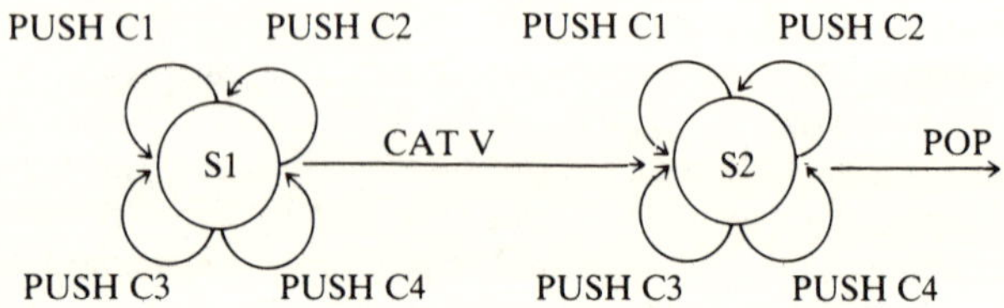

The transition from the first of these to the second consumes the verb. In this way we recognise the possibility that some cases can occur before the verb: this is clearly so with whatever case is acting as surface subject (not necessarily Agent, note); but in a sentence like (19a), notice that there are several 'adjunct' cases also before the verb, while (19b) demonstrates the sort of disregard for word-order prescription that has encouraged semantics-based parsing.

(19a) Yesterday at Lords' because of bad weather the umpires cancelled the game.

(19b) Over the wall jumped Fred.

The PUSH transitions for each case might look something like (20), which shows a sub-network for INST.

(20)

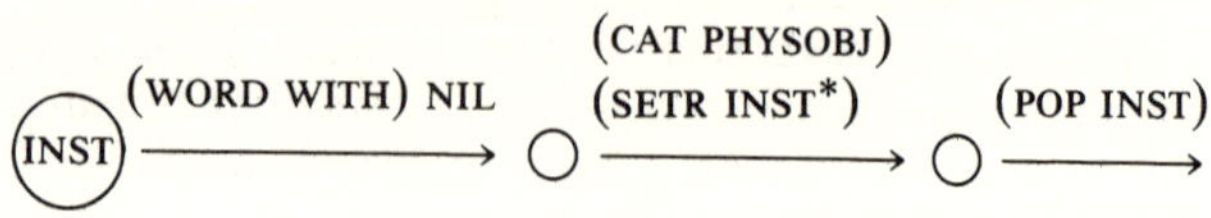

It may be that the set of cases that can occur before the verb is not exactly the same as those which occur after, so that the transitions leading from and to S1 and S2 in (18) may not be identical.

With the use of hold registers (Bates, 1978:202), we could perhaps do a little better, by delaying analysis of any elements before the verb until after the verb has been found (21). In this way, we could make use of information associated with the verb to indicate which variants of a given case network were appropriate, and indeed which cases to look for. That is to say, we could take advantage of knowledge about the cases expected for a given verb and their typical signalling preposition (if any) and associated semantic features, just as Hendrix *et al.* do. In (21) the transitions from S2 to S3 are determined by Chafe-like (1970) features for each of which there is an associated sub-network (e.g. (21b) for action verbs). Here, the complement cases are first sought, and then the adjuncts. For each case it is necessary to look both at input and at the HOLD register (21c), since any case, whether complement or adjunct, may occur almost anywhere in relation to the verb. The PUSH for each case will resemble (20).

(21a)

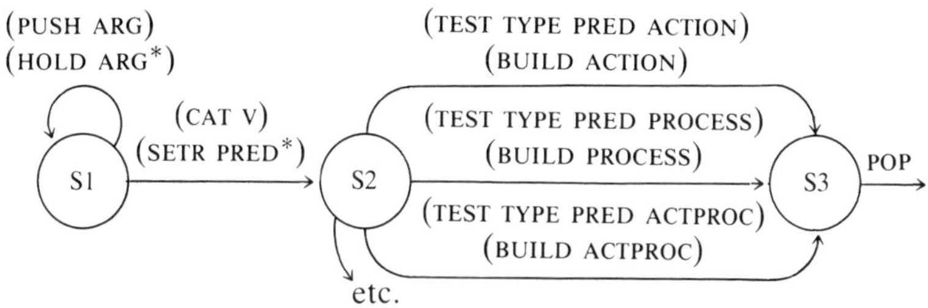

(21b)

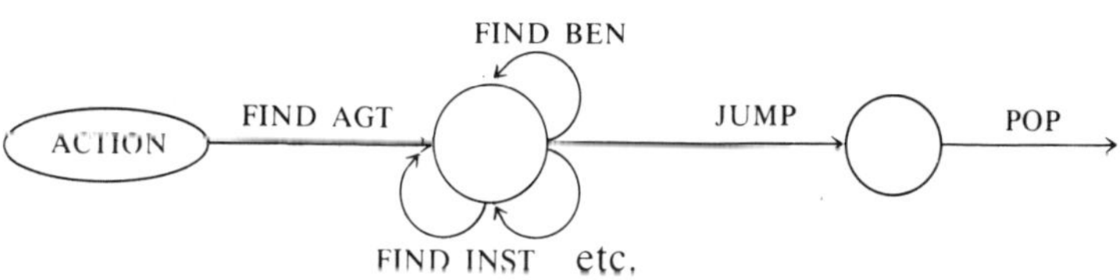

(21c)

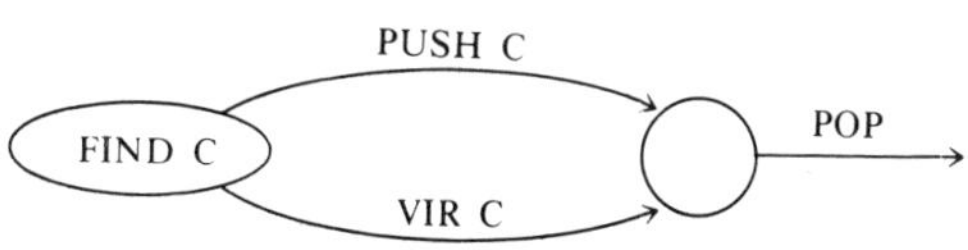

To conclude this sketch, let it be said that this adaptation of a now standard device does not seem extraordinary. Clearly, there remain a number of details to be worked out, and the proposal would carry a lot more weight if it could be shown whether and how well it works. This is an interesting project for a small pilot project in the near future.

Our putative Case-driven ATN is not unlike the 'semantic ATN' of Burton (1976) and Woods *et al.* (1976) illustrated by Ritchie (1983:205) (22). A more complex, but similar example, possibly from the same original source, is given by Bates (1978:238f).

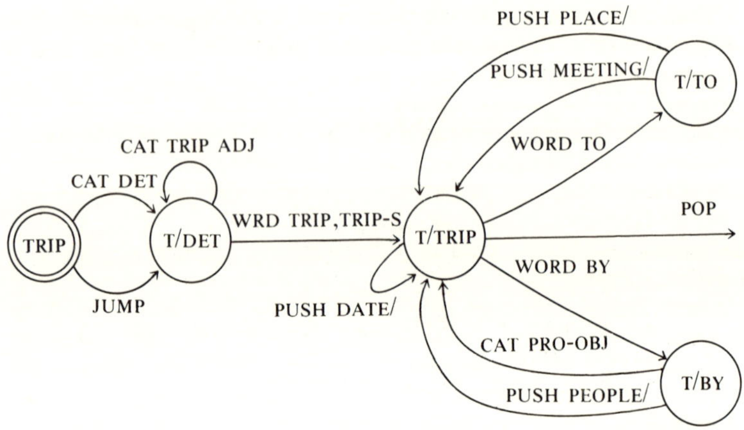

(22) [from Burton (1976), as shown by Ritchie (1983:205)]

Here again we are clearly avoiding the necessity of building syntactic structure, but notice that the network in (22) is domain-specific, and that the sub-networks – if their names are anything to go by – define semantic categories rather than semantic roles. In fact the network in (22) appears to be significantly 'deeper' than our own case-based approach. As Ritchie notes, '. . . it is not clear how the various sub-networks for different semantic categories are to be designed. Is the sub-network for parsing a "trip" radically different from that for parsing a "meeting"? The range of ways of expressing these referential items are roughly the same (traditional noun phrases, in fact)' (Ritchie, 1983:205). This criticism is perhaps also valid for the case-ATN proposed above, though at least the case sub-networks are fairly general, or at least of a generality comparable with that of syntactic categories in a syntactic ATN. One worry is indeed that the approach might necessitate reduplication of the same or similar sub-networks for different cases, though it is hoped that some way to minimise this could be found.

5. *'Specialised' case systems*

In most of the systems we have looked at so far, whatever the specific approach or purpose was, the case system used tended to be fairly traditional in nature. One exception was Hendrix *et al.* (1973), where we saw cases like Buyer, Seller, Thinggiven and Thingbt attaching to predicates like *buy* and *sell*. In this section we shall look at some more examples of non-standard case systems which I want to call 'specialised' systems.

There are two ways in which a case system can be regarded as specialised. The first is exemplified by CHRONOS (Kulikowski and Weiss, 1971; Chokhani, 1973) where a set of relations between predicates and arguments form a close analogy to Case grammar, except that these relations are not the usual Agent, Patient, etc., but are relations that are specially relevant to the domain. A further example – though not one we shall look at in detail – is the PROLID system (Harbusch and Rothkegel, 1984), which analyses texts from a corpus of German EEC decisions: here there is a more or less even mixture of traditional and text-type specific cases and predicate classes. The second type of case specialisation is exemplified by PLANES (Waltz, 1978), the system of Hendrix *et al.* already seen, and, above all, in Bobrow and Winograd's (1977) KRL. Here again we have predicates with slots filled by arguments in a more or less strictly defined way, but the 'specialisation' lies in the fact that the slot names ('cases') and their characteristics (case defining features) differ from predicate to predicate. We shall discuss in Section 7 whether or not this is still 'Case'. PLANES is interesting from this point of view in mixing specialised and general cases.

CHRONOS is a system developed at Rutgers University by a large team of researchers. It is essentially a medical expert system, concentrating for experimental purposes on the eye disease glaucoma (Kulikowski and Weiss, 1971). Our interest centres on the 'causal network model' (Chokhani, 1973) and in particular on the representation of sentences input to the system.

This representation is Case-like, in the sense that it consists of predicates with dependent arguments. In fact, Chokhani calls these 'verbs' and 'cases', though one of the interesting features of CHRONOS is that the physiological primitives that are taken as the 'verbs' are not necessarily expressed as surface verbs. For example, in the sentence (1a), the predicate is taken to be *flow*, with *increases* filling one of its argument places (1b).

(1a) Flow of aqueous humor in the anterior chamber increases.

(1b)

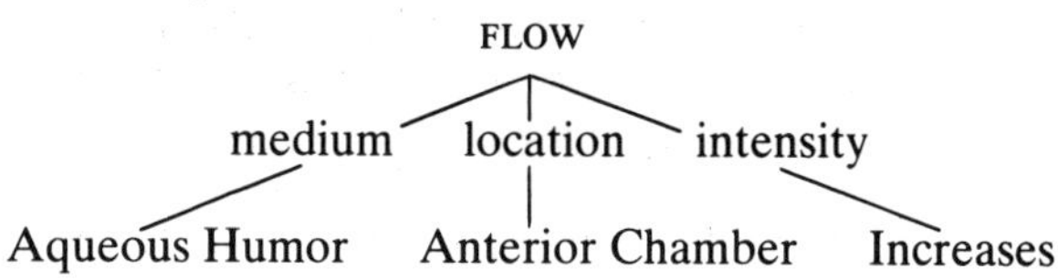

Just as in standard Case, each physiological primitive or verb defines its own 'paradigm', i.e. the number of cases dependent on it (Chokhani, 1973:7). From the list of 'primitive descriptors' (verbs) given by Kulikowski and Weiss (1971:8), we can see the range of cases proposed for CHRONOS (2).

(2) PRESSURE (Medium, Location, Magnitude, Time)
TIME (Frequency, Local duration, Global duration, Velocity)
FLOW (Medium, Location, Magnitude, Time)
ATROPHY (Object, Magnitude, Distribution, Time)
ABNORMALITY (Location, Type, Distribution, Time)
SIZE (Object, Magnitude, Time)
etc.

An important feature of CHRONOS is that the case-frame-like structures are not only used as a representation of input to the system, but also for propositions in the diagnosis model of the expert system. The model is essentially one in which a network of causalities is set up, these causalities differing in such features as probability, implication, and so on. So, for example, we have a relatively weak causality rule (3a) (Kulikowski and Weiss, 1971:12) which can be read as (3b).

(3a) Pressure (blood, cardiovascular system, ⩽low, ~) $\rightarrow^{2}$ Flow (blood, central retinal vessels, ⩽low, ~)

(3b) Minimal or zero blood-pressure in the cardiovascular system over any period of time ['~' means 'irrelevant'] sometimes results in minimal or zero flow of blood in the central retinal vessels.

Note that these rules are part of the system (not part of the language processing), and that the system functions by taking statements in natural language like (1a) or the first half of (3b), and using its knowledge about implications and causes, derives its model for diagnosis. But the key point is that the mapping between the representation of input sentences and the representation of the facts they express is very straightforward.

PLANES (Waltz, 1978) is a natural language front-end for the question-answering function of a large relational database consisting of information about military aircraft maintenance and flight data. It processes casual users' queries using a traditional ATN parse and the output is converted into sets of 'semantic constituents' for matching against the database via the use of '*concept case frames* (semantic sentence patterns)' (p. 530) [emphasis original]. It is these 'concept case frames' (CCFS) that concern us. The database itself is arranged in 'record formats' '. . . each containing between ten and twenty attributes (fields), where each attribute draws its values from one of the 80 underlying domains, such as date of the action, type of aircraft, serial number of the aircraft, type of malfunction . . .' (p. 258). It is these attribute domains which the CCFS map onto, and this is the sense in which the 'cases' in PLANES are specialised. As Waltz explains, 'Our concept case frames are somewhat different from ordinary case frames [Bruce (1975)]; each concept case frame consists of an *act* (typically relating to the verb [in the request being analysed]) and a list of noun phrases (. . .) which can occur meaningfully with the act. Unlike ordinary case frames, we do not store information about the role (e.g. agent, patient, instrument) played by the various phrases, . . .' (p. 252) [emphasis original]. Apart from 'cases' specifically associated with certain verbs, there are some more general cases – 'phrases which occur in every case frame, such as "time period"' (*idem*) – which are not specified in the particular case frame.

Few examples are actually given, other than the two concept case frames for the two uses of *require* (4) and four for *fly* (5). One can imagine that the sort of request for which these CCFS are appropriate might be as in (6).

(4a) *require (*planetype, *maintenancetype)
(4b) *require (*component, *maintenancetype)
(5a) *fly (*planetype, *flighthours)
(5b) *fly (*planetype, *shiptype)
(5c) *fly (*planetype, *catapult-flights)
(5d) *fly (*planetype, *flights)
(6a) What skyhawks have needed engine maintenance since May 1, 1973? [→(4a)]
(6b) Find phantoms which had fewer than 15 flight hours in February 1974. [→(5a)]

We need not consider here in detail how such queries are mapped from their CCF representations onto the formal query expression – a type of predicate calculus – or its execution on the relational database, details of which are given by Waltz. But it is interesting to note that the CCFS are also used to generate paraphrases of the user's query, for confirmation. Unfortunately, further details of this function are not provided.

Waltz claims that this use of case frames helps to make the system as a whole easily extendable: 'To add the ability to handle a new type of sentence, one must only add a concept case frame which expresses that sentence, and verify that the query generator produces the appropriate query for the sentence' (p. 533). In addition, the case frames assist in pronoun resolution, in that they act as predictors of the expected arguments to a given predicate. The general attraction of the system is, as in CHRONOS, the ease with which case frames map onto the predicate calculus, and the homogeneity of these representations and the form in which the knowledge is stored in the database.

We now wish to discuss one aspect of Bobrow and Winograd's (1977) Knowledge Representation Language KRL and the experimental GUS (Genial Understander System) of Bobrow *et al*. (1977) which shares many of the design features of KRL. It should be stressed that in AI, KRL is an important artefact far beyond the one small (Case-like) aspect we shall be discussing here. KRL was designed not simply as a theory of knowledge representation but also as a high-level AI programming language, and even as only the former it touches a number of important issues beyond the scope of the current discussion. Many of these are dealt with in Lehnert and Wilks's (1979) critique of KRL and in Bobrow and Winograd's (1979) reply thereto. In this section we shall only consider, therefore, those aspects of KRL that bring it within the perview of this discussion on Case in AI.

Some the relevant presuppositions stated by Bobrow and Winograd are reproduced here: 'Knowledge should be organized around conceptual entities with associated descriptions and procedures . . . An important method of description is comparison with a known entity, with further specification of the described instance with respect to the prototype. Reasoning is dominated by a process of recognition in which new objects and events are compared to stored sets of expected prototypes, and in which specialized reasoning strategies are keyed to those prototypes' (Bobrow and Winograd, 1977:5).

These notions of 'expected prototypes' and 'further specification' are the ones which provide a basis for comparison of KRL and Case, since, as we shall see, the way that prototypes and realisations are expressed are quite reminiscent of linguistic case frames for predicates and sentences. We can see this immediately by looking at the prototype or 'abstract unit' for the event TRAVEL (7a) and the specified unit for the event in which Rusty flies to San Francisco to visit Danny and Terry (7b) (*ibid*., p. 10).

(7a) [Travel UNIT Abstract
<SELF (an Event)>
<mode (OR Plane Auto Bus)
<destination (a City)>]

```
(7b) [Event 137 UNIT Individual
             <SELF {(a Visit with
                         visitor = Rusty
                         visitees = (Items Danny Terry))
                       (a Travel with
                         mode = Plane
                         destination = San Francisco)}>]
```

(7a) is comparable to a set of case-frame features (in the Fillmore (1968*a*) sense) for *travel*, specifying two 'cases' and the types of entity that can fill these cases. (7b) is like a case frame for a particular event, again with 'cases', this time filled with actual objects or entities.

If we accept this analogy, there are several aspects of KRL that make an interesting comparison with Case. First, the objects that fill the 'case slots' are not words: we shall return to this distinction in Section 6. Next, there are a number of features that do not form part of Case theory, but are clearly compatible with some computer implementation of Case. One of these is the notion of 'default assumption', by which case-slots are filled automatically in the absence of further specification: compare the filling of an Agent slot with 'some unknown human' in a system like that of Wilks (see above). There is also a distinction between 'typical' and 'expected' properties that recalls the distinction in linguistic Case between complement and adjunct cases. Perhaps the most interesting feature of KRL as seen as an implementation of a Case-like theory, however, is the notion of 'procedural attachment' to slots: '. . . associated with each slot is a set of procedures which can be activated under certain conditions of use of the unit' (*ibid.*, p. 9). In fact, these procedures can be activated either in order to fill the slot, or once the slot has been filled (cf. Rosner and Somers, 1980:12). These procedures are subdivided into '. . . *servant*[s] which provide[] the method to carry out some operation, [and] *demon*[s] which cause[] a secondary effect of some event' (Bobrow and Winograd, 1977:33) [emphasis original]. In fact, servants and demons have a wider application than that associated with slot filling, but these need not concern us here.

The most important respect in which KRL differs from Case is that the case-like elements – the 'slots' – and especially their names, are 'unique within the unit, and significantly *only* with respect to that unit' (*ibid.*, p. 9) [emphasis mine]. This is the feature of KRL that makes it a specialised Case-system in the extreme, and this close association of the slots and the units they attach to is underlined in the example (p. 16) of the TRAVELLER unit and the PERSON unit, both of which have slots named Age, with associated values Infant, Child or Adult in the former case, but an integer in the latter; in other words, the 'same' slot name has a different meaning depending on the unit it attaches to. A further example is the prototype for GIVE (8a), which contrasts with the Fillmorean case-frame features for *give* (8b).

(8a) [Give UNIT Abstract
<SELF (an Event)>
<object (a physobj)>
<giver (a person)>
<recipient (a person)>]

(8b) *give* [Agt Pat Ben]

'The constraints in [(8a)] (e.g. that the filler of the [Giver] slot must be a person) "belong to" the abstract GIVE unit, but [the quotation from Fillmore (1968*a*:26) that "any N in an A . . . phrase must contain the feature [+animate]"] states a constraint which applies to all agents of all verbs. The equivalent statement could not be made directly in KRL and would have to be expressed by putting constraints like that in [(8a)] into *all* events which happen to have [this] slot' (Rosner and Somers, 1980:15) [emphasis original]. This is comparable to the situation in Case where the Instrument relation, say, with regard to a verb of perception (= stimulus) is quite different from that with an action verb (= tool). This does of course happen, but is felt to undermine Case as a general theory. We will consider this point further in discussing Charniak's (1975) remarks in Section 7.

On this point, Charniak's (1981) 'case-slot identity theory' is also of interest. He too makes the comparison between AI representation languages incorporating a 'frame'-like representation, of which KRL is a paradigm example, and especially the notion of 'slots' therein and 'cases' in Case theory. He initially contrasts a frame-like representation for READING (9a) with a case-frame representation for the verb *read* (9b).

(9a) [frame: reading
slots: reader . . .
read . . .]

(9b) *read* (agent, patient)

Charniac gives two versions of the 'case-slot identity theory'. 'The minimal hypothesis says that this mapping [between cases and slots] is completely arbitrary. That is, given that an item is in, say, the patient case, there is no way to predict what slot the item will fill in the semantic frame. Hence, for every verb we must include a mapping between the cases in its case frame and the corresponding slots in the semantic frame' (Charniak, 1981:287). This mapping is given in (10).

(10) *read*

frame = reading
agent = reader
patient = read

'The other possibility, the maximal hypothesis, states, simply enough, that cases and slots and one and the same, so no mapping is needed' (*idem*).

There are other benefits in the maximal hypothesis, especially if slots are 'inherited via the isa hierarchy'. This is a property of many recent frame representations (Hayes, 1977; Brachman, 1979) and is comparable to Chafe's (1970) linguistic model where case frames are implied by verb features. Thus, because *read* is a transitive act (frame) or an action verb (Case), we know automatically that it takes an Agent. Charniak notes that besides such inherited slots, there may also be more specific slots that need to be specified: 'For example, one fact which is very important in the reading frame (but which obviously would not be relevant at the level of *transitive act*) is the language which is being read' (*ibid.*, p. 288). This, according to Charniak, is problematic in Case, and has led to a proliferation of cases to handle such individual problems. We could add that alternatively it leads to vaguer and vaguer characterisations of the small number of cases posited. In the case-slot identity theory however no such problem arises: there are indeed a set of general cases which are inherited as properties of higher order frame abstractions, but these are supplemented by more specialised cases/slots introduced for individual predicates. There are problems with this theory however which have to do with the lack of isomorphism between slots and cases. Charniak gives the example of *paint*, whose Instrument might be either an appliance like *roller*, or a substance like *latex paint*: assuming these are the same case – and the coordination test (11) suggests they might be – then we have a single case mapping onto two different slots.

(11) I painted the wall with a roller and some latex paint.

The inverse is found with verbs like *buy* and *sell*, which are distinguished according to the mapping between slot and case (12).

(12a) *to buy*

frame = buy-sell
agent = buyer
source = seller

(12b) *to sell*
frame = buy-sell
agent = seller
destination = buyer

This time we have the same slot mapping onto different cases. Charniak does suggest solutions to both problems. For the *paint* example is Brachman's (1979) proposal to allow slots to 'differentiate' slots inherited from a higher frame (13).

(13) [frame: deliberate-act
isa: transitive-act
slots: instrument . . .]
[frame: painting
isa: deliberate-act
slots: applier (differentiates instrument)
applied (differentiates instrument)]

The solution to the second problem is to distinguish between roles like Source and Destination which are the same for both *buy* and *sell*, and, at a separate level between Agent and non-Agent. This is a solution we have discussed above (Chapter 8) and is a key benefit of the 'case grid' proposal (Chapter 10). Charniak attributes it to Jackendoff (1972), though in fact it is considered by several Case grammarians too.

We could not consider a discussion of KRL complete without at least passing reference to the general concept of 'frames'. We shall attempt not to distance ourselves too far from Case, and in paying tribute to the considerable influence on AI of Minsky's (1975) concept, we may also note its apparent influence on the later works of Fillmore (1976, 1977*c*) too, as both Lehnert and Wilks (1979:26) and Rosner and Somers (1980:23) have remarked.

Minsky originally conceived of his 'frames' concept in the context of computer vision, the key notion being the interpretation of given data in terms of expections. The idea was quickly applied to more general domains of knowledge processing, and several derivatives appeared, notably 'scripts' (Schank and Abelson, 1977). The important feature of frames, as seen in KRL, is that of slots and fillers, with procedures attaching to the slots. This combination of the possibility of capturing both declarative and procedural knowledge is very attractive. Another important feature, not so obvious in KRL is the way in which frames are linked together in a knowledge representation system. Often slots in frames are filled with other frames, or rather with pointers to other frames. The basic elements that otherwise fill slots are also often accessed by pointer rather than copying mechanisms, giving frame systems the properties of relational databases or networks. Tennant (1981:220) likens frames to data types in a formatted database, while Bobrow and Winograd (1979:33) allude to the record type in programming languages like Pascal as a simple precursor of the frame. Of course, neither of these constructs is associated with the range of powerful devices that are common in frame-based systems.

Frames are used for describing objects, as in the CHAIR frame (14) exemplified by Barr and Feigenbaum (1981:216), or might include sequences of events, as in the RESTAURANT frame (15) (*ibid.*, p. 217). Scripts are usually representations of event sequences, and in themselves have little of the (Case-like) slot-and-filler character of frames.

(14) CHAIR Frame

Specialisation of:	FURNITURE
Number-of-legs:	an Integer (DEFAULT=4)
Style-of-back:	straight, cushioned . . .
Number-of-arms:	0, 1 or 2

(15) Generic RESTAURANT Frame

Specialization of: Business-Establishment
Types:
    range: (Cafeteria, Seat-Yourself, Wait-To-Be-Seated, Fast-Food)
    default: Wait-To-Be-Seated
    if-needed: IF plastic-orange-counter
            THEN Fast-Food
        IF stack-of-trays THEN Cafeteria
        IF wait-for-waitress-sign OR
            reservations-made
            THEN Wait-To-Be-Seated
        OTHERWISE Seat-Yourself
Location:
    range: an ADDRESS
    if-needed: (Look at the MENU)
[. . .]
Food-style:
    range: (Burgers, Chinese, American, Seafood, French)
    default: American
Times-of-Operation:
    range: a Time-of-Day
    [. . .]

Payment-Form:
  range: (Cash, Credit Card, Check, Washing-Dishes-Script)
Event sequence:
  [etc.]

Frames have, as was hinted above, caught the imagination of the AI community, and numerous implementations and developments of the concept have appeared. Several overviews and discussions are available, including those of Charniak (1976:147-54), Winston (1977:179-203), Tennant (1981:216-26) and Barr and Feigenbaum (1981:216-22). The relationship between frames and Case is brought out in two of these discussions. Winston suggests that Case grammar is frame-like: '. . . a case grammar sentence analyzer renders sentences into the verb and associated objects. We have only to draw attention to the frame-like quality of the case-slots to see that case representation fits the frame idea rather well. For a general verb, there is the bare, open frame . . . More specific verbs have some of the slots filled by tightly bound defaults inasmuch as the fundamental meaning of the verb itself has absorbed case presumptions, . . .' (Winston, 1977:189).

Barr and Feigenbaum on the other hand contrast the essentially narrow scope of the case frame with the much broader (Minskian) frame: 'Where case representations deal primarily with *single sentences or acts*, frames are applied to whole situations, complex objects, or series of events. In analyzing a *sentence*, *narrative*, or *dialogue*, a frame-based language understanding system tries to match the input to the prototypes of objects or events in its domain that are stored in the database' (Barr and Feigenbaum, 1981:231) [emphases mine]. Barr and Feigenbaum touch here on two key issues which we shall take up shortly. The first is the application of case frames to 'sentences or acts', a quiet reference to the important distinction between the linguistic and cognitive conceptions of Case and case frames. The second point is not unrelated. We can draw only a fuzzy distinction between case analysis of sentences or simple events, and deeper analyses of narratives and event sequences: in the former we may only be interested in immediate roles, whereas in the latter we will almost certainly need to make a more abstract analysis involving various inference mechanisms (not ruled out for simple sentence/event analysis either, note). Both these contrasts will be seen in Section 6. But before that, we will take a brief look at GUS.

Genial Understander System is the dialogue-system developed by Bobrow *et al.* (1976) which plays the part of a travel agent participating in a 'mixed initiative' conversation with a client. GUS analyses input in a three-stage process: it first uses Kaplan's (1973) General Syntactic Parser to perform a strictly syntactic parse which is then input to a case-frame analyser, the output of which is mapped onto a 'frame reasoning' component. It is this last part of the system, related specifically to KRL, which provides the main body of the GUS article. But we shall concentrate briefly on the case analysis and the use of the results of this phase as input to the frame reasoner. Like some of the commentators mentioned above, Bobrow *et al.* stress the linguistic nature of case frames as compared to the cognitive nature of the reasoning component: 'The case-frame analysis uses linguistic knowledge associated with individual lexical items to relate their appearance in canonical syntactic structures to their uses in a semantic environment. It uses a dictionary of case-frames based on the ideas of case grammar originated by Fillmore [(1968*a*)]; . . . This component uses knowledge about such things as selectional restrictions and the mapping between surface cases (including prepositions) and semantic roles' (Bobrow *et al.*, 1976:161).

By way of example we are shown the case-frame structure (16b) produced for the statement (16a):

(16a) I want to go to San Diego on May 28.

(16b) [CLIENT DECLARE
 (CASE FOR WANT/E (TENSE PRESENT)
 (AGENT (PATH DIALOG CLIENT PERSON))
 (EVENT (CASE FOR GO (TENSE PRESENT)
 (AGENT (PATH DIALOG CLIENT PERSON)
 (TO-PLACE (CASE FOR CITY (NAME SAN-DIEGO)))
 (DATE (CASE FOR DATE (MONTH MAY) (DAY 28]

The interpretation of the case frame is given by domain dependent knowledge given by KRL-like frames. Thus the *want* case-frame is mapped onto the CMD (command) frame, and the *go* case-frame onto part of the TRIP frame (17).

(17) CMD: (CLIENT DECLARE
 (FRAME IS A TRIP-LEG
 (TRAVELLER (PATH DIALOG CLIENT PERSON))
 (TO-PLACE (FRAME ISA CITY (NAME SAN-DIEGO)))
 (TRAVEL-DATE (FRAME ISA DATE (MONTH MAY) (DAY 28]

In (17) we see a number of instantiated frames: at the highest level there is the frame for CMD, and then the frames for TRIP-LEG (which most closely resembles a linguistic case-frame), and for CITY and DATE (18).

(18) [DATE
MONTH NAME
DAY (BOUNDED INTEGER 1 31)
YEAR INTEGER
WEEKDAY (MEMBER (SUNDAY MONDAY TUESDAY
WEDNESDAY THURSDAY
FRIDAY SATURDAY]

The article goes on to discuss the attachment of procedures to these frames, filling necessary slots or as a result of values for certain slots and thus driving the dialogue. This need not concern us however. Let us look again at (16b) and (17). Note that in (16b) we have a case frame with case slots filled by words, while in (17) we have a frame with slots filled by concepts etc. The fact that some of the slots in both have the same name (To-Place, Date) should be quite coincidental, because, for example, while there are procedures attaching to the DATE frame in (17), we can scarcely conceive of the equivalent, at least of a 'when-filled' procedure, in (16b); and note the distinction between the imaginable 'to-fill' procedures attaching to slots in the case frame (expected syntactic forms and semantic features) and to the frame slots (generate appropriate dialogue). So we must assume that there is some mapping algorithm from case frames to KRL frames, a mapping made more obvious by the name change between AGENT and TRAVELLER, and DATE to TRAVEL-DATE. Little is said about this 'translation' (p. 162), except that in the experimental GUS it is 'very limited' and that '. . . in a more realistic system, the purposes of the client would have to be understood more deeply' (Bobrow *et al.*, 1976:162). We need say no more about GUS. Its interest for us lies in the clear indication that the difference between the two types of frame is recognised, and the mapping between the two made explicit.

6. *Linguistic versus cognitive representations*

The name of Simmons is generally associated with the notion of 'semantic networks' as a cognitive model. In this section we shall see how Simmons proposes a level of representation for sentences in English, and how this representation can be used as the basis for a meaning representation, a basis from which to generate sentences, or as an intermediate representation in question-answering. Simmons's ideas are set out in a number of works: Simmons (1973) is the most detailed description, while other articles focus on the different uses envisaged: his (1972) article discusses the use of his semantic structures in distinguishing word senses, Simmons and Slocum (1972) deal with sentence generation, and Simmons and Bruce (1971) compare their semantic net formulation with the predicate calculus. Brief surveys and discussions of Simmons's work are found in Scragg (1976) and Wilks (1977).

For Simmons, '. . . the theory and model of semantic nets [is] a computational theory of superficial verbal understanding in humans' (1973:63). The key elements here are that it is computational and superficial. Simmons admits that there is not (yet) enough psycholinguistic evidence that his model is a psychological one, but it is a strong computational linguistic theory. Its superficiality stems from the fact that representations are never too far removed from the surface forms of words and sentences: the semantic nets are made up of nodes representing primitive concepts, interconnected by semantic relations, but note that 'Primitive concepts . . . are *word*-sense meanings. Primitive semantic relations are those that the *verb of a sentence* has with its subject, object and prepositional phrase arguments' (*idem*) [emphases mine]. The semantic network is made up of triples *a*R*b* where R is a relation and *a* and *b* the names of nodes in the network. Among the relations used for representing meaning are 'deep cases', Simmons using those of Celce-Murcia (1975) as seen in Section 3, although there are also connectives, modality relations, attributive relations and so on (1973:79). The case relations in Simmons's example sentence (1a) can be represented as in (1b), or its equivalent in triples notation (1c).

(1a) John broke the window with a hammer.

(1b)

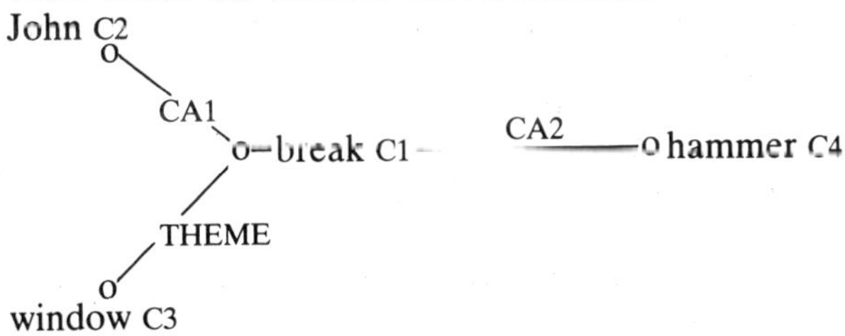

(1c) (C1 CA1 C2) (C1 CA2 C4) (C1 THEME C3)

The diagram in (1b) is given by both Scragg (1976:121) and Wilks (1977:362) and, as both authors point out, is slightly misleading in having words at the nodes, since these are given by a special relationship TOKEN as in (2).

(2) (C1 TOK break) (C2 TOK John) (C3 TOK window) (C4 TOK hammer)

The full representation would also specify number and determination for the noun phrases, and modality for the verb, but we need not dwell on that here. The triples in (2) are still slightly misleading, since the third element in each is not strictly a word, but should be an index to an individual word-sense in the lexicon: this sense of *break* might be L47 or whatever. This is actually an important point, because it means that the basic elements in the network are nodes, relations, and a range of units that correspond one-to-one with concepts (not lexemes, note), yet which are clearly word-senses rather than the semantic primitives of the sort that Schank (see next section), Wilks (Section 4) or Hendrix *et al.* (1973) (Section 4) have. This can be seen quite clearly in Simmons's (1973:81f) discussion of *buy* and *sell*: sentence pairs like (3a-b) are represented by different networks (3c-d respectively; Simmons uses the formalism seen here, which must be assumed to be a convenient shorthand with no theoretical implications), though their quasi-synonymy (paraphrase relation) can be computed using a 'paraphrase rule' like (3e) which maps the roles of one onto the other.

(3a) John bought the boat from Mary.
(3b) Mary sold the boat to John.
(3c) C1 TOK buy, SOURCE (Mary), GOAL (John), THEME (boat)
(3d) C2 TOK sell, SOURCE (Mary), GOAL (John), THEME (boat)
(3e) RO1 (BUY (S-S) (G-G) (T-T) SELL)

That paraphrase rules of the type shown in (3e) are not always so straightforward can be seen in (4a) mapping *lose* onto *defeat*, accounting for the paraphrase relationship between (4b/c) and (4d/e) (1973:99f).

(4a) (LOSE (C-G) (T-S) (L-T) DEFEAT)
(4b) Napoleon lost the Battle of Waterloo to Wellington.
(4c) lose, SOURCE (Napoleon), THEME (Battle of Waterloo) GOAL (Wellington)
(4d) Wellington defeated Napoleon at the battle of Waterloo.
(4e) defeat, CA1 (Wellington), THEME (Napoleon), LOC (Battle of Waterloo)

Simmons distinguishes (1973:81) the deeper representation in which (3a,b) or (4b,d) would have identical representations, and his own shallower approach which, together with paraphrase rules, is equivalent: 'It is probable that the deeper structure forms a *more satisfactory psychological model* of conceptual structure as well as one which will answer questions more *economically*. The argument for the shallower structure is that it neatly defines a *distinction between syntactic and semantic transformations* at the level of *lexical choice* . . .' (1973:81) [emphases mine]. Simmons distinguishes (1973:80f) between semantic paraphrases as seen above and syntactic paraphrases with the same underlying semantic representation and the same verb, but with alternating modality (active/passive) or thematisation structure.

This general position is compromised slightly by some of Simmons's remarks in his (1972) article. For example he states that 'In my opinion, a semantic representation should probably be *completely free* of its natural language representation' (1972:74) [emphasis mine]. This sounds like an argument for the sort of representation we will look at shortly (i.e. Schank's CD), but his ensuing remarks seem to suggest that what he means is that the burden of semantic interpretation should be shifted onto the grammar and lexicon. Although the lexicon is arranged in terms of word senses, Simmons does not rule out the inclusion of deeper semantic representations (including inference, generic relations and so on), these being triggered by particular individual word senses. That the grammar too has semantic significance is given by the fact that the relationships defined can also have inferences: 'Agent (*a*,*b*) for example, implies that *a* is animate, that *b* is a process, and that *b* has some effect on *a*' (1972:76).

We need not spend too much time looking at the various implementations of Simmons's semantic networks. The three main purposes, as stated above, are as a general parser, as a basis for generating sentences (this aspect is discussed in detail in Simmons and Slocum, 1972), and in a question-answering system. Fairly standard techniques are used (syntax-first ATN), followed by the same kind of syntactic and semantic feature mapping algorithm seen in several systems already. Considerable detail is given in Simmons (1973) – see especially p. 90 for case assignment. There is one puzzling feature that we should mention finally though: in his main description of the process, Simmons implies that case assignments are guided by information due to the lexical entry for the verb (this is quite normal); yet in his concluding remarks (p. 106) he suggests that correctly assigning case roles assists in distinguishing different word senses of verbs (cf. Marcus's (1980) case frame interpreter – Section 3). There seems to be conflict here: verb paradigm information is presumably available only once the correct verb-sense has been found: to use this information to find the correct verb-sense seems to be, like pulling yourself up by your own shoelaces, impossible. The only way I can see it working is that the recognition that there is some word-sense ambiguity leads to the setting up of parallel hypotheses concerning the role structure of the sentence: whichever best fits the data is confirmed as correct.

We turn now to the Conceptual Dependency (CD) theory of Schank already alluded to on several occasions above. CD is described in a large number of papers (Schank, 1972, 1973*a*, *b*, 1975, 1977; Schank and Abelson, 1977; Schank and Riesbeck, 1981) and by several commentators (e.g. Wilks, 1977:365-9; Barr and Feigenbaum, 1981:211-5). Of Schank's own descriptions, his (1975) book is the most thorough, while Schank and Abelson (1977) and Schank (1977) contain the most concise summaries. Because CD is so well-known and well documented, we shall not spend time here recapitulating the details, but shall consider the main features of it as regards our own consideration of Case in AI.

The important aspect of CD that distinguishes it from other Case-like systems is the depth of representation. This stems from Schank's desire to have a 'language-free' representation of conceptualisations which are unambiguous and uniquely capture the underlying meaning of any utterances which can be said to be synonymous. This is achieved by reducing all utterances to combinations of primitive 'predicates' chosen from a set of twelve 'actions' plus state and change of state, together with the primitive 'causation', and seven role relations or 'conceptual cases'. These cases, together with their graphic representation, are given here.

1. Object (in a state) <≡≡≡>
2. Object (change of state) <≡≡≡ [→ new state / ← old state]
3. Object (of action) —O→ action
4. Actor <≡≡>
5. Recipient <—— / Donor —— [—R→ action]
6. From-Directive —— / To-Directive <—— [—D→ action]
7. Instrument —I→ action

Schank stresses that the actions, actors and objects correspond to concepts in the real world, which is why many linguistic verbs must be analysed as complex conceptualisations, the example often given being *hurt*: this is not a 'real world' action, but a physical or mental state resulting from some real action.

A key difference between CD cases and the Fillmorean concept is that there are essentially no optional cases : '. . . conceptual cases are part of a given action and therefore are always present whenever that action is present' (Schank, 1977:577). This often-stated constraint is actually compromised somewhat in practice: referring to the fact that every ACT has an obligatory Instrument, which is very often an ACT itself, Schank notes that '. . . we can see that it should therefore be impossible to ever actually finish conceptually diagramming a given sentence. That is, every ACT has an instrument and so on. . . . Since an analysis of this kind *is not particularly useful* and is *quite bothersome to write*, we do not do so. Rather, whenever we represent a conceptualization, we only diagram *the main conceptualization* and such instrumental conceptualizations *as might be necessary* to illustrate whatever point we are making' (Schank, 1977:578f) [emphases mine]. It is not quite clear if this is a diagramming convention, or is actually implemented in the model. If the latter, then this is clearly a serious compromise of the notion of obligatory cases and the stated need for their presence in the representation (for possible inferencing etc.); furthermore, we might ask what criteria can be used to determine *a priori* the necessity to include some instrument in the conceptualization.

We should at this point briefly illustrate with the familiar example of *buy* and *sell* the difference between CD and other representations we have been looking at. For Schank, these two verbs are synonymous at the conceptual level, and so a pair of sentences like (5a,b) will both be represented as in (5c).

(5a) Mary sold the car to Beth.

(5b) Beth bought the car from Mary.

(5c)

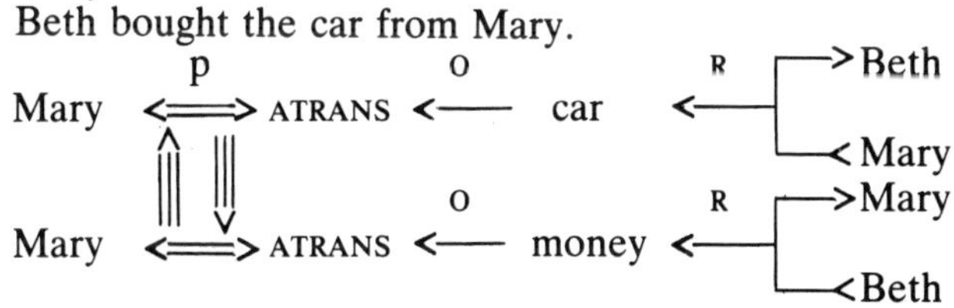

[p = past tense]

The means by which sentences of English are transformed into CD representations is described by Riesbeck (1975), though Ritchie complains of '. . . the lack of a clear theory of the relationship between surface form and conceptual meaning' (Ritchie, 1980:109).

CD has been used as a model for understanding simple stories (in the MARGIE system – Schank, 1975), this understanding being demonstrated by the production from the CD representation of English sentences stating the inferences that were drawn from the analysis of the input. More recently the use of CD-based scripts has been suggested for Machine Translation (Carbonell *et al.*, 1978; see next chapter).

CD is undoubtedly Case-like. However it is difficult to compare it to other formalisations of Case because of the lack of information regarding the strategies for computing CD representations. The complexity of the mapping between text and representation means that CD is never regarded as a serious linguistic model, and indeed Schank never intended it to be, claiming the model to be relevant to cognitive rather than linguistic science. With regard to our occasional reference to Case as a useful bridge between syntax and semantics, it is evident that CD falls outside this category. But note that it is not because of the nature of the cases Schank proposes, but his insistence on reduction of lexical predicates to a small set of primitives. The roles Schank uses are no more primitive than those found in many case systems which are much more surface-oriented, and it is interesting to ponder the implications of this. To what extent is the nature of a given case dependent on the status of the predicate to which it attaches? In Section 7 we shall discuss questions like what it means to call something 'Agent', but there we will be concerned with the difference, for example between the Agent of *dance* and the Agent of *hit*. But here we have a different conflict. Given that all the predicates correspond to primitive acts, it is conceivable that the associated cases are primitives of the same order. An alternative (and diametrically opposed) view might be that as we have a small number of primitive acts, and a small number of cases, even if each case were interpreted differently with regard to each primitive, we would still have a reasonably small number (thirty-seven) of primitive relations, some of which might turn out to be conceptually identical after all. This seems to me a more plausible approach to the cases in CD, or at least to some of them: consider for example the difference between the actor of one of the three 'mental ACTS' (MTRANS, MBUILD, PLAN) and that of, say PTRANS or INGEST. It is interesting that whereas Schank has paid a lot of attention to the explanation and characterisation of the nature of the primitive predicates, the question of cases has barely been raised.

Throughout this chapter we have seen a number of systems using Case in a variety of ways. In this section in particular we have concentrated on distinguishing between surface-oriented or 'linguistic' versions of Case, and much deeper 'cognitive' versions.

To complete the discussion I want to reiterate here some points that were originally made in Rosner and Somers (1980) on the importance of this distinction.

The paper just cited in fact grew from our concern with the use of the term 'case frame', as we noted that sometimes it referred to a frame with its slots filled, sometimes to the 'virtual' frame implied by some predicate. Cutting across this distinction between actual and virtual case frames is the distinction between case frames for sentences and verbs, and those for events and event types. We called these four different types of case frame CF1 to CF4, as in Figure 2, with associated typical statements as in (6).

	actual	virtual
linguistic	CF1	CF2
cognitive	CF3	CF4

Figure 2: Four types of 'case frame'

(6a) The case frame for sentence s is (some CF1).
(6b) The case frame for verb v is (some CF2).
(6c) The case frame for event e is (some CF3).
(6d) The case frame for event type E is (some CF4).

We can now add to this classification (from Rosner and Somers, 1980:3) examples from the systems we have been looking at. For instance, it is clear that the Case parsers seen in Section 3 – PARSIFAL (Marcus, 1980); Celce-Murcia's (1975) sentence recogniser; PTOSYS (Somers and Johnson, 1979; Somers, 1980*a*) – are producing CF1s. To do this, Marcus has CF2s stored in the dictionary though for the other two systems, 'blank' CF1s are inferred from syntactic or semantic verb features. By contrast, systems using a deeper representation, where typically 'synonymous' verbs and sentences get the same analysis, produce CF3s, with slots filled not by words but by objects, from abstract CF4s. In Bobrow and Winograd's KRL, prototype frames (Abstract UNITS) are CF3s. By the same token, Schank's CD representations can be regarded as CF3s (though because of the fact that all cases are obligatory, there is no need for any CF4s). Simmons's case frames, although closely related to surface forms, are also CF3s, since the elements at the nodes in his semantic nets are not strictly words but concepts associated with words. Since Simmons follows Celce-Murcia's idea of 'paradigms', there are no CF4s in his system.

Let us recall now some of the important distinctions that can be captured by this separation of CF*n*s. First, the actual/virtual distinction: note that two sentences that have the same CF1 can be said to be synonymous, and two events that have the same CF3 can be said to be identical events. The same cannot be said of verbs having the same CF2 (e.g. *rotate* and *bend*) or CF4. In the case of KRL, this distinction in CF4s is underlined by the fact that different event types have associated with them differently named roles. This distinction is obscured in a system that has general concepts like Agent for different verb/event types, as we shall see in Section 7. Furthermore, notice the different interpretation of the notion of optionality in actual and virtual case frames. In the latter, a role marked as optional means that the corresponding instantiation or actual case frame can be considered complete without it. With a CF2 this clearly describes a range of acceptable sentences (CF1s) that the given verb can be part of. But we noted in Rosner and Somers (p. 14) that the corresponding notion for events is less clear, for a GIVE without an Agent is presumably a RECEIVE. One possible interpretation for optionality in a CF4 however is that it implies that a CF3 can be built in which the 'optional' role is unspecified.

As this point demonstrated, there are clear differences along our other axis: linguistic/cognitive. One particular distinction we noted (pp. 5ff) was the different status of the tree-like diagrams often used to represent CF1s and (perhaps less often) CF3s: position in a linguistic tree is usually significant, reflecting surface word-order. This is particularly the case in Fillmore (1968*a*), where branches get moved around by transformations. In a CF3 however, moving branches around is typically a meaningless operation, as confirmed by the fact that different but equivalent notations can be suggested for CF3s (e.g. those in (7), from Charniak, 1975:3).

(7a)

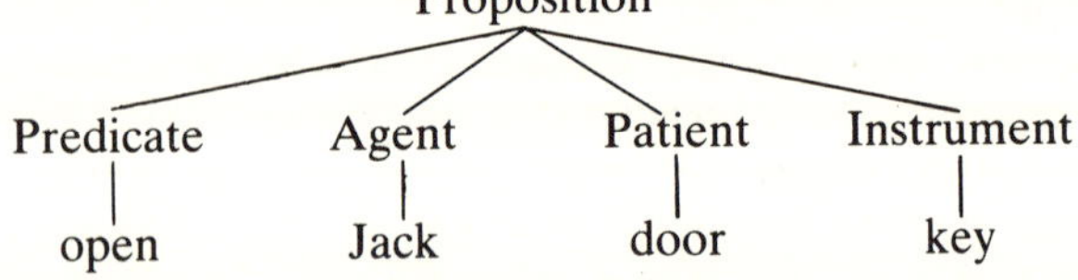

(7b) (Predicate open) (Agent Jack) (Patient door) (Instrument key)

(7c)

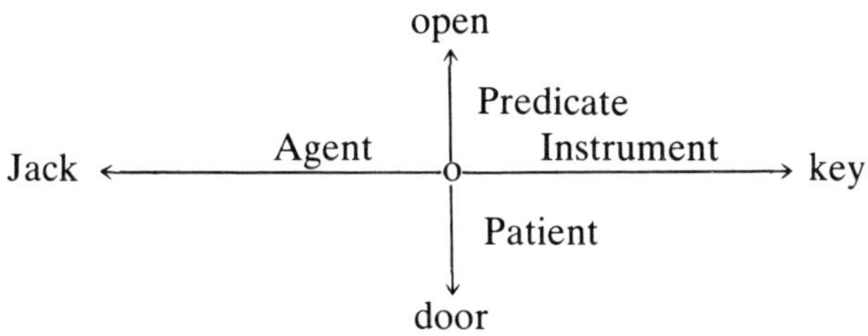

More significant though is the status of the objects filling the slots. In CF1s, they are generally words, or at least syntactic constructs like noun-phrases. In CF3s however they are generally pointers to concepts (as in Simmons) or to actual entities. This can be brought out in comparing the CF1 for the sentence (8a) and the CF3 for the event it describes. In the CF1 (8b) the Patient node is filled by the linguistic element *himself*: any representation in which this node has a pointer to the filler of the Agent slot is a more cognitive representation (8c).

(8a) Ernest shot himself this morning.

(8b)

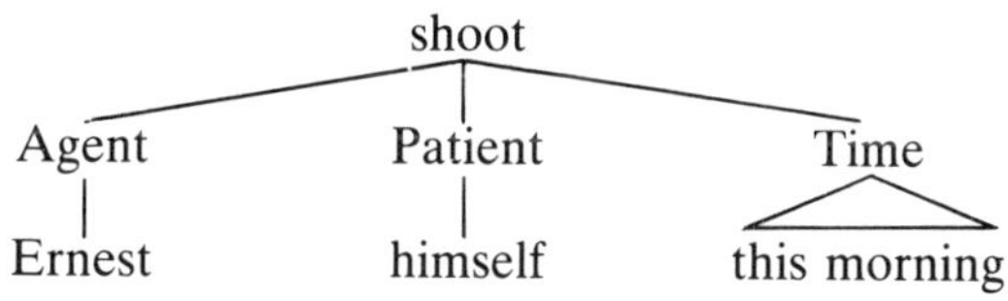

(8c)

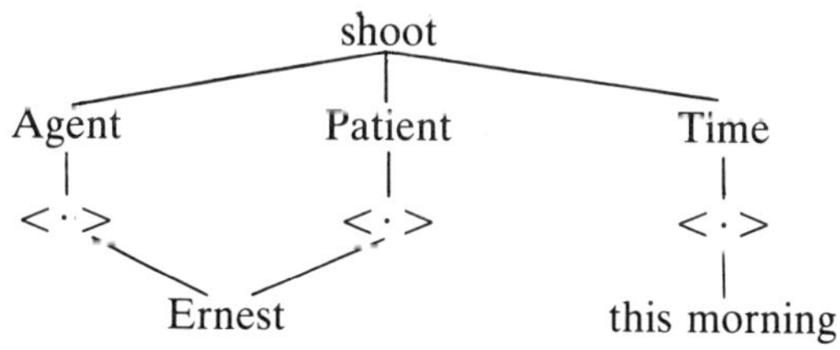

Notice that the word/concept distinction also applies to virtual case frames. CF2s will generally imply some syntactic constraints – whether expressed as general constraints applying across the board (Fillmore's (1968*a*:33) subject selection rule) or on a verb-by-verb basis – as well as word-level semantic constraints. Clearly for CF4s there will be semantic constraints, but anything equivalent to syntactic constraints is difficult to imagine. But as we have pointed out, the distinction can be blurred: '. . . certain natural language systems (e.g. Simmons, 1973; Norman *et al.*, 1975) employ case labels in a distinctly ambiguous way. Thus it is not at all clear whether the "leaves" of [a Simmons case frame] represent words or objects. For the parser that builds [it], they are clearly words, but for the paraphrase rules, they are presumably objects, implying that what we have been calling a CF3 has the chameleon quality of looking like a CF1 under the wary eye of the parser' (Rosner and Somers, 1980:16). This very quality is in fact the thing that, I suspect, makes Case so attractive to AI. Mention has been made on several occasions of Case acting as a bridge between syntax and semantics, and here we see precisely why that is: as long as the desired representation is not independent of some of the words, and that these words can be associated in some useful way with more cognitive notions, then Case can perform this function. To use another zoological metaphor, Case is like a dolphin, which looks like a fish but is actually a mammal, and has much of the best of both worlds. In the same way, Case sometimes looks like it is syntactic, and sometimes semantic, and functions in both 'habitats'. The problems only arise when you pretend the dolphin has gills or that it can live on dry land: that is, if you try to stretch the capabilities of Case in either of the two areas.

7. *What constitutes using Case?*

In his (1975) paper, Charniak argues that the use of Case notions in AI systems which analyse language is not really using Case at all. His arguments are discussed at some length in Wilks (1976*a*). I would like here to take up the discussion again, bearing in mind systems we have looked at in the foregoing sections of this chapter, and attempting to arrive at some conclusions.

Charniak (p. 4) first contrasts what he calls 'case notation' and 'positional notation', noting that the case names in a representation for a sentence like (1a) as (1b) might just be mnemonic identifiers for arguments to a predicate, wholly equivalent to (1c).

(1a) Jack opened the door with a key.

(1b) ((PREDICATE OPEN)
(AGENT JACK)
(PATIENT DOOR)
(INSTRUMENT KEY))

(1c) OPEN (JACK, DOOR, KEY)

Charniak notes that if the case names in (1b) have no independent meaning, we would have 'case notation' without 'case use'. Conversely, if the argument positions in (1c) were associated by some mechanism with such meanings, then we would have the inverse: 'case use' without 'case notation'. Wilks confirms this claim, emphasising the proviso that 'one knows that the "first argument is the agent etc. etc."' (p. 59). We can imagine such a notation in which the 'virtual' case-frame for some verb or event, as in (2), defines the mapping onto the positions in some 'actual' case-frame like (1c).

(2) OPEN (AGENT, PATIENT, INSTRUMENT)

Charniak goes on to discuss one of the obvious 'case benefits', that of comparing and contrasting the meanings of related predicates. He takes the example of *look* and *see*, suggesting that these verbs 'have the same basic meaning, but different case frames' (p. 5), *look* taking the Agent and *see* an Experiencer. He suggests that by doing this 'we avoid the need for two separate meaning representations' (*idem*). But one wonders what part, if any, the case frame plays in establishing the meaning representation. It is conceivable, for example, that in some systems the case frame is itself in some sense the meaning representation. And would it be possible to have two distinct verbs with the same meaning (in Charniak's sense) and the same case frame? Charniak summarises his position by suggesting that *look* and *see* have something in common (say, the concept OBSERVE) and their difference is due to the AGENT/EXPERIENCER concept. This is summarised as in (3) (ignoring the role of the Patient):

(3a) meaning (*look*) = meaning (OBSERVE) + meaning (AGENT)

(3b) meaning (*see*) = meaning (OBSERVE) + meaning (EXPERIENCER)

This seems fair enough at first sight. By simple subtraction we can capture Charniak's view that the difference is due to the difference between the two cases, as in (4).

(4) meaning (*look*) – meaning (*see*) = meaning (AGENT) – meaning (EXPERIENCER)

So far, says Charniak, the equations are 'linear'. But in reality, that is in AI systems, the equations should be non-linear (5).

(5) meaning (*look*) = meaning (OBSERVE) + meaning (AGENT) + meaning (OBSERVE, AGENT)

That is to say that for AI systems it is important to establish the connection between the basic meaning and the associated case. However, Charniak notes that if the system is unable to function without looking to see whether the OBSERVE has an Agent or Experiencer, i.e. in a linear fashion, we might just as well have simply (6), with no linearity at all.

(6) meaning (*look*) = *meaning* (OBSERVE, AGENT)

In this scenario though, the cases have no meaning independent of the predicate with which they occur, and therefore are not cases, but again mere argument names. Charniak concludes that linearity in meaning definitions is a necessary feature in a true Case-using system. Wilks agrees that '. . . it would clearly be a defect in a system if, every time an inference about AGENT was made, the system had to look and see what verb it was the agent of, or what the primitive action coding the verb was' (Wilks, 1976*a*:60). In this respect, we have to conclude that KRL (Bobrow and Winograd, 1977; see Section 5), with each predicate defining its own set of cases, is not a true 'Case' system at all.

This concept that the cases should have some 'meaning' independent of the predicates with which they occur seems quite reasonable, and recurs in several general discussions (e.g. Welin, 1975:33; Ritchie, 1980:114). But it is interesting to note that none of Bruce's (1975) five possible criteria for distinguishing cases necessarily implies this constraint:

1. 'A case is a property which must be used to distinguish different senses of a word.' (p. 333)
2. 'A case is a property which must be used for unique specification of an event.' (p. 334)
3. 'A case is a property whose value needs to be known, even if it is not expressed.' (*idem*)
4. 'A case is a property whose value is usually specified for a given type of event.' (p. 335)
5. 'A case is a property which is particularly relevant to the domain of discourse.' (*idem*)

Let us dwell for a little while on this question of linearity, because there is in Charniak's characterisation something of an oversimplification of matters which is clouding the issue. The main problem is his use of a quasi-formalism, and in particular the use of the 'predicate' *meaning*. He only vaguely glosses this at first, though later he is a little more precise: 'Meaning (CASE) = The set of inferences one can make about X, knowing only that X is in case CASE' (Charniak, 1975:19). That is all very well, but how does that definition apply to expressions like 'meaning (OBSERVE)' or 'meaning (OBSERVE, AGENT)'?

We shall attempt to clarify matters with a slightly more rigid formalism. Let us try to capture our intuitions regarding interpretation of Case frames. We shall begin with the definition (7), which states that a meaning (M) is a function over a concept (C) which gives an application or abstraction (A).

(7) $M : C \rightarrow A$

Our A is deliberately vague, because its exact nature will depend on the nature of the system. Let us gloss A as 'whatever you want to do with it'. In a trivial sense, our concepts are *n*'s (nouns or their 'real-world' equivalent), *v*'s (verbs or events) and cases (*k*). This would give us (8), and the trivial definition (9), which simply says that the desired abstraction is the combination (○) of the meaning M of the *n*, *v* and *k* in a given proposition.

(8) C = {N,V,K}

(9) A = M(N) ○ M(V) ○ M(K)

Taking the example sentence (10a) we can see that (9) does not capture everything we want it to say: in (10b) there is no expression of the relational nature of the *k* Agent to the *n Willy* or the *v run*.

(10a) Willy runs.

(10b) a = M(*Willy*) ○ M(*run*) ○ M(Agent)

The problem is that K is not a simple concept like N and V, but is itself a function: we want to be able to express notions like 'Agent of *run*' or '*Willy* acting as an Agent'. So clearly we must redefine C, abandoning (8) in favour of (11).

(11) C = {N,V}

Note that we do need K. A definition like (12) simply lacks any notion of the relationship of *n* to *v*, and could not distinguish between (13a-b) for example.

(12) A = M(V) ○ M(N)

(13a) Harry loves Jane.

(13b) Jane loves Harry.

At this point it is appropriate to note why Charniak's formulations are unacceptable. He has a predicate *meaning* which variously operates over words like *look*, over atoms like OBSERVE and over cases like AGENT. Additionally, it appears to be able to have a variable number of arguments, as in (5). Having noted that K is not a concept like N or V, let us now define it as a function operating on a *v* to give an *n* (14). This will enable us to define *Willy* as the Agent of *run* as in (15).

(14) $K : V \rightarrow N$

(15a) $n = k(v)$

(15b) *Willy* = Agent (*run*)

Now we can represent (10a) as in (16), that is as the combination of the meaning of *run* and the meaning of the Agent of *run*.

(16a) A = M(V) ○ M(K(V))

(16b) a = M(*run*) ○ M(Agent(*run*))

But note that K(V) evaluates to an *n*, so that (16a) is just equivalent to (12). What we need is some function that relates a *k* to an *n* and a *v*, i.e. that defines what it means to be an Agent and what it means to be the Agent of some verb. These are given in (17). Note that these correspond to the two ideas contrasted by Charniak and

Wilks: (17a) is the independent meaning of K; (17b) the predicate-oriented one.

(17a) $\text{M}' : \text{K} \times \text{N} \rightarrow \text{A}$

(17b) $\text{M}'' : \text{K} \times \text{V} \rightarrow \text{A}$

Now we can say (18), that is the combination of the meaning of *run* and the meaning of *Willy* and that there is an Agent and that *Willy* is the Agent.

(18a) $\text{A} = \text{M}(\text{V}) \bigcirc \text{M}(\text{N}) \bigcirc \text{M}'(\text{K},\text{N}) \bigcirc \text{M}''(\text{K},\text{V})$

(18b) $\text{a} = \text{M}(\textit{run}) \bigcirc \text{M}(\textit{Willy}) \bigcirc \text{M}'(\text{Agent},\textit{Willy}) \bigcirc \text{M}''(\text{Agent},\textit{run})$

Note that M′ is the example of non-linearity that Charniak gives. What is interesting about (18) is that it expresses Tesnière's most elementary notion, that of 'connexion': 'When I say: *Alfred speaks* . . . I do not mean to say on the one hand that "there is a man called Alfred" and on the other that "someone is speaking", but I mean to say at the same time that "Alfred performs the action of speaking" and that "the one who is speaking is Alfred". A result of this is that a sentence like *Alfred speaks* is not composed of the *two* elements *Alfred* and *speaks*, but indeed of the *three* elements *Alfred*, *speaks*, and the "connexion" which unites them and without which there would be no sentence. . . . "Connexion" is *indispensable* for the expression of thought. Without "connexion" we would not be able to express a single continuous thought at all, and would only be able to utter a succession of isolated images and ideas one after the other without any link between them' (Tesnière, 1959:11f) [emphases original]. We may well ask whether we need the function M defined in (7). Without it we could express the abstraction as simply the combination of what it means to be an Agent (independent of any predicate) and what it means to be the Agent of *run* (19).

(19a) $\text{A} = \text{M}'(\text{K},\text{N}) \bigcirc \text{M}''(\text{K},\text{V})$

(19b) $\text{a} = \text{M}'(\text{Agent},\textit{Willy}) \bigcirc \text{M}''(\text{Agent},\textit{run})$

I feel that this is perhaps going too far: while I could be prepared to lose the function M(N), it seems that the importance of M(V), bearing in mind the special nature of a *v* as the 'predicator' in a proposition as compared to the *n* as an argument, requires us to retain it as in (20).

(20) $\text{A} = \text{M}(\text{V}) \bigcirc \text{M}'(\text{K},\text{N}) \bigcirc \text{M}''(\text{K},\text{V})$

If M(N) is not so crucial, we can perhaps amend our earlier definitions (7) and (11) as in (21).

(21a) $\text{M} : \text{C} \rightarrow \text{A}$

(21b) $\text{C} = \{\text{V}\}$

This seems well founded, because after all perhaps we should distinguish the M function for *v*'s from a not entirely similar one for *n*'s (22).

(22) $M''' : N \rightarrow A$

To complete the picture, let us see how to generalise to multiple arguments. We can introduce a general function G for the case-argument pairing as in (23), so that a more complex proposition as expressed by the sentence (24a) can be represented as (24b) which expands to (24c).

(23a) $G : K \times V \times N \rightarrow A'$

(23b) $G(K,V,N) = M'(K,N) \bigcirc M''(K,V)$

(24a) Jack opened the door.

(24b) a = M(*open*) ○ G(Agent,*open*,*Jack*) ○ G(Patient,*open*,*door*)

(24c) a = M(*open*) ○ M′(Agent,*Jack*) ○ M″(Agent,*open*) ○ M′(Patient,*door*) ○ M″(Patient,*open*)

The important point that we must come back to is the desire to avoid defining the meanings of the cases in terms of the predicates to which they attach. Charniak's point, remember, is that if the cases have no meaning of their own, then they are just names for positions in a positional notation. But Charniak points out that AI systems tend to lack 'case meanings': 'While all of the papers describing these systems give *intuitive* meanings to the cases, there is never any indication of how such intuitive meanings are to be coded into the system, or what the precise definitions are' (Charniak, 1975:12) [emphasis mine]. But as Wilks points out, this is a common problem: 'This criticism is true far beyond case: it applies equally to notions of thinghood, causation and movement, etc. It is just a fact that basic semantic notions are vague, and perhaps necessarily so. . . . Provided, therefore, that a programmed system can perform precisely using these vague notions, we can demand no more. The fallacy is to imagine that underneath the vague notions used in thought, speech and writing, there *must lie* precise criteria for their use' (Wilks, 1976*a*:60f) [emphasis original]. He goes on to argue that we do give specifications of, say, the Agents of particular actions, and that the general notion of Agency is '. . . if anything, the union of all such agents, but that will not, and cannot, yield an intentional definition of the notion' (*ibid*., p. 61).

One of the distinctions Charniak suggests between the use of Case in Linguistics and AI is that, because of the depth of representation in the latter, certain 'case benefits' in terms of relating the syntactic and semantic levels are lost. It is clear however that this view stems from his concentration on the systems of Schank and Norman and Rumelhart, ignoring many of the much 'shallower' systems we have considered here.

Charniak concludes by stipulating four conditions which must be met if we want to say that a system does indeed 'use' Case. The first is that the meanings of the cases must be independent of the meanings of the predicates to which they attach. We have already discussed this at length. The second is that each case must apply to more than just one predicate. This stipulation particularly applies to Schank's CD, where there is a limited and small number of predicates. But in any view, this second condition seems to go hand in hand with the first: for if a case is only used with a single predicate (or even a single class of predicates), it is obvious that it will not have any meaning independent of that predicate. The opposite is obviously not true, so it is only this condition two that is superfluous, not condition one. The third condition is that inferences that the cases enable you to make be 'beneficial'. This seems quite uncontroversial, and is simply a stipulation that the introduction of particular cases must be well motivated. This would seem to be an obvious yardstick for any system employing any theory, and does not seem to be a particularly special requirement of a Case-using system. Charniak's fourth condition is the difficult one, both to prove and to understand: 'There must not be a better way to do things which invalidates conditions one through three' (Charniak, 1975:22). A charitable view of this condition would be to say that it is acceptable to go against the first three conditions if that provides a good solution, but Charniak will not call that 'Case'. But this is a hard line to take, and we shall attempt in summary to take a softer line, indicating what appear to be common features of the systems that have been discussed in this chapter.

It seems first that the condition that a case have some interpretation independent of the predicate is a valid one. We may follow Wilks (1976*a*) in suggesting that part of the meaning of a given case will depend on the predicate it attaches to, but that there will be some aspect of the meaning of, say, all Agents that is common. This approach is found, perhaps surprisingly, in Fillmore: 'Sometimes we find in different sentences semantic functions which in detail are partly alike and partly different, their differences being systematically relatable to differences in the semantic properties of the lexical material they are in construction with. (I refuse even to mention the terminological horror of speaking here of "allo-cases" of the same "caseme")' (Fillmore, 1971*b*:41). He may shrink away from this 'terminological horror', but that does at least capture the idea rather well!

Our next condition is that the case set should probably be a relatively small set of intuitively 'comfortable' relations, this 'comfort' being defined in terms of the ultimate aims of the system: the grouping together of slightly different roles must be made on the basis of similarities in their comportment as regards the system they are part of. Case distinctions should not be made on the basis of inherent features, because these can be stated as a function of the predicate the case occurs with: let us call these 'inherited' features. For example, all Agents, say, are not inherently animate, but this feature might be inferrable for a given Agent when it happens to be the Agent of, for instance, *dance*.

Our final condition is that Case must not be merely notational, that is the cases must not be simply names for something else, or to put it another way, they must add something to the representation. This again is necessarily vague, because what Case adds to a representation will depend on the ultimate aims of the system. But one consequence of this condition is that we cannot expect cases to map trivially onto other things that are around, for example surface case, or lexical features (on the linguistic side) or deeper concepts and resulting inferences (on the cognitive side) – always assuming any of these are important notions in a particular system. If the mapping is trivial, then case labels are just different names for the things that map onto them.

The overall picture can be summed up as follows: Case users should be conscious of the possibilities that various versions of Case can offer, and should use them if they offer a solution to some problem. The cases themselves should be distinguished and defined on purely pragmatic grounds only, that is, according to whether some benefit accrues from such-and-such a distinction – if necessary with disregard to theoretical wholesomeness. In nearly all the systems we have looked at, Case does have a role to play. Some of the problems that occur stem from ignoring this pragmatism constraint, where some Case users try to bend some given case system to a use it was never designed for.

TWELVE

CASE AND VALENCY IN MACHINE TRANSLATION

In this final chapter we shall be considering the use – possible and actual – of Valency and Case in MT. We shall not give here a detailed history or overview of the state of the art in MT, though as MT gains popularity a number of such articles are becoming available. Hutchins has provided two early (1978, 1979) surveys as well as (1986) the most detailed general review to date. More recent general surveys include Slocum (1984), Whitelock (1985) and Bennett *et al.* (1986:64–99), while collections of papers concentrating on individual approaches include Kittredge (1981), Lawson (1982), Loffler-Laurian (1984) and King (1987).

The major distinction between transfer-based and interlingua-based MT systems has an important bearing on our discussion. As I have stated elsewhere, 'The former can be characterised by the use of bilingual transfer modules which convert the results of the analysis of the source language into a representation appropriate for a specific target language. This contrasts with the interlingua approach in which the result of analysis is passed directly to the appropriate synthesis module' (Somers, 1983:151). Most of the systems we shall be looking at employ some version of the transfer approach, though in Section 3 we shall look briefly at the possibility of using Case as the basis of an interlingual approach to MT, and we shall discuss this distinction further there. However, for the other systems we shall be looking at, it is important to stress the role played by Transfer in mapping linguistic structures of one language onto those of the other.

1. *Valency in MT*

Before we consider Case in MT, we should first look at some notions borrowed from Valency that are used in quite a widespread manner in MT systems. The two notions that we find are Valency-like lexicon entries for verbs; and the distinction between complements and adjuncts. Both these notions are employed in a fairly predictable way in the analysis phases of the various MT systems that use them. Typically, the lexicon will contain information equivalent to that given in a Valency dictionary like that of Helbig and Schenkel (1973) (see Chapter 1 Section 2). Indeed in the work of Rothkegel (1976, 1977) and of Weissgerber (1983), the affinity is very close. The lexical information is used to assist in the computation of structured representations for the source text, with the complements predicted by the verb's dictionary entry labelled appropriately (recognition being a question of matching expected features with lexical entries for the nominals), and the adjuncts likewise. In this way, sentence pairs like those in (1) can be differentiated, as can the two place adverbials in (2).

(1a) He keeps his car in the garage.
(1b) He washes his car in the garage.
(2) In Berlin he stays at the Hilton.

It is in the bilingual transfer stage (or equivalent) of the system that the use of these distinctions becomes interesting, and it is appropriate at this point to provide a set of example translation pairs (3)-(5) that illustrate the first problem that Valency can help with.

(3a) He likes the girl.
(3b) La fille lui plaît.
THE GIRL TO-HIM PLEASES
(4a) The farmer supplies the innkeeper with eggs.
(4b) Le fermier fournit les oeufs à l'aubergiste.
THE FARMER SUPPLIES THE EGGS TO THE INNKEEPER
(5a) Charles entered the restaurant.
(5b) Charles entra dans le restaurant.

Each of the sentence pairs in (3)-(5) illustrates a change in argument structure between English and French. The example with *like* and *plaire* is something of a classic, involving a double argument change; any suspicion that this is a special exception should be dispelled by examples (4) and (5), which, while less extreme, have similar properties.

The Valency approach to this problem recognises each of the three verb pairs in (3)-(5) as having the same valency but in having different valency patterns, which must be mapped onto each other. In Helbig and Schenkel's terms, the verbs match at level I and in their selection restrictions (level III), but differ in level II (e.g. (6) for *supply/fournir*). (I have loosely adapted Helbig and

Schenkel's formalism: N=nominal, s=subject, o=direct object, i=indirect object, p=preposition. Also, I am ignoring the alternative pattern for *supply* which maps exactly onto *fournir*.)

(6a) I. $\text{supply}_{1+(2)=3}$
II. supply → Ns, (No), (pN)
III. Ns → +Anim
No → +Anim
p = with
pN → +Physobj

(6b) I. $\text{fournir}_{1+(2)=3}$
II. fournir → Ns, (No), (Ni)
III. No → +Anim
No → +Physobj
Ni → +Anim

In the case of Rothkegel (*cit.*), this mapping is achieved by simply juxtaposing the two entries, with equivalent arguments next to each other, roughly as in (7).

(7) *supply* Ns (animate) No (animate) Np (*with*, physobj)
fournir Ns (animate) Ni (animate) No (physobj)

Alternatively, in GETA (Vauquois, 1975, 1978) and TAUM-AVIATION (Lehrberger, 1981), the complements are assigned distinctive labels: in both systems the label ARG(ument) is used with a distinctive affixed numeral, roughly as in (8).

(8a)	The farmer	supplies	the innkeeper	with eggs
	ARG1	PRED	ARG2	ARG3
(8b)	Le fermier	fournit	les oeufs	à l'aubergiste
	ARG1	PRED	ARG2	ARG3
or	ARG1	PRED	ARG3	ARG2

Notice here the two possible uses of these numbered ARG labels: either they are assigned more or less arbitrarily, and an ARG-for-ARG mapping defined for the particular verb pair (9),

(9)

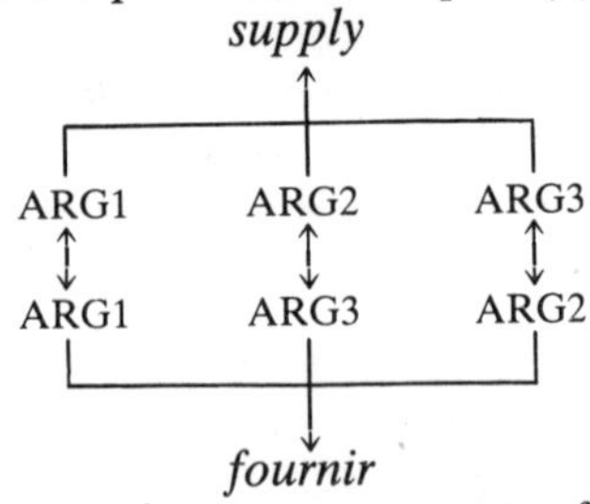

or the ARG labels correspond to some aspect of the analysis (typically deep syntactic function). In this latter approach, which in fact appears to be the one adopted, there are several advantages. First, it is possible to assign ARG numbering in a non-arbitrary manner: the ARG labels therefore take on some significance which can in fact be used for other tasks too. Second, in the frequent cases of exact mapping, there is no need to define an algorithm like (9): the default mapping is of ARG*i* onto ARG*j* ($i=j$), and this indeed works for a large number of verbs. However, there remains the disadvantage when ($i \neq j$), where we need a specific mapping algorithm. We shall return to this question and to these examples in the next section, because the introduction of Case notions gives us a third possibility, with non-arbitrary labels but without special mapping algorithms either.

Let us consider now, however, the other use Valency is put to in MT systems: distinguishing complements and adjuncts. Again we can look to GETA and TAUM-AVIATION for exemplification, for crucial in these systems is the ARG-CIRC(*onstanciel*) distinction. Nominals that cannot be matched against the valency pattern of the verb are marked as CIRC, and this distinction gives rise to different transfer strategies. The key area here is the translation of prepositional phrases: the theory is that the preposition in a valency-bound element (ARG) is semantically void, and governed by the verb. Thus for example we have in English-German translation a many-to-many mapping of strongly governed prepositions, a mere sampling of which is given in Figure 1.

	at	in	of	on	to
an	*arbeiten* work	*glauben* believe	*denken* think	*stecken* stick	*gewöhnen* accustom
auf	*blicken* gaze	*trauen* trust	*zutreffen* be true	*rechnen* count	*weisen* point
für		*s. interessieren* be interested	*zutreffen* be true		*sorgen* see
in	*ankommen* arrive	*kleiden* dress		*einsteigen* get	*einwilligen* agree
mit		*handeln* trade	*prahlen* boast	*rechnen* count	*geschehen* happen
zu			*gehören* be part	*gratulieren* congratulate	*führen* lead

Figure 1: Prepositional objects in English and German

Prepositions in adjuncts (CIRC) (e.g. *under the table* versus *on the table*) on the other hand are meaningful, and so participate in the translation process. This neat correspondence between ARG and formal preposition versus CIRC and functional preposition is very convenient, though unfortunately it does not always hold. On the other hand, we have valency-bound directional elements with verbs of movement, where the preposition is meaningful (*go to/in/on* etc.). Interestingly, GETA treats these as 'valency bound circumstantials', perhaps after the fashion of Tesnière (1959:128) (see Chapter 1 Section 2), and this makes sentence pairs like (5) problematic, since in English *the restaurant* is ARG, but in French *dans le restaurant* CIRC. On the other hand we do not always have isomorphy between a given circumstantial relationship and the preposition that expresses it: for example, 'location at' is expressed by any of *on*, *at*, *in*, *by* in English depending on the nature of the location, while in French the dependence is given by quite different factors (see Chapter 7 Section 1).

In Somers (1984) I discuss at length the question of whether the complement-adjunct distinction is simply binary, or perhaps forms part of a larger hierarchy, and parts of this discussion are recapitulated in Chapter 1 Section 6. The conclusion drawn there was that there seemed to be a call for the recognition of some 'middle' value between the complement and adjunct, for elements like *with a hammer* in (10) as compared to the clear complement status of *Nick* and *vase*, and the equally clear adjunct status of *yesterday*. Essentially the same point was repeated briefly in Chapter 9.

(10) Nick smashed the vase with a hammer yesterday.

Two further degrees of valency binding – 'integral complement' and 'extra-peripheral' – were also introduced to give the hierarchy in Figure 2:

integral complement
|
complement
|
middle
|
adjunct
|
extra-peripheral

Figure 2: Hierarchy of valency binding

It is now an appropriate moment to consider the effect of this concept on mapping of arguments in transfer in MT. Let us assume that the general transfer algorithm has the possibility of correctly matching complements in corresponding valency patterns (never mind if this is achieved by arbitrary numbering, on a verb-by-verb basis, or using case labels). Let us also assume that adjuncts and extra-peripherals can be dealt with satisfactorily. We must now consider what to do when, on a bilingual basis, there is some mismatch between the valency bindings of corresponding elements.

The most likely realisation of this problem seems to be as follows: assume that, in source-language analysis of (10), *with a hammer* has been assigned our 'middle' label, whereas in the target language either (i) the equivalent argument is considered to be part of the valency pattern of the equivalent predicate; or (ii) the equivalent argument would be regarded as wholly circumstantial. Of course if in the target language the element is also considered to be 'middle' there is no problem: but what are we to do in either of the above scenarios? In the case of (i) we can treat the element as if it had been a complement all along: the valency pattern for the translation equivalent of *smash* will tell us what to do with it. Likewise in the case of (ii) we can treat it as if we always knew it was an adjunct really: depending on the nature of the algorithm for treating adjuncts, we may be required to compute some more information about it (its case role for example), but this is no problem.

It is easy to see that a generalisation of this solution is one in which each degree of valency binding in Figure 2 is allowed to map onto either itself, or its nearest neighbour in either direction. Thus, integral complements and ordinary complements should be compatible, as should adjuncts and extra-peripherals. This blurring of the distinctions up and down the hierarchy accords well with intuitions, which suggest that because the syntactic (and semantic) behaviour of elements at neighbouring points on the hierarchy have aspects in common, partial compatibility should be achievable. If we add at the very top of the hierarchy a notional empty or 'zero' binding, we are even able to account for those cases where a verb plus integral complement in one language is expressed as a simple lexical verb in another, as for example with the English and French pairs *take part — participer, make a mistake — se tromper, catch cold — s'enrhûmer, welcome — faire accueil, reverse — marcher en arrière, stroke — donner une carresse*, etc.

Problems would arise if analyses of two languages were so different that a complement in one was regarded as an adjunct in the other, or an integral mapped onto a middle and so on. Nothing much could be done in such a case, and it can only be said that the single condition upon which this system depends for success is that that situation simply does not arise (though see below).

However, there is a second problem arising from the question of non-matching valency patterns, a problem for which Case seems to offer a solution. The problem is this: in language A, verb V is considered to have two valency-bound arguments, but in language B, it takes three complements. When we come to transfer between A and B, how do we know which two of the three complements specified for V in language B map onto the two specified for V in language A?

2. *Case in MT*

Despite its popularity in AI, there are relatively few systems that use Case in MT, even though there are a number of problems, as we have seen, with the bare Valency approach. Yet Case obviously has attractions for MT, especially due to its character stressed in Chapter 11, as a bridge between syntax and semantics. There is some dispute as to what amount of 'semantics' is needed for successful translation: for example, one school of thought has it that a translator (human or otherwise) must understand a text in order to translate it, while the opposite view is that for most translation tasks the degree of understanding needed is relatively superficial, being limited to problems like prepositional phrase attachment as in (1)-(2), or pronoun reference resolution as in (3).

(1a) I saw the man with my own eyes.
(1b) J'ai vu l'homme *de* mes propres yeux.
(2a) I saw the man with red hair.
(2b) J'ai vu l'homme *aux* cheveux rouges.
(3a) I threw a stone at the mirror and it broke.
(3b) J'ai jeté une pierre dans le miroir et il s'est cassé.

Certainly there are examples where this kind of disambiguation is unnecessary, since the ambiguity is reflected in the target language: this is the case in the German translations of (1)-(2), the Dutch translation of (3), and in Agent-Patient ambiguities as in (4).

(1c) Ich sah den Mann mit meinen eigenen Augen.
(2c) Ich sah den Mann mit roten Haaren.
(3c) Ik wierp een steen aan de spiegel en hij brak.
(4a) The shooting of the soldiers shocked us.
(4b) Das Schießen der Soldaten erschrock uns.

Nevertheless, we have seen in the previous section at least two problems which, we suggested, could be solved using Case. The first was the *like/plaire* example, where we had to have a special mapping algorithm, whether between arbitrary ARG labels, or between numbered ARG labels interpreted in terms of syntactic function. The point about case labels in this example is that they will provide a non-arbitrary transfer medium which is intuitive in both languages. If we extend the system to make it multilingual, the case for Case is even stronger, since it provides a single language-pair independent mapping in contrast to the necessary $n(n-1)$ (for n languages) bilingual mappings, which might, remember, need to be replicated for almost every verb. Even in the problem case above, where analyses required non-neighbour mapping, a solution in terms of case labels suggests that where they do not help us, the valency-binding labels can be ignored. And the Case solution to the final problem – how to identify which arguments are considered in both languages to be valency-bound – is again quite obvious.

The point about Case is that it exactly meets the need in MT for a level of representation that is both deep enough to serve in a manner relatively independent of surface form, while still being shallow enough to be compatible with these other levels of description (i.e. surface syntax, canonical form, etc.). This view is countered by Tsujii (1982), who claims that with only the shallow meaning representation afforded by Case, one does not avoid the necessity of looking at specific verbs in order to interpret the case labels and so to determine the appropriate strategy. Tsujii gives the example of *go into* and *enter* as in (5), and points out that since *the auditorium* is in the same case with both verbs, that information cannot be used to tell us whether or not to introduce the preposition *into*.

(5a) John enters the auditorium.
(5b) * John enters into the auditorium.
(5c) John goes into the auditorium.

'If the rules [for transfer mapping] refer to specific verbs, the names of deep cases are not significant because the same deep case is differently interpreted depending on individual verbs' (Tsujii, 1982:382). But Tsujii is wrongly attributing to advocates of Case for MT the idea that it should replace other forms of labelling in the representation of analysis: 'Why should we reduce the rich structures such as multi-level analysis trees into poor ones? We don't claim that semantic cases are completely useless, but only claim that a single level structure based on them is not rich enough to select appropriate target equivalents and that surface level information is also useful to specify usage patterns' (*idem*). It is quite clear, at least to me, that indeed information about syntactic configuration goes hand in hand with case structure information. Furthermore, the verb-specific approach of Tsujii, and in the GETA system upon which his system is based, means that certain significant generalisations cannot be stated. Consider that the surface case form of each argument has to be specified for each and every verb. If numbered ARGS are used for this purpose (e.g. ARG1 = deep subject etc.), then we are back with our problem of non-matching valency patterns. But if case labels are introduced, there are certain generalisations that can be used as defaults to reduce the amount of information to be expressed for each verb. While it is clear that the notions of a case-hierarchy for subject selection, or the association of prepositions with cases expressed in Fillmore (1968*a*) were overstated, this does not mean that they do not apply at all. Quite the contrary: the sort of observations Fillmore was making are indeed typical to some extent. His only error was in trying to make them hard and fast generalisations. Of course, Case does introduce new problems, not least of which is the definition of a comfortable case set. But this is not a design problem, but a development problem, and those of us who have a certain confidence in Case like to believe that the appropriate case distinctions will become evident during a period of experimentation with a prototype system. Like in any engineering (as opposed to theoretical) undertaking, one must be prepared for a period of flux where the appropriate tools are developed and modified.

In the rest of this section, we shall look at a number of MT systems that have included Case among their set of tools, so as to see more clearly some of the ways in which it can be employed.

Nishida *et al.* (1980) have an experimental English-Japanese MT system in which Case plays an important role. Translation between English and Japanese presents particular problems because of the rather different sentence patterns found in the two languages, which encourage a fairly deep representation. Case is felt to be especially appropriate because of the alleged strong mapping possibilities between deep and surface case: the relationship between deep cases and the surface postpositions that express them is said to be considerably simpler in Japanese than in western languages (cf. Taylor, 1971), and it is conceivable that Fillmore's enthusiasm for his (1968*a*:32) notion of 'associated preposition' might have been strengthened by his familiarity with Japanese. Indeed, Nishida *et al.* are not alone in adopting a Case-based approach to Japanese MT (cf. Shimazu *et al.*, 1983:719; Iida *et al.*, 1984; Nitta *et al.* 1984). Nishida *et al.* claim that their representation is 'closely related to surface structures' (p. 447) but at the same time 'almost independent . . . of respective languages' (*idem*). This apparently contradictory view turns out to be accurate, since their intention in the first comment is to suggest that the case structures built contain 'surface' verbs rather than, say, lexical decompositions.

Nishida *et al.* employ a system of 'categories of predicates' somewhat like those described in Chapter 11 Section 3 (cf. Celce-Murcia, 1975 and PTOSYS (Somers and Johnson, 1979; Somers, 1980*a*)), though based on yet another classification of verb types, that of Hornby (1975). These categories can be used to infer both the syntactic and semantic patterns for the sentence, and enable a relatively straightforward parsing strategy; they also contribute to the choice of appropriate postposition in Japanese, since 'a good correspondence generally holds' between postposition, case label and verb category (Nishida *et al.*, 1980:448). The verb categories are also helpful in assigning case labels to 'optional' constituents (that is, 'adverbial phrases and clauses outside [the] verb patterns' (p. 449)). This concurs with our own findings with regard to 'weakly expected cases' (Somers, 1982*c*:240f). The treatment of noun phrases, and particularly nominalisations of verbs, by the construction of case structures is particularly appropriate for Japanese too, given the close affinity in Japanese between verb phrases and a large range of other constructions (e.g. adjectival phrases).

Finally, a specific translation problem for Japanese that particularly lends itself to a Case treatment is the 'non-living subject problem': 'Japanese sentences avoid sentential forms in which non-living objects bring [=perform] actions such as causative and perceptive ones especially when the actions directly affect human beings. . .' (p. 451). Thus for example, various 'transformations' like those in (6)-(7) must be triggered.

(6a) Our limited budget will not allow us to start a new project.

(6b) Owing to our limited budget, we cannot start a new project.

(7a) A few minutes walk brought me to the place.

(7b) By walking for a few minutes, I arrived at the place.

This is achieved by careful association of Agent with animacy, and the use of a range of cases like Cause, Means and Source (which together with Agent make up a kind of 'supercase' – cf. Chapter 7

Section 1), which are associated via the predicate-type with an appropriate structural modification. Nishida *et al.* seem quite enthusiastic about their experiments with Case, and their necessarily brief description of the system makes interesting reading.

METAL is a translation system developed by the Linguistics Research Center (LRC), University of Texas, Austin, which translates telecommunications texts from German into English. A version of Case grammar forms a fundamental part of the linguistic theory underlying the system, and fairly full details are provided in the system documentation (Lehmann *et al.*, 1980). Less detailed descriptions of METAL are to be found in Slocum (1983, 1985) and in Whitelock (1985).

The version of Case used in METAL is reasonably straightforward, though with some unusual additional aspects. METAL is significant in being the only operational (rather than principally experimental) MT system using Case, and so it is appropriate to look at this aspect of the system in some detail. We shall not, however, say much about the overall system design, except where strictly necessary.

The system is basically transfer-based, with analysis, transfer and synthesis modules written directly in INTERLISP. Source text is analysed with a context-free syntactic parser the results of which are passed to the 'case frame processor'. Case frames are also used in transfer.

Lexical entries for verbs contain information regarding '. . . five features which are used to express restrictions which the verb places upon the form and function of associated nominals' (Lehmann *et al.*, 1980:I.24), as follows:

1. Role of argument (RA): these are the cases in the system, which are divided into two types, 'central' and 'peripheral'. A key difference between the METAL conception of central and peripheral RA's and other similar distinctions (cf. Chapter 9) is that these form two discrete sets of cases. This means that each of the RA's that are recognised is regarded as either typically 'conditioned by the particular verb' or not verb-specific. However, 'One might note that a few classes of verbs may be closely associated with arguments which are usually considered peripheral for most verb classes' (*idem*), the example given being verbs of motion which often specify a locative complement. Note that this conception that centrality or peripherality is an inherent rather than inherited property of a case is one we have argued against in various places above (Chapter 1 Section 2; Chapter 9). On the other hand, there

are certain advantages in the method adopted here where, as we shall see, there is a distinction in the degree of abstraction of the central and peripheral RA's.

2. The semantic type of argument (TA) is used to indicate selection restrictions on the RA. This is an improvement on the original Fillmorean concept where such features were regarded as implicit, a misconception noted early on by Fillmore (1971*b*:42) himself, though still adopted by many Case users (cf. for example Chapter 7 Section 2 on the requirement that Agents be animate).

3. The syntactic marker of argument (MS) indicates the syntactic role (surface case) associated with each RA.

4. The form of argument marker (FA) indicates the kind of constituent expected for the RA, e.g. clause, noun-phrase, prepositional phrase, adverb. These last two pieces of information – MA and FA – together are fairly reminiscent of Helbig and Schenkel's (1973) Valency dictionary entries, and the idea that syntactic form as well as function is an important feature to be associated with each RA is, in a Case grammar, unusual and obviously profitable.

5. The transitivity type (TT) is a feature very much like the 'paradigm' marker in Celce-Murcia's (1975) system (see Chapter 11 Section 3), giving the 'potential configuration of arguments', that is, relating the RA's defined as in [1] to the MA's in [3] according to the mood and voice of the verb. The TT feature does add information not expressed in the other features, even though at first sight it would appear only to corroborate the RA–MA correspondence: it is according to TT that rules regarding sentence forms other than simple active indicative can be generalised. Thus for example if the TT corresponds to transitive and the verb is passive, we will expect the Agent RA to be realised by a prepositional phrase, and the Target (=Patient) RA to be subject, whereas for some other TT these correspondences might not apply.

The manner in which these five features interact can be seen when we consider the way the case frame processor proceeds. With each RA is associated a 'case function', which '. . . will pick the appropriate restrictions for the case roles according to voice (active or passive) and mood (indicative or imperative) of the clause. The restrictions for a particular argument are its semantic type, its form (noun phrase or prepositional phrase), and its grammatical case or its preposition respectively. These restrictions can be general . . . or be specific to the individual verb' (Lehmann *et al.*, 1980:I.13). The case frame processor attempts to 'use up' the available arguments by matching them to the specifications given by the five features for the verb, and then applies case functions associated with the peripheral RA's to the remaining arguments. If all the arguments can be legally assigned to RA's, then the clause is considered well-formed. Otherwise, the rule is deemed to have failed, and an alternative frame processor is tried (p.I.39). Case frames are also used in transfer, primarily to order the constituents and assign them appropriate MA's. Sometimes, if an RA is 'marked', there might also be a change in FA, most often (presumably) from noun-phrase to prepositional phrase or vice versa.

We may conclude this description of METAL with a look at the list of RA's used, and some comments on the interesting proposals therein. As mentioned earlier, the RA's divide up into central and peripheral roles, though some of the latter occasionally function as 'obligatory' (='valency bound') constituents. The following central roles are used: Agent, Instrument, Target, Benefactive, Recipient, Reflexive, Topic, Commutative, Body-part.

Apart from noting that Target corresponds to the Objective or Patient case in many other systems, only the last four of these RA's require special comment. But before doing so, it should be said that Lehmann *et al.* give a reasonable 'definition' of each of the cases, including rules of thumb regarding their surface form, and informal 'tests' for some of the RA's: for example, 'The agent can often be identified by answering the questions "Who did it?" or "What made it happen?"' (p.II.123). The Reflexive is introduced 'for certain obligatory reflexive pronouns which are not true targets' (p.II.125). The Reflexive in (8) is constrasted with the Target in (9a) – compare (9b).

(8) The child behaved *herself* today.
(9a) John saw *himself* in the mirror.
(9b) John saw *Mary* in the mirror.

It is noted that while non-Target reflexives are rare in English, they are quite common in German. Herein lies the motivation for differentiating the two RA's (for, after all, any such idea must be motivated by some translation problem). First, many reflexive verbs in German are non-reflexive in English: in these instances the Reflexive can be simply eliminated, whereas the Target reflexive should not be. Note also that, apart from in the third person, reflexive and non-reflexive pronouns are not distinguished in German, so that the difference between (10) and (11), taking these two factors into consideration, is quite crucial.

(10a) Ich drehte *mich* um. (Reflexive)
(10b) I turned (*myself) round.
(11a) Er drehte *mich* um. (Target)
(11b) He turned me round.

Topic is the RA for 'the thing described', and is exemplified as the prepositional object of *talk* as in (12). *On* and *about* are cited as typical markers of Topic, though it can be direct object (presumably of verbs like *discuss*). Topic is also the RA for the subject of *be* as in (13).

(12) We talked about the plans.

(13) The book is here.

Bearing in mind our criterion of practical necessity for RA distinctions, it is difficult to see why Topic and Target must be distinguished. It is true that incorporating Topic into Target would make the latter more disparate and difficult to characterise (hints of 'waste-basketry'?), but this is already true of Topic as it stands, its two stated uses being quite distinct conceptually.

The Commutative RA is rather like the traditional Comitative (see Chapter 7 Section 6), and is used in METAL 'to represent coagency and co-objectivity' (p.II.125). The strangeness of this concept is acknowledged, and the characterisation recalls comments above regarding the fact that Comitative is a 'subcase' of Agent or Patient (Chapter 7 Section 6; Teng, 1970:334; Buckingham, 1973:115; Nilsen, 1973:48). Lehmann *et al.* note the '. . . wide variety of syntactic structures that may be used for it . . . In many instances it can be represented by a conjoined subject [(14a)], often with a phrase like *each other* in the object slot [(14b)]. Or the relationship can be identified with *with* [(14c)]' (p.II.125).

(14a) Joseph and Mr. Smith shook hands.

(14b) John and Mary kissed each other.

(14c) The Johnsons are sitting with the Smiths.

The final central RA Body-part, is perhaps the most unexpected. The fact that its name looks more like a feature (TA) than an RA should probably not mislead us. Lehmann *et al.* (p.II.126) admit that the role may seem questionable, but justify its separation on the grounds of the anomalous behaviour of such elements, though no such anomalies are convincingly illustrated.

Lehmann *et al.* propose fully thirty major and additional peripheral roles. A characteristic of these is that they tend to be rather less abstract than the central roles, and some are very precise roles indeed. Some of these RA's form hierarchies, and removal of the non-terminal RA's in these hierarchies leaves us with twenty-five peripheral RA's. What is slightly bizarre about some of these roles is that although they are allegedly typically peripheral, the examples given show them being used as 'obligatory' RA's, somewhat undermining the central-peripheral distinction.

Because Lehmann *et al.* (1980) is a relatively inaccessible document, and because METAL is such a good example of the use of Case in MT (especially since it is probably the best operational MT system around at the moment), I feel that it is reasonable to reproduce here the list of RA's used in METAL. In order to economise on space a little, I will first simply list without comment those RA's which are unremarkable and whose characterisation can be correctly inferred from their name and the accompanying example († indicates example provided by me). Notice that Characteristic [1] and Partitive [14] are exemplified by noun-phrases (as is Possessor [13] in the original), a reminder that Case can function at levels other than verb-phrase.

[1] Characteristic/Composition	a book *of poems*
[2] Effect/Result	†He flogged her *to death.*
[3] Material	John built the wall *out of bricks.*
[4] Measure	The fish weighed *seven pounds.*
[5] Method/Means	Bacteria reproduce *by binary fission.*
[6] Purpose/Reason	He resigned *because of ill health.*
[7] Similarity	†She swims *like a fish.*
[8] Contrary	He did it *against my wishes.*
[9] Despite	He came *despite bad weather.*
[10] Environment/Context	He heard her *above the din.*
[11] Exception/Exclusion	All was lost *beside this.*
[12] Manner	He did it *without any help.*
[13] Possessor	†That book belongs to *John.*
[14] Partitive	the chairman *of the board*
[15] Respective/Comparative	John is taller *than Mary.*

We should at least make comment regarding this list that some distinctions seem very fine indeed, and one could reduce the number of RA's by collapsing some of them together (e.g. Similarity [7] and Comparative [15]).

The remaining RA's are made up of eight cases, which form two hierarchies headed by Locative and Temporal, plus two rather strange RA's, State-of-Being and Transitional. The Locative RA (LOC) heads a hierarchy encompassing Station (STA) and Motion/ Mobile (MOT); STA indicates static location, while MOT specifies the direction of motion. Each of these two is further subdivided as follows:

[16] LOC-STA-Place	The book is *on the table.*
[17] LOC-STA-Proximity	The book is *next to the telephone.*
[18] LOC-MOT-Origin/Source	The man came *from New Haven.*
[19] LOT-MOT-Destination/Goal	The girl went *to the store.*
[20] LOC-MOT-Circumferential	The moth flew *around the candle.*
[21] LOC-MOT-Area-transversed	We traveled via *New York.*

As far as the Station RA's are concerned, we may ask why Proximity [17] is singled out as distinct from Place [16], and why there are not also RA's for 'Superiority' *above*, 'Inferiority' *below* etc. Alternatively, it may be that the intended distinction is really that of *at* versus *near*, with physical contact being the distinguishing feature (e.g. *below* versus *underneath*).

Three of the LOC-MOT RA's seem to correspond to the traditional Source [18], Path [21] and Goal [19] (cf. Chapter 7 Section 5), with the fourth [20] a useful additional type of Locative. We might ask though whether a verb like *surround* would have to be distinguished between its stative use, as in (15a) and its motional use as in (15b).

(15a) Italy surrounds *San Marino.*

(15b) The Indians surrounded *the wagon train.*

The hierarchy headed by temporal (TMP) is less complex, consisting of just two sub-cases:

[22] TMP-Punctual	We will go *after the movie.*
[23] TMP-Durative	It rained *during the night.*

It is interesting to note that in METAL the Source-Path-Goal distinction recognised for Locatives is not carried over into the Temporals, as it is in some other systems (cf. Chapter 7 Section 5) except that TMP-Durative [23] seems to be a 'Temporal-Path' in parallel with the 'Locative-Path' [21]. We therefore wonder what RA would be assigned to the Temporals in (16), which seem good candidates for the non-existent 'TMP-PUN-Source' and 'TMP-PUN-Goal' by analogy with [18] and [19].

(16a) *Since the last election* unemployment has risen steeply.

(16b) I will be on holiday *until July 14th.*

The final two RA's are both a little problematic. State-of-being [24] is said to indicate 'a state which characterises the referent' (p.II.129), and is exemplified as in (17).

(17) He is *on duty/at war/under age/at our mercy.*

This analysis seems to be an uneasy treatment of the problematic phenomenon of a prepositional phrase acting as a predicate, and seems to add to the number of fairly unsatisfactory case analyses associated with the verb *be* (cf. Chapter 7 Section 6). Last of all, we have Transitional [25], which is 'used to indicate a change of state' (*idem*). Unfortunately, there is no way to tell in the examples given (18) to which element this RA is assigned, and it is even conceivable that it applies to the entire phrase *water into steam* or *from grave to gay*. Since there are no Source or Goal cases apart from [18] and [19], no obvious alternative suggests itself, so this does seem to be a weakness in the RA set.

(18a) Heat can change water into steam.
(18b) His mood went from grave to gay.

The most important comment to be made in general is with regard to the central-peripheral distinction. There is a serious problem, if we admit the possibility of using these RA's also for 'obligatory' roles, of conflict between these more specific RA's and the slightly more general central RA's. For example, Exception [11] seems a good RA for the object of *exclude*, but so does the vaguer RA Target. Similarly Material [3] and Instrument both seem possible for *use* in a paraphrase of the example given for [3]. My own inclination in the METAL setup would be to uphold more strictly the distinction between central and peripheral RA's allowing the former to function as if they were the latter, but not vice versa. This would involve moving some RA's into the 'central' list (e.g. Measure [4] and the Locatives [16]-[21]), and perhaps allowing the remaining peripheral RA's – when they are appropriate as 'obligatory' RA for some particular verb – to function as secondary RA indicators attaching in some way to a central RA – probably most frequently Target (though not of necessity, note). This approach accords with my general feeling that the role of Case-like labels is different for (what I have been calling) 'complements' and 'adjuncts', a difference that is properly reflected in the nature of the cases associated with each. I shall elaborate on this, and especially on why it is a valid distinction in language processing, in the next section.

3. *Personal approaches*

In this final section I take the opportunity to explore some personal approaches to the use of Case in MT initially in the context of a transfer-based system, but I shall also discuss briefly the feasibility of interlingua-based MT.

Let us first set a context for our discussion by imagining an MT system with the following design principles, corresponding to the 'state of the art' in MT system design (cf. Somers, 1983:149f). We assume the system to permit definition of the linguistic processes in a modular fashion, using a more or less 'linguist-friendly' formalism: the underlying software will take care of controlling the interaction of the processes (cf. for example Johnson *et al.*, 1983) so that the algorithmic aspect of the system is strictly separated from the linguistic part.

As a design principle, we suppose that source-language analysis should be essentially independent of any given target language, and similarly target-language synthesis procedures should make no assumptions about data based on knowledge of the original language of the text. This requirement is essential in a multilingual system (in which one would aim to use the same analysis procedures regardless of the intended target language), though it has several important repercussions. In particular, it implies that only in the bilingual transfer state can both source- and target-language information be used.

It also implies the necessity for a carefully designed 'interface structure' as common output from the various source-language analyses and another not necessarily but probably similar interface structure as common input to synthesis, since the analysis and synthesis modules are language-pair independent. This interface structure should not be confused with an 'interlingua' (see below). In the transfer-based system, the structure produced by the analysis module will still be recognisably a representation of the particular source language, and the input to synthesis will likewise already have some target-language specific features: by having a bilingual transfer stage we permit ourselves the possibility of reorienting the representation away from the source language and towards the target language.

As a final remark, we might note that the constraints discussed here, which are serious, make this set-up unnecessarily complex for a strictly bilingual MT system, in which it would obviously make sense to develop the analysis stage strictly in terms of the known target language, more or less combining the two stages of analysis and transfer.

The exact nature of the Interface Structure (IS) is not crucial to what I wish to suggest here, though it must have certain basic properties to make my proposals feasible. These are first that it reflects constituency in a traditional manner, so that, for example, noun-phrases can be regarded as units; and second that it incorporates the dependency notion of governorship, so that in each constituent, one (and only one) element is singled out as the governor or head of that constituent. Of primary interest is the structure of the sentence-constituent, in which the governor will be the main predicate or verbal element, though, as we shall see, my proposals extend to other constituents.

My proposals are therefore compatible with a number of representations, including the interface structure found in the GETA MT System (Vauquois, 1975, 1978), and those of most contemporary linguistic theories – particularly 'f-structures' in Lexical-Functional Grammar (Kaplan and Bresnan, 1982), but also the representations found in Generalised Phrase Structure Grammar

(Gazdar *et al.*, 1985) and in recent versions of Government and Binding theory (Chomsky, 1981).

One of the features of a multilingual transfer-based system is the necessity to keep transfer as small as possible. This being the case, we can see the motivation for introducing the degree of shallow semantics offered by Case. We saw in our discussion in Section 2 the problems associated with transfer based solely on labels distinguishing only between valency-bound and peripheral elements as in GETA and TAUM, and as advocated by Tsujii (1982). We also saw how the additional information carried by case labels simplifies the mapping of arguments in transfer. We should take into consideration our discovery in Chapter 9 that all the traditionally proposed cases (with the exception of Patient) can occur both as complements and adjuncts, even simultaneously.

It seems therefore that the key to transfer is a label on each of the non-head nodes in the IS indicating both a case relation and the valency-binding of that element with regard to its head, so that each constituent is uniquely identifiable.

A system of values for valency binding has already been proposed and discussed (Chapter 1 Section 6 and Chapter 12 Section 2).

For guidance as regards the choice of a set of cases, it is interesting to look again at the METAL system (Lehmann *et al.*, 1980; Slocum, 1983, 1985; see Section 2 above). In METAL, it will be recalled, a distinction is made between essentially central and peripheral cases. I would like to propose here however that this approach in METAL may be of interest if adapted slightly. We saw in our discussion above that some uneasiness results from the combination of general and specific cases, since often both a general (traditional) and a specific case assignment seems appropriate. I would propose the definition of a range of traditional cases (which may or may not be defined according to principles I elaborated in Chapter 10 above) which may function as either complements or adjuncts. A further range of cases may be defined strictly for adjuncts and extra- peripherals, as desired. These will typically be more specific, and their character determined by particular translation problems as they arise, though one can imagine that some of the role types seen in METAL will figure on the list. Given the existence of these specific cases, it would be quite acceptable to use them as secondary labels in conjunction with the traditional cases, again as and where necessary or helpful, though their presence in the IS would not typically be a requirement for transfer. They might, for example, be found to be of assistance in choosing appropriate surface structures in generation for some target language, though not for another.

There remains the problem of constituents below the level of verb-phrase, since these too have structure, with head and non-heads in some relation. Furthermore, the recognition of the nature of this relationship is often essential with translation. Compare the noun groups in (1), all of which have a similar syntactic structure (2), but which represent different translation patterns in French, depending on the relation between the modifier and the head (3).

(1a) a steam train
(1b) a football pitch
(1c) a cotton shirt
(1d) the baby linen

(2)

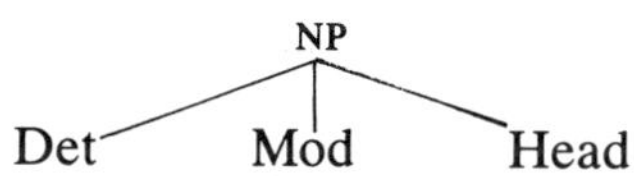

(3a) un train à vapeur
(3b) un terrain de foot
(3c) une chemise en coton
(3d) le linge pour bébé

Although it might be argued that some of the noun-phrases in (1) are strictly 'terms', and could be treated as individual compound lexical items, the type of construction they exemplify is typical, widespread and such 'compounds' occur freely in novel combinations, often involving a larger number of elements (4)-(6).

(4a) the Geneva peace talks
(4b) les négociations pour la paix à Genève
(5a) Labour election campaign promises
(5b) les promesses de campagne électorale des Travaillistes
(6a) North Sea oil field offshore rig administration
(6b) la gestion des installations offshore des champs de gaz dans la Mer du Nord

These pose considerable problems when they are to be translated into languages in which such opaque compounds cannot be formed; the relationships between the elements are made more explicit by the use of prepositions. Therefore, these relationships must be represented in the IS resulting from analysis. Indeed this has been recognised as a problem in translation, whether mechanical or human, and Case has been invoked for a linguistic description of such structures (Bauer, 1978; Mackenzie, 1983). Given these relationships, general (though not hard and fast) rules can be applied to choose the appropriate preposition – for example in (3) we have *à* for Instrument, *de* for Purpose, and *en* for Material. As regards my own approach, I would propose that the case set would need to be supplemented by a number of relations specifically suited to noun groups: these should be compatible with the cases already introduced for complements and adjuncts, so that there would be as large an overlap as possible. Clearly, in the case of complex noun groups whose head is derived from a verb, either as a direct nominalisation (7a), as a cognate form (8a), or even perhaps where there is a semantic link (9a), there is no reason why the range of cases (and valency bindings) that would apply in the corresponding verbal predication (7b, 8b, 9b) could not be employed within the noun group.

(7a) the possible future *dismissal* of teachers for incompetence
(7b) Teachers will possibly be dismissed in future for incompetence.
(8a) my mother's temporary *loss* of memory
(8b) My mother has temporarily lost her memory.
(9a) Everton's recent *victory* over Liverpool
(9b) Everton recently beat Liverpool.

It is not my intention here to establish, discuss and justify such a set of relations. In any case, only by extensive research and experimentation with a working system could one expect to be able to discover the range of cases needed. Whereas I have argued that the set of cases for complements should be a small closed set, I see no need for such a restriction on the more specific relations used for adjuncts, extra-peripherals, and within noun-groups. The number and range of these that prove necessary will emerge during this experimentation. It is probable, nevertheless, that one of the cases for noun-groups will be an essentially neutral one, since there will inevitably be instances, as Mackenzie – following Piťha (1980:93) – states, '. . . where there is no specific semantic function detectable and the speaker makes appeal to the addressee's pragmatic information to supply the full information . . .' (Mackenzie, 1983:38). In the context of MT, this will be the case where there turns out to be no need to compute the relationship – particularly for example between adjectives and nouns – because the structure can be simply transferred to the target language. This is not an example of 'wastebasketry', but simply a recognition that it is not always necessary to establish a relationship in great depth when a shallow representation is sufficient.

My proposed strategy for computing the IS representation discussed above is a combination of the linguistic theories concerning verb types, discussed at length in Chapter 4, together with an approach to Valency not dissimilar to the one seen in METAL. The first stage is a syntactic parse which delimits the main verb and its arguments, labelling them for surface syntactic function, and calculating a value for mood and voice (e.g. imperative, active, passive). A relatively straightforward algorithm can be developed to calculate from this information the likely deep syntactic functions of the arguments. At this point information associated with the verb comes into play.

The dictionary information for each verb specifies its 'verb type' in the form of a (set of) features like those of Chafe (1970), Cook (1972*b*) or Longacre (1976), seen in Chapter 4. From these features is inferred by general rule a set of cases with associated valency-bindings, i.e. integral, obligatory and optional complements, and also middle arguments. General rules also associate with the cases typical semantic features for potential fillers as well as their expected (deep) syntactic functions and morphosyntactic categories. In this way we incorporate the kind of information captured in Helbig and Schenkel's (1973) Valency dictionary entries, in a manner similar to that seen in METAL (previous section). Again as in METAL, these general rules may be overridden for particular verbs. Furthermore the Chafe/Cook-type classification may be extended to subdivide major verb types according to other criteria: for example experiential process verbs may be subclassified according to whether the associated Experiencer is the deep subject (e.g. *like*) or whether the Patient takes this function (e.g. *please*); or action process verbs may subdivide into those allowing the ergative paradigm (i.e. optional Agent) and those not doing so. The general strategy is then to attempt to match these expected label configurations to the text, with criteria at different levels weighted according to their overall significance, to enable conflicts to be resolved. For example, for a given verb, it may be a more important criterion that its Agent be animate than that it be the deep subject, or that it be expressed as a noun phrase, whereas for another verb these weightings may be reversed. Once the complements and middles have been recognised, the remaining elements must be dealt with. Whereas the valency-binding and case labelling for complements and middles is guided by the verb, the labelling for adjuncts and extra-peripherals is more independent, and often clues will be sought from within the argument to be analysed. So, for example, a locative-source adjunct (in English) may be recognised by the combination of preposition *from* together with a noun head marked with the semantic feature 'place'. It cannot be expected that all assignments will be as straightforward as this, and any combination of facts already computed may be expected to help, including information about cases already assigned. For example, co-occurrence of 'inner' and 'outer' cases might have specific repercussions for word-order or other surface realisation properties; the tense of the main verb may help in confirming or rejecting a possible temporal adjunct; semantic and pragmatic compatibility between complements and adjuncts may be a factor; and so on.

The IS representation so produced can now be passed to transfer, where first substitution of target lexical items for source lexical items takes place. Even at this stage, the various types of information reflected in the IS may be criterial. For example, *leben* may be preferred over *wohnen* as the German equivalent of 'live' if the IS shows that there is no element marked as being in the appropriate Locative case (cf. (10)-(11)). Or else the semantic features of the filler of a certain case role may determine choice of target lexical item, as when German distinguishes between *fahren* with a vehicle as Instrument and *reiten* with an animal as Instrument for 'ride' (12)-(13). As a final example, we have German *sagen* which with a noun-phrase deep object translates as *tell* (14), but with a relative clause as deep object (if there is no Experiencer expressed) must be rendered as *say* (15).

(10a) He lived in the nineteenth century.
(10b) Er *lebte* im neunzehnten Jahrhundert.
(11a) He lived in a dingy attic.
(11b) Er *wohnte* in einer düsteren Mansade.
(12a) He rode to town on his bicycle.
(12b) Er *fuhr* mit seinem Fahrrad in die Stadt.
(13a) She rode a white horse to Banbury Cross.
(13b) Sie *ritt* auf einem Schimmel nach Banbury Cross.
(14a) Er sagte immer die Wahrheit.
(14b) He always *told* the truth.
(15a) Er sagte, daß er nicht kommen wollte.
(15b) He *said* he didn't want to come.

Once the target lexical verbs have been chosen, there may then be an amount of structural transfer, that is to say, rearrangement of the shape of the IS, which may include adding new branches, deleting branches, or in the extreme case choosing a significantly different sentence pattern. This last will typically arise as part of lexical transfer, and can be expected when some construction in the source language has no direct equivalent in the target language. A typical example is involved in the translation of the

Dutch particle *graag* ('gladly') into English, where a sentence like (16a) will preferably be translated as (16b) rather than the more literal (16c) (cf. Krauwer and des Tombe, 1984*a*, *b*).

(16a) Hij zwemt graag.
(16b) He likes swimming.
(16c) He swims gladly.

Here we are introducing a new verbal element *like* plus an embedding, and a rather complex mapping between the arguments of *zwemmen* ('swim') and the arguments of *like* must be defined. This can be done in terms of the case and deep syntactic function configuration of the source structure, and is a good example of a very particular language-pair and lexical-unit-specific transfer rule, which contrasts with more general structure transferring rules which would operate, for example, on an English passive which, in translation into French, can be transformed into a reflexive (17) or an impersonal (18). Again this transfer of structure could be expressed in terms of case and deep syntactic function labels: in the case of (17) it involves only changing the latter, whereas in (18) it is necessary to introduce an impersonal Agent as deep subject.

(17a) Cigarettes are sold in many bars.
(17b) Les cigarettes se vendent dans beaucoup de bars.
(18a) English is spoken here.
(18b) Ici on parle anglais.

The introduction of arguments to express cases not found in the source language is also necessitated when the valency-binding of arguments differs between optional and obligatory from source to target language. This can be exemplified with verbs that in German require a Patient, which, when not expressed in English can be taken to be coreferential with the Agent. This is the case with verbs like *wash* and *shave* as in (19)-(20), where the English intransitive use is rendered in German by a reflexive construction.

(19a) He is washing (the car).
(19b) Er wäscht sich / das Auto.
(20a) He has not shaved (a single customer) today.
(20b) Er hat heute sich / keinen Kunden rasiert.

A further example of argument insertion comes from Italian where the deep subject, if pronominal, is not always expressed (21a) and so must be inserted for transfer into English (21b).

(21a) Suona il violino.
(21b) *He* plays the violin.

Deletion of arguments will of course occur in transfer in the opposite direction, but can also be exemplified by verbs which incorporate in one language a 'covert role' (cf. Cook, 1973;

Chapter 4 Section 5) which must be expressed as a separate argument in another. Thus for example we have various verbs in German which translate into English as *paint* with a specific Instrument or Material: *pinseln* (with a brush), *aquarellieren* (in water colours), *lackieren* (with varnish): when translating into German, the argument expressing Instrument or Material can be deleted once the correct verb has been chosen. Similarly, verbs taking integral complements in one language which translate as full lexical verbs in the other – as exemplified in Section 2 – will incur argument deletion.

Generation should be relatively straightforward, consisting principally of assigning deep and surface syntactic function labels according to rules of a parallel nature to those used in analysis, indicating the relationship between the case fillers and their surface realisation: again these may be general rules, or specific to individual verbs.

So far we have looked only at MT operating on the principal of bilingual transfer. In this final section I wish to consider the possible use of Case in an interlingual MT system. The key difference between transfer and interlingua is that the representation aimed at in the latter should be passed immediately to generation without the possibility of simultaneously taking into account particular features of the source and target languages. The relative merits of transfer and interlingua for MT have been discussed in detail by Otten and Pacak (1971), Vauquois (1975:142ff), Hutchins (1978) and more recently Barnes (1983). In fact, for general-purpose MT, the interlingua approach is now largely disfavoured, but under certain restricted conditions, it seems that a quasi-interlingual system might be possible: this is the view put forward in Somers (1983).

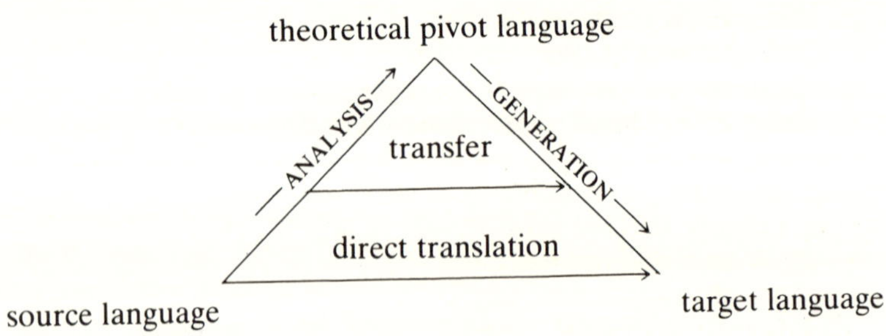

Figure 3: 'Pyramid' diagram (based on Vauquois, 1976:131)

The distinction between 'direct translation', transfer-based and interlingual systems is fairly well captured by the now well-known 'pyramid' diagram (Figure 3) probably first found in Vauquois (1976:131). The diagram shows that the deeper the analysis of the source text, the less complex is the mapping from source language to target language, with, at the top, the theoretical interlingual pivot representation with no mapping as such at all. Early (second generation) approaches to MT were based on this concept of an interlingua (e.g. Veillon, 1968), but the problems involved in defining an entirely language-free representation turned out not to merit any saving in effort over the transfer method, and so the approach was largely abandoned. It is hardly surprising that such problems arose, since the development of an interlingua, not only for translation purposes, has been the subject of philosophical debate for many years; proposals for an interlingua for MT have included the use of formalised natural language (e.g. Andreev, 1967; Melčuk, 1974), artificial languages (like Esperanto), or various symbolic representations, whether linear (e.g. Bölting, 1961) or otherwise (Carbonell *et al.*, 1978). Mostly, research has concentrated on the representation of lexis, with language-free structural representation receiving very little attention, even though this is where most of the problems lie.

The main advantage of using an interlingua lies in the reduction of the number of modules required, and this is especially clear in a multilingual system, where, as we have seen, for *n* languages there are *n*(*n*–1) language-pairs. However, as Barnes (1983:47) points out, this advantage only applies where all possible pairings are required, and it is quite conceivable, for example, that a business in Japan, say, might require a Japanese-English-French-German MT system with only the language pairs involving Japanese – i.e. six language pairs. A further advantage that is claimed for interlingual MT systems is that addition of extra languages is facilitated. But it turns out in practice that, since a truly language-independent interlingua is an impossible ideal, interlinguas tend to be defined in terms of the languages in the system, and the addition of a further language can sometimes lead to a complete redefinition of the interlingua (Barnes, 1983:40).

In view of this negative evidence as regards interlingual MT, under what conditions then could it be feasible? In Somers (1983), I proposed that the two key concepts of 'restricted syntax' and 'controlled vocabulary' could provide an environment in which 'transfer-free' MT could take place. I preferred this terminology, because I did not wish to claim anything more than the possibility of a representation of texts in subsets of fairly closely related languages and translation between any of them without recourse to any language-pair dependent processing.

The proposed interlingua consisted of a canonical representation of the text in which valency-boundness and case played a key role in much the same way as I suggested above. The need for bilingual transfer was to be avoided by restricting permitted sentence types to those which map relatively easily (i.e. by general rule) from one language to another, and by having a similarly straightforward mapping of lexical units onto 'universal' lexical values incorporating Wüster's (1971) concept of 'terminological equivalence' (i.e. the principle of one-to-one mappings between terms in the various languages): in practice, source language lexemes were to be associated with unique addresses in the system's multilingual dictionary. Elements such as time, modality and so on were to be represented by a set of 'universal' values which were calculated from or triggered generation of tense and voice markers.

One result of the missing transfer stage is that differences in valency patterns for translational equivalents are less easy to tolerate. In this respect, the controls on syntax and vocabulary would come into play, and it remains to be seen whether these controls would prove to be too much of an imposition. With text types of a chiefly technical nature, these problems should be considerably minimised, as it is rather in general language that they arise. It is further conceivable that the set of cases used could include a number of domain-specific relations (cf. Chapter 11 Section 5) in key areas.

In fact, these problems have not been put to the test, since the system was designed to run on a small microcomputer, and software problems involving data-structure design and storage constraints forced us to shelve the project as described in Somers (1983). However the general linguistic approach retains its interest, and it is significant that current developments in various MT projects suggest a move towards deeper representations with idiosyncrasies of surface syntax neutralised, and minimalisation of transfer between similar languages. Although the term 'interlingua' is out of favour, current approaches have in fact dismissed the concept to a rather lesser degree than commentators seem to imply. It is furthermore clear that MT researchers have now almost universally accepted the need to incorporate some form of Case theory for indicating 'semantic roles': in many cases however, the need to find the appropriate version of the theory, and in particular the 'right' set of cases, remains.

BIBLIOGRAPHY

Abraham, W. (1973). The ethic dative in German. In Kiefer and Ruwet (1973), 1–19.

——. (1978) (ed.). *Valence, semantic case and grammatical relations* (Studies in Language Companion Series 1). Amsterdam: John Benjamins B.V.

Abrahamson, A. A. (1975). Experimental analysis of the semantics of movement. In Norman *et al.* (1975), 247–76.

Akhmanova, O. (1973). Review of Chafe (1970). *Linguistics* 103, 105–9.

Allerton, D. J. (1982). *Valency and the English verb*. London: Academic Press.

Ananthanarayana, H. S. (1970). The kāraka theory and Case grammar. *Indian Linguistics* 31, 14–27.

Anderson, J. M. (1968). Ergative and nominative in English. *Journal of Linguistics* 4, 1–32.

——. (1969). Adjectives, datives and ergativisation. *Foundations of Language* 5, 301–23.

——. (1971). *The grammar of Case: towards a localistic theory* (Cambridge Studies in Linguistics 4). Cambridge: University Press.

——. (1972). Remarks on the hierarchy of quasi-predications. *Revue Roumaine de Linguistique* 17, 23–44, 121–40, 193–202, 319–35.

——. (1973). Maximi Planudis in memoriam. In Kiefer and Ruwet (1973), 20–47.

——. (1977). *On Case grammar: prolegomena to a theory of grammatical relations*. London: Croom Helm.

Anderson, S. R. (1971). On the role of deep structure in semantic interpretation. *Foundations of Language* 7, 389–96.

Andreev, N. D. (1967). The intermediary language as the focal point of machine translation. Booth, A. D. (ed.) – *Machine Translation*, Amsterdam: North-Holland. 1–27.

Andresen, H. (1973). Ein methodischer Vorschlag zur Unterscheidung von Ergänzung und Angabe im Rahmen der Valenztheorie. *Deutsche Sprache*, 49–63.

Apostle, H. G. (1966). *Aristotle's Metaphysics* (translated with commentaries and glossary). Bloomington: Indiana University Press.

Arbeitsgruppe Marburg (1973). Aspekte der Valenztheorie. *Deutsche Sprache*, 3–48.

Ballweg-Schramm, A. (1976). Noch einmal: Grundbegriffe der Valenztheorie. Bemerkungen zu einem Papier von S. Pape. In Schumacher (1976), 54–65.

Barnes, A. M. N. (1983). An investigation into the syntactic structures of abstracts, and the feasibility of an 'interlingua' for their translation by machine. M.Sc. thesis, University of Manchester. *CCL/UMIST* Report 83/4. Centre for Computational Linguistics, University of Manchester Institute of Science and Technology.

Barr, A. and Feigenbaum, E. A. (1981) (eds). *The Handbook of Artificial Intelligence, Volume I*. London: Pitman.

Bates, M. (1978). The theory and practice of augmented transition network grammars. Bolc, L. (ed.) – *Natural Language communication with computers* (Lecture Notes in Computer Science 63), Berlin: Springer-Verlag. 191–259.

Bauer, L. (1978). *The grammar of nominal compounding, with special reference to Danish, English and French*. Odense: University Press.

——. and Boagey, W. (1977). On 'The Grammar of Case'. *Linguistics & Philosophy* 1, 119–52.

Bauer, W. (1980). Review of Dik (1978). *Archivum Linguisticum* 11, 50–56.

Becker, D. A. (1971). Case grammar and German *be*. *Glossa* 5, 125–45.

Bennett, D. C. (1975). *Spatial and temporal uses of English prepositions: an essay in Stratificational semantics* (Longman Linguistics Library 17). London: Longman.

Bennett, P. A., Johnson, R. L., McNaught, J., Pugh, J. M., Sager, J. C. and Somers, H. L. (1986). *Multilingual aspects of Information Technology*. Aldershot: Gower.

Biere, B. U. (1976). Ergänzungen und Angaben. In Schumacher (1976), 129–73.

Binot, J. L., Graitson, M., Lemaire, P. and Ribbens, D. (1980). Automatic processing of written French language. *COLING 80* (Proceedings of the 8th International Conference on Computational Linguistics), 9–14.

Blansitt, E. L. (1977). Stimulus as a semantic role. In Abraham (1977), 311–25.

Boas, H. U. (1977). Lexical entries for verbs in a contrastive lexicon English-German. In Abraham (1977), 191–216.

Bobrow, D. G., Kaplan, R. M., Kay, M., Norman, D. A., Thompson, H. and Winograd, T. (1976). GUS, a frame-driven dialog system. *Artificial Intelligence* 8, 155–73.

——. and Winograd, T. (1977). An overview of KRL, a Knowledge Representation Language. *Cognitive Science* 1, 3–46.

——. (1979). KRL, another perspective. *Cognitive Science* 3, 29–42.

Bolkestein, A. M. (1983). Genitive and dative possessors in Latin. In Dik (1983*a*), 55–91.

——. Combé, H. A., Dik, S. C., de Groot, C., Gvozdanović, J., Rijksbaron, A. and Vet, C. (1981). *Predication and expression in Functional Grammar*. London: Academic Press.

Bölting, R. (1961). A double intermediate language for Machine Translation. Kent, A. (ed.) – *Information Retrieval and Machine Translation, Part 2* (Advances in Documentary and Library Science Volume III), New York: Interscience. 1139–44.

Boyd, J. and Thorne, J. P. (1969) The semantics of modal verbs. *Journal of Linguistics* 5, 57–74.

Brachman, R. J. (1979). On the epistemological status of semantic networks. Findler, N. V. (ed.) – *Associative networks: representation and use of knowledge by computers*, New York, Academic Press.

Braine, M. D. S. and Wells, R. S. (1978). Case-like categories in children: the Actor and some related categories. *Cognitive Psychology* 10, 100–22.

Brinker, K. (1972). *Konstituentenstrukturgrammatik und operationale Satzgliedanalyse: Methodenkritische Untersuchungen zur Syntax des einfachen Satzes im Deutschen*. Frankfurt am Main: Athenäum Verlag.

——. (1977). *Modelle und Methoden der strukturalistischen Syntax: eine Einführung* (Urban-Taschenbücher 240). Stuttgart: Verlag W. Kohlhammer.

Brinkmann, H. (1962). *Die deutsche Sprache: Gestalt und Leistung*. Düsseldorf: Pädagogischer Verlag Schwann.

Brodda, B. (1973). *(K)overta kasus i Svenskan* (PILUS 18). Stockholm: Institute of Linguistics, University of Stockholm.

Brown, G. I. (1953). *A simple guide to modern valency theory*. London: Longmans.

Bruce, B. (1975). Case systems for natural language. *Artificial Intelligence* 6, 327–60.

Buckingham, H. W. (1973). The Comitative and Case grammar. *Foundations of Language* 10, 111–21.

Burton, R. (1976). Semantic grammar: an engineering technique for constructing Natural Language Understanding systems. Technical Report 3453. Bolt, Beranek and Newman, Cambridge, Mass.

Buysschaert, J. (1982). *Criteria for the classification of English adverbials* (Verhandelingen van de Koninklijke Academie voor Wetenschapen, Letteren en Schone Kunsten van België, Klasse der Letteren 44.99). Brussel: Paleis der Academiën.

Carbonell, J., Cullingford, R. E. and Gershman, A. V. (1978). Knowledge-based Machine Translation. Research Report 146. Computer Science Department, Yale University.

Celce-Murcia, M. (1975). Verb paradigms for sentence recognition. *American Journal of Computational Linguistics* microfiche 38.

Chafe, W. L. (1970). *Meaning and the structure of language*. Chicago: University Press.

Chapin, P. G. (1972). Review of 'Integration of transformational theories on English syntax' by Robert P. Stockwell, Paul Schachter and Barbara Hall Partee, 2 volumes (Command Systems Division, Electronic Systems Division, Air Force Systems Command, ESD-TR-68-419), Los Angeles: University of California, 1968. *Language* 48, 645–67.

Charniak, E. (1975). A brief on case. Working Papers 22. Istituto per gli Studi Semantici e Cognitivi, Castagnola.

——. (1976). Inference and knowledge Part 2. In Charniak and Wilks (1976), 129–54.

——. (1981). The case-slot identity theory. *Cognitive Science* 5, 285–92.

——. and Wilks, Y. (1976) (eds). *Computational semantics: an introduction to Artificial Intelligence and Natural Language Comprehension* (Fundamental Studies in Computer Science 4). Amsterdam: North-Holland.

Chokhani, S. (1973). The definition and interpretation of a causal network model for disease within the CHRONOS system. Report CBM-TR-17. Department of Computer Science, Rutgers University, New Brunswick, N.J.

Chomsky, N. (1957). *Syntactic structures* (Janua Linguarum Series Minor 4). The Hague: Mouton.

——. (1965). *Aspects of the theory of syntax*. Cambridge, Mass.: MIT Press.

——. (1970). Deep structure, surface structure, and semantic interpretation. Chomsky, N. *Studies on semantics in generative grammar* (Janua Linguarum Series Minor 107), The Hague (1972): Mouton, 62–119; reprinted from Jakobson, R. and Kawamoto, S. (eds). *Studies in general and oriental linguistics presented to Shiro Hattori on the occasion of his sixtieth birthday*, Tokyo: TEC Co. Ltd.

——. (1972). Some empirical issues in the theory of transformational grammar. Peters, S. (ed.) *Goals of linguistic theory*. Englewood Cliffs, N.J.: Prentice-Hall. 63–130.

——. (1981). *Lectures on Government and Binding: the Pisa lectures* (Studies in Generative Grammar 9). Dordrecht: Foris.

Christie, J. J. (1970). Locative, Possessive and Existential in Swahili. *Foundations of Language* 6, 166–77.

Clark, E. V. (1970). Locationals: a study of the relations between 'existential', 'locative' and 'possessive' constructions. Working Papers in Language Universals 3. Stanford University, Stanford, California.

Clark, M. V. (1971). The case against stative (the stative the art). *Working Papers in Linguistics* 10 (Department of Linguistics, Ohio State University), 149–56.

Comrie, B. (1973). The ergative: variations on a theme. *Lingua* 32, 239–53.

——. (1975). The antiergative: Finland's answer to Basque. Grossman, R. E., San, L. J. and Vance, T. J. (eds) – *Papers from the 11th regional meeting, Chicago Linguistics Society*, Chicago: The Society. 112–21.

——. (1979). Review of Dik (1978). *Studies in Language* 3, 267–76.

Cook, W. A. (1970). Case grammar: from roles to rules. In Cook (1979), 1–15; reprinted from *Languages and Linguistics Working Papers* 1 (Georgetown University), 14–29.

——. (1971). Case grammar as a Deep Structure in Tagmemic analysis. In Cook (1979), 28–35; reprinted from *Languages and Linguistics Working Papers* 2 (Georgetown University), 1–7.

——. (1972*a*). A set of postulates for case grammar analysis. In Cook (1979), 36–49; reprinted from *Languages and Linguistics Working Papers* 4 (Georgetown University), 35–49.

——. (1972*b*). A case grammar matrix. In Cook (1979), 50–81; reprinted from *Languages and Linguistics Working Papers* 6 (Georgetown University), 15–47.

——. (1973). Covert case roles. In Cook (1979), 82–108; reprinted from *Languages and Linguistics Working Papers* 7 (Georgetown University), 52–81.

——. (1979). *Case grammar: development of the matrix model (1970–1978)*. Washington, D.C.; Georgetown University Press.

Cruse, D. A. (1973). Some thoughts on agentivity. *Journal of Linguistics* 9, 11–23.

Dik, S. C. (1978). *Functional Grammar* (North-Holland Linguistic Series 37). Amsterdam: North-Holland.

——. (1980). *Studies in Functional Grammar*. London: Academic Press.

——. (1981). Discrepancies between predication and expression in natural languages. In Bolkestein *et al.* (1981), 19–39.

——. (1983*a*) (ed.). *Advances in Functional Grammar* (Publications in Language Sciences 11). Dordrecht: Foris.

——. (1983*b*). Basic principles of Functional Grammar. In Dik (1983*a*), 3–28.

Dillon, G. L. (1977). *Introduction to contemporary linguistic semantics*. Englewood Cliffs, N.J.: Prentice-Hall.

Dirven, R. (1981). Spatial relations in English. *anglistik & englischunterricht* 14 ('Kasusgrammatik und Fremdsprachendidaktik'), 103–32.

Dougherty, R. C. (1970). Recent studies on language universals. *Foundations of Language* 6, 505–61.

——. (1974). Generative semantics methods, a Bloomfieldian counterrevolution. *International Journal of Dravidian Linguistics* 3, 255–86.

Dowty, D. R. (1979). *Word meaning and Montague grammar: the semantics of verbs and times in Generative semantics and in Montague's PTQ* (Synthese Language Library 7). Dordrecht: Reidel.

Ebert, R. P. (1974). Review of Anderson (1971). *IRAL* 12, 259–61

Edmonson, J. A. (1977). Ergative languages, accessibility hierarchies governing reflexives and questions of formal analysis. In Abraham (1977), 633–60.

Eisenberg, P. (1977). Review of Charniak and Wilks (1976). *Journal of Pragmatics* 1, 171–6.

Emons, R. (1974). *Valenzen englischer Prädikatsverben* (Linguistische Arbeiten 22). Tübingen: Max Niemeyer Verlag.

——. (1978). *Valenzgrammatik für das Englische: eine Einführung* (Anglistische Arbeitshefte 16). Tübingen: Max Niemeyer Verlag.

Engel, U. and Schumacher, H. (1976). *Kleines Valenzlexikon deutscher Verben* (Forschungsberichte des Instituts für Deutsche Sprache, Mannheim, 31). Tübingen: TBL Verlag Gunter Narr.

Falkenberg, G. and Öhlschläger, G. (1971). Einige wissenschafts-theoretische Bemerkungen zu Charles J. Fillmore. Hyldgaard-Jensen, K. (ed.). *Linguistik 1971* (Referate des 6. Linguistischen Kolloquiums in Kopenhagen) (Skripten Linguistik 1). Frankfurt (1972): Athenaion. 189–95.

Fillmore, C. J. (1963). The position of embedding transformations in a grammar. *Word* 19, 208–31.

——. (1965). *Indirect object constructions in English and the ordering of transformations* (Monographs on Linguistic Analysis 1). The Hague: Mouton.

——. (1966*a*). A proposal concerning English prepositions. Dineen, F. P. (ed.). *Report on the seventeenth annual Round Table Meeting on Linguistics Language Studies* (Monograph Series on Languages and Linguistics 19). Washington, D.C. Georgetown University Press. 19–33.

——. (1966*b*). Toward a modern theory of case. In Reibel and Schane (1969), 361–75; reprinted from *Project on Linguistic Analysis Report No. 13*, Columbus, Ohio: Ohio State University Research Foundation. 1–24.

——. (1968*a*). The case for case. Bach, E. and Harms, R. T. (eds). *Universals in linguistic theory*. New York: Holt, Rinehart and Winston. 1–88.

——. (1968*b*). Lexical entries for verbs. *Foundations of Language* 4, 373–93.

——. (1970). The grammar of *hitting* and *breaking*. Jacobs, R. A. and Rosenbaum, P. S. (eds.) *Readings in English Transformational Grammar*. Waltham, Mass.: Ginn. 120–33.

——. (1971*a*). Types of lexical information. Steinberg, D. D. and Jakobovits, L. A. *Semantics: an interdisciplinary reader in Philosophy, Linguistics and Psychology*. Cambridge: University Press. 370–92.

——. (1971*b*). Some problems for Case grammar. O'Brien, R. J. (ed.). *22nd Annual Round Table. Linguistics: developments of the sixties – viewpoints of the seventies* (Monograph Series on Language and Linguistics 24), Washington D.C.: Georgetown University Press. 35–56.

——. (1971*c*). Verbs of judging: an exercise in semantic description. Fillmore, C. J. and Langendoen, D. T. (eds). *Studies in linguistic semantics*. New York: Holt, Rinehart and Winston. 273–89.

——. (1972). Subjects, speakers, and roles. Davidson, D. and Harman, G. (eds). *Semantics of natural language*, 2nd ed. Dordrecht: D. Reidel. 1–24.

——. (1976). The need for a frame semantics within linguistics. *Statistical Methods in Linguistics* 1, 5–29.

——. (1977*a*). Topics in lexical semantics. Cole, R. W. (ed). *Current issues in linguistic theory*. Bloomington: Indiana University Press. 76–138.

——. (1977*b*). The case for case reopened. Cole, P. and Saddock, J. M. (eds). *Syntax and semantics, Volume 8: Grammatical relations*. New York: Academic Press. 59–81.

——. (1977*c*). Scenes-and-frames semantics. In Zampolli (1977), 55–81.

Fodor, J. A. (1970). Three reasons for not deriving 'kill' from 'cause to die'. *Linguistic Inquiry* 1, 429–38.

Frajzyngier, Z. (1975). Against the universality of spatial source and goal. *Foundations of Language* 13, 349–60.

Fraser, B. (1971). A note on the *spray paint* cases. *Linguistic Inquiry* 2, 604–7.

Friedman, F. (1970). A computational treatment of Case Grammar. Hintikka, K. J. J., Moravcsik, J. M. E. and Suppes, P. (eds) – *Approaches to natural language* (Proceedings of the 1970 Stanford Workshop on Grammar and Semantics), Dordrecht (1973): D. Reidel. 134–52.

Gaifman, H. (1965). Dependency systems and phase-structure systems. *Information and Control* 8, 304–37.

Gazdar, G., Klein, E., Pullum, G. and Sag, I. (1985). *Generalized Phrase Structure Grammar*. Oxford: Basil Blackwell.

Gentner, D. (1975). Evidence for the psychological reality of semantic components: the verbs of possession. In Norman *et al*. (1975), 211–46.

Gormley, H. C. (in prep). Assignment of semantic case roles to syntactic constituents. MSc thesis. Department of Computation, University of Manchester Institute of Science and Technology.

Gougenheim, G. (1960). Compte rendu de Tesnière (1959). *Le Français Moderne* 28, 142–7.

Grebe, P. (1966) (Hrsg.). *Der große Duden: Grammatik der deutschen Gegenwartssprache* (2. Auflage). Mannheim: Duden.

Grimes, J. E. (1975). *The thread of discourse* (Janua Linguarum Series Minor 207). The Hague, Mouton.

——. and Glock, N. (1970). A Saramaccan narrative pattern. *Language* 46, 408–25.

Halliday, M. A. K. (1967/8). Notes on transitivity and theme. *Journal of Linguistics* 3, 37–81, 199–244; 4, 179–215.

——. (1970). Language structure and language function. Lyons, J. (ed.). *New Horizons in Linguistics*, Harmondsworth, Middx: Penguin. 140–65.

Happ, H. (1976). *Grundfragen einer Dependenz-Grammatik des Lateinischen*. Göttingen: Vandenhoeck and Ruprecht.

——. (1978*a*). Théorie de la valence et enseignement du français. *Le Français Moderne* 46, 97–134.

——. (1978*b*). Syntaxe latine et théorie de la valence: essai d'adaptation au latin des théories de Lucien Tesnière. *Langages* 50 ('Linguistique et latin'), 51–72.

Harbusch, K. and Rothkegel, A. (1984). PROLID: ein Programm zur Rollenidentifikation. Linguistische Arbeiten (neue Folge) 8. Sonderforschungsbereich 100 Elektronische Sprachforschung, Universität des Saarlandes, Saarbrücken.

Hayes, P. J. (1977). On semantic nets, frames and association. *5th International Joint Conference on Artificial Intelligence* (MIT), 99–107.

Hays, D. G. (1960*a*). Grouping and dependency theories. Edmundson, H. P. (ed.). *Proceedings of the National Symposium on Machine Translation* (University of California, Los Angeles). Englewood Cliffs (1961): Prentice-Hall. 258–66.

——. (1960*b*). Basic principles and technical variations in sentence-structure determination. Cherry, C. (ed.). *Information theory* (Symposium on 'Information Theory', Royal Institution, London). London: Butterworths. 367–75.

——. (1964). Dependency theory: a formalism and some observations. *Language* 40, 511–25.

Heilmann, L. (1972) (ed.). *Proceedings of the eleventh International Congress of Linguists* (Bologna-Florence). Bologna (1974): Società editrice il Mulino.

Helbig, G. (1969). Valenz und Tiefenstruktur. *Deutsch als Fremdsprache* 6, 159–69.

——. (1971). Theoretische und praktische Aspekte eines Valenzmodells. Helbig, G. (Hrsg.). *Beiträge zur Valenztheorie* (Janua Linguarum Series Minor 115), The Hague: Mouton, 31–49.

——. and Schenkel, W. (1973). *Wörterbuch zur Valenz und Distribution deutscher Verben*. Leipzig: VEB Verlag Enzyklopädie.

Hendrix, G. G., Thompson, C. W. and Slocum, J. (1973). Language processing via canonical verbs and semantic models. *Third International Joint Conference on Artificial Intelligence* (Stanford), 262–9.

Herbst, T. (1984). Adjectival complementization: a Valency approach to making EFL dictionaries. *Applied Linguistics* 5, 1–11.

——. Heath, D. and Dedering, H-M. (1979). *Grimm's grandchildren: current topics in German linguistics* (Longman Linguistics Library 24). London: Longman.

Heringer, H-J. (1967). Wertigkeiten und nullwertige Verben im Deutschen. *Zeitschrift für Deutsche Sprache* 23, 13–34.

——. (1968). Präpositionale Ergänzungsbestimmungen im Deutschen. *Zeitschrift für Deutsche Philologie* 87, 426–57.

——. (1970*a*). *Theorie der deutschen Syntax* (Linguistische Reihe 3). München: Max Hueber Verlag.

——. (1970*b*). Einige Ergebnisse und Probleme der Dependenz-grammatik. *Der Deutschunterricht* 22.4, 42–98.

Hjelmslev, L. (1935/7). La catégorie des cas. *Acta Jutlandica* 7.1, i–xii, 1–184; 9.2, i–vii, 1–78.

Hoekstra, T., van der Hulst, H. and Moortgat, M. (1981). (eds). *Perspectives on Functional Grammar*. Dordrecht: Foris.

Hornby, A. S. (1975). *Guide to patterns and usage in English* (2nd ed.). London: Oxford University Press.

Huddleston, R. D. (1970). Some remarks on case grammar. *Linguistic Inquiry* 1, 501–11.

Hutchins, W. J. (1978). Machine translation and machine-aided translation. *Journal of Documentation* 34, 119–59.

——. (1979). Linguistic models in Machine Translation. *UEA Papers in Linguistics* 9, 29–52.

——. (1986). *Machine Translation: past, present, future*. Chichester: Ellis Horwood.

Iida, H., Ogura, K. and Nomura, H. (1984). A case analysis method cooperating with ATGN and its application to Machine Translation. *10th International Conference on Computational Linguistics – 22nd Annual Meeting of the Association for Computational Linguistics: Proceedings of Coling84* (Stanford, California). 154–8.

International Phonetic Association (1949). *The principles of the International Phonetic Association*. London: Department of Phonetics, University College.

Itagaki, N. and Prideaux, G. D. (1983). Pragmatic constraints on subject and agent selection. In Dik (1983*a*), 175–82.

Jackendoff, R. S. (1972). *Semantic interpretation in Generative grammar*. Cambridge, Mass.: MIT Press.

Jacobsen, W. (1982). *Transitivity in the Japanese verbal system*. Bloomington: Indiana University Linguistics Club.

Jespersen, O. (1924). *The philosophy of grammar*. London: Allen and Unwin.

Johnson, R. (1983). Parsing with transition networks. In King (1983), 59–72.

——. (1984). Contemporary perspectives in machine translation. In Loffler-Laurian (1984), 141–55.

Kanno, K. (1983). Between object and oblique: in defense of secondary object. In Dik (1983*a*), 175–82.

Kaplan, R. M. (1973). A general syntactic parser. In Rustin (1973), 193–241.

——. and Bresnan, J. (1982). Lexical-Functional Grammar: a formal system for grammatical representation. Bresnan, J. (ed.) – *The mental representation of grammatical relations*, Cambridge, Mass.: MIT Press, 173–281.

Katz, J. and Fodor, J. (1963). The structure of a semantic theory. *Language* 39, 170–210.

Kenny, A. J. P. (1963). *Actions, emotions, and will*. London: Routledge and Kegan Paul.

Kiefer, F. and Ruwet, N. (1973) (eds). *Generative grammar in Europe* (Foundations of Language Supplementary Series 13). Dordrecht: D. Reidel.

Kilby, D. A. (1978). What might a universal theory of cases look like? *University of Essex Language Centre Occasional Papers* 20 ('Universals of Language'), 59–86.

Kilby, K. J. (1982). An evaluation of lexicase theory, including its application to Machine Translation. MA thesis, Department of General Linguistics, University of Manchester.

King, M. (1981). Machine Translation: a series of talks for DG IX. *Terminologie Bulletin* 40, 11–50.

——. (1983) (ed.). *Parsing natural language*. London: Academic Press.

——. (1987) (ed.). *Machine Translation today*. Edinburgh: University Press.

——. and Perschke, S. (1982). EUROTRA and its objectives. *Multilingua* 1, 27–32.

Kintsch, W. (1974). *The representation of meaning in memory*. Hillsdale, N.J.: Laurence Erlbaum Associates.

Kittredge, R. (1981) (ed.). L'informatique au service de la traduction: Machine aids to translation. *META* (numéro spécial), 26.1.

Korhohnen, J. (1977). *Studien zu Dependenz, Valenz und Satzmodell:*

Teil I – Theorie und Praxis der Beschreibung der deutschen Gegenwartssprache. Dokumentation, kritische Besprechung, Vorschläge (Europäische Hochschulschriften Reihe 1, Band 212). Bern: Peter Lang.

Krauwer, S. and des Tombe, L. (1984*a*). Reflections on transfer in Machine Translation. In Loffler-Laurian (1984), 69–80.

——. (1984*b*). Transfer in a multilingual MT system. *10th International Conference on Computational Linguistics – 22nd Annual Meeting of the Association for Computational Linguistics: Proceedings of Coling84* (Stanford, California). 464–7.

Kulikowski, C. and Weiss, S. (1971). Computer-based models for glaucoma. Report CBM-TR-3. Department of Computer Science, Rutgers University, New Brunswick, N.J.

Kuno, S. (1973). *The structure of the Japanese language* (Current Studies in Linguistics 3). Cambridge, Mass.: MIT Press.

——. (1978). Japanese: a characteristic ov language. Lehmann, W. P. (ed.) – *Syntactic typology: studies in the phenomenology of language*, Hassocks, Sussex: Harvester Press. 57–138.

Lafitte, P. (1962). *Grammaire basque*. Bayonne: Amis du musée basque & Ikas.

Laing, R. D. (1970). *Knots*. London: Tavistock; [also Harmondsworth (1971): Penguin].

Lakoff, G. (1968). Instrumental adverbs and the concept of deep structure. *Foundation of Language* 4, 4–29.

——. and Peters, S. (1969). Phrasal conjunction and symmetric predicates. In Reibel and Schane (1969), 113–42.

——. and Ross, J. R. (1976). Why you can't *do so* into the sink. McCawley, J. D. (ed.) *Syntax and semantics, Volume 7: Notes from the linguistic underground*. New York: Academic Press. 101–11.

Langacker, R. W. (1970). Review of 'Spanish case and function'. By Mark G. Goldin, Washington: Georgetown University Press, 1968. Pp. 83. *Language* 46, 167–85.

——. (1973). Review of Anderson (1971). *Journal of Linguistics* 9, 319–31.

Lawson, V. (1982) (ed.). *Practical experience of Machine Translation*. Amsterdam: North-Holland.

Leech, G. (1981). *Semantics: the study of meaning* (2nd ed.). Harmondsworth, Middx: Penguin Books.

Lehmann, W. P., Bennett, W. S., Slocum, J., Smith, H., Pfluger, S. M. V. and Eveland, S. A. (1980). The METAL system. RADC-TR-80–374. Rome Air Development Center, Griffiss AFB, NY.

Lehnert, W. and Wilks, Y. (1979). A critical perspective on KRL. *Cognitive Science* 3, 1–28.

Lehrberger, J. (1981). The linguistic model: general aspects. Bourbeau, L. – *Linguistic documentation of the computerized translation chain of the TAUM-AVIATION system*, Montréal: TAUM, Université de Montréal.

Lehrer, A. (1970). Verbs and deletable objects. *Lingua* 25, 227–53.

Levin, B. (1977). Mapping sentences onto case frames. Working Paper 143. MIT Artificial Intelligence Laboratory, Cambridge, Mass.

Li, C. N. and Thompson, S. A. (1974). Co-verbs in Mandarin Chinese: verbs or prepositions? *Journal of Chinese Linguistics* 2, 257–78.

Loffler-Laurian, A-M. (1984) (ed.). Traduction automatique – aspects européens. *Contrastes* hors série A4.

Longacre, R. E. (1972). Taxonomy in deep and surface grammar. In Heilmann (1972), 349–65.

——. (1976). *An anatomy of speech notions*. Lisse: Peter de Ridder Press.

Lyons, J. (1967). A note on possessive, existential, and locative sentences. *Foundations of Language* 3, 390–6.

Mackenzie, J. L. (1981). Functions and cases. In Hoekstra *et al.* (1981), 299–318.

——. (1983). Nominal predicates in a Functional Grammar of English. In Dik (1983*a*), 31–51.

Marcus, M. (1980). *A theory of syntactic recognition for natural language*. Cambridge, Mass.: MIT Press.

Marino, M. (1972). A strong deep case hypothesis. *Papers in Linguistics* 5, 568–603.

Martin, W. A. (1973). Translation of English into MAPL using Winograd's syntax, state transition networks, and a semantic case grammar. Automatic Programming Group Internal Memo 11. MIT Project MAC, Cambridge, Mass.

Martinet, A. (1972). Cas ou fonctions? A propos de l'article 'The Case for case' de Charles J. Fillmore. *La Linguistique* 8.1, 5–24.

Matthews, P. H. (1981). *Syntax*. Cambridge: University Press.

McCawley, J. D. (1968). Lexical insertion in a transformational grammar without deep structure. Bailey, C-J., Darden, B. J. and Davison, A. (eds). *Papers from the fourth Regional Meeting of the Chicago Linguistics Society*. Chicago: Department of Linguistics, University of Chicago. 71–80.

Mel'čuk, I. A. (1964). *Avtomatičeskii sintaksičeskii analyz*. Novosibirsk: Nauka.

——. (1974). Grammatical meanings in interlinguas for automatic translation and the concept of grammatical meaning. Rozencveijg, V.Ju. (ed.) – *Machine Translation and Applied Linguistics*, Volume 1, Frankfurt am Main: Athenaion Verlag. 95–113.

——. (1979). *Studies in dependency syntax* (Linguistica Extranea Studia 2) (ed.: P. T. Roberge). Ann Arbor: Karoma.

Mellema, P. (1974). A brief against Case grammar. *Foundations of Language* 11, 39–76.

Meščaninov, I. I. (1967). *Èrgativnaja konstrukcija v jaznyx razlicnyx tipov*. Leningrad: Nauka.

Miller, J. E. (1970). Stative verbs in Russian. *Foundations of Language* 6, 488–504.

Minsky, M. (1975). A framework for representing knowledge. Winston, P. E. (ed.) – *The psychology of computer vision*, New York: McGraw-Hill. 211–77.

Mittwoch, A. (1982). On the difference between *eating* and *eating something*: activities versus accomplishments. *Linguistic Inquiry* 13, 113–22.

Moskey, S. T. (1979). *Semantic structures and relations in Dutch: an introduction to Case grammar.* Washington, D.C.: Georgetown University Press.

Mourelatos, A. P. D. (1978). Events, processes, and states. *Linguistics and Philosophy* 2, 415–34.

Nash-Webber, B. (1975). The role of semantics in automatic speech understanding. Bobrow, D. G. and Collins, A. (eds) – *Representation and understanding: Studies in Cognitive Science*, New York: Academic Press. 351–82.

Niéger, M. (1973). La notion de cas dans la théorie de Fillmore. *Cahiers de Linguistique* 2 ('Problèmes de Sémantique'), 39–49.

Nilsen, D. L. F. (1972). *Toward a semantic specification of deep case*. (Janua Linguarum Series Minor 152). The Hague: Mouton.

——. (1973). *The Instrumental case in English: syntactic and semantic considerations*. (Janua Linguarum Series Minor 156). The Hague: Mouton.

Nishida, F., Takamatsu, S. and Kuroki, H. (1980). English-Japanese translation through case-structure conversion. *COLING 80* (Proceedings of the 8th International Conference on Computational Linguistics, Tokyo), 447–54.

Nitta, Y., Okajima, A., Kaji, H., Hidano, Y. and Ishikara, K. (1984). A proper treatment of syntax and semantics in Machine Translation. *10th International Conference on Computational Linguistics – 22nd Annual Meeting of the Association for Computational Linguistics: Proceedings of Coling84* (Stanford, California). 159–66.

Norman, D. A., Rumelhart, D. E. and the LNR Research Group (1975) (eds). *Explorations in cognition*. San Francisco: W. H. Freeman and Co.

Okoth Okombo, D. (1983). Alpha vs non-alpha: some observations on the position of semantic functions on the SFH. In Dik (1983*a*), 143–54.

Ostler, N. (1980). *A theory of case linking and agreement.* Bloomington: Indiana University Linguistics Club.

Otten, M. and Pacak, M. G. (1971). Intermediate languages for automatic language processing. Tou, J. T. (ed.) – *Software Engineering: COINS III*, Volume 2, New York: Academic Press. 105–18.

Pak, T. (1974). Absurdities in Fillmore's Case Grammar. *Studia Linguistica* 28, 19–50.

Palmer, F. R. (1974). *The English verb* (Longmans Linguistics Library 18). London: Longman.

Pam, M. D. (1971). The case for Cash. *Working Papers in Linguistics* 10 (Department of Linguistics, Ohio State University), 172–81.

Panevová, J. (1974). On verbal frames in functional generative description, Part I. *The Prague Bulletin of Mathematical Linguistics* 22, 3–39.

——. (1977). Inner participants and free adverbials. *Prague Studies in Mathematical Linguistics* 6, 227–54.

Peterson, T. H. (1983). Semantic structure. *Journal of Linguistics* 19, 79–114.

Piťha, P. (1980). Case frames of nouns. van Alkemade, D. J., Feitsma, A., Meys, W. J., van Reenen, P. and Spa, J. J. (eds) – *Linguistic studies offered to Berthe Siertsema* (Costerus new series 25), Amsterdam: Rodopi. 91–99; reprinted in Sgall, P. (ed.) – *Contributions to Functional Syntax, semantics, and language comprehension*, Praha (1984): Academia. 225–38.

Platt, H. (1972). Case theory and its application to language teaching. *ITL* 15 (Tijdschrift van het Instituut voor Toegepaste Linguistiek, Leuven), 31–45.

Platt, J. T. (1971). *Grammatical form and grammatical meaning: a tagmemic view of Fillmore's Deep Structure Case concepts* (North-Holland Linguistic Series 5). Amsterdam: North-Holland.

Pleines, J. (1976). *Handlung – Kausalität – Intention: Probleme der Beschreibung semantischer Relationen* (Tübinger Beiträge zur Linguistik 68). Tübingen: TBL Verlag Gunter Narr.

Postal, P. M. (1968). Cross-over phenomena. *Specification and Utilization of a Transformational Grammar* (Scientific Report No. 3). Yorktown Heights, NY: IBM Research Center.

Potts, T. C. (1965). States, activities, and performances. *The Aristotelian Society Supplementary Volume* 39, 65–84.

Quirk, R., Greenbaum, S., Leech, G. and Svartvik, J. (1972). *A grammar of contemporary English*. London: Longman.

Reibel, D. A. and Schane, S. A. (1969) (eds). *Modern Studies in English: readings in Transformational grammar*. Englewood Cliffs, NJ: Prentice Hall.

Riesbeck, C. K. (1975). Conceptual analysis. In Schank (1975), 83–156.

Ritchie, G. D. (1980). *Computational grammar: an Artificial Intelligence approach to linguistic description*. Brighton: Harvester Press/ Totowa, N.J.: Barnes & Noble.

——. (1983). Semantics in parsing. In King (1983), 199–217.

Roberts, J. (1981). Rewriting a standard dictionary entry in valency dictionary format. *British Association for Applied Linguistics Newsletter* 11, 1–15.

Robins, R. H. (1961). Syntactic analysis. *Archivum Linguisticum* 13, 78–89.

Robinson, J. J. (1970). Case, category, and configuration. *Journal of Linguistics* 6, 57–80.

Rocher, R. (1964). 'Agent' et 'objet' chez Pāṇini. *Journal of the American Oriental Society* 84, 44–54.

Rosengren, I. (1970). Zur Valenz des deutschen Verbs. *Moderna Språk* 64, 45–58.

Rosner, M. and Somers, H. L. (1980). Case in linguistics and cognitive science. *UEA Papers in Linguistics* 13, 1–29; reprinted from Working Papers 40, Institut pour les Etudes Sémantiques et Cognitives, Université de Genève.

Rothkegel, A. (1976). Valenzgrammatik I. Linguistische Arbeiten 19. Sonderforschungsbereich Elektronische Sprachforschung, Universität des Saarlandes, Saarbrücken.

——. (1977). Valence frames in standard form and corresponding frames of individual languages. In Abraham (1977), 85–98.

Rumelhart, D. E., Lindsay, P. H. and Norman, D. A. (1972). A process model for Long-Term Memory. Tulving, E. and Donaldson, W. (eds) – *Organization and memory*, New York: Academic Press. 197–246.

——. and Norman, D. A. (1973). Active semantic networks as a model of human memory. *Third International Joint Conference on Artificial Intelligence* (Stanford, California), 450–7.

Russell, C. A. (1971). *A history of valency*. Leicester: University Press.

Rustin, R. (1973) (ed.). *Natural Language Processing* (Courant Computer Symposium 10). New York: Algorithmics Press.

Ruus, H. (1979). Sproglig betydningsanalyse: semantiske roller i tekster. *Nydansker Stydier & Almen Komunikationsteori* 10/11 ('Sprogteori og Tekstanalyse'), 161–97.

——. (1980). Anvendelig semantik? *Skrifter om Anvendt og Matematisk Lingvistik* 6, 343–55.

Ryle, G. (1949). *The concept of mind*. London: Hutchinson.

Saksena, A. (1980). The affected agent. *Language* 56, 812–26.

Samlowski, W. (1976). Case grammar. In Charniak and Wilks (1976), 55–72.

Sampson, G. (1972). Review of Anderson (1971). *Journal of Literary Semantics* 1, 116–18.

——. (1983). Deterministic parsing. In King (1983), 91–116.

Schank, R. C. (1972). Conceptual dependency: a theory of natural language understanding. *Cognitive Psychology* 3, 552–631.

——. (1973*a*). The conceptual analysis of natural language. In Rustin (1973), 291–309.

——. (1973*b*). Identification of conceptualisations underlying natural language. In Schank and Colby (1973), 187–247.

——. (1975). *Conceptual information processing* (Fundamental Studies in Computer Science 3). Amsterdam: North-Holland.

——. (1977). Representation and understanding of text. Elcock. E. W. and Michie, D. (eds) – *Machine Intelligence 8: Machine representation of knowledge*, Chichester: Ellis Horwood, 575–619.

——. and Abelson, R. P. (1977). *Scripts, plans, goals and understanding: an inquiry into human knowledge structures*. Hillsdale, N.J.: Lawrence Erlbaum Associates.

——. and Colby, K. M. (1973) (eds). *Computer models of thought and language*. San Francisco: W. H. Freeman and Co.

——. and Riesbeck, C. K. (1981). *Inside computer understanding: five programs plus miniatures*. Hillsdale, N.J.: Lawrence Erlbaum Associates.

Schumacher, H. (1976) (Hrsg.). *Untersuchungen zur Verbvalenz: eine Dokumentation über die Arbeit an einem deutschen Valenzlexikon* (Forschungsberichte des Instituts für Deutsche Sprache, Mannheim, 30). Tübingen: TBL Verlag Gunter Narr.

——. and Trautz, N. (1976). Bibliographie zur Valenz und Dependenz. In Schumacher (1976), 314–43.

Scragg, G. (1976). Semantic nets as memory models. In Charniak and Wilks (1976), 101–27.

Seiler, H. (1974). The principle of concomitance: Instrumental, Comitative and Collective (with special reference to German). Seiler, H. (ed.). *Linguistic Workshop II: Arbeiten des Kölner Universalienprojekts 1973–74* (Structura 8), München: Wilhelm Fink Verlag. 2–55.

Seyfert, G. (1976). *Zur Theorie der Verbgrammatik* (Tübinger Beiträger zur Linguistik 73). Tübingen: TBL Verlag Gunter Narr.

Shafto, M. (1973). The space for case. *Journal of Verbal Learning and Verbal Behavior* 12, 551–62.

Shimazu, A., Naito, S. and Nomura, H. (1983). Japanese language semantic analyzer based on an extended case frame model. *Proceedings of the Eighth International Joint Conference on Artificial Intelligence* (Karlsruhe). 717–20.

Simmons, R. F. (1972). Some semantic structures for representing English meanings. Freedle, R. O. and Carroll, J. B. (eds) – *Language comprehension and the acquisition of knowledge*, Washington, D.C.: V. H. Winston/New York: John Wiley. 71–97.

Simmons, R. F. (1973). Semantic networks: their computation and use for understanding English sentences. In Schank and Colby (1973), 63–113.

——. and Bruce, B. C. (1971). Some relations between predicate calculus and semantic net representations of discourse. *Second International Joint Conference on Artificial Intelligence* (Imperial College, London. 524–30.

——. and Slocum, J. (1972). Generating English discourse from Semantic Networks. *Communications of the ACM* 15, 891–905.

Singh, J. D. (1974). Pāṇini's theory of kārakas. *International Journal of Dravidian Linguistics* 3, 287–320.

Slocum, J. (1983). A status report on the LRC Machine Translation system. *Conference on Applied Natural Language Processing: Proceedings* (Santa Monica, California). 166–73.

——. (1984). Machinc Translation: its history, current status, and future prospects. *10th International Conference on Computational Linguistics – 22nd Annual Meeting of the Association for Computational Linguistics: Proceedings of Coling84* (Stanford, California). 546–61.

——. (1985). METAL: the LRC Machine Translation system. In King (1986).

Somers, H. L. (1980*a*). ISSCO*PTOSYS: Brief description and User Manual. Working Papers 41. Institut pour les Etudes Sémantiques et Cognitives, Université de Genève.

——. (1980*b*). The use of verb features in arriving at a 'meaning representation'. Working Papers 42. Institut pour les Etudes Sémantiques et Cognitives, Université de Genève.

——. (1982*a*). Lucien Tesnière: a review of his 'oeuvre'. CCL/UMIST Report 82/8. Centre for Computational Linguistics, University of Manchester Institute of Science and Technology.

——. (1982*b*). Thc classification of events by Vendler and Dowty compared to Chafe's and Cook's verb classification. Paper delivered at the Linguistics Association of Great Britain Autumn Meeting, Cantcrbury, September 1982.

——. (1982*c*). The use of verb features in arriving at a 'meaning representation'. *Linguistics* 20, 237–65; [substantially revised version of Somers (1980*b*)].

——. (1982*d*). The dynamic dictionary part of the sentence analyser PTOSYS. Holmboe, H. (ed.) – *Nordisk Forskersymposium om Datamatunderstøttet Leksikografi* (Sprog og Mennesker 3), Århus (1983): Institut for Lingvistik, Aarhus Universitet, 54–67.

——. (1983). Investigating the possibility of a micro-processor-based Machine Translation system. *Conference on Applied Natural Language Processing: Proceedings* (Santa Monica, California), 149–55.

——. (1984). On the validity of the complement-adjunct distinction in Valency grammar. *Linguistics* 22, 507–30.

——. and Johnson, R. L. (1979). PTOSYS: An interactive system for 'understanding' texts using a dynamic strategy for creating and updating dictionary entries. MacCafferty, M. and Gray, K. (eds). *The analysis of meaning: Informatics 5*. London: Aslib. 85–103.

——. and Nomura, H. (1987). LUTE-PTOSYS: An experimental system aiming at a deep text representation. Research Report, NTT Basic Research Laboratories, Musashino, Tokyo.

Sommerfeldt, K-E. (1973). Zur Besetzung der Leerstellen von Valenzträgern. *Deutsch als Fremdsprache* 10.2, 95–101.

——. and Schreiber, H. (1974). *Wörterbuch zur Valenz und Distribution deutscher Adjektive*. Leipzig: VEB Verlag Enzyklopädie.

——. (1975). Zu einem Wörterbuch der Valenz und Distribution der Substantive. *Deutsch als Fremdsprache* 12.2, 112–19.

Starosta, S. (1972). Case in the lexicon. In Heilmann (1972), Vol. II, 805–11.

——. (1973). The faces of case. *Language Sciences* 25, 1–14.

——. (1976). A place for case. *Language Learning* 26, 1–36.

——. (1977). The one per sent solution. In Abraham (1977), 459–576.

——. (1979). The end of phrase-structure as we know it. *University of Hawaii Working Papers in Linguistics* 11.1, 59–76.

——. (1981). Review of Anderson (1977). *Language* 57, 720–5.

——. (1982). Case, relations, perspective, and Patient centrality. *University of Hawaii Working Papers in Linguistics* 14.1, 1–33.

Steedman, M. J. (1977). Verbs, time, and modality. *Cognitive Science* 1, 216–34.

Steinitz, R. (1969). *Adverbial-Syntax* (Studia Grammatica 10). Berlin: Akademie-Verlag.

Stockwell, R. P., Schachter, P. and Partee, B. H. (1973). *The major syntactic structures of English*. New York: Holt Rinehart and Winston.

Stötzel, G. (1970) *Ausdrucksseite und Inhaltsseite der Sprache: Methodenkritischen Studien am Beispiel der deutschen Reflexivverben* (Linguistische Reihe 3). München: Max Hueber Verlag.

Stratton, C. R. (1971). The pathological case. *Working Papers in Linguistics* 10 (Department of Linguistics, Ohio State University), 221–30.

Swiggers, P. (1979). Review of Abraham (1978). *Leuvense Bijdragen* 68, 462–74.

Talmy, L. (1976). Semantic causative types. M. Shibatani (ed.) – *Syntax and Semantics Volume 6: The grammar of causative constructions*. New York: Academic Press. 43–116.

Taylor, B. H. and Rosenberg, R. S. (1975). A Case-driven parser for natural language. *American Journal of Computational Linguistics* microfiche 31.

Taylor, H. M. (1971). *Case in Japanese*. South Orange, N.J.: Seton Hall University Press.

Taylor, S. L., Krulee, G. K. and Henschen, L. T. (1977). Automatic abstracting of textual material. *5th International Joint Conference on Artificial Intelligence* (MIT). 117–18.

Teng, S-H. (1970). Comitative versus phrasal conjunction. *Papers in Linguistics* 2, 315–58.

——. (1975). *A semantic study of transitivity relations in Chinese* (University of California Publications in Linguistics 80). Berkeley: University of California Press.

Tennant, H. (1981). *Natural language processing: an introduction to an emerging technology*. New York: Petrocelli.

Tesnière, L. (1959). *Eléments de syntaxe structurale*. Paris: Librairie C. Klincksieck.

Teubert, W. (1979). *Valenz des Substantivs* (Sprache der Gegenwart 49), Düsseldorf: Pädagogischer Verlag Schwann.

Tsujii, J-I. (1982). The transfer phase in an English-Japanese translation system. Horecký, J. (ed.) – *COLING 82* (Proceedings of the Ninth International Conference on Computational Linguistics, Prague) (North-Holland Linguistic Series 47), Amsterdam: North-Holland. 383–90.

van Bakel, J. and Hoogeboom, S. (1981). Eksperiment met een Kasus-Grammatika. *Verslagen Computerlinguistiek* 2 (Katholieke Universiteit Nijmegen), 1–57.

van Langendonck, W. (1974). Internally referring prepositions and the subcategorization of space and time denominations in a Netherlandic case grammar. *Leuvense Bijdragen* 63, 1–41.

van Oosten, J. (1977). Subjects and agenthood in English. *Papers from the 13th regional meeting of the Chicago Linguistics Society*, 459–71.

van Valin, R. D. (1980). Review of Abraham (1978). *Studies in Language* 4, 293–321.

Vater, H. (1977). On the possibility of distinguishing between complements and adjuncts. In Abraham (1977), 21–45.

Vauquois, B. (1975). *La traduction automatique à Grenoble* (Documents de linguistique quantitative 24). Paris: Dunod.

——. (1976). Automatic translation: a survey of different approaches. *COLING 76: International Conference on Computational Linguistics – Proceedings* (Ottawa).

——. (1978). *Description de la structure intermédiaire* (Communication présentée au Colloque Luxembourg, 17 et 18 avril 1978). Grenoble: GETA.

Veillon, G. (1968). Description du langage pivot du système de traduction automatique du CETA. *T.A. Informations* 1, 8–17.

Vendler, Z. (1967). *Linguistics in Philosophy*. Ithaca, NY: Cornell University Press.

Vlach, F. (1981). The semantics of the progressive. Tedeschi, P. J. and Zaenen, A. (eds), *Syntax and Semantics Volume 14: Tense and aspect*, New York: Academic. 271–92.

Walmsley, J. B. (1971). The English Comitative case and the concept of deep structure. *Foundations of Language* 7, 493–507.

Waltz, D. L. (1978). An English language Question Answering system for a large relational database. *Communications of the ACM* 21, 526–39.

Warnock, G. J. (1953). *Berkeley*. London: Penguin.

Watters, J. R. (1980). Review of Dik (1978). *Lingua* 50, 155–71.

Weissgerber, M. (1983). *Valenz und Kongruenzbeziehungen: ein Modell zur Vereindeutung von Verben in der maschinellen Analyse und Übersetzung* (Europäische Hochschulschriften Reihe 1 Band 652). Frankfurt am Main: Peter Lang.

Welin, C. W. (1975). *Semantic networks and Case grammar* (PILUS 29). Stockholm: Institute of Linguistics, University of Stockholm.

Whitelock, P. J. (1985) (ed.). An in-depth study of computational and linguistic techniques in Machine Translation system design. CCL/UMIST Report 85/1. Centre for Computational Linguistics, University of Manchester Institute of Science and Technology.

Wierzbicka, A. (1975). Why 'kill' does not mean 'cause to die': the semantics of action sentences. *Foundations of Language* 13, 491–528.

Wilks, Y. (1973*a*). An Artificial Intelligence approach to Machine Translation. In Schank and Colby (1973), 114–51.

——. (1973*b*). The Stanford Machine Translation project. In Rustin (1973), 243–90.

——. (1975*a*). Preference semantics. Keenan, E. (ed.) – *Formal semantics of natural language*, Cambridge: University Press. 329–48.

——. (1975*b*). An intelligent analyzer and understander of English. *Communications of the ACM* 18, 264–74.

——. (1976*a*). Processing case. *American Journal of Computational Linguistics* microfiche 56.

——. (1976*b*). Parsing English II. In Charniak and Wilks (1976), 155–84.

——. (1977). Natural Language understanding systems within the A.I. paradigm: a survey and some comparisons. In Zampolli (1977), 341–98.

——. (1978). Making preferences more active. *Artificial Intelligence* 11, 197–223.

Willis, P. and Jeffreys, L. (1982). Participant (case) roles in lexical analysis. *Nottingham Linguistic Circular*, 11.2, 1–19.

Winograd, T. (1983). *Language as a cognitive process, Volume 1: Syntax*. Reading, Mass.: Addison Wesley.

Winston, P. H. (1977). *Artificial Intelligence*. Reading, Mass.: Addison Wesley.

Wissemann, H. (1961). Besprechung von Tesnière (1959). *Indogermanische Forschungen* 66, 176–85.

Woods, W. A. (1970). Transition network grammars for natural language analysis. *Communications of the ACM* 13, 591–606.

——. (1977). Lunar rocks in natural English: explorations in Natural Language Question Answering. In Zampolli, 521–69.

——. Bates, M., Brown, G., Bruce, B., Cook, C., Clovstad, J., Machoul, J., Nash-Webber, B., Schwartz, R., Wolf, J. and Zue, V. (1976), Speech understanding systems – Final report, Volume IV. Technical Report 2378. Bolt, Beranek and Newman, Cambridge, Mass.

Wüster, E. (1971). Begriffs- und Themaklassifikationen: Unterschiede in ihrem Wesen und in ihrer Anwendung. *Nachrichten für Dokumentation* 22, 98–104.

Zampolli, A. (1977) (ed.). *Linguistic structures processing* (Fundamental Studies in Computer Science 5). Amsterdam: North-Holland.

Zoeppritz, M., (1971). On the requirement that agentives be animate. *Beiträge zur Linguistik und Informationsbearbeitung* 21, 65–78.

INDEX OF NAMES

SUBJECT INDEX